DATE DUE

SE 16 '97			
MR 6 '98			
NO 21 '01			

DEMCO 38-296

UN MALAISE

UN Malaise

Power, Problems and Realpolitik

Geoff Simons

St. Martin's Press   New York

Printed in Great Britain

ISBN 0–312–12621–2

Library of Congress Cataloging-in-Publication Data
Simons, G. L. (Geoffrey Leslie), 1939–
UN malaise: power, problems, and realpolitik / Geoff Simons.
p. cm.
Includes bibliographical references and index.
ISBN 0–312–12621–2
1. United Nations. 2. International organization. I. Title.
II. Title: United Nations malaise.
JX1977.S4563 1995
341.23—dc20   95–2569
                                                    CIP

Contents

List of Figures

List of Tables

Preface

This book has been written to explore what has emerged as a truly historic paradox: the on-going situation in which the United Nations, still carrying a connotation of fine idealism and ethical service, has become identified with mismanagement, incompetence, corruption and various other derelictions, including illegal practices.

I confess that for me the United Nations still reverberates with idealism and hope for the global community of humankind, despite all the injustices and brutalities, genocides even, perpetrated in its name.

I do not subscribe to the plausible notion that the United Nations is no more than the sum of its constituent members. As we note the first half century of the UN's existence we should recognise that the United Nations continues to embody a vision – albeit often tarnished, obscured and suborned – that transcends the self-serving postures of individual states.

GEOFF SIMONS

x

Acknowledgements

Various people offered help and support in the writing of the present book. I am particularly grateful to: Erskine Childers, academic and reformer, for applauding this text and for generously offering the prepublication quote; Alexandra McLeod and Elizabeth Lee at the United Nations Information Centre (18 Buckingham Gate, London SW1E 6LB), for sending me copious UN documents – resolutions, reports, statements, etc.; and Christine Simons, whose swelling archive is an invaluable resource.

Introduction

The rapid and seismic collapse of the Soviet Union in the early 1990s cast the United Nations into sharp relief. No longer could UN procrastination and impotence be blamed on the debilitating exigencies of the Cold War. The likelihood of a Russian veto in the Security Council was now much reduced (though not entirely removed – as the question of UN funding in Cyprus was to show); and the possibility of contentious Soviet resolutions routinely vetoed by the Western powers was no longer an option. It seemed that the Security Council, quick to flaunt its unaccustomed consensus, would now be able to act decisively to solve regional problems wherever they occurred. Such heady optimism soon evaporated.

A central problem was that a hegemonic United States, soon to be led by a man with no experience in foreign affairs, was not in a position to orchestrate a batch of covert and overt agendas. The early shaping of the United Nations, even before the end of the Second World War, had been carried out with a keen eye focused on American strategic and commercial interests. Military power was to reside in the Security Council, where the United States was the dominant player; and the creation of such UN-linked bodies as the International Monetary Fund (IMF), the International Bank for Reconstruction and Development (the World Bank) and the General Agreement on Tariffs and Trade (GATT) was intended to strengthen the political and commercial grip of US-led world capitalism. Now, with the Soviet Union no more, it was easy for Washington to perceive a range of fresh opportunities. What did this mean for the United Nations? How was the international body to respond in a world with only one surviving superpower? Was the United Nations now able to act in ways that its idealistic founders had originally intended? Or would the post-Cold War situation bring new constraints?

It is useful to consider the background (Part I) to the United Nations: the nature of the organisation, the ideas and circumstances that led to its creation.* Chapter 1 examines such aspects as the UN as a *system*, the significance of states as building blocks for the international organisation, and the character of the challenge facing the United Nations in the 1990s. Firstly, clues are given as to how the UN can be viewed as an organic system, amenable to interpretation in terms of classical systems theory (my

---

*I have treated such matters in more detail in *The United Nations: A Chronology of Conflict* (Macmillan, 1994).

computer background and my belief in an unreconstructed philosophical determinism dispose me to such an interpretation). This approach, pregnant with possibilities, cannot be explored here in any detail.

Then attention is given to the emerging role of the United Nations, given 'the scope of its universal ambitions'. UN Secretary-General Boutros Boutros-Ghali signals that the United Nations 'must never again be crippled' as it was through the era of the Cold War. But how is the international body to escape the constraints imposed by powerful member states with their own agendas? Does the United Nations have a *supranational* status transcending the mere sum total of its members? How is that status to translate into effective action in a strife-riven world? Chapter 1 examines also the significance of states as component UN parts, with particular focus on their legal character and the nature of sovereignty. A central problem at the heart of the United Nations is how legitimate supranational authority is to be exercised in circumstances where individual members demand a substantial measure of sovereign autonomy. Finally, there is discussion of the multifaceted challenge facing the United Nations in the so-called New World Order. Boutros-Ghali notes that the demands on the UN have 'surged' since the end of the Cold War. How is this unprecedented situation to be addressed?

Chapter 2 provides a brief profile of some of the ideas and events that have been crucial in shaping the emergence and development of the United Nations. Here is advertised the age-old dream of global peace (Isaiah, when in a pacific mood, wanting to see swords beaten into plowshares), a durable vision forced to co-exist with all manner of human brutality, conquest and genocide over the centuries. Philosophers, reformers and politicians all made their contribution – as did, completely inadvertently, conquerors and traders interested in the emergence of a global order. Particular attention is given to the efforts of President Woodrow Wilson; to his seminal role in the creation of the ill-fated League of Nations, the *de facto* and *de jure* parent to the uniquely global United Nations.

The contribution of President Franklin Delano Roosevelt to the creation of the United Nations is indicated, with brief attention to the historic conferences at Bretton Woods and Dumbarton Oaks. Now the American mood was broadly sympathetic to the creation of a new international body: there would be no repetition of the League fiasco where the League architect Woodrow Wilson found himself unable to accomplish US membership. And details are included of the UN launch conference in San Francisco in 1945, a historic meeting of nearly fifty countries which, in one view, proved to be 'a mixed bag of power politics, muddy thinking, official hypocrisy, high idealism, keen good sense, legalistic nonsense, compromise and false hopes'. The scene was set for a new phase in world history, a period in which the United Nations would grow from around fifty founder members during the closing months of the Second World War to 185 members by mid-1995 and in which power politics would continue to exert the dominant influence on the course of world events.

Perhaps the most graphic instance of state power being used to exploit the United Nations in the post-World War Two order was the US-orchestrated Korean War (1950–53). Here the United States launched military action *before* the UN was enlisted to underwrite policies support-ive of American strategic interests. Chapter 2 describes what I have termed the *'Korean Paradigm'*, whereby Washington analyses an event and then judges how best the United Nations can be manipulated to reinforce American foreign policy. Here it is argued that the Korean Paradigm can serve as a useful guide to US manipulation of the UN in the post-Soviet world order of the 1990s. The chapter concludes by high-lighting some aspects of the so-called New World Order against which the problems confronting the United Nations can be assessed.

Even the most casual observer is aware that today the United Nations faces many problems: if the situation of the UN is scrutinised a wide range of difficulties, confusions and uncertainties – varying in importance but existing at all levels of UN organisation and activity – quickly becomes apparent. UN problems are constantly paraded in the media, giving some signs of the many predicaments and crises below the surface. Who is to control field operations? An on-site powerful member state or UN officials? Who has authority over UN-delegated national troops? What of the chains of command, the extent to which nation states should determine UN policy making, the authority for allocating funds? How should top UN officials be elected, monitored and directed? UN reports seem powerless to stimulate appropriate action. One UN-linked report highlights the growing UN-induced famine in Iraq; another UN report[1] advertises UN impotence in addressing the world refugee problem. In late-1993 the UN disaster chief, Jan Eliasson, indicated he would stand down because of lack of support from the UN Secretary-General.[2] Individual states ignore particular UN Conventions to which they are signatories,[3] and the United Nations seemingly has no power to act. An Amnesty International report, published on 26 January 1994, provides further evidence that UN peace-keepers often neglect human rights ('. . . human rights have been ignored and UN personnel have stood by, silent, while serious violations were taking place'). At the same time there are UN aid agency problems that may be unsurmountable. Thus some observers see the International Fund for Agricultural Development (IFAD) as near to collapse.[4] Such examples, which could easily be extended, show a multifaceted UN malaise that enervates and constrains the work of the international body.

The main categories of problems facing the United Nations are considered in Part II. Chapter 3 addresses the principal of these: the problem of power – the circumstance, already alluded to, in which powerful states feel able to pursue national self-interest against the express policies and spirit of the United Nations. Here it is shown how the UN can be manipulated (over Iraq and Libya), ignored (over Israel and Cuba) and deployed in circumstances of collapsing consensus (Bosnia) or confused objectives (Somalia and Haiti). Here one of the main problems is that there is no counterbalance to American power, no bulwark to US manipulation of the Security Council. In the post-Soviet world it was easy to see that the UN could well become 'a tool of US domestic politics', since it is clear that 'the American public approves of spectacular acts of international violence . . . provided . . . that they are perceived as virtuously motivated'[5] – and what better agency than the United Nations to provide the necessary cloak of virtue?

A consequence of US power is that the UN has been traduced to bring starvation to the ordinary people of Iraq and Haiti; with UN General Assembly resolutions ignored as Washington seeks to bring starvation to Cuba. In 1990 the World Health Organisation (WHO) recorded that 92 per cent of ordinary Iraqis had access to free and sophisticated health care, with malnutrition, cholera, typhoid and polio almost entirely eradicated. Today, because of the UN sanctions insisted on by Washington, there are virtual famine conditions in much of Iraq. UN-linked bodies have known about this for some time; and deplored it. In mid-1993 a report published jointly by the UN Food and Agriculture Organisation (FAO) and the World Food Programme noted of Iraq 'all the commonly recognised signs of pre-famine conditions . . . and that large numbers of Iraqis now have food intakes lower than those in the most disaster-stricken African countries'.[6] In one estimate the sanctions alone had caused more than a quarter of a million deaths, with 4000 children under five dying every month. The presumed target of sanctions – Saddam Hussein – remained untouched.

The sanctions on Libya (enabled by one preliminary Security Council resolution and two subsequent sanctions resolutions) tell a similar (though much less catastrophic) story: a pretext is exploited by Washington, in the absence of justification in law or natural justice, to topple a national leader. Opportunities to try the two Libyans suspected of involvement in the Lockerbie bombing outrage are ignored by the West as new evidence casts doubt on Libyan guilt.[7] At the same time UN sanctions on Libya are strengthened by Security Council Resolution 883 (Appendix 5) to accelerate the progressive crippling of the Libyan economy.

Such events should be set against the abandonment of Somalia, the continuing chaos and destitution in Haiti,[8] and the characteristic confusion over the respective UN and NATO roles in Bosnia. Chapter 3 concludes by exploring the nature of American policies in the evolving new order. In an address to the General Assembly on 28 September 1993 President Bill Clinton declared that the United States 'intends to remain engaged and to lead . . .'. The problem of power was as explicit then as it remains today.

The other chapters (4 to 6) of Part II consider the various problems of management, representation and the 'other United Nations'. We may surmise that many administrative difficulties in the UN organisation could be profitably addressed by traditional management disciplines: giving attention to such questions as manpower deployment, resource allocation, project planning, budgeting and the rest. Such mechanisms are important but the overarching tasks of UN management are uniquely problematic. While the ambitions of the United Nations are vast, embracing countless subject areas around the entire globe, the UN Secretariat, headed by the Secretary-General, has few enforceable powers to demand payment of due revenues or to raise armies (for peacekeeping or whatever). The UN cannot compel its members to be obedient; rather it is forced to rely upon consent, acquiescence and sympathy. Most managers would reckon this no way to run a business.

In Chapter 4 consideration is given to many of the resulting management problems that arise: such topics as resourcing and budgets, manpower difficulties, the persistent problems of bureaucracy and corruption, the abuses of human rights. Such matters cannot be addressed adequately without attention to the structure of the UN organisation. What powers should be granted to member states? What is the proper relationship between the Security Council and the General Assembly? What member states should have permanent seats on the Council? What are the criteria? Who should be entitled to vote? Do we need a new Security Council, one that better reflects the circumstances of the post-Soviet world. Chapter 5 examines the question of representation.

Background details are included of philosophic considerations relevant to the persistent question of franchise power. What is the significance of democracy? To what extent should we be interested in the empowerment of the majority of UN member states? What can we learn from the historical evolution of the domestic franchise? In particular, to what extent does the traditional *property* criterion for adult suffrage mirror the current pressure to give Germany and Japan – as *wealthy* states – permanent seats on the Security Council? Should other, non-wealthy, states be allowed to qualify, according to different criteria (race, population, degree of commitment to social reform, and so on)? What are we to say, in this context, of the powers of the Security Council, and the extent to which current permanent members of the Council are able to ignore provisions of the UN Charter?*

The distribution of powers within the UN organisation is crucially relevant to how the international body is to serve 'we, the peoples'. It also bears directly on the extent to which powerful states – in the post-Soviet world, primarily the US – can suborn the UN into serving national, rather than supranational, policies. To some extent the new problems have arisen because the Security Council 'is feeling its way into a world without maps'.[9] This is not the only reason. The collapse of the Soviet Union has given powerful states the opportunity to exploit the UN culture to national advantage: an opportunity quickly seized. Perhaps 'harmonious chaos'[10] is an apt way of describing the current working of the UN organisation, but it should not be forgotten that some states benefit more from an element of chaos, and the inevitable degree of UN impotence that this implies, than from the unwelcome constraints of what they might perceive as excessive harmony. Put another way, a ragged inefficient United Nations can be easily traduced to serve the interests of power. Anyone interested in the development of the United Nations to serve the real international community – not the 'international community' that is invoked by White House spokespersons as a synonym for the Western consensus – must have a different agenda: one that sees democratic representation within the United Nations as a necessary condition for genuine UN focus on the interest of the global community.

There is another dimension of crucial importance. Whatever is done to bring reform to the structure of the United Nations organisation, there is a 'parallel UN', undemocratic and authoritarian, working to secure and expand the power of privileged élites throughout the world. Chapter 6 considers the 'other United Nations', the global nexus of commercial vested interest underwritten by such bodies as the IMF, the World Bank, GATT and the transnational corporations (TNCs).

No-one doubts the power of this global nexus: it can bring down governments, hold entire nations in thrall, impact on the lives of millions. Thus the current predicament of the Russian Republic has in large measure been shaped by the deliberations and decisions of the IMF and the World Bank,[11] just as countless other states are driven to a political 'restructuring of their societies at IMF/World Bank behest'. The African

---

*One important example is how the permanent Soviet seat on the Security Council was transferred, *without a vote in the General Assembly*, to the Russian Republic – so violating Article 108 of the UN Charter.

debt deepens, according to the World Bank, while IMF/World Bank policies drive millions in the Third World into destitution and despair.[12] In December 1993, with the GATT talks brought to some sort of conclusion, another prop was erected to support the global commercial order, with weak and recalcitrant states bullied into accepting further trading terms designed to benefit above all the large corporations of the developed world.

The conclusion of the Uruguay Round of GATT talks, hyped as a triumph for liberal values and free trade, did no more than consolidate and extend trading conditions designed to benefit powerful commercial interests. Now a World Trade Organisation (WTO) had been created to police international commerce: the powerful trading nations, mainly the US and Europe, were now theoretically able to compel the world's weaker trading states into acquiescence. One consequence is the likelihood that *around 40 per cent of the world's two billion rural population will be driven from their land by the GATT deregulation of the world trade in grain*. This is the shape of the new commercial order.

Few observers believed that the new GATT provisions would bring a fresh harmony to trading relations around the world. It was still necessary for the US to slash Chinese textile quotas,[13] with a recalcitrant China, outside the GATT framework, to be pressured, wooed and cajoled as necessary: it was not long before President Clinton, sensitive to the attractions of a rapidly-expanding Chinese economy, decided to remove the link between US–Chinese trade and Chinese progress on human rights. It was as if the Tiananmen Square massacre had never happened. And soon, despite all the hyperbole surrounding the GATT deal, a new trade war between the United States and Japan seemed likely.[14] After desultory US–Japanese talks, Japan dubbed Washington a shoot-from-the-hip outlaw whose attitude towards international trade 'breeds vigilantes and a breakdown of order'.[15] Washington then stated that it was prepared to use US trade laws to put pressure on the Japanese economy. In August 1994 the dollar fell sharply against the yen after the Clinton administration launched trade sanctions against Japan for its alleged violations of fair-trading practices.[16]

It seemed clear that powerful states would continue to manoeuvre to national advantage, ignoring GATT and other trading provisions when it was judged appropriate to do so, but demanding compliance from weaker states, in particular those Third World countries with no effective bargaining power. Europe, Japan and the United States would continue to maintain prudent areas of trade protection, while poor countries, under threat of sanctions and other penalties, would be driven to expose their fragile

Introduction

economies to international exploitation. There would be hidden agendas, covert plans, backstairs deals conjured in the IMF, the World Bank, GATT, G7 and the rest; with such bodies as the Central Intelligence Agency (CIA) continuing to take an interest in all such proceedings.[17] This is the shape of the *other* United Nations, the nexus of global power and privilege that all students of world politics should consider.

There is abundant scope for reform: in the United Nations organisation, in the framework of the 'other United Nations', and in all the associated agencies and bodies. Some of the reforms are obvious, others less so; some would arouse little opposition from powerful states, others would generate bitter political hostility. Chapter 7, after discussing some crucial reform considerations, offers a 50-point framework for reform. It is essential today that we advertise the need for radical reform. The real global community – *we, the peoples* – desperately needs a democratic, just and powerful United Nations.

Part I

The Background

1 The Challenge

PREAMBLE

The United Nations has endured for half a century, over which period its character has massively evolved and expanded. On 6 June 1945 the representatives of four dozen sovereign states, convening in San Francisco, signed the UN Charter; today, in mid-1995, the United Nations has 185 member states. Now no country on earth is unaffected by its existence and its activities: the United Nations is the world's first truly global organisation. Today its character and role are being scrutinised as never before. How are we to assess the unprecedented challenges facing the United Nations in the post-Cold War world?

Every social and political system constantly faces a multifaceted spectrum of challenges. The most basic of these relate to the very survival of the functional system in the real world. Is the system secure? Can it adapt to changing circumstances to avoid extinction? And to what extent does such adaptation, if possible, change the fundamental character of the system? Does substantial change matter?

Other types of challenges relate to the perceived character of the system. What is its *raison d'être*? Was it consciously created to realise particular objectives? Are these objectives mutually self-consistent? Are they differently perceived by the various players – individuals and states – within and without the system? What are the implications of such different perceptions?

Are the objectives enshrined in a charter; whether written, unwritten or part written/part unwritten? And are all elements of the charter, whatever its character, equally significant? If some parts are ignored, what are the implications for the rest? And how are the various impacts of other social and political systems to be evaluated?

What kind of system or system complex is the United Nations organisation? What can be said, albeit at this stage in broad terms, about the UN Charter? And about the complexities of the world's most ambitious global institution? What are the problems and the challenges?

3

THE INTERNATIONAL SYSTEM

If the United Nations can be seen as a complex system – comprising a hierarchy of constituent subsystems – then various inferences can be drawn. For a start, the UN organisation can be studied according to classi-cal systems theory in which a dynamic entity can be analysed in terms of inputs, outputs, adaptation, information processing and the like. A systems view of the United Nations implies that its behaviour is mediated by dis-coverable systems rules, an approach that offers insights into the organisa-tion's internal processes and the many ways it impacts on other social and political systems.

It is characteristic of systems that they change over time. The various changes can represent useful adaptations in a shifting environment or the unavoidable onset of decay and dissolution that typifies most living systems. The idea of change (movement, alteration, modification, evolution, etc.) is intimately associated with the idea of process, which itself can be of very many different types. Change can be reversible or irreversible: within a small section of space and time it may appear to run against the second law of thermodynamics; i.e. it may seem that there is a decrease in local entropy. When a broader space–time segment is surveyed, however, it can be seen that change invariably results in an increase in entropy. The implication for living systems – of which the United Nations is a complex example – is that there is a constant search for strategies that will aid survival. This does not mean that the search is always intelligent, or that there are not other system processes that are working to undermine the survival of the organisation. Thus when the UN Secretary-General Boutros Boutros-Ghali appeals for member states to pay their dues on time he is functioning to aid system sur-vival; but unilateral US initiatives in Iraq or Somalia, under nominal UN auspices, often work to weaken UN security or to adulterate what others may perceive as the proper spirit of the United Nations organisation.

Such obvious life changes as birth, growth, maturation and dying are obvious processes that vary according to the system in question. The death of a biological cell, organ or individual leaves organic detritus, but the death of an institution or an organisation does not necessarily yield corpses. This suggests the unremarkable conclusion that aggregates of social entities – humans and states – can survive in ways that are not open to individual men and women. A species may or may not endure but it is likely to last longer than a human being. Similarly, though the United Nations – impaled on the spikes of intractable problems – may expire tomorrow or in the next decade, we can reasonably debate how it might survive through millennia.

It is significant that classical systems theory has been greatly enhanced and strengthened by computer science. The emergence of cybernetics in the 1940s as a unifying discipline for biological organisms and computer-based systems has encouraged the view that living systems – from cell to international organisation – crucially depend on the processing of information. An important corollary is that the complexity of the system is intimately related to the quantitative aspect of information. Thus amounts of information help to define the complexity of a DNA molecule, the complexity of a brain cell, and the complexity of the United Nations organisation. Similarly the processes of living systems are defined in part by their capacity to process information. It may be argued that all functions – including those that define the operations of the United Nations organisation – can be interpreted in terms of the collection, processing and distribution of information. In this spirit, the American research psychologists Peter H. Lindsay and Donald A. Norman have commented: 'We believe our extension of the area of information processing research shows how the scientific analyses of this book [*Human Information Processing*] can help illuminate many *if not all* human phenomena' (my italics).[1]

A common feature of adaptive systems is that they are constantly striving after a 'steady state', a condition of equilibrium or homeostasis. The idea of homeostasis, achieved via a range of feedback mechanisms, is a commonplace of electrical and mechanical engineering; and of complex biological systems. Such systems have evolved a range of mechanisms that facilitate adjustment in a changing environment, a necessary requisite for survival. At the same time the interest of adaptive systems in maintaining a homeostatic state does not preclude the possibility of change; in fact the reverse is the case. A system may maintain an evident steady state over any small time slot, but if the system is examined again after some lengthy period it may be found to exhibit modified behavioural responses. If a system has achieved a rigid homeostasis from which it cannot be shifted it is unlikely to survive in a shifting environment.

It is easy to see how such considerations can illuminate features of the United Nations organisation. The system collects information from the external world and feeds it to the multifaceted hierarchy of internal competing and co-operating subsystems. These in turn process the information for further dissemination within the organisation and via the many interfaces to countless targets in the outside world. The character of the collected information progressively modifies the nature of the internal processes, which in turn mediate the character of the information that is subsequently disseminated. *Negative* feedback may be seen as a restraining influence, ensuring that things do not get out of hand; in extreme cases, via 'end-product inhibition', stopping a particular sub-process from achieving a newly unwelcome outcome. By contrast, *positive* feedback, acting as a reinforcing action, encourages a greater output, a more energetic response.

The types of feedback consciously applied in the context of the United Nations are not always well judged. A UN intervention may be intended as negative feedback, as a means of cooling a situation; but if the intervention is poorly conceived – as with the brutal US involvement in Somalia – the result may be positive feedback that does no more than exacerbate the tension and violence in the situation. In these circumstances, fresh feedback information is generated to influence the information-handling subsystems in both the Pentagon and the UN Secretariat, complex adaptive systems supposedly working to the same agenda but often at odds.

The character of the United Nations as a complex information-handling system is shaped largely by its status as an international body. In some sense it is able to function as a *supra*national system with licit power over constituent member states; but this superior status has to be interpreted with care (see also *The Problem of Power*, below). The United Nations includes a number of mechanisms for taking action against recalcitrant member states (and non-member states), but in circumstances where a hegemonic Washington dominates the Security Council such mechanisms are often abused in violation of both the Charter and the spirit of the UN organisation. This circumstance represents a deep problem; one before which US client states are supine and non-client states are helpless. At the same time, abuse apart, it is useful to remember the status of the United Nations as an entity that in theory can demand the obedience of member states.

This suggests that a supranational system is not the same as an international system. It is quite possible for nations to interact without being subject to the constraints of a higher authority that would characterise a supranational system. If there is no centralised decision maker (a 'decider'[2] in one version of systems theory) able to control the member states (the 'component deciders') then the system is not truly supranational.[3] Viewed in these terms, the United Nations organisation is at times an international system and at times a supranational system: the 'supranational decider', the Security Council, can sometimes deliver rulings that bear on all member states but for the most part decisions that affect various nations tend to be made by the 'component deciders' according to international agreements. Again it is worth remarking that the evolution of the United Nations organisation from an international to a supranational system – in the circumstances of US hegemonic control of the Security Council – would threaten both the spirit and the letter of the UN Charter (see, for example, Article 2, 1: 'The Organization is based on the principle of the sovereign equality of all its Members').

In a proposed taxonomy of system types (in the context of the supranational system), the systems scientist James Grier Miller identifies: empires, federations and unions, intergovernmental organisations (single-purpose and multipurpose), coalitions and blocs, security communities, and nongovernmental organisations.[4] Since all the states constituting these various entities are members of the United Nations, the UN organisation variously straddles or incorporates the particular groupings. In particular, some autonomous intergovernmental organisations are related to the United Nations by special arrangement and are co-ordinated by ECOSOC (the UN Economic and Social Council): these include the IAEA (the International Atomic Energy Agency), the ILO (the International Labour Organisation), the FAO (the Food and Agriculture Organisation), UNESCO (the United Nations Educational, Scientific and Cultural Organisation), the IMF (the International Monetary Fund), the IBRD (the International Bank for Reconstruction and Development, the World Bank), and the WHO (the World Health Organisation). It is significant that even where the United Nations does not have formal relations with an international organisation all member states are obliged to recognise the superior legal status of the UN organisation by virtue of Article 103 in the Charter: 'In the event of a conflict between the obligations of the Members of the United Nations under the present Charter and their obligations under any other international agreement, their obligations under the present Charter shall prevail.'

The social and political impact of an international organisation depends in part on how effectively it can achieve the objectives of its (written or unwritten) constitution. What powers does the organisation have? To what extent are these frustrated by the powers of other national and international bodies? The powers of the organisation help to define its culture, and the extent to which a 'legal personality' can be identified. International organisations often have a legal status analogous to that of states: they can acquire and transfer property, and enter into legally binding agreements with states and other international organisations. They can, as can states, seek legal remedies; and they may be protected and obligated under the terms of international law.

There is little reference in the UN Charter to the organisation's legal status, though the UN's legal authority is conveyed in various Articles (for example, 103). Two Articles define UN status within the territories of member states: 104 declares that the United Nations 'shall enjoy in the territory of each of its Members such legal capacity as may be necessary for the exercise of its functions and the fulfilment of its purposes'; Article 105 similarly stipulates that the United Nations 'shall enjoy in the territory of each of its Members such privileges and immunities as are necessary for the fulfilment of its purposes' (a right applicable to 'representatives of the Members of the United Nations and officials of the Organization'). Two separate conventions, designed to supplement Articles 104 and 105, provide for functional privileges and immunities for the United Nations and the specialised agencies. The UN has also entered into legal agreements with host states; as with the UN/USA Headquarters Agreement.*

The legal status of the United Nations is of crucial importance as it becomes increasingly involved in disputes around the world. The Charter defines in part the entitlement of the United Nations to take such actions as imposing sanctions or launching military initiatives; but it has not always been clear whether the UN was entitled to lodge claims for damage to its property and personnel. In fact the international legal capacity of the United Nations was affirmed in an important legal statement by the International Court of Justice, itself a UN-linked body: it was declared that the United Nations 'was intended to exercise and enjoy, and is in fact exercising and enjoying, functions and rights which can only be explained on the basis of the possession of a large measure of international personality and the capacity to operate on the international plane'. The statement followed a request by the General Assembly for the Court to advise on whether the United Nations had the capacity to espouse an international claim in respect of an injury sustained by a UN official. The affirmative Court ruling maintained that the United Nations possessed 'objective personality', signifying the capacity for enforcement '*vis-à-vis* the whole world by virtue of the purposes of the Organisation and its almost universal membership'.[5] This landmark ruling, coupled with the expanding interventions of the United Nations to maintain or restore international peace and security, has helped to secure UN ambitions for global legal status.

The evolution of the complex United Nations organisation can be approached in various ways; here some rudimentary clues for a systems analysis approach in a legal context have been proposed, but there are many other options. There is still much scope for a Marxist analysis in terms of the economic vested interests that such entities as the IMF, the

---

* The siting of the UN Headquarters in New York sometimes brings problems when the United States itself is party to a dispute: as when the access of Iraqi foreign minister Tariq Aziz to the Headquarters was impeded by the US during the run-up to the 1991 Gulf War.

World Bank and GATT are seemingly designed to protect and advance (see Chapter 6); and the liberal focus on the rights of the individual has done much to fuel UN initiatives. The various approaches to analysis highlight particular dynamics in the UN enterprise. All are relevant to any comprehensive interpretation of the United Nations organisation. However, the most illuminating approach will always be the one that draws most faithfully on empirical data about UN performance in the real world. What is it up to? How is the world's most ambitious global body to define, justify and realise its role – or complex of roles – in a post-Cold War world in which the early facile certainties were soon fatally damaged by the politics of a history that had most evidently *not* come to an end?

SEARCHING FOR A ROLE

There has always been confusion about the role and purpose of the United Nations. Many people, groups and authorities – all with disparate interests and emphases – have influenced its evolution, and the resulting tensions and dislocations have been plain for half a century. Individual contributions in such areas as law, government and human rights led first to the founding of the League of Nations and then to the birth of the United Nations. The German philosopher Immanuel Kant was perhaps one of the most significant early contributors to the theme of a global system of government.[6] Others have focused on the character of a world democratic constitution and the emergence of a truly supranational world authority.[7] At the same time there are countervailing pressures: some observers, sensitive to the possibility that a global authority might become a global tyrant, have suggested an alternative route to world harmony. Thus thinkers such as Leopold Kohr[8] and E. F. Schumacher[9] have urged the need for political and economic devolution. Similarly, Jeffrey J. Segall, a founder-convenor of INFUSA (the International Network for a UN Second Assembly) and joint co-ordinator of CAMDUN (Conferences on A More Democratic United Nations), has argued that a peaceful civilisation must enshrine the right of secession in multination and federal states.[10] In fact the course of UN development has been determined largely by the perceived interests of hegemonic states: idealism and visionary dreams have played a manifest part but power politics have always been the dominant influence.

Debate about the character and direction of the United Nations has always co-existed with the organisation's practical activities in the world. Thus in 1956 the Harvard academic Inis L. Claude noted that discussion of the United Nations 'tends to be dominated by excessive passion for reopening the question of its basic design, for dealing first, last, and always with such exciting Great Issues as to whether the veto can be abolished or world federation should be introduced'. He suggested that the wisdom of this approach was 'questionable'.[11] Here it is proposed that the emphasis should be on what the United Nations can achieve rather than on endless scrutiny of its nature as an institution. The debate continues today (see Part II), given a new momentum in a post-Cold War world in which Germany and Japan, lacking permanent seats on the Security Council, are dominant economic powers. In 1946 the celebrated American journalist Walter Lippmann, later a Pulitzer Prize winner, observed that 'the potentiality of the world state is inherent in the United Nations as an oak tree is in an acorn . . . a world state . . . is inherent and potential in the embryonic organism of the United Nations'.[12] Half a century later, with the United States no longer impeded by the prospect of a Soviet veto on the Security Council, the possibility of the United Nations evolving into supranational world government is less appealing than it was to the early optimists.

The structure and powers of the United Nations – whether it exists as an international body with limited coercive powers over individual member states or as a real supranational authority able to compel obedience – should only be judged in so far as they contribute to an improvement of the human condition. Is the United Nations effective in tackling poverty and racism? Does it improve the condition of oppressed minorities? Does it prevent war? Does it bring military conflicts to an end? In general, does it further the cause of human rights – to life, peace and justice? It is significant that declarations on human rights have accompanied many important advances in political history. The doctrine of human rights derives from the philosophy of natural rights, which implies that individuals possess fundamental rights beyond those that may be prescribed in current law. A statement of human rights was formally incorporated in the US Declaration of Independence (1776); a Declaration of the Rights of Man and the Citizen was adopted by the French National Assembly (1789); and today most written constitutions contain a bill of rights. In 1948 the UN General Assembly adopted a Universal Declaration of Human Rights, detailing individual rights and freedoms, followed in 1953 by the European Convention on Human Rights (within which framework the European Court of Human Rights was established).

The Preamble to the UN Declaration recognises 'the inherent dignity' and 'the equal and inalienable rights of all members of the human family'; with the General Assembly later proclaiming the *universal declaration of human rights* as a common standard of achievement for all peoples and all nations'.[13]

The UN Declaration, while lacking legal force, has been seen as an important step towards the formulation of standards in regard to human rights in treaties that would have undoubted legal weight. The General Assembly has adopted various further Covenants to supplement the Declaration: for example, the International Covenant on Economic, Social and Cultural Rights; and the International Covenant on Civil and Political Rights.[14]

Much of the challenge facing the United Nations derives from the scope of its universal ambitions. Thus the rights stipulated in the Universal Declaration, intended to apply to the entire 'human family', include: the right of life, liberty and security of the person; freedom from slavery or servitude; freedom from torture or cruel, inhuman or degrading treatment or punishment; recognition as a person before the law; the rights to privacy; the right to nationality; the right to own property; freedom of thought, conscience and religion; the right to participate in government; the right to social security; the right to work; the right to education; and others. The rights are to be enjoyed without 'distinction of any kind, such as race, colour, sex, language, religion, political or other opinion, national or social origin, property, birth or other status': and may only be curtailed by 'such limitations as are determined by law solely for the purposes of securing due recognition and respect for the rights and freedoms of others and of meeting the just requirements of morality, public order and the general welfare in a democratic society'. The discussion that the UN Declaration inevitably invites is beyond the scope of the present book; it is cited above all to indicate the scale of UN ambitions and the daunting challenges that these imply.

The UN Secretary-General Boutros Boutros-Ghali has frequently addressed the question of how the United Nations should respond in the post-Cold War world. For example, in one important document, *An Agenda for Peace*, he signals the new circumstances of the international body:

> In these past months a conviction has grown, among nations large and small, that an opportunity has been regained to achieve the great objectives of the Charter – a United Nations capable of maintaining international peace and security, of securing justice and human rights and of promoting, in the words of the Charter, 'social progress and better standards of life in larger freedom'. This opportunity must not be squandered. The Organization must never again be crippled as it was in the era that has now passed.[15]

Here he highlights the holding of the 1992 Earth Summit ('the largest summit ever held') in Rio de Janeiro – the United Nations Conference on

Environment and Development (UNCED) – attended by representatives from some 180 nations with the declared aim of protecting the global environment; he celebrates the 1993 World Conference on Human Rights in Vienna and the 1994 Conference on Population and Development; and announces the 1995 World Conference on Women. He declares: 'Throughout my term as Secretary-General I shall be addressing all these great issues. I bear them all in mind as . . . I turn to the problems that the [Security] Council has specifically requested I consider: preventive diplomacy, peacemaking and peacekeeping – to which I have added a closely related concept, post-conflict peace-building.'

Recent years have seen a massive increase in the scale of the UN's global responsibilities. In 1987 there were about 10,000 UN peacekeepers stationed around the world; today there are more than 80,000 deployed in nearly two dozen operations on four continents. In some countries – Somalia, Bosnia, Angola, Cambodia, Iraq – the well-publicised UN involvement has a high profile; in other countries – Cyprus, Lebanon, El Salvador, Mozambique, Syria, India, Western Sahara, Sudan, Liberia – the on-going UN activities receive less attention. And in addition to the initiatives that have a clear military aspect, there are many UN involvements that focus solely on ecological matters, employment, technological development, community health, scientific research and the liberalisation of trading practices. Here it has to be emphasised that the UN efforts are frequently impeded by the very complexity of the global organisation; and by the important fact that different UN bodies are often seen to be pulling in different directions. Thus while UN aid agencies struggle to bring relief to destitute and starving Iraqis, the US-dominated Security Council insists on sanctions against Iraq that, according to a UN report, are causing 'pre-famine' conditions to develop and 'a grave humanitarian tragedy' to unfold;[16] and where the Security Council can impose sanctions on Libya over Lockerbie while Fawzi Hamed Al Sultan, the President of the UN-linked IFAD (International Fund for Agricultural Development), can present Colonel Gaddafi with an engraved metal plate as a token of UN appreciation for Libya's support in combating disease in North Africa.

The challenges facing the United Nations derive from its limitless ambitions. At one level it aims to embrace and succour every human being, and at the same time to protect and nourish the environment for the generations yet unborn; something of such grand aims is discernible in much that the United Nations attempts. But at another level the United Nations is suborned by commercial interests and powerful nation states to serve a variety of hidden agendas. If the proper objectives of the UN are to be realised, even in part, it is necessary to consider the characteristic impediments and obstacles. These are addressed largely in Part II; at this stage it is useful to profile the character of the nation state – in systems analysis terms, the sub-unit – as an obstacle to the emergence of the United Nations as a truly supranational organisation.

THE SIGNIFICANCE OF STATES

The nation state is the principal player in the United Nations organisation. Despite the opening words of the UN Charter ('We the peoples . . .'), relations within the organisation are necessarily between governments; and though it may be arguable that the will of the people influences many ('democratic') administrations this is by no means a universal rule. There is a crucial paradox in the role of the nation state in the structure and operation of the United Nations: while the Charter itself has been drafted to protect, amongst other things, the sovereignty of the nation state, it is precisely this sovereignty that impedes the evolution of the UN organisation into a genuinely supranational body.

It is also significant that whereas the evolution of the nation state has generated a degree of internal order this has not always translated into harmonious relations between countries. Again this highlights the problem of achieving international order: if states are to be truly sovereign then they may act as they wish towards their neighbours – with all the possibilities for international anarchy that this implies. In fact, states have proved willing to limit their sovereignty via the mechanism of international agreements and in pragmatic recognition of limitations on their power. But this latter circumstance demonstrates one of the main problems facing the United Nations in the modern world: the more powerful a state the less inclined it will be to limit its sovereignty (see Chapter 3). In short, 'The fundamental difficulty of subjecting states to the rule of law is the fact that states possess power'.[17]

The legal definition of a state highlights its relative stability and its capacity to function as an autonomous unit. The 1933 Montevideo Convention on Rights and Duties of States stipulated a number of indices of statehood; including a defined territory, a permanent population, effective government control, and the capacity to enter into formal relations with other like entities. There is much flexibility in these stipulations: thus state populations may be small (Nauru – population 6500 – has been considered a state), and territorial boundaries may not always be precisely defined (as with Israel in 1948). However, the capacity to enter into formal relations with other states clearly enshrines the element of national sovereignty: in such circumstances any putative supranational body that attempted to compel a state – in the absence of state acquiescence in a 'higher' agreement (which the UN Charter might represent) – could be accused of violating legitimate state rights.[18]

The principal problem of state sovereignty is that national governments are often irresistibly tempted to exploit state power. Thus J. William Fulbright, one-time chairman of the US Senate Foreign Relations Committee, has identified the 'arrogance of power' with the 'psychological need that nations seem to have in order to prove they are bigger, better, or stronger than other nations'. This implies that a nation with a stronger army 'is also proving that it has better people, better institutions, better principles, and, in general, a better civilization'.[19] State sovereignty is also significant in that states usually retain their international legitimacy in circumstances where their domestic performance may be lamentable. In 1993 the United Nations was prepared to impose sanctions on Haiti nominally because of its abuse of democratic principles. But the move, under US prompting, seemed to have more to do with Washington's hidden economic agenda than with any genuine interest in political freedom: the United States had no inclination to urge UN action against such manifestly undemocratic states as Burma, Kuwait, Saudi Arabia and China (this latter enjoying 'favoured nation' status for trading purposes). The characteristic UN interest in protecting state sovereignty has often worked to sanction the legitimacy of dictatorial and repressive regimes: there is implied approval of all member states entitled to 'sovereign equality' (Article 2(1) of the Charter). The actual inequalities of member states in the UN organisation derive not from their varying democratic credentials but from their military and economic power, and from the circumstances of the 1945 genesis of the organisation.

An interesting comparison has been drawn between the structure of the United Nations and that of the United States under the Articles of Confederation from 1781 to 1789.[20] At that time the US government had no power to regulate trade, to impose taxes, to draft troops, to establish courts or to issue money. The Articles note that each state [in the Confederate structure] 'retains its sovereignty, freedom and independence, and every power, jurisdiction and right which is not by this federation expressly delegated to the United States in Congress assembled'. If Congress wanted to levy money or men it could only make a request to the Confederate states; and if they refused Congress was helpless. These circumstances are closely analogous to those facing UN Secretary-General Boutros Boutros-Ghali as he struggles to induce UN member states to pay their financial dues and to offer troops for peacekeeping operations in Somalia and elsewhere. The United Nations has a stronger working constitution than did the ill-fated League of Nations but the Charter stipulates few powers against recalcitrant states. Article 19 declares that a member in financial arrears 'shall have no vote in the General Assembly if the amount of its arrears equals or exceeds the amount of the contributions due from it for the preceding two full years'. But this is little enough penalty. The General Assembly in any case is rarely entitled to reach conclusions that are legally binding (the real power lies in the Security Council); and even this minor deterrent is further diluted by the possibility of mitigation. Article 19 concludes: 'The General Assembly may, nevertheless, permit such a Member to vote if it is satisfied that the failure to pay is due to conditions beyond the control of the Member.' Such considerations help to explain the resourcing problems with which the United Nations is constantly afflicted.

In this context a crucial challenge facing the United Nations is the necessity to reconcile the sovereignty of member states with the legitimate needs of a genuinely supranational authority. In talking of 'the maintenance of international peace and security under the Charter', Secretary-General Boutros-Ghali has emphasised the need to square the circle:

> The foundation-stone of this work is and must remain the State. Respect for its fundamental sovereignty and integrity are crucial to any common international progress. The time of absolute and exclusive sovereignty, however, has passed; its theory was never matched by reality. It is the task of leaders of States today to understand this and to find a balance between the needs of good internal governance and the requirements of an ever more interdependent world.[21]

However, there is a further paradox that is important but seemingly rarely addressed by Dr Boutros-Ghali. The emergence of a supranational United Nations – possibly supplemented by an expanded and US-dominated North Atlantic Treaty Organisation (NATO) and a globally-imposed GATT economic order – may invite world dominance by a few US-led hegemonic states. Perhaps the traditional sovereignty of the nation state, nominally at odds with a global supranationalism, should be upheld as a useful hedge against hegemony. In the real world of practical politics UN members do not enjoy 'sovereign equality': until they do, we should be wary of the UN's supranational ambitions (see Chapter 3).

IN THE MELTING POT

The United Nations is today challenged by unprecedented political circumstances, of which the most significant is the end of the Cold War. A Swedish diplomat is quoted: 'It's all changing. You forget where people come from. Instead of working in blocs – the west, the east, the non-aligned – we just meet together, a group of six or seven colleagues, and thrash things out. You will find that the end of the Cold War is very obvious here. We don't speak about east and west any longer.'[22] It seemed easy, in the first flush of the Soviet collapse, to envisage a reinvigorated United Nations, a 'second youth' for a once 'moribund and disregarded organisation'. After the 1991 Gulf War – about which no consensual view has emerged in the world community – the United Nations saw a massive increase in the number and scale of its peacekeeping operations. Suddenly the Security Council, without the prospect of a Soviet veto (its incidence always exaggerated by the West: there were more UK/US vetoes through the period of the Cold War), could project an image of apparent harmony. At last, US observers could declare, the international body was working as had been intended by its founders. In fact it soon became increasingly clear – though some observers were perversely slow to notice – that the new American enthusiasm for the United Nations (which rarely extended to Washington paying its dues on time) derived from the fact that the international body could now be conveniently dragooned to serve American foreign policy – a role that the American founders of the United Nations may well have intended.

Even in the new global circumstances the basic questions did not generate what could be represented as a consensual response. How was the United Nations to adopt a proper strategic orientation in the changed political landscape? Put another way, 'Might not a UN revived do more harm than good?'[23] Soon the doubts were crowding in: the Rio Earth Summit had achieved little of value; the Vienna conference on human rights had proved an embarrassing fiasco; the Bosnian tragedy was revealing alarming divisions among the permanent members of the Security Council; and the US-led troops in Somalia led many Africans to perceive a fresh 'colonial' incursion. Thus Rakiya Omaar, then of the human rights organisation Africa Watch and now of African Rights, commented: 'A UN official recently told our organisation that "Somalia is the greatest failure of the UN in our time". I agree. The crisis in Somalia has been unfolding for at least three years; I have seen memos to the Secretary-General in 1990 accurately predicting what would happen.' Alex de Waal (also then of Africa Watch and now of African Rights) highlighted the UN problems of 'institutional inertia' and 'lack of accountability'. In both Kenya and Somalia the UNHCR (United Nations High Commission for Refugees) had failed to act in good time; aid operations to combat the 1988 famine in Sudan had been unaccountably closed down; starvation in Ethiopia was exacerbated by inadequate WFP (World Food Programme) estimates and tardy UN action.[24]

The growing international role of UN peackeepers was becoming increasingly apparent: by the end of 1992 the United Nations was involved in twelve major peacekeeping operations, with others in prospect.[25] At the same time it was obvious that the expanding range of involvements was testing the limits of UN intervention. It was necessary to consider fresh 'moral imperatives', to examine unprecedented 'practical risks', to address 'unfamiliar challenges'.[26] When should the United Nations intervene? Should there be consistent criteria, involving not least an estimate of current UN resources? Or should the Secretary-General launch initiatives, to the extent that his powers allowed, on the assumption that the member states would be shamed into providing support? Or would nations only be interested in circumstances that affected their own strategic policies? The US-led onslaught on Iraq had symbolised a focused initiative, but American eagerness to protect its oil supplies could hardly provide general principles that might guide proper UN interventions in the future. Moreover, the United States, unconstrained in the post-Cold War world, has tended to decide on action and to seek UN endorsement afterwards: such a route is not open to other UN member states.

It was now clear that the mix of unilateral US decision making, inadequate UN resources, poor management and inadequate analysis of the fresh challenges facing the international organisation was generating confusion and chaos; in some theatres of operations 'a fearsome shambles', where the United Nations seemed 'to be compounding misery and crisis'.[27] Some observers – including ones with access to and at least partial responsibility for UN decision making (such as the UK defence secretary Malcolm Rifkind) – were warning that the United Nations would 'soon be out of its depth' (as if permanent members of the Security Council had nothing to do with it). Such facile comment trades on the notion that the United Nations has some corporate existence beyond that of its individual member states, that the international organisation already has some supranational existence. There is an obvious sense in which this is true – the constitution of the Secretariat renders it nominally independent of any national government – but more importantly the various main pipers still call the operational tunes. In all the main UN operations the influence of dominant nation states, either with perceived interests in the area or supplying resources, can be clearly discerned in the thrust of UN policy. In Iraq and Somalia, of interest to Washington, intervention is managed at the whim of the US State Department and the Pentagon; in Bosnia it has been Britain and France, having allocated substantial resources to the region, that largely determine the drift of UN decision making.

Again it is easy to discern the dichotomy between an international body able only to request support from key members of the club and a United Nations struggling to evolve an identity beyond the sum of its parts. One consequence of this bifurcation is that differences between the governments of nation states can be afforded a prominent platform in the Security Council. Thus on the Bosnian question there were 'two UNs at war with each other';[28] the US-dominated UN in New York wanted one policy, the British- and French-run UN in Bosnia another. To the tension between the traditional nation state and the putative supranational authority another was added: that between the governments of individual UN members.

It remained essential in such circumstances that efforts be made to meld the various UN member factions, to encourage at least the degree of internal harmony without which the international body would be impotent. The UN Secretary-General Boutros-Ghali, while frequently castigating individual member states – though often obliquely – for their shortcomings, has tried to view the UN's evolving posture with resolute optimism. Thus he depicts *multilateralism* ('the voluntary cooperation of nations for peace and development') as 'working more effectively than ever before in history'. New challenges have to be confronted because member states 'have heaped new responsibilities on the organization' with the result that 'the danger, expense and scale of new operations exceed anything in the United Nations' history and are unique in the record of international affairs'.[29] The various operations – in such places as Angola, Cambodia, El Salvador, Georgia, Haiti, Somalia, Tajikistan and the former Yugoslavia – are seen as efforts to secure the state system in the context of international peace and security. And there are reasons for optimism: 'A growing number of member states are concluding that some problems can be addressed most effectively by UN efforts. Thus, collective security is finally beginning to work as it was conceived . . . such efforts are reviving hopes for achieving a workable international system . . . The people of the world have become convinced that democracy is essential to progress with justice. Multilateralism is the democracy of international society.'[30]

THE CHALLENGE

All organisations, movements and creeds – indeed all living systems – are constantly confronted with the need to adapt in new environmental circumstances, to change if they are to survive and remain effective. In the anodyne terms of many politicians it is essential for organisations to be

open to 'reform' and 'modernisation', soubriquets that can denote surrender, retreat or stalwart loyalty to principle. In the world of the 1990s it
is easy to see that a United Nations launched in 1945, and having seen few
constitutional changes in half a century, may now need to be fundamentally redefined. Thus in 1990 Sir Brian Urquhart, the UN historian,
declared:

> That the organization needs to be reformed, strengthened, and modern-
> ized should by now be obvious. After the tumultous changes of the past
> forty-five years, the world of 1990 bears little resemblance to that of
> 1945. Now that East and West are becoming reconciled, the differences
> between North and South developed and developing nations seem a
> more likely source of future difficulties. In 1945 the main common
> objective of nations was to avoid a third world war, to establish a col-
> lective system of peace and security, and to achieve an agreement on
> general disarmament . . . it now looks as if this objective may conceiv-
> ably be realized, while other problems have become dominant, chal-
> lenging many of the assumptions on which the original UN system was
> based.[31]

This species of 1990s optimism now seems to have been largely overtaken
by events. The dissolution of the Soviet empire has yielded massive new
racial and national instabilities; the United States promised a brake on the
arms race in the post-Gulf War World and is today (1994) pouring weapons
into the Middle East; more states are becoming nuclear powers, some of
them with alarming traditions of political instability and facing threats from
hostile neighbours. The United Nations needs to be reformed and
modernised but in ways that boldly address the new spectrum of hazards in
what was once piously and foolishly called the 'New World Order'.

The threat to peace and security must be regarded as the central challenge facing the United Nations: without peace there can be no secure
investment in health plans, aid programmes, industrial development, education, cultural reform and all the rest. But this circumstance cannot be
used to license UN intervention in any or every social conflict. It is
important to preserve the notion of the legitimate armed struggle and to
remember that a United Nations intent on preserving a US-approved status
quo would not necessarily be on the side of justice. Moreover, morality
apart, there is no practical way in which the United Nations could aspire to
the role of a ubiquitous world policeman.

Other challenges facing the United Nations relate to the development of
technology for the improvement of the human condition, the shifting of

scientific research away from military application (experiments that involve launching cruise missiles on Baghdad should be discouraged), the integration and development of the global economy in the interest of people rather than multinational corporations and the élites they serve (see Chapter 6 and 7), the sensitive control of population and migration, the proper stewardship of the environment (including the just and sustainable management of such natural elements as land, oil and water), the combating of disease at every level (from village infection to pandemic hazard), and encouraging progress in the catch-all category of human rights. Merely to signify the spectrum of challenge facing the international organisation conveys something of the scale of the task confronting the United Nations as it approaches the next millennium.

Secretary-General Boutros-Ghali, noting how the demands on the United Nations have 'surged' since the end of the Cold War, has identified the aims that the UN should adopt to resolve conflicts and to preserve peace:

> Situations that could produce conflict should be identified at the earliest possible stage to allow time for diplomacy.
>
> Peacemaking should aim to resolve the issues that have led to a conflict.
>
> Where a conflict has been brought to an end, the peacekeepers should work to implement the agreements for peace, however fragile.
>
> The peace-builders should aim to reconstitute the institutions and infrastructures that have been torn by civil war and strife.
>
> And 'in the largest sense' there should be an effort 'to address the deepest causes of conflict: economic despair, social injustice and political oppression'.[32]

Already, comments Boutros-Ghali, it is possible 'to discern an increasingly common moral perception that spans the world's nations and peoples, and which is finding expression in international laws', many owing their genesis to efforts of the United Nations. He emphasises the need for a commitment to human rights, observing that 'globalism and nationalism need not be viewed as opposing trends, doomed to spur each other on to extremes of reaction'. The rights of the sovereign state must be preserved, but the sovereignty, territorial integrity and independence of states 'must not be permitted to work against each other in the period ahead'. The aim should be 'to maintain the integrity of each while finding a balanced design for all'.[33]

In his 1992 report on the work of the Organisation from the forty-sixth to the forty-seventh session of the General Assembly, Boutros-Ghali highlighted his dominant theme: 'that the current international situation requires an Organization capable of dealing comprehensively with the economic, social, environmental and political dimensions of human development', an agenda that requires 'the full application of the principles of democracy within the family of nations and within our Organization'.[34] Having proposed such a universal framework, he then examines such principal aspects as the United Nations as an institution, global partnership for development, and the scope of the UN's aid and peace endeavours. Again the tone is optimistic: 'a better world is within our reach.'

There is no detail here of the massive and growing problems faced by the United Nations; of the debilitating impact of the greatly increased demands, of the corrosive effects of mismanagement and corruption, of the hazardous problems faced by UN officials and troops on the ground, of the growing tensions between UN personnel and US policy makers in circumstances where a hegemonic United States insists above all on its sovereign rights (see Part II). There is no reflection of the growing confusion and disillusion in the broad peacekeeping enterprise. Evidence supplied by the prestigious publication *The Military Balance* suggests that UN peacekeeping operations are in a state of chaos and that the UN organisation needs a drastic shake-up if it is to cope in the years ahead.[35] At the same time President Clinton asserts, in an address to the UN General Assembly on 28 September 1993, that the United States 'intends to remain engaged and to lead . . . we must and will serve as a fulcrum for change and a pivot point for peace'. We can hardly expect Secretary-General Boutros-Ghali to speculate in public about how American power may become part of the solution rather than remain part of the problem (Chapter 3).

This chapter began by posing a number of preliminary general questions. Now we are able to see that much of the work of the United Nations can only be undertaken in circumstances of international peace and security, while acknowledging at the same time that UN military intervention is not necessarily just, even where possible under current resource constraints.

It is likely that the United Nations will survive in some form as a viable international organisation; and that – in a shrinking world with ever growing pressure on natural resources – it will evolve a fabric of supranational authority. Elements of this are already in place, though predictably exploited by powerful states with interests to protect.

The character of the United Nations is of central global significance. Among its founders were not only public-spirited idealists but hard-nosed *realpolitik* cynics. Today's United Nations remains fuelled by many motives, too often by the eagerness of policy makers in hegemonic states to subsume the international body within the policy-making framework of national governments. The different players in the UN organisation necessarily perceive the United Nations in different ways, variously bringing to the international organisation their own cultural baggage and political ambitions. A central dominating problem is whether the United Nations is to evolve as little more than a satrap of Washington, or at least of the dominant world community of capitalist commerce.

The objectives of the United Nations are only partly defined in the Charter; and many states have learnt to ignore inconvenient clauses. The best elements of the United Nations are enshrined not essentially in verbal symbols, written or spoken, but in an amorphous but durable spirit that nourishes a humanistic commitment. At the same time it is still necessary to articulate the multilayered challenges facing the international organisation and to identify the mounting threats and problems – if only to encourage the emergence of a proper United Nations, one that genuinely serves 'the peoples' rather than this or that faction, élite or powerful state.

2 The Historical Frame

PREAMBLE

Many themes – in idealism, commitment to human welfare, and practical politics – were to contribute to the emergence of the United Nations. Principal among these was the age-old longing for a just world that would live in peace, a secure *pax orbis* that would encourage the gradual improvement of the human condition. Isaiah (2, 4) imagined swords beaten into plowshares, and nations that no longer warred with their neighbours; Jesus (Matthew 5, 9) blessed the peacemakers as 'the children of God' (though, with nice paradox, at times preferred the sword to peace*). In tribute to the dream, both secular and spiritual leaders were dubbed 'Prince of Peace', though often content to secure tranquillity by the destruction of their enemies. Echoing Isaiah, the celebrated Dr Montague John Rendall (1862–1950), one of the first Governors of the British Broadcasting Corporation, in 1927 composed the motto of the Corporation: 'Nation shall speak peace unto nation.'

It is obvious that the ubiquitous yearning for peace has co-existed throughout all human history with military invasions, the destruction of people and property, all the horrors of conquest and genocide. The struggle for peace has endured through aeons of gloom and disillusion, the beacon of hope kept alive in each new generation. Philip J. Noel-Baker, winner of the Nobel Prize for peace in 1959, considered the award 'the greatest honor a man can receive in this world' (a judgement he may have been prepared to modify in the light of the similar honouring of Henry Kissinger, a man most remarkable for his subversion of Chilean democracy and his massive bombing of Cambodia). In any event, no-one doubted that peace had to be worked for, hopefully protected in protocols and legislation, and enshrined in the charters of institutions. A principal aim of the United Nations was '*to save succeeding generations from the scourge of war*' (the first declaration in the preamble to the Charter).

The dream was unambiguous, but it was seldom clear how it could be attained. In the classical Vegetius, in the introduction to *Epitoma Rei*

---

*See Matthew *10*, 34; Luke *22*, 36.

23

Militaris, we find the exhortation *qui desiderat pacem, praeparet bellum* (he who desires peace must prepare for war), a notion that has echoed down through the ages and always served as justification for the profligate allocation of treasure for the production of arms. Others have suggested that if we want peace we should prepare for peace; that we should work to remove the social and political conditions that encourage war; that we should be honest in admitting the relevance of vast disparities in wealth, of the ambitions of élites, of the interests of large corporations and the nation state. The United Nations will learn to focus on such matters in its quest for global peace.

THE HYBRID HERITAGE

One of the main animating themes behind the spirit of the United Nations (and the letter of the Charter) is the idea that humanity can live in a harmonious world as one family, where all people acknowledge common interests and are subject to the rule of law. There have always been thoughts about how humankind could become united, and not all such ideas were pacific: many rulers have envisaged how military conquest could generate a single world state, and religious totalitarians have been happy to contemplate a congenial global bigotry that would facilitate the speedy extermination of heretics. It is not enough that some authority achieve global sway: the essential consideration of human rights must inform any framing of an international or global constitution. Erasmus (1466–1536), the great Dutch satirist and humanist, considered 'kingdoms of moderate power united in a Christian league', suggesting with such a concept the notion that monarchical ambition would need to be limited in the interest of a wider union. Others envisaged a secular rather than a religious focus.

Thus in the *Memoirs* of Maximilien de Béthune, Duc de Sully (1560–1641), we encounter a 'grand design' for a Universal Christian Commonwealth of Europe, which, despite the nod to religion, is essentially a secular and radical programme to bring peace and harmony to what he perceived to be the important nation states of the day. In the same spirit the Dutch jurist and theologian Hugo Grotius, or Huig de Groot (1583–1645), in *De Jure Belli et Pacis* (On the Law of War and Peace) suggested a basis for international law. In 1618 political and religious strife led to his imprisonment, but he escaped to Paris where Louis XIII awarded him a pension. The work of Béthune and Grotius was to influence the framing of the Covenant of the League of Nations nearly three centuries later.

William Penn (1644–1718), the Quaker founder of Pennsylvania, published *An Essay Towards the Present and Future Peace of Europe* in 1693, in which he urged the limiting of sovereignties in the interest of a wider harmony. There quickly followed a *Project for Settling Perpetual Peace in Europe* (1713), and later Jean Jacques Rousseau's *Judgement on a Plan for Perpetual Peace* (1761), declaring that rulers would be forced 'to be just and pacific'. In 1754 Rousseau wrote his *Discourse on the Origin and Foundations of Inequality Among Men* in which he emphasised the natural goodness of human beings and the corrupting influences of institutionalised life. His crucial work *The Social Contract* (1762) is widely seen as influencing French revolutionary thought and the development of human rights in Europe. Such notions stimulated many later thinkers; for example, Immanuel Kant (1724–1804) who proposed in his *Perpetual Peace* (1795) that 'the scourge of war' will drive men 'to do what reason could have taught them at once without so many bitter experiences, namely to give up their lawless life of savages and enter a League of Nations', where all states could 'expect security and peace'.

In the nineteenth century theoretical speculation, the cogitations of philosophers, jurists, clerics and others, was increasingly supplemented by practical actions. In 1816 the pacifist Peace Society, heavily influenced by Quakerism, was founded at the heart of British imperialism, in London. It was significant that such efforts were often condemned by mainstream Christian apologists. Thus a pious writer in 1819 in the *Northumberland Monthly* wondered whether any suggestion that war was inconsistent with Christianity would 'restrain the Turks, the pirates of Algiers, or the savage Indians of North America?' How gratifying it would be to such people to learn that the Christians had abolished war: 'every European kingdom would soon be deluged with blood, and every Christian community exterminated.' In 1828 William Ladd of New Hampshire, himself instrumental in the founding of the American Peace Society, urged the development of international law and the creation of an international court. Fifteen years later a General Peace Convention was held in London, a prelude to many similar meetings in the year that followed. John Bright denounced the pacifist 'extremism' of the Peace Society, while he and other activists, such as Richard Cobden, encouraged free trade on the ground that it would bring nations closer together.*

---

*This compares well with current efforts to secure economic agreements through the GATT negotiations. Would Cobden, Bright et al. be supporters of GATT if today they could see the problems faced by Third World countries in competition with powerful states? (See Chapter 6.)

The pressures of commerce have always encouraged a pragmatic internationalism, one inevitably interested in mercenary considerations rather than any idealistic vision of global peace and harmonious law. International economic units, influencing the affairs of nation states, have existed for centuries; as, for example Ulrich Fugger & Bros, a company with subsidiaries all over Europe, and with headquarters in Augsburg. This firm, founded by Jacob Fugger (1459–1525), ran mining operations in several countries, was a dominant copper company, had interests in banking, and drew substantial revenue from Mexico, South America and the West Indies. It befriended monarchs and popes, financed wars (e.g. the pope's war against the French), organised papal indulgences as a business operation, and worked to secure the elections of popes and emperors (e.g. Charles I). In later years such organisations as the East India and Hudson Bay companies were chartered in part to consolidate colonial gains and to assist in the conquest of new lands. Such matters are worth considering in the light of the twentieth-century impact of the multinational corporation (Chapter 6): there are many competing internationalisms, some interested in mercenary gain rather than the dream of global harmony.

The growing nineteenth-century interest in international commerce helped to focus attention on the pacific solution of disputes. Hegemonic states were less concerned with the possible constraints of international law than were their weaker neighbours – morality and law have always served in part as mechanisms whereby the weak can aim to chain the strong. Various international bodies were established and granted nominal powers over individual states: for example, the International Telegraphic Union (1865), the Universal Postal Union (1874), and the International Health Office (1907). Other developments (for example, the founding in 1873 of the Institut de Droit International in Brussels and the development of the powerful Concert of Europe) further stimulated the emergence of legal (and cynical *realpolitik*) mechanisms for the settling of international disputes without resort to military conflict.

At the Hague conferences of 1899 and 1907 efforts were made to secure international agreements on such matters as arms limitation, the use of poison gas, aerial bombardment from balloons, submarine mines, and the rights of neutral shipping. Regulations were agreed to prohibit what were seen as the most horrendous forms of warfare, but there were no effective mechanisms in place to compel observance by recalcitrant states. At the same time a boost was given to the idea of a body of international law to which individual states would be increasingly subject. One significant achievement was the establishment of the Permanent Court of Arbitration, or Hague Tribunal, which was largely superseded in 1921 by the

Permanent Court of International Justice, itself replaced in 1945 by the International Court of Justice (the World Court), one of the principal organs of the United Nations. The Hague conferences, themselves the outgrowth of many earlier discussions, also prepared the way for the creation of the League of Nations.

Thomas Woodrow Wilson (1856–1924), law professor and twenty-eighth US president, delivered a speech to Congress on 8 January 1918 in which he specified the conditions for peace at the end of the Great War. The speech preamble talks of a world 'made fit and safe to live in', one that would be 'made safe for every peace-loving nation which, like our own, wishes to live its own life, determine its own institutions, be assured of justice and fair dealing . . . as against force and selfish aggression . . .'. There then follows the celebrated 'Fourteen Points' urging open diplomacy, freedom of maritime navigation, free trade, a reduction in armaments, a settling of all colonial claims, and a resolution of disputes about territory and sovereignty. The final point (XIV) heralds the creation of the League of Nations: 'A general association of nations must be formed under specific covenants for the purpose of affording mutual guarantees of political independence and territorial integrity to great and small nations alike.'

President Wilson then worked to establish the Covenant of the League as part of the 1919 Paris Peace Agreement, and to sell the idea of the League to a sceptical United States weary of European involvements. On 10 July he presented the Versailles Treaty (which included the Covenant) for the approval of the Senate. The inclusion of the Covenant in the Treaty was seen as both a strength and a weakness: it helped to secure the Covenant, since no-one could be seen opposing the Paris settlement; but it inextricably linked the League to an agreement necessarily associated with the defeat of important states (not guaranteed to ensure their co-operation in the years to follow). The victorious powers secured the establishment of the League, but the Germans saw in the new international body little more than further humiliation. Thus Fritz Berber, Director of the Berlin-based Research Department, Hochschule für Politik, commented that the promise of a 'new world order' had 'rapidly turned out to be a terrible illusion . . .'. The League was seen as merely the 'executor of Versailles . . . the most important regulations of the Covenant seemed to be meant for nothing else but for the maintenance of the unbearable Versailles *status quo* . . .'. Here was the ultimate irony: that the League, intended to secure a 'peace of the peoples', simply prepared the ground for Adolf Hitler. The United Nations, similarly growing out of war, was later to enshrine a similar dislocation. The exclusion of Germany and Japan from

permanent seats on the Security Council – an anomaly today being
addressed (see Chapter 5) – has not however yet led to calamity. The
League, beset by a range of problems that the United Nations was able to
circumvent, was doomed from the outset. Not least was the problem of the
United States: Woodrow Wilson, a principal force behind the League,
failed to secure American support.

The League was unavoidably regarded as more a European than a world
body. US Senator Borah saw the League as 'Britain's tool – a dodger and
a cheater', while Senator Sherman reckoned the League about 'to empty
upon the American people the aggregated calamities of the world and send
the Angel of Death into every American home'. Even the moderate
Franklin Delano Roosevelt, later to become the principal architect of the
United Nations, saw the League as 'nothing more than a debating society
and a poor one at that'. Senator Henry Cabot Lodge, the main American
opponent of the League, had accomplished his objectives in the short term;
but even he realised that the United States would in due course be forced
out of its temporary isolationism. World power had not yet shifted across
the Atlantic, and until that time accommodations would have to be made
with the European powers – and with their creature, the League. The US
administration built up a number of unofficial links to the League, offering
support where deemed appropriate and later attending League Council
meetings on disarmament: for example, in 1932 Secretary of State
H. L. Stimson contributed to Council meetings, giving US views on
disarmament and the rapidly developing Far East crisis.

The League addressed such issues as the mandated territories (where
the former colonies of Germany and Ottoman Turkey were adopted by the
'advanced' nations), the problem of minorities, and the disarmament question with mixed success. Today it is easy to see that the assigning of mandates over Palestine, Iraq and South-West Africa did much to create
problems for the future. Disarmament, a constant League interest, did
nothing to prevent the holocaust that would soon shatter the fragile peace.
It was increasingly clear that tensions were growing in Europe and Asia;
and that the League, with only limited membership and no realistic coercive powers, would have no power to prevent another international conflict.
In the event, the League was broken by crises in Manchuria, Abyssinia
and Spain; events that involved military aggression against sovereign
states, and that moreover served as heralds to the impending Second
World War. If the League had been able to discipline the expansionist
powers of Japan, Italy and Germany then the War might have been prevented. In the event, the League had no power over national sovereignties:
powerful states were able to ignore both the spirit and letter of the

Covenant, just as today they are able to pick and choose in the basket of international laws and UN Charter Articles. The League, like the United Nations, worked diligently in the fields of health, education and human rights; but progress, like many of today's UN successes, went largely unsung: the failures were much larger than the triumphs, and ultimately catastrophic. The first Secretary-General of the League, Sir Eric Drummond, who served from 1919 to 1933[1], declared at the end of his term that if the League were to disappear, 'the first task which would confront the statesmen on the League's disappearance would be to reinvent the League'.

The League Assembly met for the last time on 8 April 1946 in the Palais des Nations. League funds were distributed to donor nations; and the Palace, its material possessions, the library and its archive, and the various powers and functions were transferred to the fledgling United Nations. Sir Robert Cecil, one of the original architects of the League, in his final address to the Assembly applauded the new United Nations Charter as potentially effective machinery to combat aggression as 'an international crime' and urged 'every well-disposed citizen of every state' to be ready 'to undergo any sacrifice in order to maintain peace'. He concluded with the words: 'The League is dead. Long live the United Nations!'

ROOSEVELT'S 'UNITED NATIONS'*

The League was no more. It had totally failed to counter the Japanese invasion of Manchuria, the Italian invasion of Abyssinia and what was in effect a Nazi invasion of Spain; crucially, it had failed to secure conditions in Europe that would have prevented the outbreak of hostilities – the German attack on Poland – that led to the Second World War. The League, impotent and discredited, was moribund; but even through the grim years of the early 1940s, with the League in its death throes, it was plain that a more effective international body would have to be created. It was less clear what form the new organisation would take, what its structure would be, and how its powers would be distributed. Many states had an interest in shaping the new institution; but in the event it was the United States, the most powerful nation on earth, that was to emerge as the principal architect.

---

*Roosevelt seemingly derived the name of the new international body from the alliance of 'United Nations' that had defeated the Axis powers in World War Two.

On 12 June 1941 representatives of Britain, the British Dominions, France, Belgium, Greece, the Netherlands, Luxembourg, Norway, Poland, Yugoslavia and Czechoslovakia signed the Inter-Allied Declaration, pledging their commitment to the creation of a harmonious new world. Two months later, President Roosevelt and Prime Minister Churchill formulated the Atlantic Charter, later endorsed by the Soviet Union and fourteen other allied states in battle against the Axis powers. The Charter proposed principles for the conduct of the war; and, analogous to Woodrow Wilson's Fourteen Points, came to influence the shaping of the United Nations. On 1 January 1942, at Washington D.C., twenty-six nations signed the United Nations Declaration, soon to attract a further twenty-one signatories; now the concept of a new international body, an effective successor to the League, was gaining momentum. On 30 October 1943 the Moscow Declaration on General Security, approving the basic idea of the United Nations, was signed by representatives from Britain, the United States, the Soviet Union and China. A month later, Roosevelt, Churchill and Stalin met at Tehran to discuss the conduct of the war and what would be the shape of the post-war world. It was recognised that a main responsibility of the putative United Nations would be to strive for an international order in which all peoples would be able to live in peace and security. However, there were already signs that the Allies had divergent views about the shaping of the post-war order.

In February 1943 Churchill had noted that it was the intention of the chiefs of the United Nations [the allied forces] 'to create a world organisation for the preservation of peace based upon the conceptions of freedom and justice and the revival of prosperity'. But there would not be a centralised authority; rather regional blocs to guarantee the peace:

> As part of this organisation an instrument of European government will be established which will embody the spirit but not be subject to the weakness of former League of Nations. The units forming this body will not be the great nations of Europe and Asia Minor only. Need for a Scandinavian bloc, Danubian bloc, and a Balkan bloc appears to be obvious. A similar instrument will be formed in the Far East with different membership . . .[2]

This was not the only sign of different emphases among the allied powers. The plans were already being laid for the establishment of the post-war international body, an organisation that, unlike the expiring League, would have effective powers to preserve the peace. Contributions were made, in particular, by Britain and the United States, but it was inevitable that the

US would be the more significant player. The US secretary of state Cordell Hull had begun to develop far-seeing plans soon after the start of the war; and various international organisations, geared to the needs of the post-war order, were already being developed. It was still evident that the British, under Churchill, had their own views about the shaping of the post-war world.

In May 1944 Churchill called a meeting of dominion prime ministers in London to consider how the British Empire might properly regard the prospect of a United Nations organisation. Again it was plain that the British premier favoured a regional approach to the shaping of the post-war order. Churchill proposed separate regional councils – for Europe, the Americas, Asia and Africa – which would convene to resolve disputes in their individual areas, and then meet as a world group to negotiate agreements. The dominion heads, less impressed than was Churchill with the old notion of empire and regional power groupings, saw no virtue in establishing localised enclaves, preferring to argue that now the world was more interdependent; a detrimental effect in one part of the world would soon affect all the others. Still Churchill saw virtue in a regional organisation for Europe, one that would include the United States, Britain and the Soviet Union.[3] Churchill was isolated. It was generally perceived that his preoccupation with winning the war had allowed too little time for consideration of the peace. In his minutes, not confided to Roosevelt at the time, Churchill noted: 'We have no idea of three or four Great Powers ruling the world. We should certainly not be prepared to submit to an economic, financial and monetary system laid down by, say, Russia or the United States with her faggot-vote China. The Supreme World Council or Executive is not to rule the nations. It is only to prevent them from tearing each other to pieces.'[4] Roosevelt, by contrast, imagined a global body that would have genuine peacemaking powers. He had been antipathetic to the Eurocentric League; but now, with little prospect of a return to pre-war isolation, Roosevelt was determined that the United States would be at the heart of a new world organisation.

Now the American mood was broadly sympathetic to the concept of the United Nations. There were few complaints when Congressman J. William Fulbright, then a member of the House Foreign Affairs Committee, introduced the 'Fulbright Resolution', urging the 'creation of appropriate international machinery with power adequate to establish and maintain a just and lasting peace'. Senator Tom Connally of Texas, Chairman of the Foreign Affairs Committee, introduced a similar resolution, and there were few problems – not least because it was increasingly perceived that new international machinery, with America the principal architect, could well be useful in securing the United States the fruits of victory. In fact the die was already cast: the development of the international bodies linked to the putative United Nations was already in progress, and the growing momentum for the establishment of the new global body was now irresistible. On 9 November 1943 forty-four nations together established the United Nations Relief and Rehabilitation Administration (UNRRA), and within four months Roosevelt had secured Congressional guarantees for UNRRA grants totalling $1,350 million. Roosevelt himself was now 'obsessed with the idea that a genuine new world order was being made'.[5]

Now the American president was keen to generate the same degree of commitment in the people of the United States; it was essential that the emerging international body not be allowed to go the way of the League. On 24 May 1944, at a packed press conference, Roosevelt read extracts from an invitation sent to 'the other United Nations and associated nations'. The 'monetary experts' had recommended the establishment of an 'international monetary fund', seen as 'an important step toward post-war international economic cooperation . . .'. A conference for the establishment of such a fund and a bank for reconstruction and development [what was to become the World Bank] would be held at Bretton Woods, New Hampshire. Roosevelt was aware that the Allies did not share his enthusiasm for a new international body. His far-sighted proposal 'received no applause from Great Britain and a bearish frown from the Soviet Union'.[6] To encourage international support he would propose that the United Nations include a lower house or assembly in which the strong and the weak would have an equal vote, but that there would also be an effective senate – comprising the Big Five (Britain, the United States, the Soviet Union, France and China) – that would have veto power over the assembly. Secretary of State Cordell Hull had already worked to develop the concept of an international organisation;[7] now he was asked to draw up the idea of international banking arrangements first, as bait for the potentially victorious but impoverished allies. The Russians, legitimately wary of capitalist machinations, prevaricated, though finally accepting Roosevelt's invitation. The Axis powers, with the war still running, were not invited.

The Bretton Woods Conference (1–22 July 1944) saw the creation of the International Monetary Fund (IMF) and the International Bank for Reconstruction and Development (the World Bank), important aids for international finance capitalism eager to consolidate its grip on the global economics of the post-war world. It was inevitable that the Axis powers would be excluded from such a conference (one does not combine with active enemies to protect their post-war fortunes); but nor was any attempt made to protect the interests of the Third World. At the time of Bretton Woods most of the Third World was in colonial subjugation; by the time the oppressed peoples achieved their independence there was no opportunity to reshape the international financial organisations created to further the interests of the world's most powerful states (see Chapter 6).

In the United States 1944 was also an election year, a circumstance that was bound to stimulate a degree of opposition to Roosevelt's plans. The increasingly obvious allied victories in the Pacific, the Middle East and Europe were adding to Roosevelt's popularity; and it was unlikely that his Republican opponent, Thomas E. Dewey, would gain much ground during the campaign. Already most senior Republicans were looking to 1948 when Roosevelt, now a very sick man, would be unable to run, even if still alive. John Foster Dulles, keen to see a successful Dewey nomination in 1948, realised that a good performance in 1944 would make this all the more likely. An obvious ploy in such circumstances was to exploit the spirit of idealism that Roosevelt himself was so successfully stimulating throughout the country.

Dulles had written a significant document, *The Six Pillars of Peace* (1943), in which he advocated a charter for a world order that would subordinate the separate nationalisms in a One World system. Here he envisaged a practical but idealistic League of Nations, this time to be called the United Nations and with the United States an important member.[8] Various national groups, including the Federal Council of Churches, adopted the document and gave further impetus to the United Nations movement. Roosevelt invited Foster Dulles to bring a copy of *The Six Pillars of Peace* to the White House; soon afterwards the arrangements were drawn up for the Dumbarton Oaks Conference from which the Charter of the United Nations would emerge. At the same time Dulles remained hostile to Roosevelt and encouraged Dewey to launch an attack on the Dumbarton Oaks proposals.

Throughout 1943 a series of staff briefings on the UN concept were presented to Roosevelt and incorporated in a 'Staff Charter', later revised into a 'Draft Constitution of International Organisation'. A final draft, approved by Roosevelt on 29 December, was presented to the Dumbarton Oaks Conference on 21 August 1944. In a series of meetings that lasted into October the Big Four – the United States, Britain, The Soviet Union and China – developed the detailed plans for the new international organisation. The decision was taken to establish a Security Council, a virtual UN executive, on which the Big Four plus France would be permanently represented. Here there was agreement but in other areas there was less than total accord. The Russian Ambassador, Andrei Gromyko, said to be privately in agreement with US Under-Secretary of State Edward Stettinius and Britain's Sir Alexander Cadogan, in public unambiguously supported the Soviet position – which represented international peace-keeping bodies as favouring the United States through voting procedures, and as hostile to the Soviet Union.

In Washington, under the growing stimulus of the election campaign, opposition to Roosevelt's ambitious international plans began to surface. The putative United Nations was depicted as a revamped League, with many of its attendant faults; in particular, no international body could be expected to work effectively without a substantial surrender of national sovereignty – an adjustment that would be totally unacceptable to most Americans. Others suggested that the United Nations should include an Executive Council (comprising Britain, the United States, China, the Soviet Union and some smaller nations) that would operate as a world government with every member having the power of veto. Sumner Welles, in *The Time for Decision*, proposed that an action could only proceed with Big Power unanimity and a two-thirds vote in the lower assembly.[9] At the same time candidate Thomas Dewey objected that the Dumbarton Oaks proposals were a disguised way of preserving Big-Power hegemony in the post-war world, that they would subordinate all other nations 'prematurely to the coercive power of the four powers holding this conference'. It seemed odd that a Republican candidate should be interested in protecting the weak against the strong, and that by implication he should want to discourage the growth of American power in the post-war world. However, the White House was sufficiently alarmed to issue a press statement that the administration had no plans to carve up the world; and at a subsequent press conference Cordell Hull agreed that he would be happy to talk to the Republicans about the shaping of the post-war world.

Dewey quickly telegraphed Hull to accept the 'invitation' and prudently nominated Foster Dulles as his spokesman. A meeting scheduled for 23 August 1944 almost had to be cancelled when, a few days before the confrontation, Dulles collapsed with a bad attack of thromboid phlebitis. However, the planned meeting took place: Dulles was allowed sight of the Dumbarton Oaks background documents; Hull reassured him that there was no Big-Power plan to rule the world; and then he proposed a bi-partisan agreement to refrain from campaign controversy over post-war American foreign policy. Dulles declined, sensitive to how Soviet moves in Eastern Europe, already alarming American ethnic minorities, might be exploited to Republican electoral advantage. Dulles did however agree that he would not make an issue of whether the United Nations would be able to requisition a peacekeeping army (a matter that would remain controversial through all the life of the United Nations). Dewey later complained that Roosevelt had deftly observed 'that the town hall didn't have any power unless it had a policeman, thereby satisfying a great many people who felt that there should be a United Nations army, about which I had a good many reservations'. Said Dewey, on this issue: 'I have been proved right, and he won the election.'[10]

The United States dominated the discussions at Dumbarton Oaks: the American plan, now entitled *Tentative United States Proposals for a General International Organisation*, was the only document presented in a final form and was given priority treatment. It was obvious from the start that the organisation of the emerging United Nations would be biased in favour of the victorious allies and that the United States would be predominant among them. The Security Council would have executive power, with the General Assembly offering membership to all states approved by the Council. It was also significant that the United Nations was intended by its US-led founders to hold sway not only over all member states but also over countries not currently within the organisation. Thus Article 2(6) of the Charter declares that the United Nations 'shall ensure that states which are not Members of the United Nations act in accordance with these Principles so far as may be necessary for the maintenance of international peace and security'. If the Dulles/Dewey faction were genuinely concerned about a Big-Power hegemony, there was ample evidence in the drafting of the UN constitution to confirm their worries. The Security Council had been structured and empowered to provide it with both executive and military power over the rest of the world. States outside the Council could join the General Assembly, if the Council approved; but the Assembly was only a talking shop, with real power residing in the US-led Council.

The American negotiators enjoyed a relatively easy ride at Dumbarton Oaks, a fact that has surprised some later American observers. In fact the United States went to some lengths not to propose any measures that it felt the other leading participants would be unable to accept. They were all 'out to ensure international security, which to each staff at Dumbarton Oaks meant a system to ensure the peace the Big Four was [sic] winning on the battlefield'.[11] The Chinese and the Russians were supposedly flattered at being asked to join the greatest council on earth. The British reportedly 'found much of the American wording legalistic and involved', but in any case were realistic in acknowledging that the structure of the post-war world would be based on practical power. Stettinius, the head of the US delegation proposed that the American scheme be used as the basic discussion document; and before long the *'Tentative . . . Proposals'* had evolved, without substantial change, into 'The Proposals'. When, on 9 October 1944, the agreed scheme was released to the outside world there were immediate protests from many of the nations that had not been consulted. The surge of criticism – 'from the chancellories of many smaller nations, from Australia to the Philippines' – was highly significant in that such nations had genuinely applauded the terms of the Atlantic Charter, a device that had offered them peace and protection. But nothing of the explicit provisions in the Atlantic Charter nor of the imagined American idealism about the rights of small nations was evident in the publicised output from Dumbarton Oaks. Now 'the crystal-clear fact that the Big Four intended to keep the real power of decision in the future as they had held it during the war horrified many statesmen from small or weak countries'.[12]

Dumbarton Oaks advertised above all what would be the shape of power politics in the post-war world; though few observers could have imagined the mounting implications of the Cold War. The *Time* magazine conveyed the common perception in noting that while the Proposals 'have many serious flaws' there was really no alternative: 'the plain reliance on Big-Power agreement is so desperate that no peaceful alternative is envisaged'. It was far from clear in these circumstances, as it is today, how the rights of small nations could be protected. The US Congress, happy to note American predominance in the new world body, was happy to give its approval. At least one of the fault lines so clearly evident in the League of Nations structure was absent from the fledgling organisation of the United Nations.

During the closing stages of the Second World War, Roosevelt, Churchill and Stalin attended the Yalta Conference (4–11 February 1945) in the Crimea. Here the principal topics for discussion were the course of the war, the post-war shape of Europe, and the development of the Dumbarton Oaks proposals. The idea of the Big-Power veto in the Security Council of the United Nations was reaffirmed, emphasising the fact that the major powers were prepared to accept no limit on their sovereignty. Discussion also focused on the question of representation in the General Assembly. Should the Soviet Union, by virtue of its power, or the British Commonwealth, by virtue of its six separate sovereignties, be entitled to more than one seat? Churchill seemed unconcerned at the prospect of a multiple Soviet vote, reminding the Americans that a pro-Western majority in the Assembly was guaranteed (the position would change as the colonised nations gradually gained their independence). On 7 February the secret voting clauses for the United Nations – agreed by only three states – were finalised and signed. Other discussions focused on the trustee lands left over from the League mandate, with Churchill keen to preserve the essential structure of European colonialism; and the preparations for the forthcoming San Francisco Conference at which the founder members of the United Nations would convene. The Yalta Conference was at an end, concluded in an atmosphere of cordiality. Sir Alexander Cadogan observed that Churchill and Anthony Eden 'are well satisfied – if not more – and I think they are right'. Churchill had toasted the British Empire; Roosevelt had expressed the hope that the world would have peace 'for fifty years, if not for eternity'; and Stalin had declared that 'the difficult time will come after the war'.

Roosevelt, now very frail, returned to the United States and began preparations for the San Francisco Conference, scheduled for 25 April 1945. However, on 12 April, while working on his Jefferson Day speech, he suffered a massive cerebral haemorrhage and was pronounced dead at 3.35 p.m. Roosevelt had died three weeks before the German surrender, and two weeks before the formal establishment of the United Nations. Harry S. Truman, sworn in as the 33rd US president four hours after Roosevelt's death, later commented that his decision to press ahead with the United Nations conference in San Francisco was the first decision he made as President of the United States.

The San Francisco Conference, at which delegates from nearly fifty nations convened on 25 April, began with broadcast good wishes from President Truman in Washington. The delegates then began their consideration of 547 amendments to the Dumbarton Oaks proposals; the 'United Nations' was acclaimed as the name of the new international body; and already there were clear signs of the tensions that would emerge between large nations and small and between the victorious allies themselves. The scene was set for the strategic and economic manipulation of the Third World by the Big Powers; and for the rapid escalation of the Cold War. The Conference had proved to be 'a mixed bag of power politics, muddy thinking, official hypocrisy, high idealism, keen good sense, legalistic nonsense, compromise and false hopes'. It was obvious that people 'could take from it almost anything they wanted'.[13] However, the real victor was power politics: this would be the clear message in the years to come. The Conference ended on 26 June 1945 with the ritual signing of the Charter of the United Nations.

The small nations, with few delusions, tended to assume that the new international body would do little more than consolidate the grip of the major Powers on the global politics of the post-war world. In the United States it was similarly assumed that the United Nations would be useful in protecting American values around the world, that the new international body and its institutions were 'devices to make the world safe for basically peaceful, satisfied, and progressive – if not entirely democratic – nations; the UN Charter implied the American Way of Life writ large'.[14] After debate about the merits of such locations as Boston, Philadelphia and San Francisco, the decision was taken to locate the UN headquarters in New York. The Rockefeller family was contacted with the idea that they might like to contribute to a prestigious development in the Turtle Bay area bordering the East River, whereupon John D. Rockefeller Jr offered the United Nations a gift of $8,500,000 to aid the project. Now it was clear that the centre of world power had shifted from Europe to the United States. A new pivotal centre had been recognised by the international community, and a new phase in world history was beginning.

THE KOREAN PARADIGM

The United States had benefited greatly – in both strategic and economic terms – by the Second World War. It had seen no conflict on its own mainland territory; there was massive industrial investment, though inevitably focused on armaments; and many overseas bases had been established, not least at the expense of the British.[15] Already Washington had pressed for significant advantages at the San Francisco Conference, despite the broadly conciliatory Soviet posture: the American journalist James Reston noted the 'ten concessions by Russia which have contributed greatly to the liberalising of the Dumbarton Oaks proposals'.[16] However, the Soviet concessions had done nothing to discourage the United States from pursuing its own perceived interests in the post-war world. Here a principal task was to convert the fledgling United Nations into an effective anti-Soviet device, a vital tool in the developing Cold war.

The US attitude to the Soviet Union at this time was well symbolised by President Truman's blunt attack on Soviet Foreign Minister Molotov when the two men met for the first time in Washington on 23 April 1945. Charles Bohlen, a senior US diplomat, recorded that 'he had never heard a top official get such a scolding'; with Arthur Vandenberg, a top US official at the San Francisco Conference, noting that he found Truman's abuse of Molotov 'thrilling'. Winston Churchill, soon to deliver his anti-Soviet 'iron curtain' speech at Fulton, Missouri, did not help US efforts to demonstrate Russian perfidy when he commented: 'The impression I brought back . . . is that Marshal Stalin and the Soviet leaders wish to live in honourable friendship and equity with the Western democracies. I feel also that their word is their bond. I know of no government which stands to its obligations . . . more solidly than the Russian Soviet government.'[17] The American posture was clear: there would be no compromise with the Soviets, even if this led to a massively increased level of international tension. There was even the prospect at one time that the American attitude would force the Soviet delegation to withdraw from the San Francisco Conference. Thus Senator Vandenberg, speaking in his diary (24 April 1945) of 'Frisco', noted: 'Russia may withdraw. If it does the conference *will proceed without Russia*. Now we are getting somewhere!' (original emphasis). Tensions now focused on such issues as the composition of the Polish government, the possibility of aid to a ravaged Soviet Union (20 million dead, with 14 large cities, 1710 towns and 70,000 villages partially or totally destroyed), and the greatly increased American presence in Asia following the Japanese collapse.

The Truman administration was keen to prosecute perceived American interests around the globe. On 24 February 1948 the US Policy Planning Staff in Washington emphasised that with the United States owning about 60 per cent of the world's wealth but with only 6.3 per cent of the world's population, 'our world task in this position is to devise a pattern of relationships which will permit us to maintain this position of disparity'. To this end the United States 'should cease to talk about such vague and unreal objectives as human rights, the raising of living standards and democratisation'. At the same time – via such instruments as National Security Council (NSC) memorandum 68 (April 1950), in which the 'slave state' of the Soviet Union is contrasted with a sublime United States; the creation of the North Atlantic Treaty Organisation (NATO), which stimulated the forming of the Warsaw Pact; and the development of the Marshall Aid Plan, in part a cover for CIA penetration of Europe[18] – Washington began to build the economic and strategic framework that would guarantee first the containment and later the rollback[19] of Soviet influence. In this grand scheme the newly hatched United Nations was destined to play an important role.

Throughout most of the history of the United Nations the international body was subject to the strategic pressures of the Cold War. In practice this has often meant that the United Nations was enlisted to serve American foreign policy. The UN was essentially an American creation, though drawing on many international themes and traditions; it was largely American financed, until Washington deliberately withheld due payments when it saw its Assembly majority eroded by the emergence of newly independent states; and the United States was always the dominant

member of the Security Council. The State Department official Robert
Murphy summed up the prevailing US attitude when he commented that
the United Nations could be used to serve American foreign policy; and
when the UN could not be exploited in this way it could then be ignored.[20]
The Soviet veto, absent in the Security Council of the 1990s, put some
constraints on US manipulation of the United Nations; but there were
many occasions through the period of the Cold War when Soviet wishes
were circumvented. The most glaring of these was when the United
Nations – during a brief Soviet absence from the Security Council in
protest at the improper exclusion of Mao Tse-tung's China – was enlisted
by Washington to support American strategy policy in Korea.* The
Korean War, the first substantial UN military involvement, was essentially
a US-run intervention. Today we can see how this event serves as a paradigm for current UN involvements, under US prompting, in circumstances
where there is no longer any real prospect of an anti-American veto in the
Security Council.

In 1945 the agreements made between the allies at Cairo, Yalta and
Potsdam facilitated the occupation of Korea by Soviet and American
forces upon the collapse of the Japanese occupation. The Koreans, having
suffered under Japanese rule for forty years, were now keen to govern
their own land, but this seemed an unlikely prospect. The United States
judged that the Koreans were 'incapable of assuming governmental control over their own country'[21] – and so began making other arrangements.
Washington succeeded, in the teeth of Soviet and Korean opposition, in
establishing a demarcation line at the 38th Parallel. Then, on 10 October
1945, the United States Military Government in Korea (USAMIGIK)
declared itself the only legitimate government in South Korea; at the same
time demanding the silence of 'irresponsible political groups', typically
comprising nationalist Koreans struggling for independence.

The new occupation by the US forces 'crystalized a large part of Korean
thinking into an anti-American mold', causing the people to feel that 'the
liberators had become the oppressors'.[22] On 14 February 1946 the US
authorities launched what they dubbed a 'Representative Democratic
Council', an undemocratic group headed by the authoritarian Syngman
Rhee with the support of the capitalists and the large landlords. Efforts to
establish a puppet Rhee regime in South Korea met with massive popular
opposition, whereupon the US forces rounded up hundreds of protestors
until the jails were crammed. At the same time the nationalist Kim Il-Sung

---

*See my *Korea: The Search for Sovereignty* (Macmillan, 1995).

in the North was distributing one half of the land to 725,000 landless peasants, and so achieving a measure of popular support.[23] In the South the puppet status of Rhee (who had lived for thirty-seven years in the United States) was increasingly obvious in circumstances where the ordinary Korean was disillusioned with the US presence. In 1947 the US Assistant Secretary of State was forced to concede that 'many Koreans feel they are worse off than they were under the Japanese', and a public opinion poll showed that most South Koreans preferred Japanese occupation to American.[24]

It was American initiative, despite the *de facto* circumstances of the US and Soviet occupation, that resulted in the division of Korea, against the wishes of the bulk of the Korean people. In 1943 the Big Four, meeting in Cairo, had pledged themselves to achieve the independence of Korea, with Roosevelt suggesting at Yalta a four-power trusteeship for the country. At Potsdam the principle of Korean autonomy was reaffirmed, though Washington was increasingly wary about Soviet intentions. The day after Stalin declared war on Japan, to US approval, Soviet troops began entering northern Korea, with American forces beginning to assert their own presence in the South. Later the Red Army, having occupied Seoul and Inchon, withdrew north of the 38th Parallel, leaving the forces of General Douglas MacArthur to receive the Japanese surrender in the south of Korea.

At this time there was a growing US preoccupation with how American strategic advantage could be secured in the area. In one account, 'several one-star generals hurried into an office of the Pentagon' demanding the division of Korea ('We have got to divide Korea. Where can we divide it?'); a colonel with knowledge of Korea objected that Korea was an economic and social unit and that there was no place to divide it, whereupon the generals insisted that a division was essential 'by four o'clock this afternoon'.[25] Soon afterwards, Dean Rusk, then a young officer recently returned to the Pentagon, found that the 38th Parallel had been designated as the administrative dividing line.[26]

The division of Korea was 'America's [38th] parallel', devised to secure a strategic US hold on the peninsula. This was more important to Washington policy planners than the eventual reunification of Korea, a country that had already suffered massively under the long period of the Japanese colonial occupation. In one communication, Lieutenant General John R. Hodge, an Occupation Commander in Korea, declared to General Douglas MacArthur that 'there is a growing deap-seated distrust of Allied intentions concerning . . . the division of Korea . . . many intelligent Koreans have already reached the conclusion that the Allied powers have no intention of building up a Korean nation . . . there is little to encourage them in the belief that the Allied promise of independence is sincere . . .'.[27] Hodge concluded that the allied powers had created a situation 'impossible of peaceful correction'. But though Washington was responsible for the division of Korea, the fact had to be disguised: 'Though it was *America's Parallel*, the United States would not say so. Instead, policy makers attributed all the problems ensuing from the country's division to Soviet intransigence, or marked them up to downright Soviet malevolence.'[28]

It was inevitable that Washington would see its strategic efforts as essentially a virtuous enterprise, a noble attempt to save the world from the force of darkness. General Douglas MacArthur, 'American Caesar', never doubted the righteousness of the American mission, and even the more sceptical General Hodge was well prepared to believe that in Asia the United States had the opportunity to establish 'something of the way of life which has made America the haven to which all the rest of the world looks with admiration and with longing. It has been given to us, as the world's greatest democracy, a post of leadership in the all-important task of establishing our doctrines of civil liberty throughout the world . . .'. It was widely perceived that the American presence in Korea was unwelcome but the Washington policy planners believed that perseverance would eventually bring popularity. By contrast, one American observer noted that 'America, which in China complained of the bad luck of having inherited the Kuomintang* through no fault of its own, has in Korea manufactured its own Kuomintang'.[29]

In 1947 the Washington policy planners began to see advantage in exploiting the United Nations to disguise US strategic plans. In September it was decided that the UN, under suitable American guidance, might usefully become involved in the Korean question. John Foster Dulles thereupon created an Interim Committee (or 'Little Assembly') in the United Nations to sidestep the anticipated Soviet veto. On 14 November Washington managed to induce the General Assembly to agree a United Nations Temporary Commission on Korea to resolve the outstanding political difficulties. When, as had been anticipated, the Soviet authorities refused to allow the Commission access to the North, it reported that the elections that had been held in the South 'were a valid expression of the free will of the electorate of that part of Korea'; and in such a fashion the United Nations, directed by Washington, had given its stamp of approval to the Rhee dictatorship, still dominated by 'landlords and mem-

---

*The corrupt, incompetent and authoritarian political faction of Chiang Kai-shek, long a darling of Washington.

bers of the old aristocracy', responsible for the 'near-extinction of civil liberties' and apt to employ such measures as the razing of villages on 'a vast scale'.[30] (It is of interest that in January 1950 the US secretary of state Dean Acheson publicly declared that a US defensive perimeter, from the Eleutians through Japan to the Philippines, did not include South Korea – a statement that has been taken as a possible 'green light' to the subsequent North Korean invasion of the South.*)

There were now growing tensions between the two halves of Korea, with mounting propaganda and frequent incursions over the 38th Parallel by one side or the other. The government of China – now massively aided by the United States in the increasingly desperate war against Mao's Communists – followed Washington's prompting and submitted a resolution to the Security Council for the admission of South Korea (represented as a 'peace-loving state') to the United Nations: there was no longer any US pretence at eventual Korean reunification. The Soviet delegate predictably vetoed the resolution on the ground that the UN had given no authority for the establishment of a puppet regime in South Korea; and it further charged Washington with violating the UN Charter by creating the unauthorised Interim Committee. Such events did nothing to ease the mounting tension, and it was not long before the frequent incursions across the 38th Parallel erupted into a major war – the first substantial military conflict in which the United Nations, orchestrated by Washington, was to become involved.

There remains much controversy about the responsibility for the starting of the Korean War, a circumstance that is heavily disguised in the bulk of mainstream Western literature in this area.[31] The actual onset of the major military conflict was not witnessed by the UN Military Observer Group in the field or by the Seoul-based UN Commission on Korea. Statements subsequently made by the Observer Group were based on information supplied either by the US military or the South Korean administration. On 27 June 1950, the day after the start of large-scale hostilities between North and South, the UN Commission proposed that : '[the Security] Council give consideration either invitation both parties agree on neutral mediator either to negotiate peace or requesting member governments undertake immediate mediation.' The abbreviated cable made no effort to assign responsibility for the outbreak of hostilities: the Commission was urging mediation, rather than sanctions or force, as the proper UN response to the crisis. In a leading article *The Manchester Guardian*

---

*We may compare this 'green light' with the one given by various US officials to Saddam Hussein in the days before the Iraqi invasion of Kuwait on 2 August 1990.

(26 June 1950) noted that the procedure for dealing with the matter was 'familiar from past experience'; the aims of the Security Council must be 'the cessation of hostilities, withdrawal of troops, and, above all, the exclusion of the Great Powers from the conflict'; the leader emphasised that 'neither the United States nor the Soviet Union has any direct military commitment to take part in the defence of either North of South Korea'.

The United States, seemingly eager for conflict, ignored the recommendations of the US-sponsored UN Commission, and – in the absence of any immediate UN authorisation – ordered armed US intervention. Truman instructed American air and sea forces to give 'cover and support' to the South Korean troops, ordered the Seventh Fleet into the zone between China and Formosa, and increased the military assistance to the French fighting their own war against the Vietnamese nationalists. Washington then called upon the Security Council to impose sanctions on North Korea. It was highly significant that this speedy use of the Council contrasted markedly with Washington's indifference to the possible role of the United Nations in other disputes. Until that time 'enforcement of the United Nations Charter had not been a compelling motive in Washington'. Thus the UN 'was brushed aside in Greece . . . no troops and planes were sent to fight the Dutch when they defied a UN cease-fire order in Indonesia . . . Nor did the United States mobilise the UN to save the infant Israeli Republic . . . The US gave no armed support to Israel as the ward of the UN'.[32] The pattern was already clear: then, as today in the 1990s, the United States would only support the United Nations when it calculated that American strategic interests were at stake.

It is also significant that the Security Council resolution went far beyond the imposition of sanctions. The Council, faced with the *fait accompli* of US military intervention (at a time when the Soviet delegate was absent from the Security Council), responded by authorising 'such assistance to the Republic of Korea as may be necessary to repel the armed attack and to secure peace and security in the area'. The Security Council had moved hastily at American instigation, on the basis of only slender information (some of which was later found to be inaccurate) and against the advice of the UN Commission, to underwrite the US intervention and to encourage a further escalation of the conflict. One important factor was the support offered by UN Secretary-General Trygve Lie for Washington's position. Lie's account[33] of the circumstances of the Korean War was 'so heavily biased, emotive and loaded, his charges against Communist countries so unsubstantiated, as to be more appropriate for a US State Department spokesperson than for a Secretary-General of the United Nations'.[34] Again the pattern was one that would later become plain: Washington would work to enlist UN Secretaries-General where possible or brush them aside where not (just as Secretary-General Javier Perez de Cuellar was brushed aside over the US-led war on Iraq in 1991).

Any efforts to determine the precise causes of the outbreak of hostilities between North and South Korea – which soon led to a massive North Korean incursion into the South – were subverted by propaganda. In fact there is evidence to suggest that the responsibility for the outbreak of the war cannot be easily assigned to one side or the other. On 30 May 1950, less than four weeks before the start of the war, Syngman Rhee had been decisively defeated in elections in the South (out of a total of 210 Assembly members only twelve Rhee supporters were elected). For months Rhee and his defence minister had been threatening to invade the North, saying they were ready to 'take Pyongyang within a few days' and 'do all the fighting needed'.[35] Now, with Rhee totally discredited and the regime 'left tottering',[36] desperate measures were needed. On the first day of the war, John Gunther reported from MacArthur's headquarters that 'one of the important members of the occupation [was] called unexpectedly to the telephone. He came back and whispered, "A big story has just broken. The South Koreans have attacked North Korea!" '[37]

The US ambassador reported that fighting had not broken out all along the 38th Parallel but in the Ongjin peninsula at the western end, an assessment that both the North and South Koreans supported in subsequent statements. However, this detail suggests that the South Koreans started the conflict, since a Western attack would give the North Koreans no access to Seoul but would give the South Koreans an obvious strategic advantage in a military incursion towards Pyongyang. In fact, US military intelligence confirmed the speedy capture by the 17th regiment, a crack South Korean unit, of Haeju, five miles north of the 38th Parallel.[38] Despite such matters the United States moved quickly to condemn North Korea; though when Charles Noyes, the US delegate to the United Nations showed the American draft resolution to the Security Council representatives of Great Britain, France, India, Egypt and Norway, all five indicated 'considerable hesitancy to take a position on which party was responsible for the invasion' (according to Noyes himself). Egypt and Norway declared that there was insufficient evidence to condemn North Korea, and objected also to the use of the word 'aggression' in what they saw as a civil war. In the event the resolution was passed – with lukewarm British support for Washington and after the United States had spread false information about Russian involvement in the fighting.[39] Now the US, despite domestic opposition, had UN authorisation to wage war as it wished.

The United States made no pretence of observing the UN Charter requirement (Article 47) that a Military Staff Committee (comprising 'the Chiefs of Staff of the permanent members of the Security Council or their representatives') be established 'to advise and assist the Security Council on all questions relating to the Security Council's military requirements for the maintenance of international peace and security'. There was no UN supervision of the American military involvement in Korea: the vast bulk of the forces were commanded by US officers answerable only to Washington; there were no blue berets, helmets, vehicle markings or other insignia to suggest that the operation was taking place under UN authority. In particular, the so-called UN forces were made subject to the orders of General Douglas MacArthur, with no UN constraint on his freedom of action. In fact the American control of the operation was made explicit in the UN resolution (7 July 1950) drafted by Washington. It demanded that 'all members providing military forces and other assistance . . . make such forces and other assistance available to a unified command under the United States'; and that 'the United States . . . designate the commander of such forces'.

The ensuing war, appallingly destructive, resulted in various violations of the UN Charter and of the specific resolutions that had authorised so-called UN intervention. The Security Council, manipulated by Washington, had authorised the United Nations forces to re-establish the 38th Parallel as a legitimate divide between North and South Korea; but it was soon clear that MacArthur had much greater ambitions – namely, the 'liberation' of North Korea, and a possible attack on China, recently 'lost' to the Communists. Four-fifths of all US casualties were suffered *after* the authorised UN aim of expelling the North Koreans from the South had been accomplished. One estimate suggests nearly 2,500,000 casualties, excluding North Korean civilians;[40] another suggests four million.[41]

The unauthorised US invasion of North Korea brought China (now Communist and without representation in either the General Assembly or the Security Council of the UN) into the war. There was now growing American enthusiasm for using the atomic bomb against China (General Emmet O'Donnell: '[the Chinese will] understand the lash when it is put to them'), with Truman himself at times seeming responsive to the idea.[42] Prime Minister Clement Attlee hurried to Washington to discourage the use of the atomic bomb, and in the event it was not used: the US forces had to be content with experimentation on a massive scale with a new weapon called napalm. Here was a new method of burning hundreds of thousands of innocent human beings to death: it would later be used to appalling effect in Vietnam in the 1960s and 1970s, and in Iraq in 1991.

The Korean War serves as a useful paradigm to illuminate aspects of Washington's relationship with the United Nations and the position of the United States in the developing world community. The paradigm is less applicable to the decades of the Cold War – even though the Korean conflict was a manifest Cold War phenomenon – than to events in the post-Soviet 'New World Order'. What the Korean conflagration had in common with the 1990s disputes over Iraq, Libya, Somalia, Haiti and others was the absence of a veto threat to American initiatives in the Security Council. The Council, as the virtual executive of the United Nations, always enshrined immense potential power, not only over the (initially) small number of UN members but over the entire world community. The only historical brake on such power was the veto in the Security Council, used for decades by both the Soviet Union and the US/UK axis. Today – as for a brief period in 1950 – the absence of the veto threat puts vast power in the hands of the dominant factions in the Council; that is, in the hands of the United States.

From the Korean Paradigm it is possible to extract a broad multiphase agenda that provides a framework for the interpretation of US foreign policy initiatives in the 1990s:

1. Washington becomes aware of a significant event in the world. The event may be well publicised and known to the world community; or it may only be known to the recipients of intelligence information derived from human assets, satellite systems or other sources.

2. Washington estimates the strategic importance of the event. The analysis will only rarely have to begin from scratch; in most cases the new information will be injected into an established policy assessment framework.

3. Depending on the results of the rapid strategic analysis, Washington moves into action on whatever fronts are appropriate. There will almost certainly be propaganda initiatives to massage the information for wider consumption by both domestic and foreign audiences. Allies will be contacted 'to keep them on board'; and military forces may be mobilised. At the same time various approaches will be made to the United Nations, with focus on both the rotating and permanent members of the Security Council.

4. The United Nations (primarily the Council) is activated, but only in circumstances where its conclusions and decisions can be suitably manipulated. If the Security Council cannot be relied upon, then

Washington will act anyway. It acted on Korea *before* it had UN
authorisation; and it invaded Grenada and Panama, without the
smokescreen of UN approval, because it could not rely on a Security
Council vote on those issues.

5. The UN, following the manipulated vote of affirmation, is enlisted
   for sanctions initiatives, military intervention or other measures
   judged helpful to American foreign policy interests. The UN is,
   however, always kept in its place. Inconvenient Articles of the UN
   Charter (for example, Articles 2(7), 19, 45, 47 and others) are
   ignored; any deployed US forces under nominal UN authorisation
   are kept under American command; and the UN Secretary-General
   is either enlisted or side-stepped.

6. The political, military and strategic gains are consolidated. Military
   bases may be established and puppet regimes reinforced.
   Commercial contractors are given fresh opportunities. The propaganda continues. When US spokespersons describe the events for
   the benefit of domestic audiences they talk about the 'American
   victory', of the 'US successes'; when they intend their comments to
   have an international flavour they talk about 'UN forces', 'the
   international community' and 'UN peacekeeping'.

This does not mean that each phase of the agenda is always given the same
emphasis, or that the necessary activities and operations are invariably
conducted with skill. Mistakes are made, actions often poorly judged:
there are usually many players in the field, so tensions and dislocations –
even between people working nominally to the same goals – are
inevitable. However, elements of each particular phase of the Korean
paradigm can be detected in most New World Order situations where
Washington has decided to enlist the United Nations. There is always the
incessant propaganda, the characteristic mix of endless drip-drip and
sudden cacophony designed to subvert sober analysis. We may speculate
on why Washington gave a 'green light' to North Korea before the onset
of hostilities, just as it did to Saddam Hussein before his attack on Kuwait;
and remember how theatres of conflict have served as laboratories for new
weapons (napalm in Korea, cruise missiles in Iraq), new communications
technologies, new war-game software, and new intelligence gathering
systems (for example, via satellite remote sensing).

The lessons learnt by the policy makers are fed into the computerised
methodologies for future conflicts. It is assumed that Washington's pursuit
of commercial and strategic interest will continue in the years ahead; and

that this will sustain the on-going investment in armaments research and production, the characteristic political manoeuvring, and the continuous manipulation of the United Nations.

OTHER MATTERS

Most international crises through the period of the Cold War involved the United Nations at some level, though its voice was seldom the decisive one.[43] The UN impact was often significant but invariably constrained by what the major powers would allow. Washington involved the United Nations in circumstances where its presence could be turned to US advantage, ignored the UN at other times, and on occasions seemed uncertain what course to adopt (US confusion over the proper role for the international body was not freshly generated in the 1990s). Washington vacillated over the creation of Israel, delayed the admission of (Communist) China to the UN for more than two decades, undermined UN efforts in such areas as the Congo and the Lebanon, and ignored the United Nations over such conflicts as Vietnam, the Cuban missile crisis and the Iran/Iraq War. Washington acted without proper authorisation in Korea (at first taking unilateral military action and then going far beyond the terms of the Security Council resolution), insisted that the US-sponsored invasion of Guatemala was no business of the United Nations, ignored the 1986 World Court condemnation of the United States over Nicaragua, and – with its invasions of Grenada (1983) and Panama (1989) – violated Article 2(4) of the UN Charter ('All Members shall refrain . . . from the threat or use of force against the territorial integrity or political independence of any state . . .'), as well as violating a number of other international agreements.

Through most of the early years of the United Nations the United States could guarantee itself a majority in the General Assembly, though this facility had more symbolic than legal weight. Thus Senator J. William Fulbright, long-serving Chairman of the Senate Foreign Relations Committee, noted: 'Because we had lots of money . . . we could send aid all around the world to gain the support and allegiance of various countries . . . That is, in part, how we got so many votes on our side in the United Nations. We could usually win on any question.'[44] Hence Washington developed a flexible approach to the United Nations through the period of the Cold War: simply put, the UN could be ignored or subverted, according to the circumstances of the case. Votes could be bought in the General

Assembly, and any pro-Soviet initiatives could be vetoed in the Security Council. In the unprecedented circumstances of the post-Cold War world, with the collapse of the Soviet Union and the global drift in the direction of free-market economics, there is little prospect of an anti-West veto in the Security Council. At the same time the debtor United States is today uncertain of its role and how it should operate within the world community. It remains to be seen how Washington's relatively untrammelled posture in the Security Council will translate into practical actions in the years ahead.

'NEW WORLD' DISORDER

Throughout the 1980s irresistible pressures for change were building up in the Soviet Union and Eastern Europe. Events in one region quickly fed into another and they combined to feed the growing sense of crisis. President Leonid Brezhnev died on 10 November 1982 and after the brief interregnums of Yuri Andropov and Konstantin Chernenko a younger man, the energetic Mikhail Gorbachev, became the new General-Secretary of the Soviet Communist Party in March 1985. Now the scene was set for a fresh political agenda, one that would lead irreversibly to the demise of the Soviet bloc. In August 1991 an attempted 'old-guard' coup against Gorbachev led to his resignation and the emergence of Boris Yeltsin, darling of the West, as the new Russian president. In September 1993, having defended the elected Soviet parliament against the coup only two years before, Yeltsin defied the Soviet constitution and abolished the parliament. This in turn led to violent protest, the bombarding of the Moscow White House by tanks, the killing and wounding of hundreds of Russians, the banning of political parties and newspapers, a massive crackdown on any anti-Yeltsin opinion, and the prospect of early rigged elections. The West declared itself well pleased at this new protection for the emerging culture of the free market in the former Soviet Union.*

Elsewhere in the region the shattered fabric of the old order seemed to yield nothing but chaos and conflict. Civil tensions ran to military confrontation in the republics of the erstwhile Soviet Union, while the ethnic war in the former Yugoslavia exposed the relative impotence of both the

---

*The West, in applauding Yeltsin's resort to violence, declared that the Russian parliament had been elected under an 'undemocratic' constitution. Western pundits seemed less keen to mention that Yeltsin had been elected president under the same constitution.

European Community and the United Nations. At the same time UN sanctions on Iraq were bringing famine to an entire people, the civil war in Angola (caused by a former US client who refused to accept the results of a UN-sponsored general election) was claiming one thousand lives a day, the UN/US intervention in Somalia was bringing carnage and confusion, and the prospect loomed of further US-prompted United Nations involvements in Haiti, Libya, Georgia, Bosnia and elsewhere. Observers talked of the 'world disorder', 'the New World Disorder', 'New World chaos' and the 'New World what?'. Now the growing demands on the United Nations for intervention around the world were throwing the Clinton administration into uncertainty and equivocation. Some of the policies seemed clear enough: there was little doubt that Washington would work hard to starve Iraq, Libya, Cuba and any other 'pariah nation' into submission; but broader matters remained unresolved. The United States was still determined to 'lead' in the post-Cold War world. But it could scarcely be active everywhere. How was Washington – now strapped for cash but still with immense and unrivalled military power – to evolve a coherent foreign policy true to US interests but within America's increasingly uncertain economic grasp?

In this context how was the United Nations to respond? What *was* the United Nations beyond its constituent members? How was it to frame effective policies that could minister to its best instincts? What types of problems does the United Nations face in the new world disorder of the 1990s, in the post-Cold War world inhabited by one surviving superpower that characteristically works to its own agenda?

Part II

The Problems

3 The Problem of Power

Power has many forms, not all of them of interest to the political philosopher. The cook has power over his culinary ingredients, the sportswoman over the various accoutrements of her sport. In political matters – as with human relationships in general – it is power over people that is important. This sort of power, in turn, is of various types.

The state has *naked power* when it can command the police or the army to coerce the individual, social groups or other states; and it has *propaganda power* when it can influence or determine public opinion or the opinion of particular individuals or minority groups in a position – by virtue of their own characteristic types of power – to shape the course of events. Power over minds is of crucial importance. Thus the state, whatever the colour of the government, is particularly interested in the ideological orientation of the armed forces, the police, and the principal propaganda organs. The armed forces are useless to the state, or even threaten its survival, if they cannot be relied upon; and it is cheaper and less problematic for the state if propaganda can be used to shape public opinion to avoid recourse to naked power.

The possession of focused power, of whatever sort, necessarily has the power to corrupt. Lord Acton, whose celebrated nineteenth-century observation[1] has been over quoted and too little heeded, noted both the expansion of power in the world and the wholesome resistance that it provoked. He claimed to perceive a movement 'away from force and cruelty to consent and association . . .'; and praised writers – including William Penn, the Jesuit Sarasa and Bishop Butler – reckoned to be opposed to arbitrary power, against Carlyle's notion 'that great and salutary things are done for mankind by power concentrated, not by power balanced and cancelled and diffused'. Such writers, noted Acton, had combined to create a 'rampart of tried conviction and accumulated knowledge, a fair level of general morality, education, courage and self-restraint . . . the reign of opinion, security of weaker groups, liberty of conscience which effectively secured, secures the rest'.[2]

In particular, for our purposes, Acton declared that the unbridled sovereignty of the national or supranational state – particularly when based on racial unity – was the most dangerous type of arbitrary power: 'If we take the establishment of liberty for the realisation of moral duties to be the end

55

of civil society . . . the theory of nationality . . . is a retrograde step in history.' Nationality, wrote Acton, sacrifices liberty and prosperity 'to the imperative necessity of making the nation the mould and measure of the State. Its course will be marked with material as well as moral ruin'.[3]

The threat posed by the nation state, particularly in the context of strong racial factors, is one that the United Nations has not yet learned adequately to address. The essential paradox is that the UN is primarily concerned with the sins of nation states – sins that *by their nature* they are almost bound to commit – and yet it goes to great lengths to uphold the principle of state sovereignty. In this context it is the states, not the putative supranational UN organisation, that have the power; and so the central dislocation in the world culture is bound to persist. States can only be compelled to observe UN authority when more powerful states oppose them – a nice analogue of the power politics that prevailed in the days of the League of Nations and before. So UN Secretary-General Boutros Boutros-Ghali is driven to talk, not of the legal power of an international body backed by supranational force, but of the 'persuasive power' of the organisation, of the Security Council's 'influence', of how the Council 'chose to authorize Member States to take measures on its behalf [in the situation between Iraq and Kuwait]'.[4] In the same vein he talks elsewhere of the 'voluntary cooperation of nations', of a 'cooperative and healthy international state system'[5] – signalling not least the reliance of the United Nations on the whims and prevailing policies of individual nation states.

The problem is that states have interests; and power necessarily brings 'temptations'.[6] Reliable military power is the most significant form of power – since it can be used to acquire other forms of power. But extreme wealth, in the individual or the state, can be deployed to purchase naked power. This suggests that any putative supranational body aiming to transcend the interests of nation states must learn how to confront vast military and economic power in the hands of individual nations. It is not enough for the United Nations to rest on the inviolability of powerful states intent on pursuing their own interests. The United Nations must learn how not to be suborned by power.

THE SOVEREIGNTY OF STATES

The military and economic power of the leading nation states means that they are only rarely required to subordinate their own interests to that of the United Nations in its role as a putative supranational organisation. At the same time it is well perceived that a UN imprimatur can often lubricate the prosecution of national goals: a course of action may be portrayed as much more moral if it is 'authorised by the United Nations' than if it is undertaken unilaterally by a single state. The rule is simple:

> *If you can exploit the UN to your own national advantage then do so; otherwise keep it at arm's length to avoid unwelcome constraints.*

The rule has been well observed by most powerful states in the world, including the Permanent Members of the Security Council. The United States, as befits the world's most powerful military state, has been the worst culprit (see examples below), but the other Permanent Members have been far from guiltless.

Margaret Thatcher, Britain's erstwhile prime minister, was quick to approve the forming of the UN 'Coalition' of nations after the Iraqi invasion of Kuwait on 2 August 1990; but she had been less willing to see a diplomatic involvement by the United Nations after Argentine forces had invaded the Falkland Islands (Spanish: Islas Malvinas) in April 1982. Thatcher noted in her memoirs that Britain needed to win its case against Argentina in the Security Council but otherwise the United Nations should not be allowed to intrude: 'in the longer term we knew that we had to try to keep our affairs out of there as much as possible. With the anti-colonialist attitude of many nations there was a real danger that the UN might attempt to force unsatisfactory terms upon us. *This remained a vital consideration throughout the crisis*' (my italics). Later she remarks that the Haig peace negotiations – which she effectively sabotaged by sinking the Argentine cruiser *General Belgrano* – 'worked in our favour' since they had at least 'precluded even less helpful diplomatic intervention from other directions, including the UN'.[7]

The Falklands War, like many other conflicts before and since, stimulated discussion about the proper relationship between nation states and the United Nations in the event of aggression occurring against a country. It has been argued that when the Security Council passed Resolution 502 (demanding the immediate withdrawal of all Argentine forces from the Falklands) the United Nations had no power to compel observance – a limitation that did not appear quite so decisive after Iraq invaded Kuwait. Had an international armed force under UN control existed in April 1982, it is argued, the outcome would have been quite different. Conceivably there would have been no invasion in the first place; but, had it happened, Argentina would have been forced to withdraw, not by Britain acting under Article 51 of the UN Charter but by mobilisation of the standing UN force. Such a scenario also has the advantage that the UN force could be used to protect small states unable to mobilise significant forces of their own.

Thus Sir Shridath Ramphal, the Commonwealth Secretary-General, declared in the Central Hall, Westminster, on 27 April 1982 that the Commonwealth supported the establishment of an effective system of collective security within the UN framework, not least to remove the need for small countries to divert precious resources to defence. In the same spirit and on the same theme, during a mass lobby on disarmament, Peter Blaker, Minister of State for the Armed Forces, stated that the force sent to relieve the Falklands should have been an international one organised by the United Nations and including US ships. In writing he later commented: 'it is regrettable that the military enforcement provisions of Chapter VII of the Charter are likely to remain a dead letter. I see no grounds for thinking that there would be a consensus . . . in favour of strengthening the 'UN's enforcement role.' The Secretary-General has called for the creation of such a standing force; to act as a permanent deterrent to aggression and to remove the need for individual states to take unilateral action. Again it is clear that any such suggestion would be opposed by powerful states keen to keep matters in their own hands.*

The determination of states to retain their own freedom of action is particularly evident in areas that affect trade. In 1981 the United Nations drew up a convention limiting the deployment of mines and other weapons that primarily targeted civilians. Both Britain and the United States failed to ratify the convention, with only thirty-two countries signing, but today Washington appears to be supporting a fresh ban on anti-personnel mines. In October 1993 the United Nations laid plans to stamp out a trade that has left some 100 million uncleared land-mines in fifty-six countries, with thousands of victims every week.[8] It was predicted that Britain, not wanting to lose its share of a valuable export market, would oppose the export ban on trade grounds. On 17 December the General Assembly, without a vote, adopted a non-mandatory resolution calling for a moratorium on the export of anti-personnel land-mines.[†]

---

*UN Secretary-General Boutros Boutros-Ghali has been quick to recognise the cynical attitudes of member states: 'You may be shocked for ethical reasons, but we have to accept this. This is a political body and the member states have national interests . . . they will obtain a resolution in their favour which interests them and not pay attention to [another issue]. My role is to correct this distortion, to put things in the limelight' (*The Independent*, 31 October 1994).

†Britain, shamed into compliance, voted for the resolution *and then deceitfully tabled a note stating that the resolution did not apply to Britain since its secret sale of mines to 'responsible' countries did not 'pose grave dangers'*. British MPs then lied to their worried constituents, saying that the British government supported the UN ban on sales of mines (*Red Pepper*, November 1994).

The British government is also unsympathetic to UN efforts to strengthen the fight against racism. An investigation by the United Nations Committee on the Elimination of Racial Discrimination has concluded that Britain is not doing enough in such areas as housing, employment and law enforcement.[9] Professor Rudiger Wolfrum, a German nominee to the committee, declared that the efforts being made by the British government were not enough: 'We were not very impressed with them.' In particular, the committee urged the British authorities:

to take stronger action to stop racial violence;
to introduce laws banning racist organisations and tackling racist violence;
to extend the Race Relations Act to cover Northern Ireland;
to improve the training and equipment of the police to deal with racist attacks;
to address discrimination against non-whites in housing and employment.

Marc Wadsworth, the national secretary of the Anti-Racist Alliance, who gave evidence to the UN committee, said that his group felt vindicated by the committee's conclusions: 'Perhaps this will lead the Government to take firm action to stop racial violence and murders.' The British Home Office said it would consider the report 'carefully', but since that time various government ministers announced that they would not want to ban racist groups 'in a free society'.

Other issues have focused attention on differences between the United Nations and member states and between various states themselves. In Bosnia, for example, tensions have grown between various Permanent Members of the Security Council (see below), and the civil war in Georgia has exposed the rift between UN policy and the wishes of President Yeltsin's Russia, a Permanent Member. In January 1993 the Georgian leader Eduard Shevardnadze asked for UN peacekeepers to be sent to Georgia to quell fighting in Abkhazia where government forces were struggling to repel Abkhazian guerrillas. By March, Shevardnadze was claiming that Russia was backing the rebels, a circumstance that might demand 'general mobilisation'. Four months later UN officials were trying to mediate in the conflict, while one foreign ambassador in Tbilisi was quoted: 'The Russians are running faster than the UN and they don't want anyone else meddling in their backyard.'[10] At the same time it was reported that US special forces had helped train security forces associated with President Shevardnadze, and that, according to *The Washington*

Times, Georgian paramilitaries were being trained at Fort Bragg. Whatever UN mediators, such as Boutros-Ghali's envoy Eduard Brunner, were to accomplish they would have to cope with the separate agendas being operated by Washington and Moscow.

In August the Security Council unanimously approved sending an advance team of UN military observers to help verify compliance with a ceasefire between Georgia and the Abkhazia rebels. The team was given a three-month mandate, after which it would become part of the proposed UN Observer Mission in Georgia (UNOMIG). In September, in the conditions of a rapidly deteriorating situation, Shevardnadze urged the United Nations to intervene more actively to prevent the escalation of a guerrilla war. Soon afterwards, he was forced to flee from Sukhumi, the Abkhazian capital, with little prospect of UN action to bring the fighting to an end. There were reports that the Abkhazian commander Nodar Khazba was continuing a campaign of ethnic cleansing of Georgian civilians in Sukhumi and elsewhere. By October the mandate of the few United Nations observers no longer had any meaning: the ceasefire had collapsed, fighting was escalating, and the Security Council seemed reluctant to pronounce on 'the fiasco that is the UN's first peacekeeping effort in the former Soviet Union'.[11]

The Security Council had failed to act decisively in Georgia; in part because this was yet another demand on an overstretched United Nations organisation increasingly strapped for cash and short of human and other resources, but also in part because the interests of Russia, a Permanent Member with the power of veto, were involved. There were signs also that the United States had an interest in supporting President Shevardnadze, though not to the point that Washington would push for a UN intervention against the wishes of Yeltsin's Russia.

Again it seemed clear that possible UN mediation had been stymied by powerful states with their own agendas. The message was advertised yet again: the United Nations would only be allowed to act effectively in ways that were consistent with the most powerful members of the Security Council. Georgia was in Russia's 'backyard', and Washington had no substantial interest that demanded UN action. In other disputes however the United States was keen to orchestrate UN intervention.

MANIPULATING THE UN: OVER IRAQ

On 2 August 1990 President Saddam Hussein of Iraq launched an invasion of the small but oil-rich state of Kuwait, an event that was to have massive regional and world consequences. Many of the facts were not in dispute: the aggression against a member state of the United Nations was a gross violation of international law; the interests of many of the developed nations of the world focused on the secure supply of oil from the Middle East; and the US-led 'international community' would be compelled to respond to this grave challenge to its authority.[12]

It was clear from the beginning that the issue was less a matter of principle than one involving the security of powerful states. Washington, the main agent behind the response to the Iraqi aggression, had been well prepared to tolerate a range of invasions against sovereign states that equally challenged international law and the human rights of suffering populations. No serious UN actions had been taken to reverse the long-standing and illegal occupations of Northern Cyprus by Turkey, Southern Lebanon by Israel, West Beirut by Syria, East Timor by Indonesia, etc. In such disputes the US-dominated Security Council was prepared to wait years, decades even, for a resolution of the dispute. And in such pro-crastination UN Secretaries-General have appeared largely pliant, but perhaps reluctant accomplices. One example will suffice here: consider the case of East Timor, subject to a brutal invasion in 1975 by an Indonesian army equipped with US armaments. The subsequent occupation led to the slaughter of 200,000 people, the genocide of a third of the entire East Timorese population by 1980. Washington supported the Indonesian action throughout, as it continues to support the Indonesian occupation today, supplying armaments and blocking any effective UN response. Thus in September 1993 all Secretary-General Boutros Boutros-Ghali is able to say on the question of East Timor is that 'efforts for a comprehensive and internationally acceptable solution to the question of East Timor are continuing'.[13] No urgency, no UN sanctions against aggressor Indonesia, no UN Coalition to evict an illegal occupying force, no American interests at stake.

The Iraqi invasion of Kuwait was an altogether different matter. Here Washington quickly saw the national interest and began orchestrating the response: the relatively few 'No Blood for Oil' protest banners in the United States, Europe and elsewhere would not be allowed to influence the course of events. At times President George Bush made it plain that oil was the issue; and many other American politicians and commentators were in no doubt.[14] The general rule – *exploit the UN or keep it out* – would be systematically applied. A vast military force, largely American, was organised under the nominal sanction of the United Nations; but, as with Korea forty years before (see Chapter 2), the international organisation was allowed no part in the management of the 1990/91 crisis and the ensuing 1991 Gulf War.

The Security Council response to the Iraqi invasion was prompt and unambiguous. Resolution 660 (the first of nearly two dozen on the Iraq issue), adopted by fourteen votes to none (with Yemen abstaining), condemned the invasion and demanded an immediate and unconditional Iraqi withdrawal.[15] Subsequent resolutions variously imposed sanctions on Iraq, put demands on the 'international community', authorised 'all necessary means' to enforce the stranglehold on Iraq, authorised 'all necessary means' to launch a war against Iraq (nominally to evict it from Kuwait), discouraged Iraq from persecuting its minorities, and defined the terms of the eventual ceasefire and the subsequent conduct of affairs. It is useful to consider Resolution 678 (see Appendix 2), the resolution nominally embodying the Security Council decision, adopted by twelve votes to two (Cuba and Yemen) with China abstaining, to authorise the 1991 Gulf War.

Resolution 678, passed under Chapter VII of the UN Charter, has generally been taken as authorising the various air and land assaults on Iraq to force a withdrawal from Kuwait. There are few signs that subsequent commentators saw any value in scrutinising the terms of 678, the requirements of Chapter VII, or the circumstances in which 678 came to be passed. In fact there are a number of questions that should be considered.

The initial drafting of 678, a task carried out largely by the Americans, included the words 'use of force'. The then Soviet foreign minister Eduard Shevardnadze objected: the Soviet government had agreed the use of force but any explicit mention of it, evoking memories of the unhappy Soviet experience in Afghanistan, had to be avoided. It was better, Shevardnadze declared, to keep the resolution vague, whereupon US Secretary of State James Baker tried various other versions. Eventually there was agreement on 'all necessary means' (a formulation that had already been used in Resolution 670 for the enforcement of sanctions and other measures specified in Resolution 661 as early as 6 August). Baker was not enthusiastic about the wording, concerned that it was ambiguous, but gave the clear American interpretation in his later address to the Security Council: 'Today's resolution is very clear. The words authorise the use of force . . . .'.[16] However, it remains significant that both Baker and Shevardnadze did not regard 'all necessary means' as synonymous with 'the use of force': Shevardnadze welcomed the euphemism that avoided the suggestion of military action, and Baker felt it necessary to clarify matters by means of supplementary observations in the Security Council. Such considerations are more than pedantry, not least because 'all necessary means' is open to further analysis.

There is no stipulation in Resolution 678 as to who should judge what action is or is not 'necessary'. Was it to be the Security Council? The UN

Secretary-General? Or any and every UN member state, as it saw fit? Clause 2 of the resolution authorises 'Member States' to use all necessary means to uphold the key Resolution 660 and all subsequent resolutions. So presumably they were all entitled to act unilaterally in any way they judged 'necessary'. There was nothing in 678 to involve the Secretary-General or any other leading official in the Secretariat. Nor was there any attempt to give the UN sanctions committee a role in determining what further measures might be necessary. In fact, as was plain to everyone, it would be the Americans who would decide what was necessary; other states would not be allowed to interfere with the decisions of James Baker and George Bush, and American commanders would be given charge of any military 'coalition' that might be launched against Iraq. The plans had already been laid. The US forces and their allies had already poured into Saudi Arabia, long before the passing of Resolution 678 in the Security Council. The UN 'flag of convenience' was now flying, though – as with the Korean War – Washington judged that the United Nations had no practical role to play. The United States would run the show, despite the provisions specified in Articles 45 to 47 in Chapter VII of the UN Charter for the establishment of a Military Staff Committee (consisting 'of the Chiefs of Staff of the permanent members of the Security Council or their representatives') to be 'responsible under the Security Council for the strategic direction of any armed forces . . .'.

The ambiguities and gaps in Resolution 678, a key Security Council product in the emerging 'New World Order', invited unilateral action by the United States and its key allies: there can be little doubt that 678 was drafted with this in mind. At the same time it was necessary to achieve the maximum degree of consensus in what was frequently dubbed the 'international community': the desired UN 'flag of convenience' would impress no-one (UN member states, domestic constituencies, pliant journalists) if it only fluttered at half mast. The methods used by Washington, largely threat and bribery, to guarantee 'consensus' have been widely reported. For example, the journalist Martin Walker observed that the UN Security Council 'was brought round by a mixture of intensive personal diplomacy, wheedling and bullying by the US' (*The Guardian*, London, 3 December 1990).

The Saudis had been bullied into accepting the massive inflow of American troops, despite the little reported detail that King Fahd believed that it was Kuwaiti inflexibility that had provoked the Iraqi invasion.[17] To ensure Egyptian compliance, a debt to the amount of $14 billion was 'forgiven', while other governments – including Canada and Saudi Arabia – were encouraged to 'forgive' or delay repayment of much of the rest of the Egyptian debt. President Turgut Ozal of Turkey observed that the United States had generously donated $8 billion-worth of military hardware, so there was little doubt that Turkey would remain part of the international 'consensus'. In a similar vein, arms and aid were offered to Syria; a World Bank loan to Iran suddenly materialised; the Bank also donated $114 million to Peking; and various punitive threats were made to recalcitrant states. When Yemen, using its proper entitlement under the UN Charter, voted against Resolution 678, the World Bank and the IMF moved to block loans, 800,000 Yemeni workers were abruptly thrown out of Saudi Arabia, and massive additional suffering was brought to the poverty-stricken Yemeni people.*

The 1991 Gulf War was launched, despite various peace efforts, to achieve its largely predictable results. The United Nations had been kept out of the operational frame: the sad figure of Secretary-General Perez de Cuellar, often unable to disguise his deep unhappiness about American policy, had been prevented from playing any significant role in the dispute. The US-led allied forces had violated the Geneva Conventions[18] in many respects, and also gone far beyond the terms of UN authorisation, in their conduct of the war. But the manipulation of the United Nations was far from at an end: there was still abundant scope for the exploitation of UN authority in the interest of perceived Western strategic interest. Fresh moves at the United Nations, following growing awareness of the appalling plight of the Kurds in northern Iraq, resulted in further Security Council resolutions mainly designed to give the West a handle on the 'peace'. Resolution 688 (adopted by ten votes to Cuba, Yemen and Zimbabwe against, with China and India abstaining) condemned 'the repression of the Iraqi civilian population in many parts of Iraq', demanded that Iraq end the repression, and insisted that Iraq allow 'immediate access by international humanitarian organisations to all those in need of assistance . . .'. This resolution, not passed under Chapter VII, had no provision for further action in the event of Iraqi non-compliance. However, the Resolution was frequently cited as justifying the creation by the West of the 'no-fly' zone in the south of the country.

The West created the southern no-fly zone in the absence of any UN authorisation, a detail that was suitably reported at the time ('UN was bypassed over no-fly zone', *The Independent*, London, 19 August 1992) but largely ignored afterwards. The UK foreign secretary Douglas Hurd had conceded that the no-fly zone did not have United Nations authorisation,

---

*One estimate was that the 'no' vote had cost the impoverished Yemen about $1 billion.

commenting that 'not every action that an American government, a British government or a French government takes has to be underwritten by a specific provision in a UN resolution'; but subsequent (uncorrected) reporting on the no-fly zone characteristically described it as a 'UN' measure. Now, long after the end of the war, Western aircraft continued to make sporadic attacks on sites and personnel in southern Iraq, citing as justification Resolution 688 (which was not passed under the enforcement provisions of Chapter VII) and the unauthorised no-fly zone policed by allied aircraft. The whole episode of the no-fly zone in southern Iraq was a graphic illustration – to anyone who cared to notice – of how UN 'authorisation' could be invented when it suited powerful member states in the Security Council: in this case to provide 'justification for the West to continue punitive and surveillance operations over southern Iraq'.[19]

Further manipulation of the United Nations is shown by the West's continued insistence that harsh sanctions be maintained on Iraq, despite the growing disquiet of many UN-linked aid agencies. Sanctions were first introduced under the authority of Security Council Resolution 661 (6 August 1990), designed 'to bring the invasion and occupation of Kuwait by Iraq to an end and to restore the sovereignty, independence and territorial integrity of Kuwait'. Today, in mid-1995, long after the principal aims of sanctions have been accomplished, the Iraqi people are still being systematically starved to death. The Western excuse is that without effective sanctions Iraq will move to develop 'weapons of mass destruction', a catch-all phrase that in reality has prevented the Iraqi authorities from buying food and medical provisions, specifically allowed in UN resolutions, for the good of its population. The growing calamitous impact of UN sanctions on the Iraqi population has been known to various United Nations agencies for some time.

In February 1993 the United Nations Children's Fund (UNICEF) commissioned Eric Hoskins, a Harvard expert on public health, to compile an analysis of the food situation in Iraq. The 32-page preliminary draft, obtained and publicised by *The Independent* (24 June 1993), purports to identify 'the impact of war and sanctions on Iraqi women and children'. The report finds that 'nearly three years of economic sanctions have created circumstances in Iraq where the majority of the civilian population are now living in poverty', and that 'by most accounts, the greatest threat to the health and well-being of the Iraqi people remains the difficult economic conditions created by nearly three years of internationally mandated sanctions and by the infrastructure damage wrought by the 1991 military conflict'; and the Executive Summary includes the observation that '*politically motivated sanctions (which are by definition imposed to create*

The Problems

hardship) cannot be implemented in a manner which spares the vulnerable' (my italics).

A later report, produced under the auspices of the United Nations Food and Agriculture Organisation (FAO) and the World Food Programme (WFP), describes the food supply situation in Iraq and provides an estimate of the basic food import requirements for the 1993/94 marketing year.[20] The report comments on a country 'whose economy has been devastated by the recent war and subsequent civil strife, but above all by the continued sanctions since August 1990, which have virtually paralysed the whole economy and generated persistent deprivation, chronic hunger, endemic under nutrition, massive unemployment and widespread human suffering'; and notes 'with deep concern the prevalence of the commonly recognised pre-famine indicators such as exorbitant prices, collapse of private incomes, soaring unemployment, drastically reduced food intakes, large scale depletion of personal assets, high morbidity levels, escalating crime rates and rapidly increasing numbers of destitute people'. Here it is acknowledged that 'a grave humanitarian tragedy is unfolding', an observation that bears out the claim by Umeed Mubarak, the Iraqi health minister, that in late-1993 about four thousand Iraqi children under five were dying every month as a result of sanctions.[21]

Thus the effects of the continuing UN sanctions, insisted on by the US-dominated Security Council, stand exposed by officials from such United Nations bodies as UNICEF, WFP and FAO. In these circumstances it appears that Security Council moves to allow Iraq to sell some of its oil are primarily a device to enable the United Nations – and so the Western powers – to gain access to key Iraqi resources. It is unlikely that any plan that created mechanisms for channelling Iraqi revenues through UN accounts would be soon revoked; and that in consequence Iraq would have surrendered any hope of regaining its sovereignty. In his annual report (September 1993), Secretary-General Boutros-Ghali spoke of 'the suffering of the Iraqi civilian population' and notes the 'deterioration of living conditions throughout Iraq'; but there is no talk of abandoning the punitive sanctions. Instead Boutros-Ghali records that legal advice has been supplied on whether 'Iraq's frozen assets might be used as payment for the sale or supply to Iraq of medicine and health supplies, foodstuffs and materials and supplies for essential civilian needs . . .'; and he draws attention to the existence of an escrow account into which the proceeds from the sale of Iraqi oil might be paid to cover the costs of UN operations, compensation claims and aid efforts in Iraq. In this context much has been made of Security Council Resolution 706, drafted supposedly to allow Iraq to sell up to $1.6 billion of oil to relieve the suffering of its people. In fact the plan would have given Baghdad only about a half of this amount, about $40 per head. Nor would Iraq have had immediate access to even this paltry sum: a request would have had to be submitted to the UN-administered escrow account, whereupon the (probably American) UN officials would judge the request. At the same time, with a manifest demonstration of Iraq's loss of sovereignty over its own resources, the rest of the oil revenue would have been paid to US contractors in Kuwait and as US-approved compensation to American allies in the Gulf War. The paltry aid provisions signalled by Resolution 706 and the associated measures had little to do with relieving the suffering of the Iraqi people. We need to remember what miseries the prolonged US-inspired sanctions have brought to a helpless nation.

Many UN-linked bodies and independent aid agencies have testified to the appalling impact of economic sanctions – by 1995 of nearly five years' duration – on the Iraqi people. For example, the London-based charity Medical Aid for Iraq (MAI) has regularly reported the deteriorating conditions in Iraqi hospitals. Thus an MAI report following a medical mission during January and February 1993 noted that 'as always, it has been the children who have been hit hardest'. The report notes:

> Shortages of milk powder, cannulae, antibiotics and syringes have been a problem since the Gulf War but now a lack of insulin has become a major problem . . . children with diabetes are arriving at hospitals in comas and dying . . . foods containing protein are too expensive to buy. The result is an ever increasing number of children with kwashiorkor . . . the children's wards are full of malnourished children, many of whom also have chest infections or gastroenteritis.

The Kerbala Children's Hospital had received no insulin for four months:

> Children were dying as a result of this. Children were also dying because of a lack of other medicines such as salbutamol (treatment for asthma) . . . Some incubators were out of order . . . No lactose free milk powder for babies suffering from gastroenteritis and diarrhoea. No milk powder for babies who are not in-patients. Shortage of cannulas.

At the Samawa Children's and Obstetrics Hospital there was 'no milk powder of any kind, no high energy (protein) food, no antiseptics'. The hospital's director, Dr Saad Al Tibowi, had given his own blood 'three times in the past week'. Wards at the Alwiyah Children's Hospital in Baghdad had been closed because of water and sewage problems; and there was also a 'lice and worm infestation' due to the shortage of soap and antiseptics. At these and the other hospitals visited there was a growing incidence of hepatitus, polio, diphtheria, mumps, diarrhoea, marasmus and kwashiorkor.

Later MIA reports (for example, for September/October 1993 and April 1994) indicated a deteriorating situation. Basic supplies (cannulae, syringes, catheters and surgical gloves) were being reused, in the absence of soap and disinfectants. In the absence of paper, prescriptions and medical notes were being written on cardboard. There was a chronic shortage of milk powder, vitamin drops for babies, and drugs. There was a growing incidence of aplastic anaemia and cancers, especially leukaemia, among children. No vitamin D was available for the soaring number of children with rickets. Rags were pushed into holes in damaged incubators in an attempt to maintain the internal temperature. The Medical City Children's Hospital in Baghdad was 'full of dying children because of a lack of basic antibiotics and cytoxic drugs' (used to treat cancer). Children's resuscitaires were 'black with dirt, because of the shortage of cleaning and disinfecting fluids'. On one occasion a woman was left open for several hours after an emergency caesarean operation while medical staff went in search of catgut from another hospital. The MIA workers watched a child die of hydrocephaly, denied the intracranial shunts that would have saved his life. There are no oxygen cylinders because Iraqi factories are now denied the necessary components. Neonatal units suffer from 'rife septicaemia'; and babies 'cannot be ventilated; there is no blood gas machine. Many are left to die . . .'.

Independent estimates have suggested that economic sanctions on Iraq have killed about half a million people, with the toll of children in 1994 expected to reach something in excess of 100,000. In May 1994 the United States and Britain managed to withstand mounting international pressure for a relaxation of sanctions on Iraq, at a time when MAI workers were reporting a continued deterioration in the conditions facing the Iraqi people: 'Malnutrition and the increases in infection rates associated with it have resulted in a worsening situation and an increased shortage of medicines' (MAI report for 3–22 April 1994).

By late 1994 the dire plight of the Iraqi people, forced to suffer under the seemingly endless US-orchestrated 'UN' sanctions, was common knowledge: reports on their privations and miseries appeared even in peak-time US and UK television broadcasts. And other factors were beginning to weigh heavily in the balances: for example, countries such as Russia and Turkey expected to reap considerable economic advantage once sanctions on Iraq were relaxed. In these circumstances, where the merciless regime for the punishment of the Iraqi people seemed increasingly insecure, Washington was forced to invent new reasons for the continuation of sanctions. One ploy was to suggest – as did the United States and its pliant allies in October 1994 – that Iraqi troop movements close to Kuwait represented a new threat to the emirate. A tide of US-orchestrated propaganda swept through the media. Was a new invasion of Kuwait imminent? What did Saddam intend? How could he be effectively deterred from another reckless adventure? Soon Western forces were again flooding into the Gulf region – not to deter Iraq but to create a climate in which it would be easy to maintain sanctions. The new Iraqi 'threat' was a total fabrication, a new torrent of black misinformation, soon exposed for the sham it was by perceptive observers.

Thus the reputable journalist Robert Fisk commented (*The Independent*, 24 October 1994) that reporters on the Kuwait-Iraq border had been able to detect no signs of aggressive Iraqi intent. UN officials disclosed that their reconnaissance aircraft, which give them a 20km view across the frontier, had not observed a single Iraqi tank or personnel carrier. Even Israel, usually a reliable propaganda ally of the US, suggested that the 'crisis' had been manufactured by Washington. Yitzhak Rabin and senior Israeli army officers stated that Saddam did not have the resources to invade Kuwait, and that the Republican Guard divisions were not deployed in an aggressive posture. What *was* indisputable was that Iraqi children were continuing to die in large numbers because of US-sustained sanctions. *The United Nations Development Programme (UNDP) reported that infant mortality in Iraq had tripled since the Gulf War; and UNICEF stated that 2.5 million nursing mothers, pregnant women and babies faced 'severe malnutrition' in late 1994.* Major picture agencies refused to use photographs of Iraqi babies that had died of starvation because they were 'too gruesome'. 'Thus did a non-existence war receive more coverage than real death . . .' (Fisk).

Then, early November 1994, the Iraqi government announced it was recognising Kuwait and the UN-defined demarcation border – so depriving Washington of yet another pretext for genocide. Madeleine Albright, the US ambassador to the UN, responded by showing the Security Council satellite pictures of 'pleasure palaces' being built in Iraq: if Iraqi babies were starving, it was Saddam's fault. This new US ploy was dismissed. Said Sergei Lavorv, the Russian UN envoy: 'I don't recall that building palaces was prohibited by Security Council resolutions.' Now the US posture was transparent: any lie and any absurdity would be used if the Washington strategic planners judged that they would serve the continued torture of the Iraqi nation. The allies of the United States could largely be relied on: though the French foreign minister, Alain Juppé, had felt obliged to remind Washington that it was up to the UN, not the United States, to decide on whether fresh military action should be taken against Iraq; after visiting Kuwait, Juppé stated: 'I think it belongs . . . to the Security Council to decide what must be done' (*The Guardian*, 18 October 1994). In any event, by dint of the usual lies and manipulations, Washington managed to prolong sanctions on Iraq: the starving mothers and babies would be allowed no respite.

In these circumstances it is ironic that the UN Special Commission on the disarmament of Iraq announced in November 1994 that it was so short of funds that it had started to plan for the closure of its operations (UN Information Centre *Newsletter*, 16 November 1994). Doubtless, once this body has been forced through US parsimony to leave Iraq, Washington will argue that it is no longer possible to guarantee that Iraq is not building 'weapons of mass destruction'.

The multiphase manipulation of the United Nations over Iraq illustrates the most substantial instance of the 'Korean Paradigm' in the so-called New World Order. The characteristic features were all evident: monitor the event, estimate its strategic significance, organise propaganda, activate the United Nations, define its proper role, and then move in to exploit the various gains. At the same time the general principle – exploit the UN or ignore it – was signally at work during the particular phases of the 1990/91 crisis. UN resolutions were useful but not essential: unilateral interpretations could be given to such Security Council decisions, when necessary; and unilateral actions, in the absence of even vague UN authorisation, could always be taken (as with the creation of no-fly zones). The United Nations was totally ignored when Washington launched a number of post-war attacks on Iraq, including the various cruise missile bombardments of Baghdad (here it was useful to invent the idea of an Iraqi plot on the life of George Bush).

Washington's experience through the period of the crisis – acquisition of fresh information on armament performance, the pliability of allies, the malleability of public opinion, the character of the United Nations after the Cold War – was useful for the analysis of post-Gulf War issues (including those that continued to involve Iraq). The lessons would be learned, though often badly. After the Gulf War there were soon fresh opportunities to manipulate the United Nations.

MANIPULATING THE UN: OVER LIBYA

Libya was next.[22] On 15 April 1986, at 2 a.m. Libyan time, American aircraft flying from bases in Britain and carriers in the Mediterranean had

bombed six main targets in Tripoli and Benghazi. In these raids, ordered on the pretext of earlier Libyan terrorist acts, there were several hundred Libyan casualties, including Colonel Gaddafi's wife Safia and three of the couple's children, all of whom suffered severe pressure shock from a 2000lb bomb that hit their house. The injured children were rushed to hospital and some hours later Gaddafi's sixteen-month-old adopted daughter, Hanna, died from her brain injuries. Gaddafi himself was unharmed but few observers doubted that Washington had planned an assassination attempt. Officials from the National Security Council (NSC) had prepared a prior statement describing Gaddafi's death as 'fortuitous', and an official who had helped to plan the bombing raids admitted that 'We hoped to get him'.[23] The attempt on Gaddafi's life had failed but Washington was keen to target Libya at the first new opportunity. The success of the onslaught on Iraq had convinced the United States that in the New World Order it would be possible to use the United Nations again.

It was decided in mid-1991 that Libya was to be charged with full responsibility for the Lockerbie and UTA DC-10 bombing outrages, in which a total of several hundred passengers and crew members had been killed on 21 December 1988 and 19 September 1989. Many observers were surprised that other likely suspect countries (primarily Iran and Syria) and various Palestinian groups were now discounted, despite many earlier accusations made by American and British spokespeople. Libya was now urged to hand over two suspects, Abdelbaset al-Megrahi and Amin Fhimah, for trial in Scotland or the United States. There was already talk of sanctions being called against Libya if the two men were not delivered to the West. And, significantly enough, there was also talk of involving the United Nations; what had worked with Iraq might also work with Libya.

London and Washington then explicitly planted the idea of a worldwide trade embargo on Libya, and repeatedly declared that the option of military force could not be ruled out – so violating Article 2(4) of the UN Charter ('All Members shall refrain in their international relations from the threat or use of force against the territorial integrity or political independence of any state'). Western charges against Libya were lodged with the United Nations; and on 20 January 1992 the Security Council unanimously passed Resolution 731 urging the Libyan government to respond to the 'requests' being made upon it. UN Secretary-General Boutros-Ghali then prepared his own report on the mounting crisis, noting a 'certain evolution' in the Libyan position. His suggestion that this should be recognised before action was taken against Libya 'irritated London and Washington'.[24] After a brief delay, to allow time for appropriate arm-twisting in the Security Council, the West secured Resolution 748 (though now there were five abstentions in the Council vote), calling for a range of actions against Libya. This fresh resolution (Appendix 3) made it clear that the UN-approved measures were only a start: 'every 120 days, or sooner should the situation so require', the measures would be reviewed. The West now had a handle on the situation: Saddam had been humbled and now it was Gaddafi's turn. There was little prospect that in the foreseeable future the sanctions would be removed, every likelihood that the West would exploit the situation to tighten the noose.

There was now little chance of the two suspects being brought to trial in Scotland or the United States, but in any case that was hardly the point. The West was less interested in trying two minor Libyan officials than in putting pressure on the Libyan regime. If a trial might expose Gaddafi to further measures then all to the good; but sanctions, progressively strengthened to create intolerable pressures, might be the preferred option. In any event the overthrow of Gaddafi, pending a new assassination opportunity, was the prime objective. Then the possibility of bringing the vast resource of Libyan oil once again within the comforting embrace of Western capitalism would be firmly on the political agenda.

The relative indifference of Washington, London and France to the possibility of trying the two Libyans was clearly demonstrated by their total neglect of the 1971 Montreal Convention (Appendix 4), the obvious instrument in international law which would have guaranteed a speedy trial. The Lockerbie and UTA outrages, and all similar terrorist acts, are properly addressed by this Convention,* an agreement that was enacted on 23 September 1971 under the auspices of the International Civil Aviation Organisation (ICAO), a specialised UN agency. Both Britain and the United States were founder members of the Convention, and today they and Libya are signatories. This Convention was the device that could have been observed to bring al-Megrahi and Fhimah to trial, and which – for reasons best known to the Western powers – was totally ignored by the accusing states.

The relevance of the Convention (properly lodged with the United Nations under Article 102 of the Charter) to the Lockerbie and UTA outrages is clearly shown in the explicit wording of Article 1(1c): 'Any person commits an offence if he . . . places or causes to be placed on an aircraft . . . a device or substance which is likely to destroy the aircraft.'

Convention for the Suppression of Unlawful Acts against the Safety of Civil Aviation (Montreal, 23 September 1971).

The Convention (Article 7) obliges Libya, 'if it does not extradite' the two suspects, to prosecute them in Libya:

> The Contracting State in the territory of which the alleged offender is found shall, if it does not extradite him, be obliged, without exception whatsoever and whether or not the offence was committed in its territory, to submit the case to its competent authorities for the purpose of prosecution. Those authorities shall take their decision in the same manner as in the case of any ordinary offence of a serious nature under the law of that State.

In this context it should be noted that Libya has no extradition treaty with Britain, France or the United States; and that Article 8(2) of the Convention protects the right of Libya not to extradite the suspects ('If a Contracting State . . . receives a request from another Contracting State with which it has no extradition treaty, it may at its option . . .').

It is important also that the Convention requires the various Contracting States to co-operate in bringing the accused people to trial. Thus Article 11(1) obliges the Contracting States to 'afford one another the greatest measure of assistance in connection with criminal proceedings . . .'. States, even accusing states, that refuse to assist the proceedings are thus in opposition to the terms of the Convention. It is significant that Libya encountered nothing but obstruction and condemnation by the Western powers in its handling of this case; and yet, if lawful procedure were all that mattered, the behaviour of the Libyan authorities is hard to fault. Throughout the episode the Libyan government complied with the demands of the Montreal Convention. It promptly arrested the suspects named by the Western powers; it notified the accusing states; it invited them to submit their evidence; it instructed lawyers to begin an enquiry; and it invited the West to send lawyers to observe the propriety of the proceedings.

The West, by contrast, refused to observe any of the provisions of the Montreal Convention. Instead, London and Washington threatened economic and military action (in violation of the UN Charter); and consistently ignored their responsibilities in law. Thus Professor Francis A. Boyle, professor of International Law at the University of Illinois at Urbana-Champaign, prepared a detailed Memorandum of Law on the dispute. Here he commented that the United States and Britain had rejected all Libya's efforts to resolve the matter peacefully, noting that 'both the United States and the United Kingdom have effectively violated most of the provisions of the Montreal Convention when it comes to the handling of this dispute with Libya'.[25] In their flagrant refusal to co-operate with Libya, and in their other dismissals of the Convention terms, the United States and the United Kingdom have acted in direct violation of international law. It is not enough for the West to protest that the suspects would not be given a fair trial in Libya. Frequently they have been branded as guilty by leading Western politicians, including President Bill Clinton and the UK foreign secretary Douglas Hurd, so the chance of a fair trial in the West may be judged equally unlikely. However, the Montreal Convention – with wording originally approved by the United States, Britain and other countries – made provision for the possibility of dissatisfaction among the accusing states. Article 14 allows recourse to arbitration and the World Court. Thus Professor Boyle notes: 'Libya has repeatedly offered to submit this dispute to international arbitration, to the International Court of Justice, to an international commission of investigation, or to some other type of *ad hoc* international institutional arrangement for the impartial investigation and adjudication of these allegations.'[26]

The position was plain: London and Washington had no interest in bringing the two accused Libyans to trial *per se*, only in exploiting the issue to bring pressure on the Gaddafi regime. To this end, the United Nations – with a pliant Security Council conveniently dominated by the Western powers – was a better bet than the relatively unhelpful terms of international law.

The two Libyan suspects were first targeted by the West more than six months before the passing of the first sanctions resolution (Resolution 748) in the Council. The resolution was passed only after members of the Council had been bullied by Washington and its allies, with China threatened with loss of 'favoured nation' trading status if it used its veto. Marc Weller, a research fellow at St Catherine's College, Cambridge, England, observed: 'the claimant states had to expend considerable political capital and good will in the Security Council, bullying fellow members to obtain the necessary votes, and enraging many non-members of the Council who keenly observed this spectacle.'[27] China, seemingly against its inclination, agreed not to veto the crucial resolution (748), but thereafter took steps to help Libya cope with the impact of sanctions imposed in such a fashion.[28]

The Western powers had again managed to manipulate the Security Council but at much political cost and in violation of international law and the spirit of the United Nations. Weller notes that the United States and Britain 'may well have contributed to, or brought about, an abuse of rights by the Security Council'; and suggests that the International Court of Justice might be able to determine that such an abuse had taken place. He concludes that 'it is perfectly possible to seek judicial review even of decisions of the Security Council . . . it may in fact be necessary for the Court to exercise such competence if the constitutional system of the UN Charter is to recover from the blow it has suffered in this episode'.[29]

The illicit sanctions on Libya remained in place through 1993, with the prospect of yet harsher measures. On 18 August the Jamahirya News Agency (JANA), the official Libyan agency, reported that the Security Council had prohibited Libya from using air ambulances to fly critically ill patients abroad for medical treatment. The decision was in violation of Resolution 748, Clause 4, which allows for aircraft flights 'on grounds of significant humanitarian need'. The Libyan people would continue to be punished in the Western hope that this would bring intolerable pressure on the Gaddafi regime. The possibility of bringing the two accused Libyans to trial seemed more remote than ever. Their Libyan lawyer, Ibrahim Legwell, observed that his clients could not expect a fair trial in Britain or the United States, and again there was talk of a possible trial elsewhere. At the same time London and Washington prepared fresh sanctions against Libya, while on 27 September 1993 President Clinton used his maiden address to the UN General Assembly to threaten tough new sanctions in order to bring the 'mass murderers' to justice. On 6 October Secretary-General Boutros-Ghali reported that no progress had been made with Libya on the question of surrendering the two suspects to the West. The scene was set for another turn of the screw.

On 1 October a new resolution sponsored by the US, Britain and France had been tabled in the Security Council, with the manifest aim of striking at the heart of the Libyan economy. First it was necessary to remove the possibility of a Russian veto in the Council, a task that was undertaken with the characteristic promises of financial assistance. The Russian government was expressing concern that if, under the terms of the new resolution, Libyan financial assets abroad were to be frozen Russia might not be able to recover the $4 billion it was owed by Libya. The Western powers argued that it was not their business to turn a UN sanctions decision into an aid package; but none the less some assistance would be given to Russia to bring Yeltsin on board. China, also with the power of veto in the Security Council, was expected to abstain on the new resolution but the Western members of the Council were reluctant to face a Russian abstention.

At the beginning of November 1993 President Clinton, John Major and the French prime minister, Edouard Balladur – in an obvious joint campaign – all wrote separately to Boris Yeltsin, urging him not to block further sanctions on Libya. Clinton's letter made it explicit that 'further

US aid [to Russia] would be prejudiced should it [Russia] obstruct' the proposed package of sanctions (*The Independent*, 5 November 1993). The clear financial threat was sufficient. Russia made it clear that it would not veto the proposed resolution (or even abstain), and the scene was set for the vote in the Security Council. In the event, Resolution 883 (Appendix 5) was passed in the Security Council on 11 November with eleven in favour and none against (with four abstentions: China, Djibouti, Morocco and Pakistan). A total boycott of Libyan oil sales had been avoided but the new resolution was clearly intended to hit Libyan oil refining and exports. Paragraph 5 (Resolution 883) bans the exporting to Libya of a wide range of equipment listed in the Annex: pumps, loading buoys, flexible hoses, anchor chains, inspection tools, cleaning devices, metering equipment, boilers, furnaces, fractionation columns and so on. The revenue from oil sales would not be blocked but Libya's capacity to produce and export oil products would be progressively crippled.

It was possible to speculate also on another aspect of the newly imposed sanctions. Paragraph III of the appended Annex to Resolution 883 bans the export to Libya of 'equipment not specially designed for use in crude oil export terminals but which . . . can be used for this purpose'. This meant that a range of equipment intended for non-oil sectors of the Libyan economy would fall within the scope of Resolution 883. Thus the West was now in a position to block the import of much-needed equipment for Libya's agricultural and other projects; in particular, for the development of the Great Manmade River Project, the heart of Gaddafi's plan for Libyan food self-sufficiency. This possibility was confirmed in a letter (18 January 1994) from the British foreign minister Douglas Hogg to Labour Member of Parliament Tam Dalyell (following an enquiry of mine): 'It is likely that the very large water pumps and other items conforming to the specifications in Section 3 [of the 883 Annex] would be prohibited from being exported to Libya . . .'. Thus the West had contrived a means – through the subtle mechanism of Resolution 883 – to hit not only the Libyan oil industry but also the plans for agricultural (and other) projects: Libya, it was conceived, would be less able to import food, because of the progressively diminishing oil revenues; and less able to achieve food self-sufficiency, because of the progressive crippling of its agricultural technology. It remains to be seen whether gradual starvation will be used against the Libyan people (with the covert purpose of toppling Gaddafi) as it has been used for five years against the Iraqi people (to topple Saddam Hussein).

It is clear that the US-sponsored campaign in the United Nations against the Libyan regime has nothing to do with Western opposition to international terrorism and the associated demand for the surrender of the two

Libyan suspects. There have been many opportunities to bring the suspects to court, all blocked by the West; and many signs that the West is not interested in international law (see above consideration of the 1971 Montreal Convention). Moreover, by 1994 it was evident that the case against the two Libyans had been known for three years to be extremely weak: in December 1993 it emerged (*The Sunday Times*, 19 December 1993) that the timer that triggered the Lockerbie bomb 'may not have been supplied to Libya after all' and that 'investigators were told this three years ago'. Now it was being suggested that the prosecution case against Libya 'may now be on the verge of collapse' – at a time when the United Nations was being coerced by the West to impose new sanctions on Libya to strike at its oil industry and agricultural development.

The investigative film *The Maltese Double Cross*, made by Allan Francovitch in 1994, suggests an official cover-up by Western governments interested above all in blaming Colonel Gaddafi: the film, denied a public showing, was shown in the House of Commons on 16 November 1994. This investigation argues that the Lockerbie bombing was financed by Iran and planned by Ahmed Jibril's Popular Front for the Liberation of Palestine–General Command (PFLC–GC), in revenge for the US's shooting down of the Iranian civil airliner in July 1988. It is suggested that the bomb was unwittingly carried on board by the Lebanese Khalid Jaafer, a drug-carrier for the CIA and the DEA. Martin Cadman, who lost a relative in the bombing, declares in the film that an official under President George Bush told him: 'Your government and ours knew exactly what happened but they are never going to tell' (*The Guardian*, 16 November 1994). It is clear that Western governments will continue to lie – and to defy international law – in their justification of punitive sanctions against Libya.

IGNORING THE UN: OVER ISRAEL

Israel, by virtue of the powerful Jewish lobby in the United States, has always enjoyed a unique relationship with the United Nations. In particular, it has always been immune to UN demands: resolutions critical of Israel, and making demands upon it, have frequently been passed – often despite great US reluctance – but there has never been any real prospect of UN-mandated sanctions against Israel, much less UN-authorised military intervention, in the event of non-compliance.

One of the main Security Council resolutions on Israel, which it has successfully resisted for nearly three decades, is Resolution 242

(22 November 1967), which stipulates the application of two crucial principles:

(i)   Withdrawal of Israeli armed forces from territories occupied in the recent conflict;

(ii) Termination of all claims or states of belligerency and respect for and acknowledgement of the sovereignty, territorial integrity and political independence of every State in the area and their right to live in peace within secure and recognised borders free from threats or acts of force . . .

After further Arab/Israeli conflict, Resolution 242 became transmogrified into Resolution 338 (22 October 1973), which in turn (Clause 2) called upon all parties 'to start immediately after the ceasefire the implementation of Security Council Resolution 242 in all of its parts'. In fact, Israel, citing the need for national security above all else, made no effort to withdraw from the occupied Arab lands (it remains to be seen whether the accords of 1993 will yield practical and lasting results). Resolutions 242 and 338 were not the only Security Council products that Israel decided to ignore for many years.

Israel has ignored also the terms of Security Council resolutions that address the conditions of the Arabs in the occupied lands. Thus, with tacit approval from Washington, there has been no attempt to observe the demands and conditions laid out in:

*Resolution 465** (1 March 1980), which condemns Israel's restrictions on freedom of travel, its illegal changes to the status of occupied Arab territories, and its 'flagrant violation' of the Geneva Convention relative to the Protection of Civilian Persons in Time of War;

Resolution 476 (30 June 1980), which condemns the prolonged occupation of Arab lands, illegal changes to the status of Jerusalem, and its 'flagrant violation' of the Geneva Convention;

Resolution 478 (20 August 1980), condemning a violation of international law over Jerusalem, the continued violation of the Geneva Convention, and the consequent 'serious obstruction to achieving a comprehensive, just and lasting peace in the Middle East';

---

*The failure of Israel to obey, or the Security Council to enforce, the requirements of 465 led directly to the Hebron massacre of 25 February 1994.

Resolution 672 (13 October 1990), condemning the killing in Jerusalem of more than twenty Palestinians and the injuring of more than 150 people, 'including Palestinian civilians and innocent worshippers', and demanding that Israel observe its obligations under the Fourth Geneva Convention;

Resolution 673 (24 October 1990), noting 'the continued deterioration of the situation in the occupied territories', and deploring the refusal of Israel 'to receive the mission of the Secretary-General to the region'.

Resolutions 672 and 673 are of particular interest since the Security Council passed them unanimously after the 1990 Iraqi invasion of Kuwait and during the run-up to the 1991 Gulf War. Here was a situation in which Israel's flouting of international law, its ignoring of UN resolutions, and its denial of human rights – as expressly recorded in the relevant resolutions – were met by no more than a reprimand; whereas Iraq's manifest derelictions were to bring a massive military response, leading to the total devastation of a country and several hundred thousand Iraqi casualties, a toll that continues to mount four years after the end of the Gulf War. It is important to remember the circumstances in which the two key resolutions (672 and 673) on Israel failed to bring a characteristic American veto or abstention.

In early October 1990 the Temple Mount Faithful in Jerusalem, an organised group of about one thousand pious Jews, moved to reclaim the Mount, the holy shrine to which they were allowed only limited access. On 5 October Sheikh Fadhallah Silwadi, the preacher of the Al Aqsa mosque, urged his followers to congregate at the Noble Sanctuary on 8 October to resist the efforts of the Temple Mount Faithful. The resulting confrontation quickly erupted into a major crisis involving the Israel security forces: by 11.30 a.m., after the heavily armed Israelis had used tear gas, plastic bullets and live ammunition, about twenty Palestinians lay dead and some 150 were injured. In an appeal to the Security Council, Palestinian leaders from East Jerusalem declared: 'We do not understand how the Security Council can ignore our plea for protection when it is prepared to send troops to fight a war in the Gulf region. Once again we issue a plea to the civilised world . . . Protect us against Israeli soldiers, settlers and armed religious zealots.'

The United States was in a dilemma. Its traditional support for Israel was unaffected but Washington had gone to some pains to construct an anti-Iraq Coalition, seen as a pragmatic alliance that usefully included Arab states. The principal Arab members of the Coalition – Egypt, Kuwait and Saudi Arabia – were horrified at a fresh slaughter of Palestinians; so it was necessary from Washington to make some gesture. When Iraqi troops had fired on protesting Kuwaitis, killing one woman, the Americans had dubbed the act 'murder'; now President George Bush brought himself to declare that the Israeli killing of twenty Palestinians was 'saddening'. In addition Bush persuaded President Mitterand to moderate a draft resolution condemning the Israeli action. The subsequent watered-down resolution (672) was passed in the Security Council, with the US delegate supporting it. The follow-up resolution (673) was even less consequential. Washington had decided that this particular dispute was at an end: the Israeli security forces would be allowed to behave as they wished and the long-suffering Palestinians could expect no protection from the Security Council.

The next resolution on Israel (Resolution 681), again supported by a pragmatic Washington keen to preserve the fragile anti-Iraq Coalition, expressed grave concern 'at the dangerous deterioration of the situation in all the Palestinian territories occupied by Israel since 1967, including Jerusalem, and at the violence and rising tension in Israel'; expressed 'grave concern' over Israel's rejection of Resolutions 672 and 673; deplored Israel's decision to resume the deportation of Palestinian civilians; and urged Israel to accept its legal obligations under the Fourth Geneva Convention (1949). There was no prospect that Israel would take more notice of this resolution than it had of any of the others, but one of its clauses – (3), deploring further Palestinian deportations – was to have particular relevance to a fresh violation that was to occur in the congenial atmosphere of the emerging New World Order. Israel was set to organise a fresh batch of deportations that would outrage much of the international community and yet again demonstrate Israel's immunity to both the spirit and the letter of Security Council resolutions.

On 14 December 1992, after further actions by Hamas, the extremist Palestinian organisation operating in the occupied territories, the Israeli authorities sealed off the West Bank and Gaza. Three days later Israel deported more than four hundred Palestinians, dumping them in southern Lebanon. To this gross violation of international law and human rights, Washington expressed 'strong objections'; whereupon the Security Council passed Resolution 799 (Appendix 6), denouncing the Israeli outrage. This important resolution noted Israel's fresh violation of the Fourth Geneva Convention, reaffirmed the sovereignty of Lebanon, and demanded that Israel 'ensure the safe and immediate return to the occupied territories of all those deported'. The world could now see that the deportees had been left – with few supplies of food or clothing – in a wilderness. US President-elect Bill Clinton announced that he was 'con-

cerned'. No serious effort was made to force Israel to observe the requirements of international law and the unambiguous demands of Resolution
799. Secretary-General Boutros-Ghali indicated that he might urge sanctions on Israel to force compliance, but few observers imagined that
Washington would support such a course.

Eventually, after many international expressions of outrage, the Israeli
government offered a compromise. Perhaps a quarter of the deportees –
some of them sick and admittedly deported in error – might be allowed to
return. This move, clearly inconsistent with the demands of Resolution
799, allowed Washington to squash any further UN talk of sanctions on
Israel. The resolution had demanded a return of '*all those deported*' (my
italics), and Israel was offering to take back perhaps one hundred out of
four hundred. The US Secretary of State Warren Christopher declared:
'The US believes that this process is consistent with UN resolutions . . .
further action by the Security Council is unnecessary and could even
undercut the process under way . . .'.[30] Now the international community
would be discouraged from any further consideration of yet another Israeli
violation of human rights, UN resolutions and international law.

Israel had demonstrated yet again that it could act with impunity – in
clear violation of international law – to pursue its perceived strategic interests. It was now obvious that the *débâcle* over Resolution 799 would act as
a 'green light', if another were needed, for further illegal initiatives. On
25 July 1993 Israel launched a new military invasion – by land, sea and air
– of Lebanon, with the intention of crushing the Hizbollah groups lodged
in the south of the country. The protracted onslaught brought the number
of displaced people to around a quarter of a million, with hundreds of
civilian casualties. Resolution 799(3) had declared 'the independence,
sovereignty and territorial integrity of Lebanon'. So what was to be done?
After all, the United States had supported the resolution. So what were the
options? Comprehensive UN-mandated sanctions, drawn up in a speedy
new resolution? A military anti-Israel coalition to guarantee that the new
aggression 'will not stand'? In fact no serious approach to the Security
Council was made. Washington did not urge a fresh consensus to resist
aggression. Instead Washington urged restraint on both sides.

A procession of UN resolutions had been ignored, Israel remained an
occupying power in Arab lands, and the Middle East peace talks – with no
real US commitment – were stalled. Then it was revealed that PLO/Israel
talks, secretly conducted in Oslo, had reached a measure of accord. The
Palestinians would be granted some degree of autonomy in Gaza and in
the Jericho region of the West Bank. On 13 September 1993 the Israeli
premier Yitzhak Rabin and PLO leader Yasser Arafat shook hands in

Washington to signal the new agreement. The Americans – for once side-lined in the talks – soon saw the advantage in staging a new piece of theatre. None of this had anything to do with the United Nations, which, having authorised the creation of Israel, was largely ignored thereafter. The future shape of the Middle East has yet to emerge but it is easy to make some predictions. For one, the United Nations will be involved only when it suits the principal players in the region.

THE COLLAPSE OF CONSENSUS: OVER BOSNIA

The conflict in what was Yugoslavia broke out in August 1990, soon after elections had ended Communist rule in Croatia and Slovenia. The mounting turmoil derived not simply from the escalating collapse of Eastern Europe but also from deep ethnic and territorial tensions that had often brought conflict in the past. Now the region was set for a new horrendous war, with all the obscene paraphernalia of civilian slaughter, 'ethnic cleansing', mass rape, prison camps and torture that had characterised the Second World War and which Europeans had resolved would never happen again in their lands.[31]

On 25 September 1991 the UN Security Council unanimously adopted Resolution 713, calling on all states to implement a 'general and complete embargo on all deliveries of weapons and military equipment to Yugoslavia'. So began a United Nations involvement that was to deliver substantial aid to suffering peoples, but which was to have little impact on the scale of the conflict and which was destined to expose deep divisions among the Permanent Members of the Security Council. Resolution 724 approved the Secretary-General's proposals for a peacekeeping operation, and on 15 February 1992 Perez de Cuellar recommended the creation of a United Nations Protection Force (UNPROFOR), subsequently authorised on 21 February by the Security Council's adoption of Resolution 743. An early aim was to establish the United Nations Protected Areas (UNPAs), an optimistic goal that was not accomplished. Throughout the conflict the impression grew that the United Nations was largely impotent, incapable of timely and decisive action. Divisions among the members of the Security Council – and within NATO and the European Community – meant that initiatives to resolve the turmoil were invariably low-key, tardy and unproductive. The Security Council issued a flood of resolutions, statements and warnings from the beginning of the conflict to the eventual virtual abandonment of Bosnia in mid-1993. A detailed history of this war has yet to be written but there are few involved individuals – either within the former Yugoslavia or in the international community – who will emerge with credit.

The UN involvement began with a seemingly shared resolve among the Permanent Members of the Security Council. But before long the consensus had collapsed: differences were paraded in public, to the point that much of the United Nations effort was discredited. The underlying cause was easy to see. Washington, with no overwhelming strategic interest in the former Yugoslavia, had no reason to whip unco-operative Permanent Members into line. They in turn lacked the muscle to compel American acquiescence in politics that had a European focus. From the beginning the fault lines in the Security Council were discernible but by 1993 they were gaping wide.

One key difference between the Permanent Members related to how the post-war situation would be supervised, given the optimistic scenario of a negotiated peace. When it was suggested that the putative peace plan drawn up by Cyrus Vance and David Owen would require substantial NATO forces, including at least 5000 British and 10,000 US troops, to remain in Bosnia until the next century the Americans reacted with stunned disbelief. President Clinton, at the same time eager to cut military commitments, had backed Secretary of State Warren Christopher's support for a Vance–Owen scheme that proposed a loose federation in Bosnia with ten autonomous ethnic provinces. Seemingly, few Washington policy makers had thought through the implications of the plan, long since abandoned.

In February 1993 there were deep divisions among the Western allies – and so in the Security Council – about the extent to which there should be external military intervention in the Yugoslavian turmoil. Washington sources spoke of a potentially disastrous fracturing of Western policy, while Secretary-General Boutros-Ghali seemed unable to sustain a consensus. On 22 February the Security Council set up an international war crimes tribunal to prosecute those responsible for atrocities in the Balkans, while at the same time British and other Western diplomats discounted the idea, suggesting that the tribunal might serve as an obstacle to peace.

When President Clinton then proposed dropping aid to besieged Muslim towns the other Western powers were less than enthusiastic. British officials noted that it was 'very unlikely that the UK will provide aircraft for parachute drops'; and it was suggested that any such initiative could threaten the peace process. A senior British official declared that air drops would not work, while the Foreign Office added that there was 'much to be said for creative thinking'. Soon, however, Foreign Secretary Douglas Hurd 'warmly welcomed and supported' the US move – though emphasising that no British aircraft would be involved. In February there were also talks about the possibility of bombing Serbian targets, an option favoured by Washington but discouraged by Britain and France with their own personnel active on the ground. On 7 March 1993 Secretary-General Boutros-Ghali suggested for the first time that UN troops might have to be sent into the region to remove Serbian forces from disputed territory: 'there is only one solution, which is enforcement. And again, the members [of the United Nations] . . . must be ready to send troops on the ground.' He added, speaking on US television, that he was 'not a technician' and could not estimate how many troops might be needed, but 'certainly it will be a major operation'.

Further difficulties were now emerging about the structure of any peacekeeping operation; and about the details of any projected peace plan. It was reported that the Russians would be reluctant to serve under NATO command in the event of a NATO force being used to supervise the postwar situation. Boris Yeltsin, it was announced, would have difficulty in putting Russian troops under the command of a former Cold War adversary. And at the same time Washington was rejecting the current drafting of the Vance–Owen peace plan: the Americans were unwilling to accept the degree of Serbian 'ethnic cleansing' that the scheme apparently endorsed. Furthermore, a draft UN resolution to tighten the noose around Serbia had been diluted by the Russians – so that it now failed to satisfy the demands of the European Community. Here it was suggested that if the Security Council could not agree on the level of anti-Serbia measures the European Community might be prepared to act on its own. Thus Neils Helveg Petersen, the Danish foreign minister and then President of the EC Council of Ministers, declared: 'We should apply maximum pressure on the Serbs and I would not exclude unilateral action.'

In May further problems about the command of troops were exposed in the Security Council. Secretary-General Boutros-Ghali had 'surprised the Security Council and unnerved the US' by suggesting that forces implementing a peace plan in Bosnia would be controlled by his office through the UN special representative, Thorwald Stoltenberg, who had replaced Cyrus Vance as UN mediator. One Western diplomat commented that 'Boutros-Ghali's plan for overall political and strategic control has to be fudged if the US is to come on board'.[32] The problem was a familiar one. Washington would always insist that US troops, acting under nominal UN auspices, remain under American command. At the same time there were signs that Washington was tiring of the Bosnian conflict. On 17 May it was suggested that the United States might not even attend a meeting of foreign ministers at the Security Council, a circumstance that caused temporary 'diplomatic confusion'. UN sources declared that American objections existed 'because the real problem was disunity with the other allies over Bosnia'.[33] A week later, deep disagreements surfaced between Boutros-Ghali and the Security Council on the question of supplying further aid to the Bosnians; and between NATO members disputing the practicality of the 'safe area' plan. And already it was clear that the US/EC differences over the war were deepening.[34] Washington continued to contemplate the option of bombing the recalcitrant Serbs in Bosnia; and now was urging that the arms embargo on the Muslims be lifted. UK Foreign Secretary Douglas Hurd squirmed: having bitterly opposed the arming of the Bosnian Muslims, he now conceded that the arms embargo might be ended ('It may become inevitable').

In July the pressures mounted for the provision of an air defence of the so-called 'safe areas' in Bosnia. The Bosnian President, Alija Izetbegovic, was complaining that, despite UN resolutions and UN declarations, nothing was being done to protect the besieged Muslims. NATO aircraft were in place and ready to act, but Boutros-Ghali had insisted on a delay because the UN air controllers were not yet in place. On 27 July France urged the United Nations and NATO to provide prompt air cover to protect the UN peacekeepers from attack. Already, the French Foreign Ministry emphasised, there was UN authorisation – via Security Council Resolution 836 – for defensive air attacks and troop reinforcements. Now President Clinton was again threatening to bomb the Serbs, though few observers thought that any action would be taken. Britain and France continued to register strong objections to any such initiative, with Russia's special envoy, Vitaly Churkin, declaring that the US posture was having a 'very negative' impact on the peace talks. The dispute dragged on into August, with fresh arguments about whether the United States or the United Nations would have control over the planned air strikes.[35] On 7 August some Serbian withdrawals were agreed, making the prospect of UN and NATO air attacks on Serbian positions unlikely. To many observers it seemed clear that the Serbs had manipulated the situation to their own advantage. The 'international community' had huffed and puffed – with Clinton repeatedly announcing that air strikes were imminent – but no action was taken. Divisions both within and between the United States, NATO, the United Nations and the European Community had caused a total collapse of consensus. UN Secretary-General Boutros-Ghali, whatever his instincts, was impotent in the face of such factional discord.

The Bosnian Muslims now felt betrayed on every front. The United Nations had passed its resolutions, but they were increasingly perceived as

empty verbiage. Various states had urged and promised military intervention but no practical initiatives had been taken. The Bosnian Muslims
had no option but to 'await their fate'.[36] Anti-Serb air strikes, active UN
peacekeepers on the ground, arms for the beleaguered Muslims – all
options were off.

Britain then acted by arranging for an RAF Hercules to fly an injured
five-year-old girl, Irma Hadzimuratovic, out of Sarajevo for treatment at
Great Ormond Street hospital in London. This initiative, organised by
John Major, was soon seen as cynical propaganda, more concerned with
advertising the benevolence of a government than with offering real help
to the desperate people of the former Yugoslavia. Commented one journalist on Prime Minister Major and Foreign Secretary Hurd: 'there is a
chilling cynicism in their actions. The men who have consistently stood
against any real change in the West's policy towards Sarajevo and have
blocked crucial European and American initiatives for intervention now
have the gall to climb onto a white horse and drag 5-year-old Irma
Hadzimuratovic on to their saddle.'[37]

The event stimulated fresh efforts to bring some of the wounded victims out of Bosnia for treatment in the West. It also generated recrimina-
tions between medical staff working in the afflicted areas and outside
personnel seemingly operating to a different agenda. The 'rescue' efforts
were increasingly perceived as a public relations affair, 'good advertising for the outside world to make them look like humanists' (according
to a Sarajevo paediatrician, Dr Olga Anic). Little publicity was given to
the fact that some 10,000 children had been killed since the start of the
war; or that, even now, little effort was being made to improve the
appalling conditions of Sarajevo hospitals. There were even complaints
from Downing Street that there were few children in a fresh batch of
evacuees, prompting Sylvana Fox, a spokeswoman for the United
Nations High Commissioner for Refugees (UNHCR) in Geneva to comment on the 'public opinion' that 'only wants 10-year-olds with blonde
hair and blue eyes'. Prime Minister John Major was reportedly 'upset'
and 'fed up' about the small number of children among the forty-one
people earmarked for rescue.[38] Michael Meacher, the overseas development spokesman for the British Labour Party, commented that the rescue
mission – now dubbed 'Operation Irma' – was 'a tombola', with children as prizes. The rescue operation, called a 'cynical piece of political
theatre' by British medical staff working in Sarajevo, was increasingly
seen as a front to disguise failed policies. Operation Irma, few could
deny, was a poor substitute for proper international initiatives that might
have brought an end to the war.

Bosnia, long deprived of the means to defend itself, had been abandoned to its fate. At a poignant meeting of the Security Council on 8 September 1993 the president of Bosnia, Alija Izetbegovic, made a final appeal: 'Defend us, or let us defend ourselves.' The plea was met with silence. The US ambassador to the UN, Madeleine Albright, was moved to comment: 'I was surprised that people didn't say anything to him . . . He spoke eloquently to say that the international community had let him down. Then the fact that nobody spoke . . . it was just sad.' Soon, however, the Permanent Members of the Security Council were addressing their proper priorities, arguing about who would have authority for supervising the eventual peace in Bosnia.[39]

In an interview in *The Washington Post* (15 October 1993), President Bill Clinton roundly criticised his Western allies for their policies on Bosnia, declaring that he 'had the feeling that the British and French felt it was more important to avoid lifting the arms embargo' on Bosnia's Muslims 'than to save the country'; and he added that John Major had told him that he 'wasn't sure he could sustain his government' if he agreed to lift the embargo. (In another interview, Secretary of State Warren Christopher commented that 'Western Europe is no longer the dominant area of the world'.) In London the Prime Minister's office retorted that in a 'mature relationship' there were bound to be disagreements, such as those over Bosnia.

On 26 October the UN announced, following the death of the tenth UN relief worker since the war began, it was indefinitely suspending relief operations in central Bosnia, so imperilling the lives of 1.5 million Muslims and Croats. As winter threatened, the UN High Commissioner for Refugees (UNHCR) predicted that 2.74 million Bosnians would need emergency assistance. Said Jorge de la Mota, UNHCR head in the Muslim town of Zenica: 'It's going to be a catastrophe because of a lack of food, adequate infrastructure and medical services.' In the event, the winter was less severe than had been feared, and soon the bulk of the aid convoys were moving again. The war itself seemed set to continue.

On 5 February 1994 a mortar bomb hit a Sarajevo market, killing 70 civilians and wounding many more. This in turn led to a UN-agreed NATO ultimatum demanding that the Serbs withdraw their artillery outside a 12-mile exclusion zone around the city; and an unprecedented Russian intervention to help oversee the withdrawal. The tensions remained. When the ultimatum expired on 20 February, NATO took no action, but had the Serbs really complied? Soon the issue of the marketplace massacre receded into history, to be replaced by fresh unresolved crises. There were still no signs of a coherent UN policy with defined objectives and a clear strategy. The principal UN-mandated players in the situation (the United States, Britain, France and Russia) were often at odds, interpreting matters in their own national terms and frequently taking unilateral decisions with little or no consultation with the authorised UN representatives. The UN itself was frequently humiliated: its troops variously killed, taken hostage, or denied access to the so-called 'safe havens'. The UN aid programme had brought relief to tens of thousands of people but through 1994 there was little hope that UN efforts would bring a just solution to the war.

In March there were fresh signs of uncertainty among UN officials. Extra soldiers were desperately needed in Bosnia but Britain, France and the United States were resisting UN requests. Should the UN accept Russia's offer of a further 300 troops, so strengthening Moscow's influence in the region and ignoring the long-standing UN policy of rejecting peacekeeping troops from neighbouring states? It was now obvious that the UN effort was staggering from crisis to crisis, inadequately resourced and constantly manipulated by the warring factions.[40] The Clinton administration continued to vacillate, in one breath ruling out the likelihood of punitive NATO air strikes against the Serbian forces and in the next breath announcing that such strikes were imminent.[41] In May, in contemptuous disregard for UN instructions, the Serbs drove tanks across the heavy weapons exclusion zone around Sarajevo. The UN humiliation was compounded by the unclear posture of Yasushi Akashi, the UN Secretary-General's special representative in the area – who first gave permission for the tank movements, then withdrew permission, only to grant it again before yet again changing his mind. Akashi's vacillations encouraged the Serbs to act with impunity and led to repeated calls from the Muslim-led Bosnian government for his resignation.[42] For his part, Akashi dubbed the American leadership 'timid and tentative' – drawing a rebuke from Madeleine Albright, Washington's UN ambassador. The situation was clear: the United States was reluctant to support UN efforts in Bosnia, while at the same time Washington criticised the UN for its manifest failures and opposed suggestions that the United Nations create its own resource pool, including a standing peacekeeping army.[43]

The Clinton administration had no hesitation in encouraging Britain and France to maintain their troop commitments in the area ('until we have exhausted all possibilities of a settlement'), while still refusing to commit US forces on the ground. And there was the further irony that, at a time when Clinton was encouraging a continued troop commitment *by other states*, he was contemplating easing the sanctions against Serbia and lifting the arms embargo against Bosnia – moves that would immediately undermine the British and French presence in the region. On 9 June the

US House of Representatives voted (244–178) to approve a congressional order for an end to US support for the arms embargo against Bosnia. Britain, with no longer any heart to oppose such developments, announced that it was planning to withdraw its forces from Bosnia.[44] UN Secretary-General Boutros Boutros-Ghali, now increasingly frustrated at the further demonstration of UN impotence, wrote to the Security Council acknowledging that the 21,000 troops based in Bosnia might have to be withdrawn. President Clinton, in manifest indifference to UN endeavours, then instructed the CIA and the Pentagon to prepare a covert arms pipeline and weapons-training programme for the Bosnian Muslims.[45] Washington – through its vacillations and indifference – had encouraged the collapse of the entire UN enterprise; as the UN command in the former Yugoslavia drew up its plans in September 1994 for an emergency withdrawal the humiliation of the United Nations was transparent.

In November 1994 the US compounded the disarray in UN policy by announcing that it would no longer help police the arms embargo and would no longer provide satellite information to its NATO allies. This clear violation of Security Council resolution 724 further undermined UN authority. Alain Juppé, the French foreign minister, declared that this was 'the first time that a country like the United States has unilaterally exonerated itself from a United Nations Security Council resolution that it has voted for . . .' (*The Sunday Times*, 13 November 1994). The UN was further humiliated when, at the end of November, the seemingly impotent United Nations watched as Bosnian-Serb forces invaded the UN 'safe area' of Bihac.

UN OR US? IN SOMALIA

On 3 December 1992 the UN Security Council voted unanimously to send a multinational force, with a US contingent of up to 28,000 troops, to Somalia. So began a UN-sponsored initiative that would quickly generate massive confusion about the respective roles of the UN authorities and the American forces on the ground, and that would rapidly build up tensions between the various contingents in the multinational force. President George Bush expressed the hope that the US-led intervention intended to protect the distribution of food and medical supplies would be concluded before he left office in January 1993, but the specific UN resolution set no time limits. Marlin Fitzwater, the President's spokesman, declared that all the forces would be withdrawn from Somalia as soon as the supply corridors had been secured. The aims seemed clear, but already some observers were suggesting that American troops were likely to become enmeshed in an impossible situation. Thus Representative John Murtha declared in the US Congress: 'We have to know what the consequences are. We just cannot afford to be the policeman of the world.'

It was clear from the outset that the intervention in Somalia would be under American rather than UN control. Sir David Hannay, the British Ambassador to the United Nations, commented that an option proposed by Secretary-General Boutros-Ghali 'clearly envisages a US general in command'; and it was now obvious that the Pentagon was insisting that the United States have command of any operation. It was announced at an early stage that the force's likely commander on the ground would be Marine Lieutenant-Colonel Bob Johnson, who had been one of Norman Schwarzkopf's top aides in Operation Desert Storm in the 1991 Gulf War; and that Marine General Joseph Hoar, the chief of Unified Command, would be in charge of the overall strategy. Already General Hoar had drafted a mobilisation plan requiring 1800 Marines to make an amphibious landing at Mogadishu and then to secure the international airport and parts of the port. It was expected that the American forces would include 16,000 troops of the Marine Expeditionary Force at Camp Pendleton in California; 10,000 soldiers from Fort Drum, New York; and an unspecified number of Special Operations covert teams. An aircraft carrier, the USS *Ranger*, and two other ships, a cruiser and a destroyer, were quickly despatched to the area; and it was reported that about twelve other countries – including France, Canada and Nigeria – would be sending troops to the region. Britain declined to offer a troop contingent but promised transport aircraft.

The US-led initiative – now dubbed 'Operation Restore Hope' – was advertised as an essentially humanitarian venture, designed solely to bring food and other supplies to a starving population. But already some doubts were being expressed about the wisdom of the intervention. Aid agencies, in particular, were concerned that the massive US-led invasion would disturb the fragile relationship that the international aid agencies had managed to build with the contending Somalian clans. Thus Brigitte Doppler, of Médecins Sans Frontières, commented: 'The troops are going to completely shatter the equilibrium that has been established. The figures of 95 per cent malnutrition and 80 per cent of food being looted are months out of date, and are being used to justify the arrival of the troops.'[46] Already President Bush was indicating how the clans would be treated: 'Our mission is humanitarian, but we will not tolerate armed gangs ripping off their own people.' It was significant that neither the clan leader nor any UN relief agency staff in Somalia had been consulted by the US military over its plans, despite the key role that such organisations were playing in distributing the food that the US troops were being sent to protect. A top United Nations official in Mogadishu summed up a wide-spread feeling: 'The operation stinks of arrogance. All this bullshit about 80 per cent of food being looted and all that – it's all very well stage-managed by the United States. That's why there is no co-ordination with the UN or the relief agencies. This whole operation is a test case for future conflict resolution. It's as if the US had a new vaccine they wanted to test. Now they have found an animal to test it on.'[47]

Already there were widespread suspicions about a hidden American agenda. Aid agencies in Somalia were questioning what seemed to be US propaganda about the state of the country. No-one doubted the need for a continuing aid effort, but the gravity of the situation seemed to be exaggerated. Thus Geoff Loane, the co-ordinator of the International Committee of the Red Cross, the largest food distributor in Somalia, reckoned that a maximum of 30 per cent of food aid was lost to looting; and Justin Forsyth of Oxfam, while agreeing that some relief aid had been looted, said he did not know where the 80 per cent figure had come from. It was also clear that the US forces were keen to pursue a course of action without seeking the agreement either of local UN officials or of key figures in the Secretariat in New York. UN Secretary-General Boutros-Ghali was soon expressing his dissent from how the US-led forces were approaching their tasks. According to Boutros-Ghali, the US troops were supposed to be disarming the clan factions, as a prelude to creating secure corridors for aid; but seemingly the US command had no such intention. By mid-December 1992 there were some 4000 US marines in Mogadishu, rapidly being joined by troops from France, Belgium, Botswana, Italy and Saudi Arabia. The German Luftwaffe was also playing a significant role, having already flown a number of evacuation missions to rescue Western relief workers from dangerous areas.

By early 1993 it was clear that Operation Restore Hope was achieving only limited success: the clan factions were still disrupting aid efforts, the US-led forces seemed uncertain how to proceed, and there were growing tensions between UN officials and Somali factions in Mogadishu and elsewhere. In these circumstances, with little prospect of further political theatre to improve the humanitarian image of US troops in the country, Washington seemed well prepared to hand over the operation to nominal UN control. On 26 March 1993 the UN Security Council voted to transfer the US-led peacekeeping operation to the United Nations. The original United Nations Operation in Somalia (UNOSOM) had been established by Resolution 751 (24 April 1992); and the subsequent US-led Unified Task Force (for Operation Restore Hope) was authorised by Resolution 794 (3 December 1992). Now Resolution 814 (26 March 1993) launched a new initiative, under nominal UN control, to secure peace in Somalia and to rebuild the country. The ambitious terms of Resolution 814 were unprecedented for the United Nations. Here was authorisation for a UN force, expected to cost some £1 billion, to run the country. Troops acting under nominal UN-command would be authorised to maintain the peace, to disarm warring factions, to protect relief workers, to return thousands of refugees to their homes, to clear land-mines, to set up a police force, to help rebuild the economy, and to take steps to establish a new and democratic national government. Few observers thought that much of all this would be accomplished.

Again there were many ambiguities in the respective roles of UN officials and American commanders on the ground. The UN-authorised forces had been transferred to nominal United Nations control, but US officers were still in charge. There were frequent military encounters in Mogadishu, with both UN and Somali casualties. Tensions were also growing between the various national contingents in the UN force and the overall American command. In June, after the deaths of twenty-two Pakistani UN soldiers, Pakistani officials criticised the United Nations and the United States for failing to ensure that peacekeeping troops in Mogadishu were adequately equipped. In addition to the fatalities, at least ten Pakistani soldiers were missing, with more than fifty wounded; and now Pakistan was seeking a commitment that its 4000-strong contingent would be equipped 'with the necessary equipment, such as armoured personnel carriers and helicopters' to enable it to operate safely and effectively. At the same time the Security Council went into emergency session and authorised the UN forces in Somalia to 'take all measures' against those responsible for the attacks 'including to secure the investigation, arrest and detention for their prosecution, trial and punishment'.

Now dissatisfaction was growing in other national contingents of the UN force. Following the deaths of three Italian peacekeepers, Italy continued to resist opposition demands to withdraw its troops from Somalia; but it was plain that both the Italian government and much of the opposition wanted Italy to have a greater role in the command of UN forces. On 12 July 1993 the United Nations rejected calls from the Italian government that combat operations in Mogadishu be suspended after US helicopter gunships had blasted buildings said to be the command centre of the faction leader, Mohammed Farah Aideed. The attack resulted in the deaths of at least thirty Somalis, with dozens more wounded and two photographers killed by enraged Somalis after the event. Fabio Fabbri, the Italian defence minister, commented: 'A choice of this nature, with its extremely high risk, indeed certainty, that human lives will be lost is shared neither by public opinion nor by parliament in our country.' Joe Sills, a spokesman for the UN Secretary-General, retorted that 'the mandate of any UN operation is up to the Security Council and is not up to individual member states.' On 17 July the Italian government declared that it would pull its troops out of Somalia unless the participating states could agree on a single command and a single policy. It was now emerging that *contingents from several countries, unhappy with the US-led command in Mogadishu, had defied the nominal UN command and instead were taking orders from their own capitals.* The Italian daily newspaper *Il Giorno* commented that for the United States there were two things too many in Somalia, 'the Somalis and the Italians. Without these Somalia would be perfect'; it suggested that American troops were there to get rid of these two inconveniences, while the United Nations was 'a little dog on the American lead'. Similarly, *La Republica* denounced the American raid as 'incomprehensible and unjustifiable'.

The United Nations responded by trying to evict the Italian commander, General Bruno Loi, from Mogadishu, though Italy refused to bow to the US-orchestrated pressure.[48] A top Pakistani officer observed that disagreements between the Italians and the US-dominated UN command had wrecked the cohesion of the UNOSOM force and that a fundamental review of strategy was now essential: 'The US handed over the leadership to the UN, but they continue to dominate. We are coalition partners, but we are very very much hurt that the US didn't disarm the gunmen last December, when they had the might and the public support to do it.' Such criticism from Pakistan, traditionally a firm ally of the United States, was seen as a serious blow to the US command; and the strictures gained support from another source, this time one close to Washington. In August a confidential UN document, prepared by Ann Wright, a United States state department legal expert seconded to UNOSOM, questioned the legality of the unannounced military attacks against General Aideed: 'From the legal, moral and human rights perspective, we counsel against conducting military operations that give no notice of attack to occupants of buildings.' The report was seen as signalling the widening gulf between the US-led command in Mogadishu and American and other civilian strategists interested in developing a more constructive approach to the Somali problem. The American commanders were further embarrassed when in early August they launched a determined attack on what turned out to be a United Nations building in Mogadishu: for three hours, members of the

UN Development Programme (UNDP) were manhandled, blindfolded and interrogated by US troops trying to determine the whereabouts of General Aideed. The crack American force had succeeded in capturing innocent UN officials, after which Jonathan Howe, the retired US admiral heading the UN effort in Somalia, felt obliged to apologise to the UNDP; privately Pentagon officials agreed that the crack Ranger force had 'cocked up'.[49]

Now the emphasis was shifting. The frequent US *débâcles*, leading to hundreds of Somali casualties, had achieved nothing. The renegade factions had not been disarmed; General Aideed was still at large, despite a UN-offered price on his head; the aid relief had been comprehensively obstructed; and – worse to the sensitive American public – 'our boys' were returning home in body bags. Some sixty-two UN soldiers had been killed since 4 May, and the situation was deteriorating. Now President Clinton was hinting at the possibility of a political deal with Aideed: after all, the United Nations had originally paid protection money to him, so some sort of accommodation might be possible.[50] When Secretary of State Warren Christopher suggested that perhaps it was time to ease up on the hunt for Aideed, the UN Secretary-General immediately denounced the shift in policy. So the American policy makers decided that Aideed would still be sought – in order to try him for war crimes – while at the same time negotiations to improve the situation could not be ruled out. The hunt for Aideed was still on, but now the US-led UN intervention in Somalia appeared to be in mounting disarray.

On 4 October fresh street battles in Mogadishu resulted in more than 500 Somali casualties, with 12 US dead and 75 wounded. The US Defence Secretary Les Aspin announced that some two hundred more US troops, backed by tanks and armoured vehicles, would be sent to bolster the American contingent. These events stimulated fresh US demands for a withdrawal of troops, in turn stimulating a new call from Boutros-Ghali for Washington to stay the course. President Clinton, before these new tragic events already seeming at a loss, now appeared even more confused and indecisive. Now he reportedly felt let down by those responsible for US policy in Somalia. The Pentagon and the State Department were criticising Admiral Jonathan Howe, and tensions were developing between the White House and Boutros-Ghali, now struggling to maintain the disastrous US-led intervention on track. He complained to the Security Council that the UN force in Somalia was still 6000 to 7000 short of the numbers promised, and that it was too early to say that the ambitious UN initiative had failed.

On 7 October 1993 President Clinton, trying to satisfy every constituency, announced that he would withdraw all American troops by 31 March 1994, but that in the short term he would send 1700 more soldiers to Somalia, with another 3600 Marines to be stationed offshore. At the same time he announced that he would be sending Robert Oakley, the former US special envoy to Somalia, back to the region to try to bring an end to the fighting, while presumably US troops continued to hunt for Aideed. Then there followed an extremely tough meeting between Boutros-Ghali and the US ambassador to the UN, Madeleine Albright. The Secretary-General complained that Washington was not entitled to send an envoy unless the Security Council passed a fresh authorising resolution: the United States was trying to muscle in on a UN show.

It now seemed clear that President Clinton was facing little less than humiliation at the hands of the Somali factions.[51] None of the declared policies had come to fruition; and now Washington had been driven to the absurdity of proposing fresh troop reinforcements as a prelude to total withdrawal. The faction leaders needed to do no more than sit tight, and then the war-lord Washington would be out of the picture. Robert Oakley succeeded in negotiating the release of an American soldier held hostage by supporters of General Aideed's Somali National Alliance (SNA). Said the SNA's Issa Mohammed Siad: 'The man that the SNA supporters took was a man who was killing and bombing innocent people and destroying homes. He was fighting against people who haven't hurt his country, his life or his children.' The soldier, Warrant Officer Mike Durrant, was released; the US command in Mogadishu continued to hold more than thirty alleged Aideed supporters, having killed many hundreds.

The United States ran the Somali intervention under UN auspices. For reasons not yet fully explored, Washington judged this a useful enterprise to undertake. The UN Secretary-General Boutros Boutros-Ghali reckoned that he could not afford a confrontation with the United States ('such an important member'),[52] though by now it was increasingly apparent that in Somalia as elsewhere the United States and the United Nations were functionally one and the same thing: 'For UN read US'.[53] Somalia had become 'an albatross, obscuring Mr Boutros-Ghali's goal for his five-year term at the UN: securing for the UN a "central place in the infrastructure" of the post-cold-war period'.[54] The United Nations was now being cast as a 'whipping-boy',[55] a rerun of its frequent role as scapegoat. Where Washington wanted to run affairs in Somalia, as elsewhere, the UN *was* the US; when things went wrong the two entities were suitably and conveniently distinct.

There were now suggestions that the planned US pull-out at the end of March 1994 would result in a total collapse of the UN effort in Somalia: on 26 October the UN Secretary-General Boutros Boutros-Ghali declared that if the member states 'are not ready to do peace enforcement then we have to withdraw'. French, Belgian and German units were already planning a withdrawal, adding to the burdens on the Pakistani and Indian troops. On 18 November the Security Council renewed the UNOSOM II mandate until 31 May 1994, but there was little doubt that the UN involvement in Somalia was rapidly running down. There was no longer any attempt to apprehend Mohamed Farah Aideed (who in any case had only served as a scapegoat), and the ambitious UN efforts at social and political engineering had been largely abandoned. By now it was widely assumed that by 31 March, following the withdrawal of the US, French and Belgian troops, the country would be back in the hands of the so-called war-lords. Some $1.5 billion had been designated to save Somalia: most of this had been spent on a compound for the protection of US and UN personnel in Mogadishu.

The 80-acre armed camp included 'reserved parking, take-out pizza and manicured flower gardens . . . street signs and shuttle buses . . . electric power, a telephone network and sewerage'. A shark net costing $60,000 had been erected to protect the beach, and a general store set up to sell 'whisky, espresso machines and pornographic videos'.[56] Most of the money going to Somalia was being spent on sustaining UNOSOM's 28,968 troops, with one estimate suggesting that less than $100 million would be spent on genuine development assistance. The US-led UN initiative had committed an appalling catalogue of blunders, so defining the framework of *'Operation Disaster born out of a lie'*[57] (the 'lie', used by President George Bush to justify sending in US troops, being that 80 per cent of relief food in Somalia was being stolen by bandits). The United Nations had accomplished a *débâcle*.

After the US withdrawal in March 1994 a 20,000-strong UN contingent, comprising mainly African and Asian forces, remained in Somalia, but with a much reduced mandate. No-one doubted that the US-dominated mission had lost direction, with even President Clinton's special ambassador to Somalia, Robert Oakley, forced to admit: 'There was a period when I think the United States and the United Nations were both off course. Sometimes you do make mistakes.'[58] The US-inspired operation had resulted in the deaths of 40 Americans, dozens of troops from other UN contingents, and around 2000 Somalis. On 31 May 1994 the Security Council approved yet another resolution on Somalia (Resolution 923), reaffirming 'the commitment of the international community to assisting the Somalia people to attain political reconciliation and reconstruction'. But the UN had retreated, there was talk of pulling the entire UN effort back to Mogadishu as factional fighting intensified, and there were fresh charges (not least in the memoir *Somalia: The Missed Opportunities* by the Algerian diplomat Mohamed Sahnoun) of bureaucratic impotence in the United Nations and of Secretary-General Boutros-Ghali's incompetence and arrogance over Somalia.[59]

Through 1994 the UN presence in Somalia seemed increasingly irrelevant to the affairs on the ground. The original grandiose ambitions of the UN planners had evaporated: a measure of humanitarian relief had been afforded, but the grand scheme for 'nation building' had melted away. In particular, the UN/US presence had come to symbolise incompetence and brutality, manifestly confused operational tactics and abuse of human rights.* In September 1994, with the 18,000-strong Asian/African UN contingent already withdrawn from the outlying towns, the United Nations was threatening to withdraw its peacekeeping force. Over a calamitous 2-year period, the UN – despite high costs in blood (most of it Somali) and treasure – had failed to deliver Somalia from chaos. Now the only option seemed to be retreat. Thus Kofi Annan, the UN Under-Secretary-General for Peacekeeping Operations, declared: 'Unless they [the Somalis, 'especially their faction leaders'] show evidence almost immediately of significant movement towards reconciliation and the formation of a broadly-based government, the Security Council will have no alternative but to bring [the UN's] presence in Somalia to an end.'

In November 1994 the United Nations announced that its presence in Somalia would be brought to an end by 31 March 1995, whereupon the undignified endgame began. Who would inherit the remaining UN hardware? What of the lucrative building contracts? What of the financial sweeteners ('logistical expenses') paid to the Mogadishu warlords? The *false economy* created by UNOSOM in Somalia threatened to leave further chaos in its wake. A report by the Swedish Life and Peace Institute condemned aspects of UN mismanagement: 'A potentially criminally negligent policy has been pursued by UNOSOM throughout 1994 of increasing civilian staff . . . despite the fact that UNOSOM has closed most of its zone offices and plays an extremely limited functional role in Somalia. With the real possibility of looting sprees and/or armed attack, the UN has put hundreds of international staff at risk unnecessarily and has made the withdrawal process much more difficult.' In the same vein Oxfam's Nancy Smith commented that the UN involvement had not been 'a helpful operation. . . . It has distracted the Somalis, led to false hopes, enriched very, very few people and failed to reach the poorest in Somali society'

---

*On 16 March 1993 Canadian UN peacekeepers arrested a 16-year-old Somali youth, Shidane Arone, and over a 4-hour period tortured him to death. He was punched, kicked, struck with a baton, burned with a cigar, and smashed in the shins with a metal bar. At least fifteen soldiers looked on, and some 80 heard his screams of agony. The officer, Major Anthony Seward, who had ordered his soldiers to abuse prisoners and who was present at the torture and murder, received only a reprimand. (See *The Observer*, London, 28 November 1994; *The Militant*, New York, 28 November 1994.) This appalling case was one of many.

(*The Guardian*, 10 November 1994). A dismal chapter in the saga of UN mismanagement – and US manipulation of the United Nations – was drawing to a close.

THE SPECIAL AGENDA: FOR CUBA

In January 1959 Fidel Castro finally toppled General Fulgencio Batista, the US-supported dictator of Cuba. From that time to the present day, through the administrations of nine American presidents without exception, Washington has developed a special agenda for Cuba that has involved gross abuses of human rights and many blatant violations of international law including United Nations resolutions.

It is useful to remember Article 2(3 and 4) of the UN Charter: '*All Members shall settle their international disputes by peaceful means in such a manner that international peace and security, and justice, are not endangered. All Members shall refrain in their international relations from the threat or use of force against the territorial integrity or political independence of any state, or in any other manner inconsistent with the Purposes of the United Nations.*'

For the last thirty-four years the United States has run a range of policies on Cuba that are in direct violation of Article 2, and so in direct violation of both the spirit and the letter of the international organisation. Through a variety of programmes – notably Operations Mongoose and AM/LASH – the US has repeatedly attempted, with the aid of Mafia and other factions, to assassinate Fidel Castro*; has orchestrated numerous invasions and terrorist attacks against Cuba; has run an illicit economic blockade against the island, with recent US legislation supported by President Bill Clinton; and has adopted many tactics to pressure other states to follow the American example.

The framework of Operation Mongoose, established in November 1961, involved 400 US personnel, 2000 anti-Castro Cubans, a private navy of fast boats, and an annual budget of $50 million. The scheme operated in

---

*Washington has frequently been implicated in the assassinations of foreign leaders: for example, Patrice Lumumba (Congo), Rafael Trujillo (Dominican Republic), Ngo Dinh Diem (Vietnam) and Salvador Allende (Chile). The 1986 bombing raid on Tripoli was clearly an attempt to kill Muammar Gaddafi, despite nominal US bans on such attempts; and part of the Iraqi reluctance to allow full UN monitoring derives from the suspicion that the intelligence so gathered would be used to facilitate the assassination of Saddam Hussein and other Iraqi leaders.

violation of the Neutrality Act and the American law prohibiting CIA operations on the United States mainland.[60] Through the 1960s and 1970s the US-funded and US-organised operations against Cuba included: the strafing from the sea of a hotel near Havana, killing a score of Russians and Cubans; attacks on Cuban cargo ships; the blowing up of a Cuban factory, killing four hundred Cuban workers; the sinking of Cuban fishing boats; the bombing of a Cubana civilian airliner, killing all seventy-three people aboard, including Cuba's gold medal-winning fencing team; fire-bomb air raids on Cuban cane fields and sugar mills, with American pilots dying in crashes or captured; the bombing of a French freighter in Havana harbour, killing seventy-five people and injuring two hundred; the bombing of oil refineries and chemical plants; the destruction of bridges and other infrastructure assets; the bombing of Soviet ships docked in Cuba; the offshore shelling of a theatre, and so on.[61] In addition, goods destined for Cuba have been sabotaged: machinery deliberately damaged, corrosive chemicals added to lubricating fluids, Western manufacturers bribed by the CIA to produce faulty goods intended for Cuba (West German manufacturers paid to produce ball-bearings off-centre and unbalanced wheel gears), a cargo ship carrying buses to Cuba sabotaged in the London Thames.[62] Similarly, Cuban products were deliberately sabotaged: chemicals were added to Cuban sugar exports (a CIA official: 'There was lots of sugar being sent out from Cuba, and we were putting a lot of contaminants in it'), Cuban turkeys deliberately infected with the fatal Newcastle disease (8000 died), pigs deliberately infected with African swine fever virus (500,000 slaughtered to prevent a nationwide epidemic), and so on.[63]

In recent years, despite mounting international opposition, Washington has moved to tighten the noose around Cuba. The trade embargo has been intensified; in particular, via the notorious Torricelli Act – introduced by Bush and now supported by Clinton – designed to pressure other countries into accepting a virtually total ban on trade with Cuba. However, in the post-Cold War United Nations there are some indications that the international community is no longer prepared to tolerate American policy in this matter. On 24 November 1992 the UN General Assembly passed Resolution 47/19 (Appendix 7) by 59 votes to 3 (US, Israel and Romania) with many abstentions, calling for an end to the 'economic, commercial and financial embargo imposed by the USA against Cuba'. The supporters of Cuba included France, Canada and Mexico. Britain and most of the European Community countries abstained; but on 16 September 1993 the European parliament passed a resolution calling on the Commission to condemn the US blockade of Cuba. It also called on the United States government to repeal the Torricelli Act, calling this piece of legislation an 'anachronism' and 'contrary to international law'. According to a paper submitted by the Cuban foreign minister Roberto Robaina to the UN Secretary-General on 25 June 1993, the United States policy of interference with Cuban trade has cost the country an estimated $40 billion. This factor should be considered in any discussion about the success or failure of the Cuban economy.

The historic UN resolution 47/19 was buttressed a year later by the passing in the General Assembly of Resolution 48/16 (11 November 1993), drafted to condemn yet again the American economic blockade of Cuba. It is highly significant that this new resolution (see Appendix 7) was passed with an enlarged majority: 88 to 4 (Albania, Israel, Paraguay and the United States) with 57 abstentions. The tide was running against Washington: now the United States stood condemned by two unambiguous resolutions passed with massive majorities in the UN General Assembly.

The passing of GA 47/19 and GA 48/16 – and later the passing of GA 49/24 (see below) – calling on 'all member states', is an important indication of the unacceptability of current US policy on Cuba. It is significant that the UN opposition to American policy in this regard is rooted in a long UN tradition of support for national sovereignty and the right of all states to economic and cultural development. Article 2(7) emphasises that there should be no interference 'in matters which are essentially within the domestic jurisdiction of any state'; and subsequent UN declarations have served to reinforce this principle. Thus on 21 December 1965 the UN General Assembly adopted the Declaration on the Inadmissibility of Intervention in the Domestic Affairs of States and the Protection of their Independence and Sovereignty', an important milestone intended to support the rights of peoples to self-determination. This followed the adoption in 1960 of the Declaration on the Granting of Independence to Colonial Countries and Peoples, against the opposition of the Western colonial powers. The rights of peoples to self-determination carried with it the right to pursue, without interference, economic and cultural development. Such concepts have been further reinforced by the 1970 Declaration on Principles of International Law; and by various other resolutions adopted by the General Assembly. It is significant that US policy on Cuba violates not only the crucial Resolution 47/19 (24 November 1992), but also the General Assembly Resolutions 38/197, 39/210, 40/185, 42/173, 44/215 and 46/210 – all of which condemn the taking of coercive action against the legitimate sovereign decisions of developing countries. Moreover, US legislation aimed at achieving the total economic strangulation of Cuba has adversely affected other Third World countries and significantly damaged the patterns of international trade. Again the Torricelli Act stands condemned for threatening sanctions on states that trade with Cuba.

The continuing US violation of Resolution 47/19 is shown by continuing legislative enactments through 1993. It was clear, soon after the vote on 47/19, that the United States was considering various measures to enforce the blockade against Cuba. For example, the eligibility of foreign governments to receive American economic aid now depends upon the trading relations of those governments with Cuba, as shown by the Foreign Aid Bill provisions adopted on 16 June 1993 by the House of Representatives. Similarly, a law passed in the state of Florida on 20 May 1993 imposes legal and economic reprisals on any company which trades with Cuba and is located or has interests in the state of Florida, whether the companies be private or state-run concerns. Such legislation suggests that the United States, both at the federal and the local level, is indifferent in this regard both to the spirit of the United Nations and to the associated principles of international law.

It is important to note also that, as with the hundreds of anti-Cuban terrorist attacks in the 1960s and 1970s, the United States does not rely solely on legislative mechanisms to attack the Cuban economy. Washington has adopted many measures in its long-running determination to crush the Castro regime:

The US has intimidated Latin American countries into terminating treaty negotiations with Cuba for the exchange of sugar, nickel and other products for petroleum;

A state in the European Community has been told by Washington that its interests within GATT will be adversely affected if it does not withdraw its credit to Cuba;

The US has warned various countries that if they traded with Cuba their access to World Bank and IMF loans might be impeded;

The US has informed the Total company of France that areas offered by Cuba for prospecting in fact belong to owners registered before the 1959 revolution;

The US has used the Petroconsult group at the University of Houston, Texas, to spread disinformation about the prospects of finding oil in Cuba;

The British sugar company Tate and Lyle has been pressured by the US to cut its economic ties with Cuba after company representatives attended a meeting in Cuba in May 1992;

The British Cable and Wireless company has been informed that any investment in Cuba would mean that its application for a licence to operate in Europe and Asia, using the United States as an intermediate territory, would be rejected;

US pressure on the Maria Isabel Sheraton Hotel in Mexico City caused the cancellation of a contract signed with Cuba;

US pressure on the Mexican Monterrey Group prevented the creation of a joint venture with Cuba in the textile industry;

The US has blocked the sale to Cuba of respiratory valves, connections, micro vaporiser flasks and other spare parts for the Bird respiratory machine, the most common device of its kind used in Cuba in hospital asthmatic units, intensive-care units, etc;

The US has told the Canadian company Eli Lilly Canada Inc. that because of the Torricelli Act the company is now banned from selling medicines to Cuba;

The Torricelli Act has forced the Argentine's two major grain producers, Cargill SACI and the Continental SACINF Company, to discontinue their grain exports to Cuba. Continental Grain, SACINF's main office in the US, has received visits from US officials threatening reprisals if trade with Cuba was allowed to continue.

Such examples (the list could be extended) illustrate some of the tactics being used by Washington – in the teeth of mounting international opposition – in its obsessive wish to strangle any efforts by the Cuban people to develop their trade or social provisions. The estimated losses ($40 billion) are roughly equivalent to twenty times Cuba's annual account earnings, a devastating shortfall that has had an inevitable cumulative effect on the Cuban people for more than three decades.

Today there is growing suffering throughout Cuba: a nation is being gradually starved to death. The average Cuban has lost between 15lb and 20lb since the start of the so-called 'Special Period' in 1990, with rationing more severe than it was in Britain during the Second World War.[64] There is enough milk for the sick and for children under six, but for no-one else; there is scarcely any meat, cheese, butter or eggs. In mid-1993 a mysterious illness, thought to be linked to malnutrition, spread through the country, bringing fatigue and total or partial blindness to some 50,000 Cubans. The Cuban medical system swung into action, with 18,000 Cuban physicians dispensing advice and vitamin B complex pills to

Cuba's entire population of 11 million people. Dr Bjorn Thylefors, a blindness specialist working for the World Health Organisation (WHO) praised the Cuban effort: 'Cuba has invested more in health services than almost any other country, and it has a higher health profile than the US. Cuba treats its children very well. The same goes for the old.'[65]

At the end of 1993, encouraged by the General Assembly vote on Resolution 48/16, the Cuban government called for a lifting of the illegal US blockade, repeal of the punitive Torricelli Act (itself a violation of international law), the dismantling of the US Guantanamo naval base on Cuba (illegally occupied against the will of the Cuban people), a stop to constant military threats against Cuba (in violation of Article 2(4) of the UN Charter), and the establishment of diplomatic relations with Cuba on the basis of sovereign equality (in accord with Article 2(1) of the UN Charter). Washington made no move to respond to the new General Assembly vote, to observe its obligations under international law, or to observe the letter and spirit of the UN Charter.

It was now clear that the United States, intent to maintain illegal policies in the teeth of majority UN opposition, was almost totally isolated on the Cuba question. Even *The New York Times* (8 November 1993), noting the Republican and Democratic support for the Torricelli Act, observed that the legislation had managed to isolate the United States and that it was hard to remember a similar humiliation for US diplomacy. Further, declared the *Times* editorial, many countries were firmly opposed to the extraterritorial demands of the the Torricelli Act; with Britain and some other states considering it a crime for anyone to observe these demands. Again such comments seemed to have no effect on the US posture.

Throughout 1993 many efforts were made by US Congress members to tighten the noose on the Cuban economy. The US government was urged to propose to the Security Council the creation of an international mandatory embargo on Cuba, to limit trade with Russia if that state maintained trade with Cuba, to deny federal aid to countries judged to be friendly with Cuba, and to reinforce the prohibitions on US citizens being allowed to travel to Cuba. One sponsored bill urged the supply of military aircraft to terrorist groups working to destabilise the Cuba regime, while proposals were made for funds to support a pro-US Cuban 'government in exile'. An article in *Time* magazine (20 October 1992) revealed that anti-Castro Cuban-American National Foundation (CANF) had spent more than a million dollars in recent years to buy influence in Congress. Some $26,750 had gone to Robert Torricelli himself, with some $57,000 being donated to the George Bush election campaign.

All the signs were that the Cuban people would continue to suffer under the punitive policies of a hegemonic United States, unlikely to change its posture even when its illegal anti-Cuban measures could be seen to be damaging the trade of its allies to the tune of millions of dollars (see *The Observer*, 14 November 1993). Through 1994 Washington continued to tighten its noose on the Cuban economy – until, in August, there was a massive increase in the number of Cuban refugees struggling to leave the island. The Clinton administration moved quickly to declare that there would be no repeat of the 1980 boatlift, when 125,000 Cubans were taken from the Cuban port of Mariel to Key West, Florida. Said a State Department spokesman: 'The United States will not permit Fidel Castro to dictate our immigration policy. We urge the Cuban government to carefully consider all the implications of such incitement [Castro's threat to lift restrictions on those wanting to leave].'

Washington responded in characteristic fashion. Clinton administration officials emphasised that the economic embargo would be maintained and that there was no point in talking to Castro on any substantive issues, though lower-grade official talks would be undertaken to seek a solution to the immigration problem. Now, in a departure from the decades-long policy, Washington was refusing to allow Cuban refugees to enter the United States: refugees picked up off the sea in their thousands were taken to Guatanamo naval base and there incarcerated incommunicado in concentration camps surrounded by razor wire. At the same time Clinton moved to tighten the economic strangulation of Cuba yet further, imposing fresh limits on US charter flights to Cuba and prohibiting Cubans in America from sending gift packages to their relatives on the island.

The US policy was plain: *everything possible would be done to plunge the ordinary Cuban people yet deeper into destitution while at the same time they would be discouraged, on pain of indefinite incarceration, from any attempt to flee from their privations.* There was even the hint that a *total* blockade of Cuba was being considered. Thus Peter Tarnoff, the State Department's co-ordinator for Cuba policy, said on NBC television's Meet the Press programme: 'I cannot be categorical that a blockade is not an option under consideration.'[66] Even without such a draconian act of war the effects of the American policy were clear. Already large numbers of Cuban lives were being lost,[67] and there were fresh punishments in store: it was reported that Clinton intended to stop not only cash transfers but other forms of aid, including private deliveries of medicine by Cuban exiles to their relatives on the island.[68] Thus Lisandro Perez, associate professor and director of the Cuban Research Institute at Florida International University in Miami, summed up the policy of the Clinton administration:

'The get-tough policy is based on raising the level of suffering and exasperation of ordinary Cubans.[69] The effective message from President Clinton to the Cuban people was unambiguous: *We are prepared, in the name of traditional Cold-War hatred, to offer you nothing but poverty, malnutrition and starvation.*

On 26 October 1994 the UN General Assembly yet again made it clear what it thought of US policy on Cuba. A new resolution, GA 49/24, was passed with a majority exceeding even the large majorities of resolution 47/19 and 48/16: in a vote of 101 to 2 (the United States and Israel), the General Assembly yet again voted to condemn the American blockade of Cuba. It is worth pointing out that this new resolution (see Appendix 7) draws attention to the Ibero-American Summits (July 1993 and June 1994) and to the Twentieth Council of the Latin American Economic System (June 1994), all of which condemned the US policy on Cuba. Now, via GA 49/24, a large majority in the General Assembly (apart from a self-serving Israel) was combining to deplore the squalid posture of the United States.

The broadly-based UN position (the US excepted) on the Cuba Question is today unambiguous: resolutions and declarations, the public speeches in the General Assembly, the active support given to Cuba by such UN-linked bodies as WHO, WFP and UNICEF – all testify to Washington's international isolation, to the cruel enormity of a superpower striving to pressure a small national economy into terminal collapse. But the US special agenda for Cuba, involving illegality and the gross abuse of human rights, runs deep and even today in early 1995 seems unshaken by international criticism. The case of Cuba is one of the most signally graphic indications of United Nations impotence.

THE LOW PRIORITY: BURUNDI AND RWANDA

Burundi and Rwanda have a common ethnic structure and colonial history. At the beginning of the twentieth century both countries, as Ruanda-Urundi, were part of German East Africa, one of the consequences (via the 1894 Treaty of Berlin) of the European carve-up of Africa. Before the European colonisation the élite Tutsi and the peasant Hutu in Ruanda-Urundi lived in a starkly stratified but relatively peaceful society. After the First World War the League of Nations assigned control of the region to the Belgians, who then exacerbated the tensions already fuelled by the Germans: while the Hutu were ignored, the Tutsi were given a Western-style education. At the same time identity cards were introduced to signal a person's ethnic group. Such blatant discrimination provoked Hutu unrest, which in turn led to the slaughter of thousands of Tutsis in 1959 and the Belgian decision to leave the country. In 1962 Burundi and Rwanda became two separate states. Now the scene was set for further turmoil – and for further gross manifestations of UN indifference, vacillation and incompetence.

In Rwanda the majority Hutu managed to instal Gregoire Kayibanda as the country's first president; while, despite Hutu rebellions in 1965 and 1972, the Tutsi minority retained power in Burundi. In 1973, amid more anti-Tutsi violence in Rwanda, Juvenal Habyarimana seized power, only to face a mounting economic crisis when the price of coffee collapsed. The exiled Tutsi in Uganda formed the Rwandan Patriotic Front (RPF), which invaded Rwanda in 1990 to fuel the mounting civil war; a fragile ceasefire was signed three years later. In June 1993 democratic elections in Burundi produced that country's first Hutu leader, Melchior Ndadaye. He was killed three months later in a failed Tutsi coup that led to the slaughter of more than 100,000 people. On 6 April 1994 Cyprien Ntaryamira, Ndadaye's replacement, and President Habyarimana were both killed when their plane was shot down by rocket fire. Now the region again collapsed into turmoil.

At this time there were 2500 UN peacekeeping troops in Rwanda, their presence recently extended for four months by the Security Council, but they seemed increasingly impotent in the face of the mounting violence. On 7 April the Rwandan capital Kigali collapsed into chaos. Gangs of soldiers and civilians swept through the town, killing the Rwandan prime minister, UN soldiers and scores of civilians. A Western diplomat commented: 'It is becoming messier and messier. There are a lot of people with a lot of guns taking different orders and shooting and detaining people. A casualty toll is impossible.' Another observer noted the 'general score settling going on in Kigali'. Belgian UN peacekeepers had been killed, the toll of Hutu and Tutsi dead was mounting, and the international community was well aware of what was happening; yet there was no practical response from the UN Security Council. The Belgian government demanded additional powers for the small UN observer force already present in Burundi and Rwanda, but still there was no call for direct UN intervention. The Belgian government itself began talks with France, the United States and the United Nations with a view to assembling an international force that might be used to evacuate foreigners; Belgian paratroops were put on standby, and the Belgian national airline Sabena flew a Boeing 727 jet to Nairobi for possible use in an evacuation operation. By now it was clear that the UN personnel in the region were 'no more than spectators to the savagery which aid workers say has seen the massacre of 15,000 people – mainly from the traditionally dominant Tutsi minority'.[70] Soon even the UN's observer role began to collapse.

On 14 April the UN military chief, Brigadier-General Romeo Dallaire, commented that he hoped UN troops would stay in Rwanda to oversee an eventual ceasefire, despite the mounting violence. 'What we would like to do,' said Dallaire, 'is expand our capabilities' to protect the thousands of civilians in fear of the rampaging death squads. In fact it was not long before the UN forces were depleted rather than enlarged. On 20 April more than 250 terrified Bangladeshi UN peacekeepers in Kigali scrambled onto evacuation planes as the UN mission neared collapse.[71] It was of course time for the Security Council to agree a statement: Resolution 912 (21 April 1994), after expressing the Council's shock and deep concern, variously 'takes note', 'expresses regret', 'demands', 'condemns', 'reiterates', 'commends', 'calls upon', 'invites', etc. Thousands were being killed, anarchy prevailed in substantial parts of the region, and everyone could see that fresh horrors lay in store. So the UN Security Council resolutely deplored the mounting carnage, and, in the customary jargon of UN resolutions, decided 'to remain actively seized of the matter'.

A two-day airlift began on 22 April to evacuate most of the UN peace-keeping force: fewer than 300 troops would remain to mediate between the RPF and the government forces battling for control of Kigali. Now it was estimated that around 100,000 people had been killed in two weeks of slaughter, and relief agencies were declaring that the UN pull-out would occasion yet more deaths. With death squads advancing on many Tutsi concentrations, it was reported that as the UN troops were flying out the fighting in Kigali became intensified. David Bryer, the director of Oxfam, speaking of the UN withdrawal, commented: 'We are outraged at this short-sighted callous decision.' There was no greater slaughter occurring anywhere in the world, yet the UN had cut and run. Said Salim Ahmed Salim, Secretary-General of the Organisation of African Unity (OAU): 'The UN decision on Rwanda is a sign of lack of sufficient concern for an African tragic situation.'[72] By end of April some 230,000 people, many mutilated by machetes, were fleeing to escape the slaughter. A UNHCR statement detailed reports indicating that up to 50 Tutsis a night were being taken from a group of 5000, imprisoned in a sports stadium, to be murdered. UN Secretary-General Boutros-Ghali urged the Security Council to consider the use of force to stop the carnage, but to no avail. Now a human tide of refugees was flooding out of Rwanda.[73]

The Clinton administration had ruled out the direct use of US forces (just as US ground troops had been ruled out for Bosnia), at the same time floating the idea that African states might like to intervene. The aid agencies continued to express their disgust at the seeming indifference of the United Nations (as signalled by the procrastination of the major powers) to the genocidal situation that had developed in a country in which the UN had maintained a clear (but rapidly diminishing) presence. Thus Edward Cairns, a policy adviser to Oxfam, commented: 'This is the worst example so far of the Security Council acting completely inconsistently in different crises.' The small beleaguered force of UN peacekeepers was desperately appealing for reinforcements, but to no evident effect. In mid-May the US, supported by Russia, defeated a Boutros-Ghali proposal to send 5500 troops to Rwanda – yet another 'severe rebuff' to the UN Secretary-General.[74] Yet again the United Nations was dithering about what to do. The enabling Security Council resolution (918, 17 May 1994) had authorised the enlargement of the UN Assistance Mission for Rwanda (UNAMR) but now there seemed no practical way in which this could be achieved. The US had supported Resolution 918, but was now opposing the despatch of the 5500 UN troops that 918 specified.[75]

UN Secretary-General Boutros-Ghali appeared at a press conference on 25 May 1994 to declare that the United Nations had failed Rwanda: 'I failed. It is a scandal. I am the first one to say it and I am ready to repeat it. It is a failure not only for the United Nations but for the international community and all of us are responsible. It is genocide which has been committed in Rwanda and more than 200,000 people have been killed [but] the international community is still discussing which ought to be done.'

The Security Council passed fresh resolutions, all of which duly recorded the Council's decision 'to remain actively seized of the matter'. In June, with the approval of the Council, French troops moved into Rwanda with the intention of stopping what premier Edouard Balladur called 'one of the most unbearable tragedies in recent history'. The new initiative, because of France's historical involvement in Africa, was controversial: the French intervention could not be seen as neutral – its principal aim was to defend the Tutsi – and could too easily be depicted as a reversion to a colonialist posture. In the event the French forces, facing a deteriorating situation in which little relief would be offered by the UN, was destined not to stay long.

Now, via the mechanism of Resolution 935 (1 July 1994), the United Nations was embarked upon a different policy: an effort would be made to apprehend, try and convict the perpetrators of 'humanitarian law violations' (war criminals) in Rwanda. Here too, while the overall crisis deepened, the UN ran into problems. On 10 September Karen Kenny, the Irish human-rights lawyer heading the UN investigating team, resigned amid accusations that the UN's genocide investigation was being handled with 'shameful incompetence'. The promise made by José Ayalo-Lasso, the UN High Commissioner for Human Rights, for 22 human-rights monitors to be sent to Rwanda by the end of August had not been honoured; plans for the extra monitors to be sent in September remained vague; and Kenny's team had not even been provided with vehicles to facilitate investigation of particular allegations of genocide – for a week Kenny and her team had struggled to hire cars when the UN military mission in Rwanda refused her request for transport! Moreover, France and the US were now engaged in a farcical battle for influence over the new Rwandan government.[76] It was now increasingly clear that even the new UN initiative, the relatively modest proposal that the perpetrators of genocide be brought to justice, was doomed because of lack of resources, incompetence, and the indifference of powerful states.

The tragedy of Burundi and Rwanda had signalled yet again the impotence of the UN when mere matters of human suffering, rather than the perceived strategic interests of hegemonic powers, were the issue. *The protracted human disaster was rooted in the narrow discriminatory policies of European colonialism and shaped in large part by the forced implementation of the structural adjustment programmes within the IMF/World Bank/GATT ethos.* Such shaping factors have been given little attention in the Western media. We need to remember that evident UN vacillations, incompetence and indifference are occasioned *in toto* by the postures of powerful states interested above all in seizing the free-market main chance.

WHY HAITI?

The United States has always been interested in Haiti and the other regions of the Caribbean. To signal this interest Washington has organised various invasions of Haiti over the last hundred years, not least by troops nominally answerable to President Woodrow Wilson, the revered propagandist for non-intervention. At this time the effective ruler of Haiti was Colonel L. W. T. Waller of the US Marines, charged with the task of blocking constitutional reform, suppressing nationalist movements and keeping the small country safe for American capitalist investment. Between 1867 and 1900 there were eight American invasions of the supposedly independent Haitian republic, the last leading to a US occupation that lasted nineteen years. In later years a procession of US puppets was sustained, with or without the immediate presence of American marines. We need not be surprised that in the post-Soviet world of the 1990s American policy on Haiti was merely continuing a long and much practised policy of intervention. A question mark, albeit a small one, remains. Why, in recent years, has Washington bothered to involve the United Nations in Haitian matters? If Woodrow Wilson, idealistic architect of the League of Nations, could send in the troops why should Bush, Clinton and others not act with equal despatch?

On 30 October 1990 supposedly democratic elections brought Jean-Bertrand Aristide to power, a Catholic priest, aged 40, who had won 67 per cent of the popular vote. He lasted for less than a year: in September 1991 Father Aristide was deposed in a military coup, whereupon General Raoul Cedras assumed power. On 27 June 1993 the United Nations began talks with the aim of restoring democracy to the beleaguered country. Few people were predicting an outcome but a UN spokesman declared that the attitude was 'very positive' on both sides.

The crisis had begun to escalate as desperate refugees in small boats struggled to reach the American mainland. On one occasion, on 30 May 1992, a US Coast Guard vessel stopped a refugee boat, took aboard the Haitians, and then destroyed their vessel. Said one Haitian: 'The boat belonged to all of us, but at no time did the coastguards offer us compensation for it.' At this time the UN High Commissioner for Refugees was trying to persuade Washington to alter its policy, arguing that the US Coast Guards were acting illegally by infringing Article 33(1) of the 1967 UN Protocol on the Status of Refugees, signed by the US in 1968. It is useful to remember that Lawrence Eagleburger, the last secretary of state under George Bush, declared of Vietnamese refugees in 1989 that the American government would not consider forced repatriation as being 'acceptable under international law'. Legal experts in the United States have commented that it is manifestly illegal to arrest people in international waters and to destroy their boats. During the presidential election Bill Clinton repeatedly condemned the Bush policy of forcing Haitians attempting to reach America to return home.[77] By May 1993 the Clinton administration, presumably to prevent further refugee problems, was suggesting that a UN 'police force' might be sent to Haiti, nominally to maintain order and to train Haiti's army-controlled police while Aristide's return was organised. It was predicted that Brazil and other Security

Council members would oppose the idea of US-orchestrated UN intervention.

In early October it was announced that President Clinton would be sending 700 American troops under the UN flag to ensure a peaceful transition to civilian rule, to enforce a deal that had seemingly been negotiated between UN officials and representatives of the military regime. It was also reported that some 500 French and Canadian police would be sent to Haiti as part of the UN force. The situation still remained unclear: observers suggested that the army and the police, supported by death squads, would remain in effective power whatever the new constitutional arrangements.[78] Was Haiti set for another period of foreign occupation in the name of protecting American nationals and securing the peace?

The agreement on the return of Aristide was by now looking increasingly fragile. In the Haitian capital, Port-au-Prince, the Haitian police had forced the withdrawal of the USS *Harlan County*, an American naval vessel carrying a batch of 170 US troops as part of the planned UN force. President Clinton declared that he would not endanger the lives of US soldiers, and that instead economic sanctions, including an oil embargo, would be imposed on Haiti. Now no-one imagined that General Cedras would step down, as agreed, on 15 October to be replaced on 30 October by Father Aristide. The only course, apart from a massive military intervention, was a reimposition of the sanctions authorised only a short time before under Security Council Resolution 841. Now President Clinton, already facing humiliation over Somalia, was faced with the collapse of his policy on Haiti.

On 15 October President Clinton sent six naval destroyers to Haitian waters to enforce the economic blockade. He deplored the refusal of the Haitian military to abide by what was now known as the Governor's Island agreement, but at the same time seemed at a loss as to a further course of action. The visas of Haitian military officers were revoked and Haitian assets in the United States were frozen. The regime was now isolated but it was not clear what would happen next. One Western diplomat commented: 'There is nobody left to stop the country disintegrating. Thugs prevented the greatest superpower in the world from coming ashore and they are chasing the UN out. Nobody is in charge except hoodlums run by the military.' Already congressional dissent was mounting in the United States, with observations that to send US troops into Haiti would only lead to a second Somalia. Clinton himself contributed to the debate by announcing: 'I want the Haitians to know that I am dead serious about seeing them honour the agreement they made'; while in Haiti the head of the UN human rights mission, Colin

Granderson, said that he feared for the safety of the nearly 300 human rights workers in the country. It was reported from Port-au-Prince that schools and businesses were shut, and that Aristide supporters were being killed in the streets. Clinton was rumoured to be contemplating a full military invasion, with Madeleine Albright, the US ambassador at the UN, announcing the familiar lines: 'We don't rule out anything at all.'

On 17 October, having openly disavowed the Governor's Island agreement, General Cedras declared that the Haitian people had no wish to be confronted 'by American might. We have no intention to defy the United States . . . Our country is no threat to peace. It is not at war.' Most UN personnel had now been evacuated and the embargo was being reinforced by ships from Britain, the Netherlands, Canada, France and Argentina; US navy aircraft were tracking suspect cargo ships in the area, and before long a number of vessels had been stopped for inspection. By now the embargo was biting hard and there was growing speculation about the course of events as the date approached for Aristide's return. At the same time a critical CIA assessment of the deposed president's character had been circulating on Capitol Hill in Washington. The document stated that Aristide had suffered from various psychological problems, and that he had been implicated in gang violence and politically motivated murder. White House officials dismissed the report as flimsy and out-of-date, one administration source saying that although the intelligence community regarded Aristide as a 'weird, flaky guy' there was no reason to believe him 'impeded in his ability to serve as president'. It also emerged that the CIA had been making regular payments to senior members of the military junta to gain information on political developments and cocaine smuggling (*The Independent*, 2 November 1993).

The embargo – part of 'Operation Restore Democracy' – remained securely in place; though it was reported that many supplies were pouring in from the neighbouring Dominican Republic, and at least one blockade vessel, the British frigate HMS *Active*, had apparently sailed off for routine operations elsewhere. It was conceded that the deposed President Aristide would not be allowed to return 'on time' and that the blockade would have to be maintained for the foreseeable future. On 27 October 1993 a US Coast Guard cutter docked briefly at Port-au-Prince to unload a fresh batch of refugees picked up from a makeshift boat twenty miles off the north-west tip of Haiti.

By December 1993 it seemed clear that President Clinton was backing away 'from commitment to Aristide'. Washington's unwillingness to invade Haiti – with or without a nominal UN sanction – meant that the military junta was winning the battle of wills with the US administration.

Larry Birns, director of the Council on Hemispheric Affairs, an independent Washington think-tank, commented: 'Right now, Clinton's policy on Haiti is moving backwards. In reality, they're not doing anything at all. Haiti has moved off the back-burner and into the pantry'; and an official from the US State Department admitted that 'everyone is just thrashing around . . . the [Haitian] military has us boxed into a corner. . .' (*The Guardian*, 2 December 1993). However, the sanctions continued to exact their grim toll: as with Iraq, the suffering of the ordinary people increased while the military leadership remained unaffected.

A Harvard University study asserted that the UN-sponsored sanctions designed to help restore democracy to Haiti were killing 1000 children a month: a desperately poor population was being plunged into severe hardship, particularly in the rural areas. Food shortages were causing disease, malnutrition and dramatically increased mortality rates in the young and the old: so stimulating the exodus of boat refugees heading for Florida. A succession of boycotts had done little to undermine the rich and their military allies; in fact many prospered in the growing black market. What was clear was that by 1994 the Haitian poor were being plunged into abject destitution. A worker for Care, a US aid organisation, noted: 'We know that people are already dying . . . because people can't get from their villages to the [feeding] centres and we can't spare what little gas we have to get to them [because of the UN oil blockade], we don't know the full extent' (*The Guardian*, 21 December 1993). The manager of a foreign-owned rice processing company predicted starvation 'in another month'; while the director of Catholic Relief noted that the people, selling everything in order to survive, would soon have nothing ('It is a disaster').

Washington had judged that it had an interest in restoring the 'democratically elected' Father Aristide, despite suggestions that he was mentally unstable and had advocated lynching his opponents: President Clinton, beset by foreign policy confusion and failures, had desperately needed a success near to home. It was, he decided, essential to prevent a fresh wave of Haitian boat people, with the embarrassing violations of international law that further interceptions would involve. The UN had served a useful purpose in achieving the Governor's Island agreement, and Security Council Resolution 841 had legitimised the imposition of a comprehensive trade embargo on Haiti. Few observers bothered to notice Article 2(7) of the UN Charter, forbidding intervention in a state's domestic affairs; or to wonder why Washington failed to denounce equally serious abrogations of democracy in Saudi Arabia, Burma or Indonesia. If the pious Woodrow Wilson could happily deploy American power in the region to protect US interests then perhaps President Bill Clinton could do no less. But Washington's policy in Haiti, like much of American foreign policy, appeared to be in disarray. By 1994 it seemed that the US administration had little enthusiasm for Aristide: he was no longer the 'US choice for Haiti' (*The Guardian*, 17 December 1993), and Washington was 'losing patience with' the exile (*The Independent*, 23 December 1993). It is useful in these circumstances to remember that Aristide was *not* the American choice in the 1990 election.

The favoured US choice was Marc Bazin, a one-time senior World Bank official and finance minister under the Duvalier dictatorship. Washington was disappointed when its preferred candidate received only 12.6 per cent of the Haitian vote, with Father Aristide winning some 70 per cent. The US administration was also alarmed at the fact that Aristide headed the Lavalas ('Avalanche') people's movement committed to human rights and social reforms. When we consider the emergence of such an unwelcome victor in the context of the CIA's continuing links with the Haitian military, it is not hard to see why the coup by General Cedras happened when it did. The popular Aristide had been deposed and now Washington had the excuse to use force to instal a puppet administration directly run from Washington under UN auspices. If Aristide were to be returned to Haiti, he would be usefully emasculated in the process. It was now possible to discern the self-serving logic in the US manoeuvres.

The enduring tensions between Aristide and the Clinton administration were equally obvious. Senior US officials were reportedly doubtful of Aristide's 'political utility';[79] and Aristide himself was refusing to name a new Haitian prime minister able to serve as a pliant US puppet in talks with Cedras. Moreover, Aristide moved also to repudiate the American policy of returning Haitian refugees to Haiti, declaring that the 1981 US–Haitian agreement that gave a slender legal justification for this policy must end within six months.[80] The Clinton administration responded by tightening economic sanctions on Haiti (via SC Resolution 917, 6 May 1994); and by threatening to use force to resolve the crisis. With Aristide refusing to urge his countrymen to stay put ('Haiti looks like a house on fire. I cannot ask people to stay'), the pressure continued to build in Washington for a military invasion.[81] Already, before the predictable enabling resolution from the Security Council, the USS *Mount Whitney*, a hi-tech floating command post similar to the vessel despatched to Panama prior to the 1989 US invasion, had been stationed in Haitian waters.

On 31 July 1994 the Security Council approved, by 12 votes in favour and two abstentions (Brazil and China), Resolution 940 (Appendix 8) authorising a multinational force to use 'all necessary means' to remove the Haitian military leadership; and stipulating that an administrative United Nations Mission in Haiti (UNMIH) would then replace the multi-national force. The military invasion would be controlled by the US (one estimate suggested that the 10,266-strong invasion force would include 10,000 Americans), and UNMIH would be staffed by US officials. At the same time Washington seemed in no hurry to launch the UN-authorised invasion. Clinton administration officials warned that an invasion was imminent, while efforts were made to recruit an 'international' force: Britain despatched a Royal Navy frigate to join the US-led invasion force in training in Puerto Rico, while the total of 266 soldiers pledged by Jamaica, Barbados, Belize and Trinidad and Tobago were deemed to have immense symbolic importance. The US Defence Secretary William Perry cancelled a visit to Russia scheduled for 5 September in order to oversee the preparations for the invasion.[82]

Economic sanctions had done nothing to topple the Cedras regime. What they had done, in time-honoured fashion, was to destroy the economy of a pitifully poor Third World state, bringing fresh suffering to an already immensely deprived people (causing, as in Iraq, a mortality explosion among the vulnerable young* and old). All this was insufficient for Washington's purposes: it remained necessary to impose a US solution to the crisis, with Clinton no doubt calculating (in the teeth of some Congressional dissent) that the usual mid-term war would bring him some benefit in the polls. The predictable UN authorisation had been served up (using the same catch-all wording that had helped in the Gulf): without demur the Security Council had delivered on cue. Now the United States was free to invade Haiti whenever it wished (no deadline for a Cedras step-down had been given), and to run the peace in whatever manner it chose. As with Korea, Iraq and Libya, the Security Council had offered the legal authorisation. Then, true to form, the Council had obediently vacated the scene: the superpower invasion of a tiny crippled state would be controlled by the Pentagon's military planners, and by them alone.

The subsequent peaceful US invasion of Haiti, following the Cedras-Carter talks, was advertised as a great success for American foreign policy. Little attention was given to particular important aspects of the affair: not least that the original coup that toppled Aristide had proceeded

---

*It was the Haitian children who were suffering the most under the impact of the US-imposed economic sanctions. By mid-1994 several thousand infants were in effect starving to death every month, with the child malnutrition rate continuing to soar through the year. Infant mortality was around 11 per cent, with kwashiorkor and other nutritional deficiency diseases increasingly widespread (*The Guardian*, 4 July 1994).

with the knowledge, if not the connivance, of the CIA (*Time*, 17 October 1994); and that Aristide, now sustained by the US military, would have no choice but to accede to IMF/World Bank plans for the exploitation of Haiti. It was also significant that Washington, having gained UN authorisation for the invasion, totally ignored the United Nations thereafter. This led to the resignation of Dante Caputo, the UN special envoy to Haiti, who declared in a terse letter to Boutros-Ghali: 'The total absence of consultations, and even information, from the government of the United States of America, makes me believe that this country, in fact, has taken the decision to act unilaterally in the Haitian process.' Yet again an impotent United Nations had been pressured into providing Washington with a flag of convenience for its strategic policies.

THE UNCERTAINTIES OF POWER

Soon after the victorious World War Two 'United Nations' had been transmuted into the United Nations Organisation (UNO), Washington moved to suborn the new international body in the interests of US foreign policy. This was most graphically illustrated in the case of the Korean War (see 'The Korean Paradigm', Chapter 2). Here the United States was quick to see how the United Nations could be used to further American strategic objectives, at that time – and for the next forty years – focused on the containment and rollback of Communism. Already it was clear that Washington perceived the UN Charter as little more than a set of useful guidelines – to be picked over and ignored at will – rather than as a legally binding document of international law. This was well shown by Washington's 'Uniting for Peace' scheme, whereby a force drawn from the General Assembly could be brought into areas of conflict hitherto the nominal province of the Security Council, so avoiding the embarrassing prospect of a Soviet veto.

The Uniting for Peace scheme was portrayed as a mechanism for organising collective enforcement in circumstances where a manifest aggressor might be supported by a great power; but in fact it was inconceivable that the scheme – designed by Washington as a response to the Korean crisis – would ever be exploited against the United States. It was one of a number of anti-Soviet moves made to bolster Washington's emerging global hegemony. The Uniting for Peace scheme was not in reality a disinterested amendment to improve the framework of the Charter. Rather it was 'an American initiative . . . clearly conceived as a device whereby the United

States might invoke the moral support of the United Nations for such resort to force as it might find necessary and desirable in the course of its cold war struggles'.[83] This central American interest was destined to shape Washington's relationship with the United Nations in the years that followed, first through the period of the Cold War and then in the context of the post-Soviet world. As one example, the 1990/91 Gulf crisis and the ensuing 1991 war clearly showed that the Security Council is dominated by the Permanent Members, primarily the United States, that there is no practical impediment to the breaking or bending of Charter rules, and that there is no way in which the Security Council is accountable to the wider world community represented by the largely impotent General Assembly. This means that, in effect, one nation is taking the UN's crucial decision on peace and war – a circumstance that Secretary-General Boutros-Ghali, despite all his commitment to the proper functioning of the international body, is unable to address. Thus in his 1993 report[84] there is no mention of some of the crucial factors that continue to stoke up problems in areas of considerable UN involvement. For example, he does not consider the extent to which UN-imposed sanctions on Iraq are contributing to the 'deterioration of living conditions'; the extent to which the problem over Libya regarding the Lockerbie outrage is exacerbated by Washington's neglect of relevant international law, namely the 1971 Montreal Convention; or the extent to which the requirement for reconciliation in El Salvador has meant that identifiable mass murderers have been allowed to escape justice. The reason is simple: no UN Secretary-General can afford a serious confrontation with the United States.

The scale of American power over recent decades has meant that foreign policy initiatives have been taken in virtually complete indifference to the requirements of both international and domestic (US) law. Thus John Quigley, professor of law at Ohio State University, having surveyed Washington's principal foreign involvements since the end of the Second World War, comments that much of this activity 'was unlawful under the United Nations Charter'.[85] This has meant, moreover, that such operations were illegal under American law. Chief Justice Marshall declared in 1815 that in the absence of an Act of Congress the court was bound by the law of nations which was part of the law of the land, while in 1900 Justice Gray stated that 'International law is part of our law, and must be ascertained and administered by the courts of justice of appropriate jurisdiction . . .'[86] Such judgements, applicable today, mean that many foreign policy initiatives undertaken by the United States have been illegal for the presidents of the day. The US Constitution requires that a president who breaks the law be impeached, a proper course but one for which Congress has rarely had the stomach. In short, if the requirements of law had been observed in the United States in the decades since the Second World War probably every US president would have been impeached and thrown out of office. It is one of the marks of hegemonic power that the requirements of law can be viewed with lofty and cynical disdain.

It is in this context that the relationship between Washington and the United Nations should be considered in the post-Soviet world. For a brief period it was possible to ask whether the United States could 'succeed where the UN has failed?'[87] Could America step into the peacekeeping/ peacemaking breach? Two crucial Security Council resolutions – 678 (29 November 1990) on Iraq; and 794 (3 December 1992) on Somalia – had authorised Washington to undertake military tasks on behalf of the United Nations, or so the argument ran. Was this a pattern for the future? Did the international community at last have an effective military arm, albeit one belonging in the last resort to a nation state? It was not long before such questions were answered, and in a way that quickly deflated the heady optimism of the post-Gulf and post-Soviet months. The United Nations, despite appearances, was in no position to authorise or requisition anything – without the permission of Washington. The Secretary-General was often unable to resist pressure from powerful member states, especially the United States; and in consequence the (moral) authority of the United Nations was much more likely to be requisitioned by self-serving powers, especially Washington, than were the (military) resources of any member state. The fact was that the Permanent Members of the Security Council had put 'something akin to a political stranglehold over the UN's room for manoeuvre'.[88]

The implication was the unremarkable likelihood that the United Nations would be persistently drafted to serve the interests of the major powers, themselves largely subservient to Washington. The new factor was the confusion in US foreign policy and, in consequence, in Washington's relationship with the United Nations. The disarray in turn fed through into UN initiatives and involvements: in late 1993 and on into 1994 there was mounting uncertainty about the UN's role in Bosnia, Somalia, Haiti and other specific regions and about its broader posture in the world. US uncertainties were afflicting UN efforts to develop a coherent philosophy for initiatives and involvements in the so-called New World Order. It was no longer clear how the United Nations would learn to address the post-Soviet challenges in the international environment.

President Clinton, in his address to the UN General Assembly on 28 September 1993, warned against the UN's 'reach exceeding its grasp';

and proposed various conditions for US involvements in new missions under UN auspices. The United States, declared Clinton, remained 'committed to helping to make the UN's vision a reality'; the United States 'intends to remain engaged and to lead . . . we must and will serve as a fulcrum for change and a pivot point for peace . . . our overriding purpose must be to expand and strengthen the world's community of market-based democracies . . . we seek to enlarge the circle of nations that live under those free institutions'. The United States had 'begun asking harder questions about proposals for new peacekeeping missions':

Is there a real threat to international peace? Does the proposed mission have clear objectives? Can an end point be identified for those who will be asked to participate? How much will the mission cost? . . . The United Nations simply cannot become engaged in every one of the world's conflicts. If the American people are to say yes to UN peacekeeping, the United Nations must know when to say no.

The United Nations, in short, must pick and choose when to intervene, when to observe and to do nothing. Washington, as a key player in the Security Council, would shape the choices, prepared to threaten non-payment of dues in the event of unwelcome pressures from the Secretary-General or other UN members. And perhaps Washington was paying too much: 'The assessment systems has not been changed since 1973, and everyone in our country knows that our percentage of the economic pie is not as great as it was then. Therefore, I believe our rates should be reduced to reflect the rise of other nations that can now bear more of the financial burden. *That will make it easier for me as president to make sure we pay in a timely and full fashion*' (my italics). Put simply: if you expect us to pay our obligatory dues promptly then take notice of our wishes on assessment and other matters. No other nation would come to the General Assembly of the United Nations and threaten non-payment of mandatory dues if the international body refused to behave in a particular way.

It was clear what President Clinton expected. The United Nations would have to earn American support. Washington's obligations under the UN Charter had nothing to do with it. The main aim was to increase the number of free-market democracies in the world – and in this crusade, the United Nations could expect American support. In the guise of a pro-UN activist, Clinton articulated the principal post-Soviet US message to the international community: we will fund whatever UN initiatives we agree with. And in this posture Washington could rely on supine and self-serving allies. The British foreign secretary Douglas Hurd was happy to underwrite the drift of American policy: future peacekeeping activities would have to be vetted more rigorously.[89] In practice, this meant that aggressive or undemocratic allies of the West – Turkey, Saudi Arabia, Indonesia – would be allowed to behave as they wished; whereas other states – Iraq, Libya and Haiti – would be subject to entirely different criteria. The West would continue to exploit the fresh opportunities offered by the United Nations but with minimal enthusiasm for the 'UN's vision'. Margaret Thatcher commented in her memoirs that she did not like 'unnecessary resort to the UN, because it suggested that sovereign states lacked the moral authority to act on their own behalf'.[90] Again the enduring principle: *exploit the United Nations or keep it at arm's length*. But the principle is pragmatically sound only if hegemonic states are capable of framing coherent foreign policies. And during 1993/94 this was becoming increasingly uncertain in the Washington of President Bill Clinton.

Now Clinton was the 'worrier king';[91] He was forcing the United Nations into a space between 'Clinton's rock and Somali hard place' (Boutros-Ghali; 'I cannot afford a confrontation with such an important member as the United States');[92] his foreign policy was 'in tatters';[93] and so on. The journalistic commentary was virtually unanimous: Bill had a 'big mouth'; he was only capable of 'big words, small deeds'; and the United States was squirming 'in a policy vacuum'. The problem of power for the United Nations had always been – and remained – the problem of how to protect the sovereignty of nation states while acting to render (even hegemonic) states subservient to the rule of law. The problem of power for the United States under the Clinton adminstration seemed increasingly to devolve on the problem of framing a coherent foreign policy in which a pliant United Nations could be drafted to play its proper traditional role. For Washington the problem of power had become *uncertainty* – at a time when the United States seemed unchallenged, constrained by no other nation state and by no international body, only by debt and social decay. Perhaps these were the principal factors that would come to shape the American international posture in the second half of the 1990s and beyond.

4 The Problem of Management

PREAMBLE

The principles of management at their most general level are portable from one organisation to another, whatever its size and whatever its aim. All organisations ideally require well-defined objectives, the optimum use of resources, the proper motivation of people, and so on. At the same time there are many practical and theoretical variations, different emphases, in the various management traditions. Some focus on the so-called scientific analysis of tasks, others on the relevance of bureaucratic structures, and yet others on the importance of human motivation. It is easy to see the relevance of such general considerations to the management of any large organisation, where, characteristically, human and other assets are acquired and exploited to achieve particular objectives. The organisation of the United Nations can be explored in these terms. Here management problems arise as they do in any organisation: people may be corrupt or incompetent, and the external environment may develop in unexpected directions. And there is also the crucial fact that the United Nations is often beset with difficulties that do not confront other organisations. The UN has a unique character and unique ambitions: this circumstance brings many problems.

The United Nations employs people, mainly in the Secretariat, as do other organisations. But it also relies on effective secondment, the provision of personnel from powerful nation states, often with their own political agendas. Similarly, other vital resources – such as funds and specialist information – are provided at the whim of external organisations. Thus the UN Secretariat has limited power to requisition the crucial assets without which it cannot function, a particular handicap in circumstances where the demands on the organisation are rapidly escalating. As one example, after the Vance–Owen peace plan for the former Yugoslavia was approved on 21 February 1992 there were, up to late 1993, more than 40 Security Council resolutions and no less than fifteen mandate enhancements; all signalling a rapid expansion of demands which the Security Council had no means to implement. This particular escalation was part of the growing activity of the Security Council made possible in part by the collapse of the Soviet Union and the consequent removal of the likely Soviet veto.

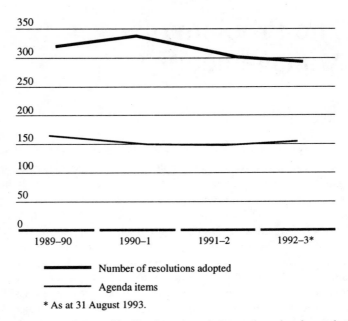

Number of resolutions adopted

Agenda items

* As at 31 August 1993.

Figure 4.1   *General Assembly: Number of resolutions adopted and agenda items, 1989–1993*
SOURCE: Boutros-Ghali, *Report*, United Nations, New York, September 1993.

Thus through a period that saw a small decrease in activity in the General Assembly (Figure 4.1), the work of the Security Council significantly expanded (Figures 4.2 and 4.3). Since it is the work of the Security Council, rather than that of the largely impotent General Assembly, that places practical demands on the organisation, it is principally the substantial growth in Council activity that has placed an immediate strain on UN resources. This has led to the Security Council treating resolutions as if they were 'self-executing',[1] an obvious absurdity that has done nothing to enhance the international authority of the United Nations.

It is also significant that the powerful member states often have an interest in scapegoating the United Nations. If the UN fails in an international operation – albeit through inadequate resources – this can be advertised to divert attention from the culpable inactivity of particular nations. Thus Secretary-General Boutros-Ghali has commented on Washington's domestic problems over Somalia and Haiti: 'The UN exists to help member countries solve their problems'; if attacking the UN helps President Clinton with Congress, 'I am not going to answer back'.[2] Similarly, the UN mediator Thorvald Stoltenberg, considering the

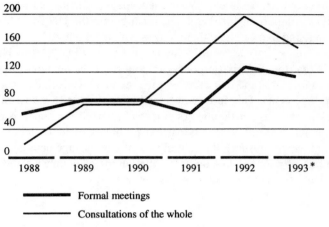

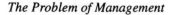

Formal meetings

Consultations of the whole

* As at 31 August.

Figure 4.2   *Security Council: Number of formal meetings and consultations of the whole, 1989–1993*
SOURCE: Boutros-Ghali, *Report*, United Nations, New York, September 1993.

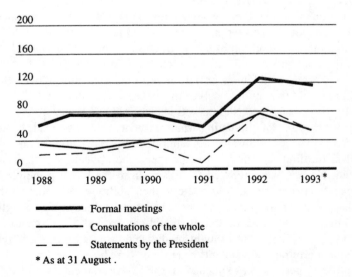

Formal meetings

Consultations of the whole

— — —   Statements by the President

* As at 31 August .

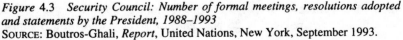

Figure 4.3   *Security Council: Number of formal meetings, resolutions adopted and statements by the President, 1988–1993*
SOURCE: Boutros-Ghali, *Report*, United Nations, New York, September 1993.

Serb–Croat conflict, declared: 'We are a scapegoat for the parties. It can be politically important for them. They can blame the UN for what has gone wrong, and that can help them to deal with each other.'[3]

This suggests that the central management problem of the United Nations is that the organisation is not in control of the resources that are essential to its tasks (and that moreover the member states find this a congenial arrangement). This in turn is bound to contribute to a host of secondary problems: the difficulties of financial control, the supervision of UN personnel in the field, the persistent problems of inefficiency, corruption and worse. In short, the central task of UN management is to cope with the fact of national sovereignties, the whims of member states, and the associated complex of problems that these bring.

RESOURCES

The Whims of States

The rapid growth in the scale of demands on the United Nations, coupled with the reluctance of many states to pay their dues on time, has stretched the UN's financial resources to breaking-point. In early 1993 the assessed contributions from the Member States for the regular budget amounted to $1.6 billion, with peacekeeping costs expected to rise from $1.4 billion in 1992 to around $3.6 billion by 1994.[4] Such sums may be considered modest in the context of the United Nations' ambitions and global posture. However, a key problem is how to determine what individual nations should pay (and thereafter to collect the assessed contributions).

At the time the United Nations was launched at San Francisco there was no agreed method for stipulating what payments should be made by individual member states. Instead a Committee on Contributions was established at the first Assembly to recommend the allocation system to be adopted. No-one was prepared to dissent from the broad principle that Members' contributions should relate to their ability to pay, though there was dispute about how this was to be calculated. The economic strength of the United States suggested that it should pay around 50 per cent of the total bill, an estimate that brought predictable protest from Washington. Subsequent arbitrary adjustments progressively reduced the American liability: first 10 per cent was knocked off the US assessment, then in 1957 a theoretical ceiling of 30 per cent contribution for any state was agreed, with this further reduced to 25 per cent in the early 1970s. Such adjustments allowed other wealthy states to claim that they should not be expected to contribute more *per capita* than did the United States, a ploy that led to further adjustments in favour of the developed nations. And at the lower end there were yet more adjustments against the interests of poor Member States: it was declared that no nation should pay less than 0.04 per cent of the total budget, so forcing the poorest nations to pay more than the strict principle of proportionality would have justified. It was clear from the beginning that the wealthy Member States, led by Washington, were determined to distort the contribution assessments in their favour. Today the United States continues to put pressure on the UN to secure a further reduction in the American assessment. Thus when President Clinton addressed the General Assembly on 28 September 1993 he declared that US contributions 'should be reduced to reflect the rise of other nations that can now bear more of the financial burden'.

The question of assessment is only part of the problem of obtaining appropriate revenues for the United Nations organisation; there is also the matter of late payment, when Member States withhold funds for political or other reasons. In fact, remembering similar difficulties in the League of Nations, the drafters of the UN Charter included the provision (Article 19) that Member States in arrears 'shall have no vote in the General Assembly if the amount of its arrears equals or exceeds the amount of the contributions due from it for the preceding two full years'; but voting would be permitted if the Assembly judged that the arrears were beyond the control of the state in question. Article 19 may on occasions act as a disincentive to late payment but it has proved to be far from a conclusive pressure.

In the 1960s the Soviet Union withheld due payments for expenditure related to the Korean War (see 'The Korean Paradigm', Chapter 2), the United Nations Trust Supervisory Organisation (UNTSO), the UN field service, and other activities. This unilateral Soviet decision was a serious matter, though far from exceptional among Member States. Various small nations have been in arrears, usually briefly, beyond the two-year limit specified in Article 19, but in general arrears have been settled to enable such states to vote in the General Assembly when they wish. Ironically, when the US-supported Taiwan illicitly held the Chinese seat in the Security Council in the 1950s and 60s its assessment was based on the total Chinese national income, not simply that of the relatively small off-shore Taiwan. In consequence, Taiwan's assessment was often burdensome and frequently led to arrears. Such problems were perhaps more understandable than decisions by states to withhold funds for political reasons. Again the Soviet Union decided to pay towards the United Nations

Force in Sinai (UNEF) authorised by the General Assembly in 1956, but not towards the United Nations Operation in the Congo (ONUC) set up by the Security Council in 1960.

The 'pick and choose' attitude among powerful Member States as to which UN operations they would support has been clearly evident also in recent years. The Oxfam Director, David Bryer, has emphasised that the current fund-raising system 'enables donor governments to "pick and choose" which UN initiatives to support, according to their own interests', a situation that is not helped by a Security Council not constituted 'to represent the interests of the international community as a whole'.[5] In 1986 Washington withdrew virtually all US funding in protest against UN attitudes, and today (in mid 1995) Washington remains in debt to the international body. The United States paid around $500 million in October 1993 to settle some long-standing budget arrears but still owed $472 million. In fact in recent years the paid contributions have generally amounted to around half of the annual assessments for all nations (Figure 4.4), a short-

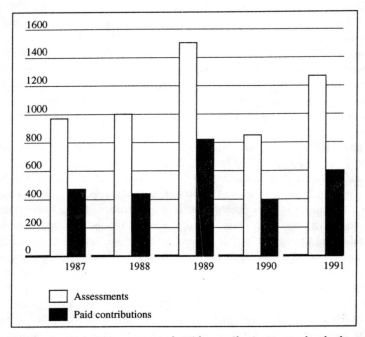

Figure 4.4 *Annual assessments and paid contributions: regular budget and peacekeeping combined, 1987–1992 (millions of US dollars)*
SOURCE: Boutros-Ghali, *Report*, United Nations, New York, September 1993.

fall for which many Member States share responsibility but where, because of the relatively high US assessment, American derelictions are particularly serious.

Many observers have noted that UN can rely on funds when Western interests are seen to be at stake, but in other circumstances its finances are less secure. Thus Conor Cruise O'Brien, one-time high UN official, has remarked that when the West's vital interests are involved, as with the Iraqi invasion of Kuwait, the impact of a Security Council decree could be 'awe-inspiring', but where Western interests are not involved, 'as over Bosnia, Cambodia or Somalia – the authority of the UN looks less impressive, because Western enforcers are not available'.[6] Here again, simply by virtue of American military power, Washington is the crucial player. UN Secretary-General Boutros-Ghali has no option but to acknowledge this central feature of international power politics: 'I cannot afford a confrontation with so important a member of the United Nations as the United States.'[7] At the same time there are hints of a shift in American policy towards the international body. President Clinton has acknowledged the requirement that the US be a timely payer to UN funds, but has stressed the need for certain conditions. There has also been some attempt to reverse the UN policies of preceding Republican administrations, though up to 1994 there were few discernible practical differences.

On 10 June 1993 the American UN ambassador, Madeleine Albright, emphasised to a Senate Panel the requirement for an 'assertive multilateralism', jargon that was becoming common parlance in the Clinton administration and which Boutros-Ghali was also adopting as signalling the UN's newly emerging international role.[8] There was also debate about the extent to which Washington would accept UN command over American soldiers serving in a UN peacekeeping capacity (in practice there were few signs of movement in this direction). It is significant that in such UN commitments as the UNOSOM II force in Somalia the command structure is essentially American, notwithstanding the appointment of a Turkish general as commander. A retired US admiral, Jonathan Howe, was the UN Special Representative; while Thomas Montgomery served as the direct tactical commander of the US Quick Reaction Force that typically carried out military operations without reference to UN officials. In fact a draft directive instructed American military commanders 'to disobey UN orders they judge illegal or militarily imprudent'.[9] Similarly, Senator Robert Byrd, the Democratic Chairman of the Senate Appropriations Committee, commented that the deaths of four US soldiers in Mogadishu showed that the operation 'was crumbling . . . that it was not

worth American lives lost and injuries sustained'. American politicians
and policy planners were, it seemed, prepared to support UN operations
only on US terms: at no level would the requirements of American control
and decision making be sacrificed. Here the debate was not confined to
Washington: other nation states – Britain, Pakistan, Canada and Italy –
were all prepared to consider pulling personnel out of trouble spots in the
light of (relatively minor) casualties. Throughout 1993 Boutros-Ghali
repeatedly appealed for secure commitments on the part of various
Member States providing personnel for Bosnia, Somalia and elsewhere;
but it remained obvious that UN operations could be carried out only at
the behest of particular contributing nations. Thus in October 1993 the UN
Secretary-General urged the Americans yet again not to abandon Somalia,
at the same time complaining that the 22,000-strong UN force was still
6000 to 7000 short of the numbers promised.[10]

In various other troubled regions it was equally possible to detect the
baleful influence of powerful Member States working to frustrate the best
instincts of the United Nations. Thus the brutal aggression of Indonesia
against East Timor – which has led to the genocide of 200,000, a third of
the Timorese population – was sustained by armament shipments from the
United States, Britain and Australia, interested above all in trade with
Indonesia and the prospect of oil in the Timor Sea. In the first decade after
the 1975 aggression the UN General Assembly passed some ten motions
deploring the Indonesian invasion and demanding a withdrawal of the
armed forces. Neither Britain nor the United States urged the implementation of such resolutions, instead taking steps to block any practical
UN initiatives. When UN representative Amos Wako visited East Timor
in April 1993 and reported to Secretary-General Boutros-Ghali, his
findings were not made public.[11] In June reports emerged suggesting that
Boutros-Ghali was suppressing Wako's report, thought to recommend
United Nations support for East Timorese self-determination. At the same
time Britain was accused of blocking European Community criticism of
Indonesian policy.[12] There was no prospect of Member States such as the
US and the UK agreeing the use of UN resources to reverse an Indonesian
invasion that favoured Western economic interests.

The UN dilemma is plain enough. Keen to protect state sovereignties,
the international body has no power to subordinate recalcitrant Member
States to legitimate human rights or the demands of international law. The
Soviet Union has withheld due funds as a political protest, as have the
United States, South Africa (in late 1993 owing some $92.9 million) and
other Member States. It has been suggested that Japanese delays in payment may be intended to put pressure on the international community to

give attention to Japan's claim for a permanent seat on the Security Council, while current Russian delays may be calculated to attract Western aid for a collapsing pro-market economy. In any event the United Nations remained chronically underfunded, unable to recoup even the assessed contributions that Member States implicitly agree by virtue of their commitment to the Charter. It is not yet clear how the UN will find a way to evolve policies less subject to the whims of sovereign states.

The Funding Question

In 1987 the Member States were billed less than $300 million for UN peacekeeping operations, in 1991 less than $500 million; but by 1993 the figure had exceeded $3 billion. Throughout 1993 the alarm bells sounded, with commentators on all sides urging the United Nations to adopt a new realism, not to take on fresh commitments that would be certain to outstrip its resources. The heady triumphalism of the so-called New World Order had long since evaporated: the collapse of the Soviet Union had not allowed the world to be remade overnight. And now the manifest UN policy failures in Bosnia, Angola and Somalia were advertising the need for vastly increased deployments that could not be financed. By mid-1993 the UN funding crisis was obvious.

In August Secretary-General Boutros-Ghali, now gravely alarmed, appealed to Member States in arrears to pay their dues. In a letter to Prime Minister John Major he begs Britain to encourage other members 'to pay their contributions in full'. The letter, dated 2 August 1993, begins with the words:

> I am writing to share with you my deep concern at the prospect that the critical financial situation of the United Nations will soon prevent it from discharging its responsibilities in the field of international peace and security. I am, of course, aware that the United Kingdom is one of the small number of member states to have paid its contributions in full, and I am most grateful for this support.

Boutros-Ghali notes that the United Nations' total cash reserves amount to $380 million, 'whereas the total monthly expense of the organisation is $310 million'. He emphasises that the troop-contributing governments are owed $360 million, and that 'it is increasingly difficult to make timely payment to contractors who provide goods and services to peacekeeping operations'. Existing operations were seen to be 'in jeopardy', with the situation 'the most critical' that the United Nations 'has ever faced'.[13]

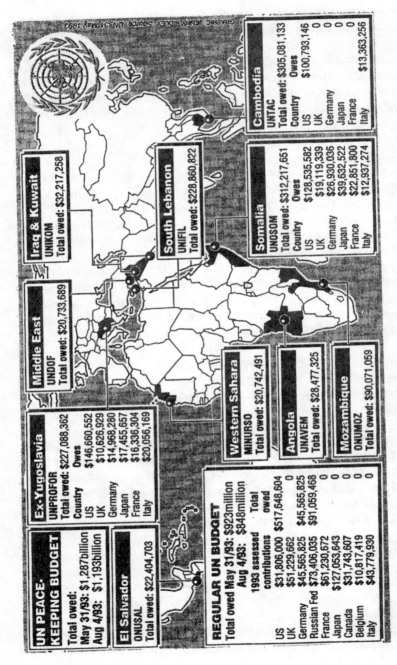

Figure 4.5   Debt situation for some key UN operations
SOURCE: *The Guardian* (London), 4 August 1993.

British officials commented that the United States owed more than $800 million, Russia more than $490 million, and Japan just over $90 million. Britain could do little beyond 'encouraging and nagging' the defaulters.

Many of the UN's members were now defaulters, leading to a serious cash flow problem in many key operational commitments (Figure 4.5). The United Nations is currently unable to raise loans, even short-term ones, and so the prompt payment of dues on a regular basis is of particular importance. Annual contributions are supposed to be paid by 31 January each year, but few countries manage this. Tokyo typically delays payments until June, and Washington until October, when only part of the outstanding debt is settled. In 1993 only 18 countries, accounting for only 16 per cent of the regular budget, paid up on time. Such tardiness in payment inevitably leads to severe cash flow problems.*

Two months after Boutros-Ghali's appeal for cash President Bill Clinton, addressing the UN General Assembly, emphasised that UN operations 'must not only be adequately funded but also fairly funded' – a prelude to a US cut (October 1995), to 25 per cent, in its peacekeeping contribution. At the same time UK Foreign Secretary Douglas Hurd launched a criticism of financial mismanagement of UN peacekeeping operations: 'The UN would be able to afford more operations if it ran the existing ones more economically'; without thrift and financial probity the UN's authority 'will weaken and vanish'.[14] The UN coffers were almost empty. Unless substantial funds arrived within a matter of weeks, key peacekeeping operations would have to be cut back.

In May 1993 Russia had unexpectedly used its veto in the Security Council to block a move to reform the financing of peacekeeping activities in Cyprus. The British-sponsored resolution aimed to apportion the costs of the 1500-strong force among all UN members instead of having to rely on voluntary contributions. Russia complained that outside any UN obligations it already had to pay for CIS peacekeeping operations in such areas as Tajikistan and Nagorno-Karabakh, and was already heavily involved in operations in the former Yugoslavia. The proposed Security Council resolution would have significantly increased Russia's liability, and reduced Britain's from an annual contribution of around £32 million to £653,000. The West appealed to Moscow to lift the veto, at the same time working to attract contingents from poorer countries to replace the

---

*The funding situation remained precarious through 1994. On 12 October of that year Boutros-Ghali announced that the UN was close to bankruptcy. Only 13 of the 184 members had paid their dues in full by 30 September; the organisation had a debt of $1.7 billion, a capital fund that 'is today virtually depleted' and a peacekeeping reserve fund dwindling toward zero.

departing Danes, Austrians and Canadians. Britain too gave notice that it was cutting its Cyprus contingent. In September 1993 a 73-man Argentinian advance party arrived in Cyprus to work alongside the British, not much more than a decade after the Falklands War. But any prospect of a significant increase in general UN funding seemed unlikely: France and China, also permanent members of the Security Council, seemed no keener than Russia to increase their UN commitments by contributing to the Cyprus peacekeeping operation.

There were signs also that funding questions were fuelling fresh controversies in Cambodia. In January 1993 the *Cambodia Times*, the country's only English-language weekly, launched an attack on Eric Falt, the chief spokesman for the United Nations Transitional Authority in Cambodia (UNTAC), and on the Western involvement:

> 'The UNTAC spokesman's office regards itself more as an agent of the Western press than as a provider of information to the local people, who time and time again come last in their order of priorities. This gives rise to a strong feeling amongst the local press that UNTAC is really a Western transplant plonked in the middle of the country, run by Westerners for the sake of good media ratings in the Western world and their bosses at UN headquarters in New York. Cambodia, it seems, is just incidental to the whole process.'

It is further charged that many UNTAC officials, 'especially those from the West', were treating Cambodians as second-class citizens in their own country and behaving like old-style colonialists.

Two-thirds of the entire UN peacekeeping budget was being spent in Cambodia; and the funding of 16,000 troops and 6000 civilians from more than 40 countries was having a dramatic effect on a desperately poor Third World country. Even the UN's own financial controllers had complained about the scale of the spending, with almost as many vehicles and computers as there were UNTAC personnel. The flood of dollars, by then a second currency in Cambodia, had created a lopsided prosperity, totally distorting the local economy. Much of money was going to foreign contractors from south-east Asia and elsewhere; and to corrupt Cambodian officials and ministers now profiting from the economic dislocation. At the same time many Phnom Penh policemen and soldiers, not paid for months, were being forced to extort what money they could from their compatriots. UN officials were earning a special allowance of $145 a day in addition to their tax-free salaries, while volunteer electrical technicians were risking their lives in remote areas for $700 a month. It has been suggested that the UNTAC spend of well over $1 billion could have been much reduced if more Cambodians had been involved in the operation.[15]

Aid to Cambodia, much of its pledged under UN auspices, seemed slow in coming. Thus Eileen Maybin, a Christian Aid journalist, reported the complaint of Yasushi Akashi, UNTAC head, that donor nations who had pledged funds at the UN Tokyo aid conference in June 1992 were now waiting to see the results of the UN peacekeeping operations. Only 10 per cent of the promised $880 million had been forthcoming. The funds that might have contributed to the stabilisation of Cambodia were waiting on the stabilisation process itself. In October 1993 it was reported that unless funds were received before the end of the month the clearing of land-mines would have to be abandoned: an immediate guarantee of $10 million was needed to prevent a withdrawal of UN personnel. At that time at least 300 Cambodians were being killed or maimed by mines every month.

In Angola the government, desperately fighting for survival, continued to charge import duties on UN vehicles for the peacekeeping operation; and on occasions even demanded substantial payments of taxes. Here, with a growing food shortage, Washington was asking the World Food Programme (WFP) to scale down its demands because of the cost, with the United Nations continuing to beg donor states to provide food assistance. Increased fighting in Sudan resulted in a reduction in food aid, while UN funding difficulties caused a withdrawal of UN guards in northern Iraq and the virtual abandonment by the UN and the West of the Afghans, desperately in need of food and other aid supplies. In Western Sahara a contingent of fifteen British servicemen had spent two years – at a cost of well over $1 million a year – awaiting a UN-brokered referendum that might never take place, with the total UN operation having cost around $70 million. By 1994 well over $3 billion had been spent on the UN involvement in Somalia, with most of the troops securely ensconced in their compounds. At the same time evidence was emerging that the UN procurement policy was out of control, the methods for supplying mineral water to the 27,000 peacekeepers in Somalia illustrating a general malaise. The contract for supply was not advertised but quietly assigned to an Israeli company that has supplied UN operations for many years. The UN office in Mogadishu buys a 46-cent bottle of Israeli water from a dealer in Tel Aviv, whereupon he ships the bottled water to Mogadishu for transfer onto leased cargo planes that cost the UN around $40,000 a day. The final result is a supply of Eden water costing more than $2 a bottle. The proven alternative was to buy supplies from Kilimanjaro Mineral Water Ltd in neighbouring Kenya at a fraction of the cost.

The UN cash crisis began to affect operations in Bosnia in early 1993, though various initiatives were undertaken in the absence of the due payments from the United Nations. Thus a NATO official emphasised that more troops would be sent to police an agreed partition of Bosnia: 'We shan't be waiting for the UN cheque. Pre-funding by individual NATO members is quite normal in this sort of situation.' However, it was emerging that any US commitment to a Bosnian involvement would depend upon the various parties agreeing to pay US costs and to an 'exit strategy' for US forces (Clinton: 'I think we did not have an adequate exit strategy in Somalia and we need an exit strategy here').

The Manpower Question

A principal task of the United Nations is to raise troops and other manpower to fulfil declared obligations and commitments. The UN Charter (Chapter VII) supposedly assists in this task by detailing the procedures to be adopted when there are 'threats to the peace, breaches of the peace, and acts of aggression'. Thus Article 43 declares that all UN members 'in order to contribute to the maintenance of international peace and security, undertake to make available to the Security Council, on its call and in accordance with a special agreement or agreements, armed forces, assistance, and facilities . . .'. It is obvious that the 'agreement or agreements' are crucial: in their absence the Security Council can make no call on the troops from soverign states. Such agreements are to be concluded 'between the Security Council and Members or between the Security Council and groups of members and shall be subject to ratification by the signatory states in accordance with their respective constitutional processes'. This means that the Security Council, despite its executive status, is powerless under the Charter to requisition troops from Member States; but this does not mean that the US-dominated Council is powerless to exert pressure in other ways. Just as the Security Council can be manipulated (see Chapter 3), so it is able to coerce Member States. The Secretary-General, by contrast, has no such *de facto* power.

Again there is the familiar situation that the UN, when raising troops under the terms of Chapter VII of the Charter, can only perform at the whim of powerful Member States. The Secretary-General can only request support, not command it, for any initiatives he may take under Article 99 ('The Secretary-General may bring to the attention of the Security Council any matter which in his opinion may threaten the maintenance of international peace and security'). If Member States, especially the permanent members of the Council, are unsympathetic the Secretary-General cannot then take further action. In Somalia it has seemed obvious that Italian, Pakistani and US troops have been subject to national commands that fall outside the UN orbit. Italy threatened a pull-out from Mozambique if Secretary-General Boutros-Ghali did not accede to their wishes in Somalia, the Pakistan government contemplated a withdrawal that Boutros-Ghali would have been powerless to prevent, and no-one doubts that the US command is a law unto itself.

The United Nations has also had to contend with post-World War Two national legislation – in the cases of Germany and Japan – that has restricted the availability of troops from powerful Member States for UN peacekeeping operations. Thus Rudolf Scharping, the leader of Germany's opposition Social Democrats (SPD), seized on the issue of German troops in Somalia to attack Helmut Kohl's government. Here it is argued that there may be a constitutional constraint on the deployment of German troops outside the NATO area (though some suggested that the prospect of German casualties may have carried more political weight). In June 1993 Secretary-General Boutros-Ghali offered to appear before the German supreme court to support the Kohl government over the presence of German troops in Somalia, so underlining the importance attached by the UN to German involvement in peacekeeping operations. At that time a 255-strong advance contingent of 1700 assigned German troops had already been deployed at Belet Huen, 200 miles north of Mogadishu: a constitutional violation, according to the SPD; essential support for the UN aid operation, according to the Bonn administration. On 23 June the German supreme court – perhaps with an eye to Germany acquiring a permanent seat on the Security Council – ruled that the Bundeswehr involvement in Somalia was legal under the constitution, at the same time declaring that the German parliament had to take the final decision on the mission.

In Japan a similar debate had focused on whether Japanese personnel should be allowed to participate in UN peacekeeping missions. On 31 October 1990 Toshiki Kaifu, the then Japanese prime minister, abandoned his detailed control over a controversial bill designed to authorise Japanese military participation in overseas peacekeeping missions. This decision, designed to accept opposition amendments, showed the confusion in the Diet at a time when Washington was pressing Tokyo to take a firmer stand against Saddam Hussein. The bill stipulated that Japanese involvement in peacekeeping would be authorised, but that Japanese troops, allowed only to carry arms for self-defence, would not be allowed to fight. A survey suggested that 53 per cent of Japanese were against the bill, with 49 per cent thinking that it violated the constitution.*

---

*Article 9 of the Japanese constitution, imposed by General Douglas MacArthur's post-World War Two administration, declares: 'The Japanese people forever renounce war as a sovereign right of the nation and the threat or use of force as means of settling international disputes . . . land, sea and air forces, as well as other war potential, will never be maintained . . .'.

On 15 June 1992 the Diet passed the bill authorising Japanese soldiers to join UN peacekeeping operations. Members applauded but outside there were several hundred hostile demonstrators and there were still constitutional questions to be answered. Makato Tanabe, chairman of the opposition Social Democratic Party (SDP), denounced the new legislation as a 'violation' of the Japanese constitution, at the same time threatening to take the issue to the people and to force a dissolution of parliament's lower house. There was now, declared Tanabe, 'a shadow over Japan's future'. The then Japanese prime minister, Kiichi Miyazawa, commented that for the first time 'Japan can now contribute physically to international affairs'. Now there was talk of sending Japanese troops to Cambodia, though some government supporters, remembering World War Two history, thought this a bad idea: 'It's too close to bad memories of the Imperial Army. We should go to Yugoslavia first where no-one has any bad memories of the Japanese.' With the Peacekeeping Operations Act now law, the Japanese government was authorised to send up to 2000 troops as non-combatants to support UN operations.

The new legal position remained controversial through 1993. The ruling Liberal Democratic Party (LDP), before its electoral defeat in July, moved to review the 1947 anti-war constitution. For years the (Article 9) prohibition on Japanese military involvement had suited the country: the United States had taken care of Japan's external security, with Tokyo, required only to maintain minimal Self-Defence Forces, free to concentrate on economic development. Now, partly under US and UN pressure, the prospect of Japan having its own armed forces was again on the political agenda. It remained certain that there would be widespread opposition to any such development. When UN Secretary-General Boutros-Ghali visited Waseda University outside Tokyo in February 1993 left-wing students greeted him with chants of: 'Don't allow B-Ghali inside our campus! Protect our peace constitution!'

The enthusiasm of the Secretary-General for Bundeswehr involvement in Somalia (and elsewhere) and for revision of the 1947 Japanese constitution to allow Tokyo to send troops on UN operations abroad signals above all the desperate UN requirement for active personnel in adequate numbers. Already individual states cannot be relied upon to supply troops in controversial trouble-spots: Boutros Ghali, subject to the whims of sovereign states, often seems impotent in his efforts to recruit for crucial peacekeeping missions. His obvious interest is in enlarging the catchment form which he can garner UN forces.

One option in these circumstances is for Member States to allocate personnel and other assets as part of a standing UN force, available for speedy deployment when the need arises. In early 1992 Boutros-Ghali proposed 'bringing into being, through negotiations, the special agreements foreseen in Article 43 of the Charter, whereby Member States undertake to make armed forces, assistance and facilities available to the Security Council . . .'. This would not be done, as happens today, 'on an ad hoc basis but on a permanent basis . . . The ready availability of armed forces on call could serve, in itself, as a means of deterring breaches of the peace since a potential aggressor would know that the Council had at its disposal a means of response'.[16] Various observers have applauded the idea of a standing UN force as an effective reinforcement of UN authority and as an element of insurance against the whims of the sovereign Member States. Sir Crispin Tickell, British Permanent Representative to the United Nations 1987–1990, has emphasised that such an arrangement would enable problems of structure and logistics to be addressed in a timely fashion; and that such standby forces might be useful also in other circumstances, for example for disaster relief operations. The lack of resources, Tickell notes, is at the heart of the current difficulties: 'The coffers are nearly always empty. Governments are happy to call upon the services of the UN, but they do not want to pay for them.'[17]

There is of course a significant difference between the provision of a unified UN standby force and the allocation of earmarked standby units in the individual contributing countries. An integrated UN force specially adapted to peacekeeping tasks and under explicit UN command would have obvious advantages; but perhaps not for the Member States who may suspect an irreversible loss of sovereignty. With current UN operations there is always the inevitable tension between UN control and control by the participating states. This in turn leads to command difficulties, a confusion about objectives, and a fractured and rancorous force where unity is essential. It still remains unlikely that the major powers would agree to fund a permanent United Nations standby force over which they would necessarily have only limited control.

In late 1992 the Security Council endorsed an initiative to develop standby arrangements for personnel, equipment and funding between the UN and the Member States.[18] Here a seven-strong Stand-By Forces Planning Group was established to develop a system whereby forces assigned in advance to UN tasks could be speedily deployed when required. Again the group encountered the indifference of Member States troubled at the thought of loss of sovereignty. The United States, essential to any such scheme, has proved reluctant to make firm commitments, and the British government has seemed equally loath to offer binding assurances. In September 1993 it was reported that the Western military powers 'refused to countenance' the idea of a standing UN force at a time when defence costs were under pressure and governments were keen to secure some economic advantage from the 'peace dividend'. Britain, seemingly content with its NATO involvement, would be unlikely to support any proposed new UN framework. Thus Group Captain David Bolton, Director of the Royal United Services Institute (RUSI) commented that the UN 'is not equipped to directly conduct military operations and it should delegate that job to NATO or a proven military organisation while it maintains the political direction of the operation'.[19]

The question of personnel remains, along with the overarching problem of funding, one of the principal difficulties facing the United Nations in the post-Soviet New World Order. If the UN is to rely solely on the good will of Member States then it will often be unable to react speedily to address a threat to international peace and security: if the interests of powerful states are involved then they may be prepared to act, or to block action. The main merit of a standing UN force would be to avoid the constraints of unhelpful national sovereignty; but this is precisely why the Member States would be unlikely to support such a development.

MANAGING THE SYSTEM

The Problem

The overall management task facing the United Nations is a nightmare. It is massively under-resourced in funds, personnel and general logistical support: beyond the needs of the Secretariat it has limited powers to appoint staff, and it is unable to raise money via normal commercial routes, as might any other large organisation. At the same time, with no power of disciplinary sanction, it is required to manage a global system involving many different factional and linguistic elements that owe their first allegiance to other masters. No manager, without a remarkable degree of optimism and commitment, would want to start from here.

It is one thing to manage the Secretariat, quite another to manage the many UN commitments around the world. It is obvious that unless the UN's own administration is efficient and cost-effective it stands little chance of acting promptly and with authority in the wider world community: a streamlined Secretariat is an essential condition if the United Nations is to properly fulfil its global role.

Bureaucracy

There have long been charges of UN incompetence and lack of accountability. In earlier days the manifest failures of the international body could be attributed to the wilful perversity of this or that permanent member of the Security Council, too ready to use a blocking veto; but even then there were frequent criticisms of the United Nations organisation, well placed to serve as a scapegoat for the baleful effects of Great Power rivalries. In today's post-Soviet world there are fewer excuses, with the consequence that the shortcomings of the newly transparent United Nations are even more loudly proclaimed: now a central and persistent charge is of bureaucratic incompetence at the heart of the United Nations organisation.

On 9 November 1992 an editorial in *The Independent* (London) newspaper surveyed the manifest failures of the United Nations and suggested the need for radical action. This in turn stimulated a call for fundamental reform of the UN's administrative machinery to improve its effectiveness and accountability. Thus in a letter reply (13 November) Alex de Waal and Rakiya Omaar, then both directors of the human-rights group Africa Watch, signalled the on-going struggle against 'the incompetence and lack of accountability within the UN bureaucracy'. There should be independent public enquiries into major UN operations – 'Somalia, Yugoslavia and Cambodia will do for a start' – with UN officials responsible for needless failures 'disciplined or dismissed'. Many observers judge that there has always been too little appetite in the UN hierarchy for the disciplining of incompetent or corrupt employees. Yet such discipline must properly be regarded as 'a basic requirement of an accountable civil service'.

Such views were further advertised on 1 March 1993 when the American Dick Thornburgh, the outgoing Under-Secretary-General of the UN Department of Administration and Management, presented his final report to Secretary-General Boutros-Ghali. Here the UN's 'deadwood' bureaucrats and outdated management methods were roundly condemned, with charges of defects existing in nearly every aspect of present personnel practice. It was suggested that recruitment was 'more or less haphazard' and that it consumed 'an inordinate amount of time', while training was inadequate and promotions 'unduly complicated to the point of being nearly unworkable'. Further criticisms were levelled at the 'almost surreal' budget practices and at internal audits that were 'chronically fragmented and inadequate'. One UN unit, the report charged, had become a convenient patronage dumping ground', and had recently spent $4 million on a study of the management of works of art at the New

York UN headquarters. Thornburgh declared that the United Nations organisation was 'almost totally lacking in effective means to deal with fraud, waste and abuse by staff members',* and that it was difficult to get rid of 'dead wood': 'discipline and dismissal procedures are encumbered to seemingly interminable appeals procedures', with the result that a 'few good staff members are doing too much, and over-extending themselves sometimes to the point where they have become counter-productive'. A major disappointment for Thornburgh was that the UN had failed to devise an effective method for evaluating performance; the present system was 'virtually useless', producing positive assessments for 90 per cent of the staff.

Significant reforms to UN organisation and administration were introduced in 1993 (see below) but there were still persistent charges of incompetence and inefficiency. An editorial in *The Independent* (28 August) highlighted what was seen as a widely-perceived shortcoming in the UN headquarters: 'Part of the trouble derives from the bureaucratic culture that prevails in New York, where officials can further their careers better by keeping their heads down and covering the incompetence or malfeasance of their colleagues than by demonstrating zeal and honesty.' The problem was compounded by the fact that many of the employees were political placements: a sacking or other disciplinary measure might have repercussions with a Member State. At the same time there 'is no effective system of control and accountancy, and far too much secrecy . . . the discrepancy between the brave and dedicated work of many UN soldiers and officials, and the rotten, creaky and overweighted structure they represent, is now too great to tolerate'.[20]

Reform

The drafters of the UN Charter were well aware of the need for adequate staffing of the Secretariat, and so detailed the requirements in Article 101. 'Appropriate staffs' assigned to the various organs of the United Nations would form part of the Secretariat: 'The paramount consideration in the employment of the staff and in the determination of the conditions of service shall be the necessity of securing the highest standards of efficiency, competence and integrity.' It is to the credit of Secretary-General Boutros-Ghali that he has worked to translate this pious aspiration into reality.

---

*An audit at the UN headquarters in New York revealed that the cost of the 51 million photocopies made on 209 machines in 1993 was three times the amount paid by comparable large organisations (*The Daily Telegraphs*, 19 September 1994).

The rapid expansion of the number of demands on the United Nations has not been matched by an equivalent expansion of resources. Boutros-Ghali himself has pointed out that in 1992 the regular UN budget had not increased significantly in real terms since the mid-1980s. This situation posed a challenge 'in requiring a search for greater efficiency in the conduct of its [the UN's] mandated activities'.[21] It was against this background that Secretary-General Boutros-Ghali began taking steps to streamline the Secretariat:

A number of offices have been regrouped, related functions and activities have been consolidated and redeployments of resources have been undertaken. Unnecessary bureaucratic layers have been reduced through the elimination of several high-level posts. Lines of responsibility have been more clearly defined by concentrating the decision-making process in seven key departments at Headquarters under eight Under-Secretaries-General. The needs of each component of the Secretariat are now being re-evaluated with a view, on the one hand, to eliminating any remaining duplication and redundancy and, on the other, to reinforcing those offices and departments with expanding mandates and responsibilities.[22]

Boutros-Ghali emphasised the need for a Secretariat 'with a streamlined structure comprising components with clearly delineated responsibilities and greater managerial accountability'. There should also be a proper balance between the activities carried out at the New York headquarters and those performed by the regional commissions and other UN organs and programmes: the focus of the UN 'must remain in the "field", where economic, social and political decisions take effect'. When the current phases of the restructuring had been completed, declared Boutros-Ghali, he would focus 'on the improvement of the conditions of service, including salaries, long-term recruitment policies, grade structure and career development opportunities'.[23] Here he emphasised the importance of staff training, and of motivating and rewarding staff for creativity, versatility and mobility. It was vital to avoid the politicisation of the Secretariat, to resist pressures that favour a few at the expense of the majority, and to give proper recognition to the many – including women – who may have been ignored in the past.

A year later, in September 1993, Secretary-General Boutros-Ghali declared that the Secretariat would continue 'to address the challenge of strengthening of the Organization's ability to manage the 29 peace-keeping and other field missions', noting that the continuing effort during the coming year would involve 'enhancing planning activities through greater coordination among departments, improving budgetary planning and financial operations, invigorating structures for audit, investigation and programme evaluation, introducing a comprehensive staffing plan and ensuring the security and safety of staff in the field'.[24] The 'restructuring and streamlining' would continue, supported by the creation in August 1993 of the new post of Assistant Secretary-General for Inspections and Investigations intended to complement the Under-Secretary-General for Administration and Management. The core of the management strategy, according to Boutros-Ghali, was to achieve 'a more rational distribution of responsibilities' between the New York headquarters and the UN centres at Geneva, Nairobi and Vienna, as well as among the many field, regional and global structures. There would be 'clear lines of responsibility in a simpler structure, together with steps to eliminate duplication and over-lapping', which would 'greatly improve coordination'.[25] In August 1994 a German diplomat, Karl Paschke, was appointed head of the newly created Office of Internal Oversight designed to tackle mismanagement and waste.

The extent to which the reforms have achieved the radical restructuring necessary for the UN's performance of the international responsibilities can be debated. In one view the existing machinery for managing peace-keeping operations – perhaps the principal UN task – remains 'wholly inadequate to meet the present and future needs of the UN'.[26] Furthermore, much of the difficulty derives from persistent (and new) problems in the New York headquarters. For example, the increased complexity of UN missions over recent years has led to an increased number of institutional participants in the various planning and decision-making processes. Today important institutional actors include the Department of Peacekeeping Operations (DPKO), the Field Operations Division (FOD), and the Department of Political Affairs (DPA). The Secretary-General nominally directs peacekeeping operations, subject to the whim of key Member States, but the DPKO has retained overall responsibility for the planning and execution of missions in the field. Any assigned task force typically includes DPKO personnel, representatives of the Secretary-General, technical staff from the FOD, personnel from the participating countries, representatives from the Office of Human Resources Management (within the Department of Administration and Management), and representatives of relevant specialised agencies.[27] There are further staffing and operational complexities within each of these participating groups. Such convoluted arrangements are not helped by what is widely perceived to be the extremely poor level of internal communication within the Secretariat.[28]

In such circumstances it is hard to imagine that current reforms to the structure and operation of the UN headquarters, as outlined by Boutros-Ghali,[29] have achieved – or will significantly contribute to – the drastic reforms that seem essential. It seems that the measures to date may amount to little more than 'improving inter-departmental consultation' with the aim of facilitating 'integration across bureaucratic boundaries and political fiefdoms'.[30] This is scarcely a radical approach to the evident management problems that afflict both the UN headquarters and the active missions in the field. Again the United Nations – beset by under-resourcing and organisational complexities – depends upon the attitudes of the Member States. They contribute staff to the Secretariat and are in a position to block significant organisational change. This circumstance has impacted also on Boutros-Ghali's efforts to introduce financial reforms into the UN organisation.

Financial Control

Secretary-General Javier Perez de Cuellar, during his term of office (1982–1992), repeatedly drew attention to the funding difficulties of the United Nations organisation. During the forty-sixth session of the General Assembly he made a number of proposals which his successor, Boutros Boutros-Ghali, was quick to endorse. *Proposal One* suggested a number of cash measures to deal both with the inadequate working capital reserves of the organisation and with the high level of unpaid contributions:

- charging interest on the amounts of assessed contributions that are not paid on time;

- suspending certain financial regulations of the United Nations to permit the retention of budgetary surpluses;

- increasing the Working Capital Fund to a level of $250 million and endorsing the principle that the level of the Fund should be approximately 25 per cent of the annual assessment under the regular budget;

- establishment of a temporary Peacekeeping Reserve Fund, at a level of $50 million, to meet initial expenses of peacekeeping operations pending receipt of assessed contributions;

- authorisation to the Secretary-General to borrow commercially, should other sources of cash be inadequate.

Proposal Two, since implemented, suggested the creation of a Humanitarian Revolving Fund of around $50 million, to be used in emergency humanitarian situations. *Proposal Three* suggested the creation of a

UN Peace Endowment Fund, in the order of $1 billion derived from both assessed and voluntary contributions, to provide investment proceeds to finance peacekeeping and other related operations.

Later suggestions, recorded by Boutros-Ghali,[31] included: a levy on arms sales that could be linked to a UN Arms Register; a levy on international air travel, itself dependent on peace; authorisation for the UN to borrow from the IMF and the World Bank; tax exemptions for contributions made to the UN by foundations, companies and individuals; and changes to the formula for assessing peacekeeping contributions. It was already clear in 1992 that the financial position of the United Nations was growing weaker day-by-day, 'debilitating its political will and practical capacity to undertake new and essential activities'.[32] Faced with this predicament, Boutros-Ghali urged the creation of the $50 million Peacekeeping Reserve Fund, an agreement that one third of the estimated cost of each new peacekeeping operation be appropriated by the General Assembly as soon as the Security Council authorises action, and authorisation for the Secretary-General in exceptional circumstances to place contracts without competitive bidding. At the same time 'the question of assuring financial security to the Organization over the long term is of such importance and complexity that public awareness and support must be heightened'.[33]

The drafters of the UN Charter had attempted to encourage Member States to make prompt payment of the assessed contributions by stipulating (Article 19) that a member would not be allowed to vote in the General Assembly if substantially in arrears (though a 'get-out' provision was included). In 1992 the General Assembly tried to strengthen this stipulation by passing Resolution 41/213, calling for prompt payment in full. But members able to ignore Article 19 were equally able to ignore 41/213. Boutros-Ghali noted that in September 1992 only 52 Member States had paid in full their dues to the regular budget, with the total unpaid contributions to the peacekeeping budget at that time amounting to $844.4 million. In August 1992 it was only possible to pay regular UN staff their salaries by borrowing from peacekeeping funds where cash was available. Boutros-Ghali commented that 'perennial shortages, the absence of reserves and a debilitating uncertainty over the immediate future are the main characteristics of the financial situation of the United Nations'.[34] This situation did not change in 1993. Boutros-Ghali recorded that as of 26 August 1993 only seven Member States had paid their assessed contributions in full.[35] Despite this shortfall he recommended 'a modest growth of 1 per cent in the level of resources' (as shown in the proposed programme budget for the biennium 1994–1995), mainly for preventive diplomacy, peace operations, peace-building, human rights, and the co-ordination of humanitarian assistance. At the same time, having sent urgent appeals to Security Council members and Member States with outstanding contributions (see 'The Funding Question', above), Boutros-Ghali took emergency economy measures that curtailed the services to the Security Council, the General Assembly, and the associated committees and subsidiary bodies.

The funding problem remained unresolved. At the request of the Secretary-General, the Ford Foundation convened an advisory group of experts to examine the financing of the United Nations, with the aim of creating a secure financial base over the long term. After three meetings between September 1992 and January 1993, the group issued a report, 'Financing an Effective United Nations', in February 1993. Boutros-Ghali made the report available to the Member States and to the General Assembly for consideration. No radical transformation in the UN's parlous financial circumstances was anticipated. Reporting in September 1993, Boutros-Ghali observed that in spite of the unfavourable financial circumstances, 'indeed partly because of the strained cash situation, the Administration has pursued its efforts to enhance its productivity'.[36]

MANAGING THE COMMITMENTS

The management of the peacekeeping missions in the field is often beset by the same problems that can be found in the Secretariat: inadequate powers of discipline and control, insufficient information, poor levels of communication. The growth in the number of 'multicomponent' missions, where military and civilian operations are juxtaposed, have resulted – as in Cambodia, Angola, Bosnia and Somalia – 'in major command, control and coordination problems for which neither contingency planning nor doctrinal guidance presently exists'.[37] One particular problem is that the UN lacks any capacity to gather and process information, whether derived from trained staff on the ground or from satellite systems. Again the Member States have an interest in preventing the UN from acquiring such a capacity. Individual states run their own intelligence networks and are keen to filter the information supplied to the international body. If the United Nations were to evolve an independent intelligence facility, its dependence on the Member States in this regard would diminish, so leading to a loss of national sovereignty. This may be seen as good for the international community but disturbing for powerful Member States. It is useful to mention some of the mission failures that more timely information might have helped to prevent, but which probably required extra resourcing, greater commitment and less political interference by interested powerful states.

A UN mission to East Timor, suffering under the cruel Indonesian occupation, yielded a report that defended the Timorese right to self-determination but was given no attention by the Security Council. The United States and Britain had supported the Indonesian aggression and – with an eye on trade and the prospect of oil in the Timor Sea – continue to tolerate the grossest abuses of human rights. In The Hague an annual $4 billion is allocated – mainly at the behest of the West – to support Indonesian development, which feeds through into increased repression and enhanced trade prospects to Western advantage. In such circumstances any UN mission intended to secure justice for a tormented people is doomed to failure.

In Western Sahara UN efforts to broker elections were constantly frustrated by inadequate resources on the ground, by inadequate information, and by Western hostility to the Polisario Front independence movement. Again US support for Morocco as a strategic ally in Africa served to block UN efforts to resolve the conflict. At the same time there was evidence of corruption among UN officials keen to aid the illegal Moroccan occupation (see below). In Angola the West's tolerance of the rebel Jonas Savimbi led to a protracted civil war that in late 1993 was claiming a thousand lives a day – and this despite a prodigious UN effort to organise elections and to oversee the intended peace. Here much of the trouble derived from Washington's historical support for Savimbi's National Union for the Total Independence of Angola (UNITA) against the ruling (initially) Marxist government of the Popular Movement for the Liberation of Angola (MPLA); but also from the UN's relative impotence in struggling to cajole the two sides. A senior UN official declared: 'There is a growing consensus that if the United Nations decides to participate in peace and electoral processes, then it must have far greater control, and the West must be prepared to pay for it.' Many Angolans, continuing to suffer through 1993 and on into 1994, mistakenly believed that the UN Angola Verification Mission (UNAVEM) had the power to intervene in the civil war, and so blamed the United Nations for the enduring conflict.[38] In October 1993 Manuel Aranda da Silva, head of UN emergency coordination in Angola, commented: 'If there is no resumption of heavy fighting, we will be able to stabilise the humanitarian crisis in Angola in three months. But we need time and we need more funding.'[39] By now, after months of procrastination, the UN Security Council had banned the supply of arms and fuel to UNITA; but now the casualties were numbered in the hundreds of thousands and three million Angolans were in danger of starving to death. At the same time there were growing signs that Mozambique was about to slide into a new civil war. Elections, originally planned for October 1993, had been abandoned because of the UN's slow progress: the operation had been 'difficult and complex', and had been hindered by unforeseen delays, observed a UN spokesman. It was now hoped that the planned elections would be held in May 1994.

The United Nations seemed equally impotent to arrest the Armenian–Azeri conflict, with Armenian forces through late-1993 and beyond to ignore a Security Council demand for their withdrawal from Azerbaijan. Similarly, the UN seemed powerless to intervene in the mounting crisis in the former Soviet republic of Georgia, with the Security Council reluctant to comment on the fiasco of its grossly under-resourced peacekeeping effort. Brigadier-General John Hvidegaard, the head of the UN military observer mission in the rebel region of Abkhazia, had made it clear that human-rights abuses were being committed against the Georgian population; but the United Nations seemed incapable of effective action in Russia's 'backyard'.[40]

Mounting UN casualties through 1993 – in such areas as Somalia, Bosnia, Angola and Afghanistan – also suggested under-resourcing, inadequate logistical support, and a far from comprehensive insight into many conflicts. In Sudan the UN-linked World Food Programme (WFP) unaccountably delayed aid shipments, with no reasons given and at least one UN official reluctant to talk to the press.[41] At the same time Secretary-General Boutros-Ghali seemed intent on keeping the United Nations out of the mounting problems of Liberia. Here Charles Taylor, the leader of the National Patriotic Front of Liberia (NPFL), complained that elements of the West African peacekeeping force (ECOMOG), supported by the UN and Washington, had been bombing civilian targets in Liberia. On 25 March 1993 there was confirmation that Nigerian aircraft from ECOMOG had used cluster bombs to attack hospitals and homes, and that the Nigerian navy had shelled civilian areas from the sea. In a report to the Security Council Boutros-Ghali acknowledged a 'general consensus . . . that the United Nations should assume a larger role in the search for peace in Liberia' – where four years of war had produced some 150,000 deaths – but insisted that the problem was a regional matter best solved by the neighbouring states.[42] It has also been suggested that hundreds of Liberians might have died from hunger and disease because the UN prevented emergency food aid entering the country, a decision taken on 30 July by Trevor Gordon-Somers, the UN Special Representative for

Liberia, and described by the Red Cross in Geneva as a 'grave violation of international humanitarian law'. Richard Dowden, the Africa Editor of *The Independent* (London), commented:

> Despite furious protests from the aid agencies working in the country, the border is still closed, leaving hundreds of thousands of people vulnerable to starvation. The incident follows a string of UN failures in Africa but in most cases they have resulted from UN inaction or delay. This is the first time that the UN has actively caused hunger.[43]

A spokesman for the aid agency Médecins Sans Frontières (MSF) was quoted: 'We have 800 tons of supplies at the border and children are starving . . . It's UN bureaucracy.' The widespread feeling that Gordon-Somers should be dismissed was ignored.

The situation in Somalia continued to deteriorate through 1993 with mounting confusion about US strategy, the UN role, and the relationship between the two. It was now clear that Washington was following one agenda, the UN Secretary-General desperately struggling to preserve another. The relatively small number of American casualties had brought panic to certain elements of the US Congress, and Clinton was being urged to order an early withdrawal of American forces. Boutros-Ghali, in a letter to US Secretary of State Warren Christopher, warned that a withdrawal 'would condemn the people of Somalia to a resumption of civil war and all the horrors that would result'. In the event President Clinton decided to send in reinforcements but with the promise that there would be a withdrawal of American troops by 31 March 1994. Washington's Somalia experience had severely dented American confidence, seemingly rendering future US military involvements less likely. Said US Defence Secretary Les Aspin: 'We are trying to understand how to do this [organise military interventions] in the new world and do it better. This is a controversial subject today. In fact the current mood in the nation would indicate that we'll be less likely to be doing these missions, rather than more likely.'

The Clinton decision to maintain a lead role in Somalia – sidelining the UN in the process – had only served to compound Washington's problems. There had been setbacks over Bosnia, with undisguised tensions between the Clinton administration and the US's nominal European allies, and the fiasco over Haiti was bringing fresh humiliation. Clinton responded by purging a number of foreign-policy advisors, a strategy that was bound to impact on US – UN relations. For example, the retired US Admiral Jonathan Howe, the UN Special Envoy in Somalia, had been forced on the UN by Washington – which made it difficult for the US to demand that Boutros-Ghali sack him.[44] Here, for once, it was hard to scapegoat the United Nations for errors made by key staff seconded by a powerful Member State. At the same time UN impotence had been demonstrated yet again: many of Washington's blundering mistakes in Somalia had been painfully predictable, and the United Nations – which had provided legal justification for the entire intervention – had been powerless to prevent them.

In virtually all its active missions the United Nations has been beset by under-resourcing, uncertain objectives, inadequate management strategies, and the hostility or indifference of powerful Member States. This has meant that UN decisions have often been tardy, inconclusive and insufficiently rooted in practical possibilities. The United Nations has often been exposed as impotent, unable to follow through its own resolutions, and with a tendency to procrastinate, keen to delay (or even block) discussions that are likely to demand action. In late 1993 there was evidence of a resurgence of death-squad activity in El Salvador, despite the protracted UN commitment to a lasting peace settlement and the unambiguous recommendations of the UN 'Truth Commission'.[45] The situation was unhappily symbolic of the wider UN malaise: the United Nations had no power to address fundamental human-rights abuses in a small country whose government had manifestly failed to observe clear UN demands. Here a key factor was that the Reagan and Bush administrations had been prepared to underwrite death-squad activities through the 1980s, by maintaining a public silence about atrocities and surreptitious funds and training.[46] Thus the strategic policies of a powerful Member State ran consistently against both the spirit and the letter of the UN Charter, a circumstance that today still casts a baleful shadow over all reform efforts in El Salvador. This particular case illustrates a general condition: the United Nations is largely impotent in confrontation with powerful vested interest. This is a fundamental management problem that the United Nations has yet to address.

THE QUESTION OF JUDGEMENT

Many of the UN's failures suggest the widespread prevalence of bad judgement. Was it sensible to undertake this or that commitment? Was it likely that the intended objectives would be achieved within acceptable time limits? Was this or that particular initiative thought through? Was there adequate contingent planning? How was the overall situation evaluated? How were allowances made for the impact of this or that decision on other UN commitments? What steps were taken to ensure that the important decision makers were well informed?

There is often the impression that UN officials and troops are inadequately prepared for their tasks, poorly trained and ill-equipped for adaptation to alien cultures. UN troops have sometimes displayed racist prejudice, an ignorance of local political structure, a hostility to foreign cultural patterns. Such details suggest that the United Nations is not adept at collecting and disseminating information that is essential to the achievement of its goals; and that the shortcoming exists at all levels of the hierarchy. Because of opposition from Member States, primarily Washington, the UN has been reluctant to develop systems for the collection, processing and dissemination of information: intelligence matters, say the Member States, are best left to us. However, it is difficult to see how decision makers can exercise good judgement, and UN personnel at other levels be adequately trained, in the absence of modern provisions for systematic information handling.

The decision to launch a peacekeeping mission, and the techniques required to manage it effectively, depend upon good information.It may be necessary to exploit local human intelligence sources and to access satellite systems. As one example, the lack of independent means of verifying information supplied by the various factions in Bosnia has often prevented UN forces from carrying out their tasks. In such an environment the absence of an intelligence capacity may threaten the lives of UN personnel.[47] Many UN casualties have been caused through intelligence failures.

A shortage of relevant information obviously helps to explain what can be seen with hindsight to have been poorly judged UN involvement and poorly executed missions. Would the UN initiatives in Western Sahara have been conducted differently had it been known that the King of Morocco was to launch a referendum in September 1992, which had the effect of undermining UN efforts to secure its own referendum? Would the UN High Commissioner for Refugees (UNHCR) have seemed quite so complacent about the numbers of Azeri refugees if there had been more information about the scale of the exodus? Would the abortive UN initiative in Georgia have been conducted differently if more attention had been given to Russia's attitude to 'its own turf'? And would the UN intervention in Somalia have been quite so clumsy if there had been more information available on the Somali clan structure and the logistical position of the various contending factions?

What thought went into the UN posture on Haiti? Was it thought likely in October 1993 that a 'mob' ('thugs') would prevent a UN peacekeeping mission from landing on the island? What contingency plans were in hand to prevent the humiliation that might arise from such an event? How did the UN assessment differ from that of the Clinton administration? And did Secretary-General Boutros-Ghali have access to information that suggested that such a *débâcle* was likely? Did he know that the CIA had made payments to key members of the Haitian military from the mid-1980s until the 1991 coup that toppled Father Aristide?[48] To what extent did this information, or the lack of it, affect the development of UN policy? Where was the crucial information shortfall that made the UN initiative on Haiti so poorly judged?

The question of judgement is central to any UN operation; and it depends crucially on timely and comprehensive information. Ideally, the information should be independently collected and independently assessed, while care should be taken in the analysis of information readily supplied from interested sources. It is a commonplace truism that we live in the Information Age. It is essential that the United Nations take steps to develop its own independent information culture.

A CORRUPT UN?

No-one doubts that there is corruption throughout the United Nations organisation, as there is in any large institution or group, but there is debate about its extent and its significance. It is inevitable that there has always been a degree of UN corruption: it did not begin in the post-Soviet world order. Conor Cruise O'Brien describes how, as UN Representative in Katanga, he was approached in April 1961 by his cook, Ngoye, inviting his participation in illicit currency exchanges. O'Brien records that he was 'senior enough, and cautious enough, not to be drawn by that one', but recognises that, had he been a young subaltern, there would have been temptation.[49] He points out that the UN characteristically operates in anarchic conditions, in turbulent countries where 'the cleverest and most successful racketeers will seek UN co-operation and UN cover . . . what is complacently called "humanitarian peace-keeping" seems particularly liable to such forms of military, political and economic gangrene'.[50] In such a context there are many pressures working to corrupt UN troops and UN officials, particularly in circumstances where national governments (for example, the Clinton administration) urge their staff under nominal UN supervision to ignore UN orders which they find 'illegal' or 'militarily imprudent'. Again the jealous protection of Member State sovereignty is necessarily subversive of UN discipline.

Sometimes UN personnel (officials and/or troops) unwisely take sides in a conflict that has invited UN involvement. Thus UN officials sympathetic to the Moroccan case over the West Sahara dispute indulged in a range of questionable practices that, no doubt coincidentally, reflected Great Power interests in the region. Confidential computer diskettes giving information about the Polisario guerrilla movement were supplied to the Moroccan authorities, fuelling suspicions that this intelligence would be used in elections and to aid the Moroccan military campaign. Senior UN officials were thought to have altered the terms of the proposed referendum in order to put Polisario at a disadvantage, and evidence emerged of links between a key UN negotiator and the Moroccan Royal Palace. *The Independent* (London) obtained copies of internal UN documents expressing concern about official UN collaboration with Morocco.[51] A diplomat aware of allegations of UN misconduct commented: 'This is potentially a serious failure in a major UN peacekeeping operation and it must cast a shadow over the reputation of the Secretary-General [Javier Perez de Cuellar] as he leaves office.'

Such matters heralded partisan UN attitudes in such involvements as Cambodia, Somalia and Haiti; with frequent accompanying charges of financial or other forms of corruption. Russian troops assigned to the UN force in Bosnia were widely accused of black marketeering, defying UN orders, skimming UN funds and illicitly colluding with Serbian military factions. Other UN soldiers accused the Russians of carousing with the Serbs, failing to follow UN orders to disarm them, and ignoring their atrocities. Russian generals were despatched from Moscow to investigate, after which two senior officers were sent home. The United Nations wanted to keep the issue quiet but many UN officials and non-Russian troops were prepared to speak anonymously.[52] The Russians, reportedly shunned by other UN personnel, ignored a direct order by General Satish Nambiar, the UN commander in Croatia, to move their base from Erdut to Vukovar (a Belgian soldier commented: 'If we had ignored that we would have been court-martialled'); were suspected of selling UN supplies, including petrol, on the black market; and – as with the Mercedes car driven around by Colonel Viktor Loginov – accepted gifts from the Serbs. The UN seemed impotent to exercise prompt and effective discipline in such matters.

It was now being suggested that problems in the management of UN peacekeeping missions derived in part from a deep malaise that ran through the entire UN organisation. A major report by the 'Insight' team of *The Sunday Times* (London) catalogued wide-ranging examples of UN corruption and mismanagement, many at the heart of the New York headquarters.[53] The report highlights:

The staging of the International Decade for Natural Disaster Reduction (IDNDR), dubbed the 'disaster decade' by critics who complained of waste, mismanagement and inefficiency;

Staff – at least 15 professionals and 24 general service employees – retained on full salary without having proper jobs. Such 'supernumeraries' (one, Neelan Merani, has a salary of £100,000 p.a.) cost the UN an annual £2m;

An American report to a UN financial committee in 1991 expressing concern over 'the seriousness and number of cases of fraud and presumptive fraud' in the Office of the UN High Commissioner for Refugees (UNHCR): 'Large amounts have been embezzled by UNHCR staff';

The case of Jean-Pierre Hocke, accused of using £300,000 from a UN fund for entertainment and first-class air travel for himself and his wife. On one occasion he ordered the destruction of 138,000 copies of the UNHCR magazine because a critical article on Germany might have spoiled his forthcoming visit to that country;

The case of Singa-Vele Lukika, the former UNHCR special representative to Uganda and Djibouti, forced to resign in 1991 after financial abuses were discovered in his office;

The investigation of Romani Urasa, head of the UNHCR supply and transport division, who had established links with the entrepreneur Mohamed Adel Gawish, a connection later admitted by Urasa to have been an 'error of judgement';

Salaries and payoffs at the top of the UN organisation now outstripping those in many multinational corporations. A former UN assistant secretary, Alan Keyes, declared: 'we lived rich by day *and* lived rich by night.'

The practice of 'double dipping' whereby UN officials who have retired on generous pensions are re-employed on a consultancy basis. One 'double dipper', Virendra Dayal, an Under-Secretary-General at the New York headquarters, was given a £300,000 payoff; and was then given £30,000 to write a report;

The report on mismanagement produced by Dick Thornburgh (see 'Managing the System', above) at the request of Secretary-General Boutros-Ghali but then 'suppressed'. Thornburgh: 'Remaining copies were confiscated and in some cases shredded. This is the kind of shoot-the messenger mentality that inhabits the upper levels . . .'.

A response from the United Nations Information Centre in London stated that the *Sunday Times* 'Insight' report 'presented a false and misleading account of what the United Nations is and how it works, and contained more than 30 factual errors'.[54] It was emphasised, for example, that Mr Urasa had been cleared and that there was no justification for the slur on the name of Sir Brian Urquhart (various comments on the 'absurdity' of the report', its 'half-truths, distortion and plain fabrication').

In August 1993, under pressure from Washington, the United Nations appointed Mohamed Aly Niazi, an Egyptian accountant, to investigate charges of corruption in the organisation (the *Sunday Times* 'Insight' team claimed to have influenced the appointment). Niazi himself declared that he would target corrupt officials and incompetent managers, tackle red tape and bureaucracy, and introduce new auditing procedures to streamline the organisation: 'I will be looking at everything. Nobody is going to be above scrutiny. If you mention ten cases I will be looking at all ten. Rest assured, I will leave no stone unturned . . . The Secretary-General is fed up with seeing reports on paper and things not being done. His instructions are very clear. He doesn't want any fooling around. He wants facts.' Some observers were sceptical (Keyes: 'I just hope that Niazi will be able to overcome some of the obstacles and roadblocks that are usually put in the way of efforts like this').[55]

On 21 July 1993 the United Nations suspended eight staff members who had been handling UN contracts in Cambodia with unspecified private contractors. At the same time the Skylink company, a Toronto-based firm that operates helicopters for the UN, was complaining the the United Nations was 90 days in arrears with its payments. The UN denied any link between the problems with Skylink and the dubious handling of some UN contracts. A statement from the office of the Secretary-General declared that following 'a number of concerns on the handling of some contracts, a number of staff members have been suspended with pay in order to enable them to provide written explanations of their involvement in these contracts'. Other reports suggested widespread corruption among UN officials.

A senior British officer who had served in Cambodia spoke of corruption being 'widespread and institutionalised by the UN itself'.[56] The British Army had paid for his air travel to Cambodia but when he arrived UN officials invited him to fill in a form to recoup the cost of the ticket 'to keep for myself, if I wanted'. When, at the end of his term of duty, he returned his motorbike to the UN compound UN officials were surprised ('why didn't I keep it, or sell it to some local Cambodians'). The officer noted that about 50 Toyota Land Cruisers, brought by the UN and valued at around £1 million, had gone missing, and nobody was concerned

('There was no accounting or accountability'). Similarly, other equipment – including computers and generators – also went missing, whereupon fresh items would be ordered via the New York headquarters. Staff were also encouraged to lie about where they spent their leave, in order to claim allowances ('the figures got astronomical'). UN helicopters were used by senior officers for their own personnel requirements, preventing their use on proper UN business, and extended lunchtimes at headquarters meant 'you couldn't raise anyone, however serious the problem'.[57]

Other reports suggested that the UN mission in Phnom Penh had lost millions of dollars-worth of assets to thieves, mostly in a three-month period since the Cambodian election. Yasushi Akashi, the UNTAC chief, warned that the losses would be deducted from the package of equipment that the United Nations would leave behind on its departure at the end of 1993.[58] At the same time there were reports that corruption amongst UN personnel in Croatia and around Sarajevo was continuing, with one Ukrainian battalion in Sarajevo unable to respond quickly to emergencies because their UN-issued fuel had been sold to civilians.[59] UN troops in Bosnia were said to be 'out of control', indulging in widespread racketeering – in cigarettes, alcohol, food, prostitution and heroin – to make 'themselves and the Sarajevo mafia rich'.[60] The Sarajevo mafia was reported to be running its Mercedes and Nissan saloon cars on petrol siphoned from UN vehicles by UN troops and sold at £20 a gallon; the mafia was then trebling the price to sell UN-supplied petrol on the streets of Sarajevo at £60 a gallon: 'it is mainly the French and the Ukrainians who do the business. The Egyptians operate on a small scale.' The trade was reported as extending over fuel, wine, cars, Coca-Cola, gold, women and heroin (a detected 300-gram consignment of heroin hidden in white UN vehicles for smuggling into Sarajevo). A senior officer in the Sarajevo police force stated: 'Since the UN came in August 1991, the amount of drugs on the market has been growing. We have information from inside the organisation that drugs are brought in to Sarajevo on supply convoys.'[61]

In August 1993 a military team was summoned to Sarajevo to investigate UN soldiers suspected of trading in food, cigarettes, alcohol and women. A senior Sarajevo police officer expressed his concern about the scale of war profiteering by UN personnel prepared to accept gold jewellery in exchange for UN-supplied goods and to pay local women to have sex with them in UN trucks. Nearly two dozen UN soldiers (19 Ukrainians and three French) had been sent home but few observers thought that this would do anything to dent the scale of the racketeering. A UN officer describes the United Nations organisation as 'the most corrupt I ever worked for; everybody is on the take'.[62] There were doubts that the investigation would get to the root of the problem: the French UN commander, General Jean Cot, had instructed a French officer to conduct the enquiry, and some senior UN figures had urged the need for an independent enquiry.

Some suggested that corruption was inevitable in a war situation and the issues should be kept in proportion. Sylvana Fox, a spokeswoman for UNHCR, suggested that people should not be 'too suprised that out of 14,000 pimply 18-year-olds a bunch of them should get up to naughty tricks'; and the English historian Norman Stone remarked that 'most armies have gone in for corruption and stealing on an often remarkable scale: the opportunities are simply too vast, given scarcities and the absence of legal machinery'. At the same time it was hard to disguise the gravity of the UN plight. With reports that Italian troops were paying out money to Somali factions to avoid confrontation (a new protection racket), that UN officials in Cambodia were professionally committed to dishonest accounting, and that UN soldiers in Bosnia were defrauding the United Nations of vast sums, it was difficult to pretend that the patterns of management in the UN were not seriously awry.

In November 1993 Melissa Wells, Under-Secretary in Charge of Management at the United Nations, agreed in interview with Mike Wallace ('Sixty Minutes', CBS) that there were serious problems in UN management and administration, that some of the criticisms were well founded, and that there were on-going (but confidential) investigations into many issues involving corruption and mismanagement. There were hints in this report of bizarre UN practices; of phantom payrolls involving imaginary staff, of inadequate auditing procedures, of hidden layers of serious mismanagement, and of a pervasive reluctance to discipline corrupt and incompetent staff.

The appointment in August 1994 of Karl Paschke as head of the UN Office of Internal Oversight was intended to achieve various objectives. By combating mismanagement and waste in both the Secretariat and far-flung field offices it was hoped that the appointment, largely an American initiative, would make it easier for Washington to pay its debts to the UN.

ABUSING HUMAN RIGHTS

There is now accumulating evidence that UN personnel in the field have often been guilty of human-rights abuses, sometimes reaching the level of atrocity. As with corruption, many types of abuse are unavoidable in a war situation, though commanders and administrators should always be expected to minimise the incidence of such dereliction. Again the occurrence of abuse can be regarded as a management problem, to be addressed by appropriate training, by creating the appropriate operational culture, by close monitoring of field activities, and by the transparent willingness of commanders to exercise appropriate discipline.

The problem has not been helped by the relatively poor state of communications in UN field missions. There has often been a lack of standardised communication equipment, a failure to develop common communications procedures, and a shortage of suitable training for field missions in an alien environment. Such difficulties are necessarily compounded in multinational military involvements: communication between the various factions may be difficult and commanders may have an interest in shielding their own troops from criticism from other units. In Cambodia, for example, several UN contingents had no knowledge of either English or French, so causing major communications problems within the UNTAC organisation (31 nations provided personnel for UNTAC, while there were 29 participating states in the Somalia intervention). But if troops are to be adequately commanded in the field it is obvious that communications should be prompt and effective.

Some types of behaviour that may signal dereliction may not amount to human-rights abuses; much less to atrocity. The use of willing prostitutes, for example, may or may not amount to abuse; but the use of children and captive women clearly does. It is alarming to find that UN personnel have been involved in all such activities. We have already indicated the Bosnian women selling sex in UN trucks, and such trade seems to be common wherever there is a large influx of foreign troops. When 20,000 UN troops arrived in Phnom Penh in 1992 there was a sudden and dramatic increase in the number of prostitutes. The girls soon realised that 'a few nights with an "Untac"' would 'keep them in rice for a year'.[63] A number of aid agencies, alarmed at the spread of disease, raised the matter with the UNTAC head Yasushi Akashi, who reportedly commented: 'I am not a puritan. Eighteen-year-old hot-blooded soldiers who come in from the field after working hard should be able to chase after young, beautiful things of the opposite sex.'[64] After a letter of protest by aid workers, an official UNTAC directive stated that UN personnel should not travel to 'areas of not very good repute' in official vehicles; nor should they wear their uniforms when patronising such places.

In late 1992 there were widespread complaints in Cambodia that the UN troops had corrupted the morals of the country, stolen its women, and spread venereal diseases (including AIDS) at an alarming rate. The World

Health Organisation (WHO) reported that 75 per cent of people giving blood in Phnom Penh were now infected with HIV; and one survey showed that a quarter of the soldiers of a French battalion tested positive for the AIDS virus when they completed their six-month tour of duty. The Khmer Rouge denounced the French for being 'too busy with prostitutes to check on the presence of Vietnamese soldiers' – a charge which led Colonel Elrich Irastorza, the commander of a French paratroop battalion, to close down a shanty-town brothel outside his camp. At the same time there were many complaints of sexual harassment of Cambodian women by UN personnel.[65]

There was also mounting evidence that the dramatic influx of UN troops into Cambodia* had caused an explosion in child prostitution.[66] According to Defence for the Child International, a Danish-based human-rights group sponsored by the UN Children's Fund (UNICEF), the number of women and children involved in prostitution in Phnom Penh rose between December 1991 and May 1993 from 6000 to 20,000, with more than 3000 UN soldiers catching sexually transmitted diseases in the same period: 'Today Cambodia is facing a wave of prostitution, in a similar fashion to that which happened in Saigon and in Bangkok after the Vietnam war. But this time AIDS is a new dimension of the problem.' The author of the DCI report, the Danish clinical psychologist Eva Arnvig, claims that UN soldiers were not tested for AIDS before they took up their posts, with the result that HIV infection quickly spread throughout Cambodia's brothels. The fear of AIDS, Arnvig claims, led to a rapid increase in the number of young girls being recruited to serve the UN personnel; within a week of her recruitment, however, the price of sex with a young girl had fallen from $400 to $15 as HIV infection became more likely.[67]

Reports from Bosnia suggested that captive Croat and Muslim women held in brothels near Sarajevo were being visited by UN personnel, with women forced against their will into UN vehicles. The Bosnian government had talked to witnesses, and the United Nations was said to be investigating the matter 'very actively'.[68] In Somalia there were signs that the use by UN personnel of local women was increasing the tensions in Mogadishu: a press photograph (*The Independent*, 27 August 1993) showed a mob confronting a Somali woman accused of consorting with UN soldiers.

---

* A letter from representatives of the Campaign to Oppose the Return of the Khmer Rouge (CORKR) pointed out that thanks largely to the legitimacy afforded them by the United Nations, the genocidal Khmer Rouge today control more territory than they did before the UN intervention (*The Guardian*, 14 November 1994).

There was also mounting controversy about the range of severe human-rights abuses by UN troops in Somalia. A report from African Rights, with co-directors Rakiya Omaar and Alex de Waal, catalogued a series of violations, some of them manifest atrocities.[69] Here – with details of abuses from Mogadishu, Kismayo and Belet Weyn – it is claimed that there is prima facie evidence 'that UNOSOM forces have committed a number of grave breaches of the Geneva Conventions', including the bombardment of a political meeting, an attack on a hospital, and firing on unarmed demonstrators. In addition:

> there are cases of killing of unarmed civilians, and forced relocation of Mogadishu residents by means of demolition of their homes. United States, Pakistani, Tunisian, Italian and other troops have been responsible. These are not cases of undisciplined actions by individual soldiers, but stem from the highest echelons of the command structure.[70]

Aerial bombardments carried out by UN forces in Mogadishu almost invariably took place at night, as a transparent terror tactic. In one attack on a house, claimed by UNOSOM to be harbouring a war council (according to Somali sources, a 'peace and reconciliation' meeting), several dozen deaths were caused (the UN at first admitted 13 deaths, later increased to 20, with the International Committee of the Red Cross ascertaining at least 54 fatalities). The dead included religious leaders, elders and intellectuals from various clans and a number of ordinary civilians, including women and children. No weapons were found in the house.

A number of other incidents are described and considered, including:

> The attack on 17 June 1993 by US, French and Moroccan forces on the Digfer hospital in the centre of Mogadishu, killing nine patients and other civilians;

> The firing, on 12 June by Pakistani troops, on a small civilian demonstration on the Afgoy road, close to the UN compound, killing two civilians and wounding others;

> The attack, on 13 June by Pakistani troops, on an unarmed crowd near to the Egyptian embassy, resulting in at least 20 fatalities;

> The arrest and detention of hundreds of civilians in 'preventive detention' without trial for periods up to 45 days;

> Frequent complaints by Somali civilians of abuse and harassment by UN troops, with reluctance to make official protest for fear of reprisals;

An unarmed man killed in Kismayo on 27 May;

Children thrown into the Juba river by Belgian UN soldiers;

Numerous reports of theft by UN personnel of money, commercial goods, documents, food and jewellery;

The killing and injury of Somali civilians, including children, by aggressive driving of UN vehicles (Belgian trucks breaking the leg of a 13-year-old boy, killing a 10-year-old girl);

The terrorising of Somali civilians (UN troops kicking a sick woman, breaking windows, blowing roofs off with explosives, demolishing houses, and so on).

The report concludes that there is no doubt that UN personnel have engaged in abuses of human rights, including 'killing of civilians, physical abuse, theft and irresponsible disposal of ordnance'. Moreover, 'unacceptable levels of racism' have been displayed; 'military actions by UNOSOM forces . . . have displayed a disregard for the basic humanitarian laws of warfare that can only emanate from the highest echelons of command'; these abuses 'are not isolated incidents . . . they are part of a consistent pattern that reaches to the senior command'. Underlying all the abuses '*is a lack of accountability which means that UNOSOM soldiers are able to commit violations with near-total impunity*' (my italics). The authors of the report judged that many of the problems derived 'from failures at the highest levels of the UN and US Government in planning the international intervention in Somalia, and in failing to take adequate initiatives for political reconciliation, disarmament and socio-economic reconstruction'. The evidence showed that these gross failures of UN/US management throughout the various organisational hierarchies had resulted in hundreds (perhaps thousands) of civilian casualties; massive impediments to the supply of aid, and the consequent discrediting of the entire UN initiative.

Many other reports have provided details that support the African Rights findings. Thus a German journalist witnessed a UN soldier from the United Arab Emirates (UAR) suddenly shoot a Somali youth in the head;[71] English journalists recorded how dozens of Somali civilians were being held without trial and denied other basic legal rights;[72] and a military investigation in Ottawa concluded that the Canadian army had sent an admittedly racist paratroops unit to carry out missions in Somalia.[73] In the same vein Amnesty International was driven to record that whereas the United Nations has taken many measures to secure the implementation of human-rights standards in many different contexts it is also true that 'UN forces have been accused of taking sides in an internal conflict [Somalia] and of direct responsibility for human-rights abuses'.[74] Here it is recognised that – as always – the ultimate responsibility lies with the Member States. When they are guided 'by narrow political and economic interests, these will be reflected in the decisions taken by the UN. The best human rights standards are meaningless if governments ignore them; the best human rights machinery is powerless if governments refuse to cooperate with it'.[75]

At the same time it is useful to emphasise the simple truism that UN officials – the permanent employees throughout the Secretariat and elsewhere – have unambiguous responsibilities. We have seen that Member States often see mileage in being able to scapegoat the United Nations. It is important that UN officials – at whatever level – do not seek to scapegoat the Member States to disguise their own failures.

5 The Problem of Representation

PREAMBLE

It may seem obvious that the United Nations organisation exists to serve the peoples of the world. The UN is not meant to make a profit for investors, nor to favour the strategic or commercial interests of this or that factional group: the Charter itself begins with the evocative words 'We the peoples . . .'. Yet it cannot be assumed that the characteristic behaviour of the United Nations necessarily contributes to the universal welfare of the global community,* or that the current structure of the United Nations organisation is well equipped to serve all the peoples of the world.

We need to consider the extent to which the collective democratic will of the Member States translates into UN policy and UN action. In fact it is easy to argue that the United Nations is far from being a truly democratic body, that its structure simply enshrines the Great Power relations that existed at the end of the Second World War. The UN was not established with the sole purpose of creating a world of peace and justice but mainly to consolidate the power of the victorious allies. Now the UN functions to sustain the power of the victors in the Cold War, an aim that cannot be assumed to benefit the majority of the Member States.

Today the central questions remain. In whose interest is UN power exercised? Does membership of the United Nations adequately translate into active influence? How, and to what extent, are 'we the peoples' served? Such questions suggest the importance of democracy, empowerment, the sovereign equality of Member States. Central to such matters is the problem of representation. How are Member States to be represented in the decision-making organs of the United Nations? In particular, on the powerful Security Council? More radically, would an entirely new UN structure more adequately serve the peoples of the world?

---

*In fact evidence is provided in this book to suggest that the United Nations and its associated bodies often work against the interest of many people (see Chapter 3 and 6).

PHILOSOPHIC HINTS

Since the end of the Cold War there has been much talk of 'democracy', 'freedom' and 'human rights', much of it serving as a smokescreen for the imposition of authoritarian free-market economies. With escalating crises in such regions as Somalia, Angola, Haiti, Burundi, the former Soviet Union and the former Yugoslavia, optimistic platitudes about a 'New World Order' quickly evaporated and complacent bourgeois philosophers were forced to admit that perhaps after all they were not witnessing the end of history. At the same time the new political environment stimulated and continues to stimulate fresh debate, much of it focused on the evolving role of the United Nations, about the age-old concept of democracy, about how the broad mass of the people might gain real political power, and about whether existing political and economic structures were best designed to benefit humanity as a whole. It is highly significant that in this debate many apologists were (and remain) available to sanctify the existing *realpolitik* structures and arrangements. The democratic ideal suggests the political equality of all the participants in the political process, just as Article 2(1) of the UN Charter protects the 'sovereign equality' of all Member States; but the realities of power politics often rise above the constraints of such a promiscuous egalitarianism. Thus most UN Member States should be denied possession of nuclear weapons, providing that powerful states retain theirs; the undemocratic and aggressive clients/proxies of Washington (Indonesia, Israel, Burma, Turkey, Saudi Arabia and so on) are protected from the demands of international law; while other states (North Korea, Iraq, Libya, Haiti, Cuba and so on), often undemocratic and aggressive but not more so, are judged in a different way. Such double (or multiple) standards suggest the post-Periclean disdain of Plato and Aristotle to the democratic form of government. Of all the political options only tyranny was worse than democracy, then reckoned to be 'a charming form of government, full of variety and disorder, and dispensing a sort of equality to equals and unequals alike' (Plato's *Republic*: Book VIII). And they suggest also the nineteenth-century Nietzschean notion that democracy, with the 'vulgar' rising over the 'noble', represents a perversion of the natural order of excellence.

It would be hard to avoid the conclusion that the United Nations organisation, as presently constructed and operated, embodies at best 'a sort of equality' and at worst a power structure that ensures that the 'vulgar' many are rendered permanently subservient to the 'noble' few. The political machinery of today's United Nations would probably have impressed Plato and Aristotle; it is likely that philosophers such as John Locke, Jean-

Jacques Rousseau and Tom Paine would have been less enthusiastic. The English philosopher John Locke (1632–1704) urged the creation of a 'supreme' legislative power elected by the people but itself bound by law; in a similar vein, Rousseau (1712–1778) proposed the equality of all people as both citizens and subjects of the state. Such approaches articulate or at least imply mechanisms whereby binding laws can be enacted to enshrine the popular will, so allowing the democratic many to prevent the despotism of the few. This principle contrasts well with the present operation of the United Nations where a Security Council of only fifteen members is empowered to enact mandatory resolutions, effective international laws, that are binding on the entire 185-strong UN membership.

There can be many impediments to the empowerment of the democratic majority. For example, it is highly significant that whereas the influence of such philosophers as Locke and Rousseau was intitutionalised in the Constitution of the United States, American democracy remained deeply flawed: there were property and other restrictions (often racial) on the franchise; and already all the elements of a plutocratic oligarchy – with all that this implied about nepotism and corruption – were in place.[1] Today well over one hundred countries have a constitution or social contract as their basis of government, though even where a constitution is nominally democratic there may well be a range of *de facto* and *de jure* mechanisms that facilitate the subversion of the democratic process. Many of the political structures of the United Nations are undemocratic and there are many factors in *realpolitik* that encourage the subversion of the democratic will: for example, we have seen (Chapter 3) that Washington can secure votes by bribery and threat.

For a political organisation to be truly democratic the participating players (individual or state members) must have equal rights under the constitution and broadly equivalent *de facto* power in the wider political environment (this latter to prevent illicit political influence through bribery or intimidation). Equal political rights for individual participants implies that the composition of the political assembly is broadly representative, a *sine qua non* of democracy. But where states themselves are the political players the situation is more problematic: for the simple reason that the states may not be democratic. An assembly that offers a consortium of dictatorships equal rights under a constitution may do little to protect human welfare, a circumstance that should be borne in mind when considering the democratic credentials of the UN organisation: a UN constitution that did no more than offer equal voting rights to Iraq, Syria, Thailand, China, Saudi Arabia and the like may have little to commend it.

If we are to be confident that the United Nations truly serves 'we the peoples' it is necessary to look beyond a charter that safeguards principally the rights of states as participating entities. And the problem is compounded by the fact that particular leaders may claim to be representative even in the absence of nominally democratic constitutions: there is a sense in which Adolf Hitler and Joseph Stalin were representative before, during and after World War Two; and in which Hafez Assad and Saddam Hussein are representative today. We cannot insist that majority electoral support within a democratic framework is a necessary condition for licit claims to representation: since, if so, the present governments in Britain and the United States would certainly not qualify.

It is significant that the European mediaeval basis of representation was similar to the one that exists in today's United Nations organisation. The mediaeval view was that the 'people' were not individual political actors but groups focused around status and occupation. Thus the representative assemblies incorporated 'estates' set in a political hierarchy: in England, for example, the estates of peers, church and commoners, all supposedly representing different factional interests and correspondingly assigned different constitutional powers. Similarly, in the United Nations it is not individuals who are represented but states (just as Article 34(1) of the Statute of the International Court of Justice stipulates that 'only states may be parties in cases before the Court'). It was a principal aim of such radical groups as the seventeenth-century English Levellers, active during the English Civil War and the Commonwealth, nineteenth-century activists on behalf of 'The People's Charter' (the Chartists), and the twentieth-century suffragettes, to extend the base of political representation (though not necessarily in the direction of universal adult suffrage). It is important to remember that traditional liberal democracy did not always advocate the extension of voting rights to all citizens, irrespective of their circumstances and background (see 'Entitled to Vote?', below). Thus Thomas Jefferson emphasised the importance of an educated majority as a prerequisite for sound representative government.[2] The successive Reform Acts in nineteenth-century Britain progressively expanded the size of the electorate, at the same time working to equalise the size of the constituencies, to guarantee a secret ballot, to attack corrupt practices, and so on. Anxieties remained, however, about the likelihood that the unenlightened many might come to rise above the enlightened few.

It is of course possible that a majority in a representative assembly might act to tyrannise the minority: there is at least an element of this in most functional parliamentary systems. Thus Alexander Hamilton declared, during the debates in 1788 on the American constitution: 'Men love power . . . Give all power to the many, they will oppress the few. Give all power to the few, they will oppress the many. Both therefore ought to have power, that they may defend itself against the other.'[3] In the same spirit the English philosopher John Stuart Mill (1806–1873), worried about the majority, suggested that the vote should be limited to the literate and that certain types of people with superior qualities should have greater voting power than the rest. Mill acknowledged that no suffrage arrangement 'can be permanently satisfactory in which any person or class is peremptorily excluded; in which the electoral privilege is not open to all persons of full age who desire to obtain it'; but Mill is quick to declare 'certain exclusions' to his general principle: 'I regard it as wholly inadmissible that any person should participate in the suffrage without being able to read, write, and, I will add, perform the common operations of arithmetic.' It may also be desirable that people entitled to vote have 'some knowledge of the conformation of the earth, its natural and political divisions, the elements of general history, and of the history and institutions of their own country', but official efforts to determine whether intending voters had acquired such knowledge 'would lead to partiality, chicanery, and every type of fraud'. So, thought Mill, it would be enough to expect basically literate and numerate voters: in the presence of a registrar they would expected to 'copy a sentence from an English book, and perform a sum . . .'.[4] Perhaps also 'the assembly which votes the taxes, either general or local, should be elected exclusively by those who pay something towards the taxes imposed', since those 'who pay no taxes, disposing by their votes of other people's money, have every motive to be lavish and none to economise'.[5] So it is right, on this principle, that the United States, as the largest contributor to UN funds (even if usually in massive arrears), should have the loudest voice in the councils of the United Nations.

Alexis Charles Henri de Tocqueville (1805–1859), the French historian and political scientist, visited America in 1831 and on his return to Paris produced his seminal work, *La Démocratie en Amérique (Democracy in America)* in two substantial volumes (1835 and 1840). Here he recognised the democratic revolution that had transformed the 'body of society', and declared that in consequence a 'new science of politics is needed for a new world'. The work ranged over the political institutions and social character of America, with one of the main themes (also dominant in his *L'Ancien Régime*, 1856) what he perceives as the persistent danger of democratic tyranny: 'I am convinced that democratic nations are the most likely to fall under the yoke of centralized administration.' He regretted, for example, the abolition of France's ancient and varied provincial institutions. Democracies, de Tocqueville suggests, are liable to spiritual degradation, which governments must counter by setting suitable standards. He does not welcome certain aspects of American democracy: 'When I survey this countless multitude of human beings, shaped in each other's likeness . . . the sight of such universal uniformity saddens and chills me, and I am tempted to regret that state of society which has ceased to be'; but at the same time he is forced to concede that whereas a state of equality 'is perhaps less elevated . . . it is more just: and its justice constitutes its greatness and its beauty'.

There is no proposal in de Tocqueville that democracy be rolled back to return society to earlier modes of political organisation; he is an optimist, though prepared to warn of democratic hazards. However, some writers perceived the hazards as necessarily conclusive, to be avoided at all costs. Thus Walter Bagehot (1826–1877), the English lawyer and political philosopher, observed (in *The English Constitution*, 1867) that 'if you once permit the ignorant class to begin to rule, you may bid farewell to deference for ever . . . A democracy will never, save after an awful catastrophe, return what has once been conceded to it, for to do so would be to admit an inferiority in itself, of which, except by some almost unbearable misfortune, it could never be convinced'. De Tocqueville, Mill and Bagehot were all worried by the gradual encroachments of democracy, but their responses to the problem were different. In Bagehot, at odds with his relatively progressive contemporaries, there was evident regret that mediaeval political arrangements no longer fully obtained: from the mediaeval parliament 'the King learned, or had the means to learn, what the nation would endure, and what it would not endure'; but there was no enthusiasm for a political system in which the people as a whole would be empowered to bend their rulers to the democratic will.

All the various historians and political philosophers agree the need for political arrangements that include representative assembles; but there has always been disagreement about who or what should be represented. The Pericleans of Ancient Greece allowed men, but not women or slaves, into their representative assemblies; Plato and Aristotle urged the importance of political privileges for élitist groups with special qualities; mediaeval assemblies enshrined the representation of estates in the realm, just as nineteenth-century liberal democrats emphasised the political importance of property. Few democrats were *full* democrats, prepared to acknowledge the claims to representation made by all adults, even if propertyless, illiterate, female or of an ethnic minority. Few were prepared to embrace the words of the *Communist Manifesto* (1848): 'All previous historical movements were movements of minorities. The Proletarian movement is the self-conscious, independent movement of the immense majority, in the interests of the immense majority'; and to develop the representational forms – parliamentary, industrial and other – that this implied. Most democrats throughout history have displayed a primary interest in how representation should be restricted, as well as in how it should be expanded. Thus most democrats who are keen to applaud the United Nations are reluctant to countenance the thought of radical change: we may tinker with voting procedures, add a couple of permanent seats to the Security Council, urge a more prudent use of resources, but little more. There is little radical debate about how the patterns of representation in the United Nations might be reformed so that the international body could better serve the peoples of the world.

The United Nations culture remains rooted in various assumptions that have historical significance rather than modern justification. One of these is the familiar nineteenth-century idea that possession of property confers legitimate political privileges. Today the Security Council is often said to be unrepresentative because some *wealthy* states do not have permanent seats on the Security Council; and the only significant agitation for reform in this area focuses on the granting of seats to Germany and Japan (see 'A New Security Council?', below). We need to remember that attempts to justify representation rights on the basis of property belong to earlier forms of democracy that today should find little theoretical support. It is significant that any plutocratic influence on democratic processes is today generally regarded as *corruption* or *subversion*. This perception should be enlisted in efforts to refine the culture of the United Nations organisation.

ENTITLED TO VOTE?

There have always been pleas from the disenfranchised for an extension to the base of political representation, though reform has usually only come after protracted struggle. The claims are often seen with hindsight to have been transparent and compelling; even though at the time there were always powerful voices raised against any substantial change. For example, the cry of the American colonies, 'No taxation without representation!', is today seen as carrying a singular force. But less attention is given to its implicit assumption, one that was to be highly influential in the subsequent evolution of the franchise in America and elsewhere: that a taxed person had a greater claim to political representation than did someone not in a position to pay taxes. Thus the old colonial slogan, nominally democratic, was implicitly hostile to any egalitarian extension of the franchise: there were the *deserving* political participants and the rest. Such an approach helped to sustain the idea that 'superior' people – white, male, propertied, well-born, etc. – were entitled to the franchise while others were not. The principle bore particularly heavily on the lengthy struggle for women's suffrage.

Thus even the radical instincts of the English Levellers – led by John Lilburne (c. 1614–1657), Richard Overton (c. 1631–1664) and William Walwyn (1600–1680) – did not extend to the enfranchisement of women. The Levellers' important document *The Agreement of the People* (1647) was based on the principle that the consent of the governed was needed for government: a man could rule over others 'no further than by free consent, or agreement, by giving up their power to each other, for their better being'. The suggestion that *the franchise should be based on rights rather than on property* was radical for the day (and highly relevant today to the assessment of voting rights in the United Nations), but there was no thought here of women's suffrage and even the enfranchisement of men was not intended to be universal: male 'servants' would be excluded since they were not householders. And in the same vein John Locke (1632–1704) seemingly excluded women from his thought on natural equality; just as James Tyrrell, an associate of Locke, was prepared to declare: 'There never was any government where all the promiscuous rabble of women and children had votes, as not being capable of it, yet it does not for all that prove that all legal civil government does not owe its origin to the consent of the people.' In short, women and children were excluded from the class of people. Thus John Cartwright (1740–1824) noted in his radical People's Barrier Against Undue Influence (1780) that 'one man [not one woman] shall have one vote'.* And when there were moves towards female suffrage it was often via the inevitable condition of wealth or property. The Chartist movement, launched in the 1830s by the London Working Men's Association and responsible for the 6-point People's Charter, emphasised the importance of universal male suffrage; but in its early days specifically advocated the franchise for women.[6]

The Reform Acts (Table 5.1) failed until the twentieth-century to address the question of female suffrage, but gradually the key requirements of wealth and property were eroded. It is significant also that the strategists of the 1832 Reform Act had not calculated that economic

---

*Just as, during the debates on Labour Party constitutional reform through 1993, Labour spokes*men* often inadvertently referred to 'one man one vote' (sometimes hastily corrected to 'one member . . .').

TABLE 5.1   *British Parliamentary Reform Acts*

1832	Extended the franchise to almost all (male) members of the middle classes
1867	Extended the franchise to all (male) settled tenants in the boroughs, so introducing a working-class vote
1884	Extended a similar franchise to rural and mining areas
1885	Created parliamentary constituencies of broadly equal size
1918	Extended the franchise to all men, and to women over 30 years of age
1928	Extended the franchise to all adult women
1969	Reduced the minimum voting age from 21 to 18

growth would quickly extend the franchise to many people formerly unqualified to vote. When electoral statistics were presented to the House of Commons many of the traditional parliamentarians were alarmed, persisting in the attitude that the people best fitted to vote in both local and national elections were those with a long-standing traditional and material stake in society and those – as John Stuart Mill was keen to advertise – with sufficient knowledge and education to exercise their voting rights with due wisdom and prudence. A common fear was that any extension of the franchise would increase the opportunity for political corruption, an anxiety that appears to have infected even the radical reformers of the 1980s.[7] It also seemed self-evident that no man who depended upon the state for his maintenance should be allowed to vote for the government; so until 1918 men in Britain in receipt of aid from the Poor Law Guardians were excluded from the enlarged franchise. And it seemed equally self-evident that if it was representation that people required they could be best represented by prominent people in the community.

At the philosophic level the debate about the franchise was publicly conducted in terms of principle, duty and the rights of citizens, with due attention paid to whether or not particular groups of people were fit to exercise the vote. There was also the inevitable hidden agenda (with nice parallels in current debate about ways of enlarging the UN Security Council): how would any specific extension of the franchise help or handicap the most powerful parties or political factions? In fact some extensions followed a government's need to secure support from nominally hostile groups in parliament (just as the United States might support a Japanese permanent seat on the Security Council in return for a freeing-up of the Japanese economy). Thus when Disraeli was unable to patch together a Commons majority in 1867, he offered concessions to Liberal backbenchers and so sanctioned a dramatic increase in the size of the borough electorate.

At the beginning of the twentieth century, in Britain and elsewhere, many categories remained excluded from any sort of voting rights: women (the 1832 Act specified 'male persons'), lunatics, aliens, criminals, peers, receivers of poor relief, some election officials, servants, men living in their parents' home (and so not householders), and those who had behaved corruptly in elections. This means that by 1914 1.5 million men in Britain were excluded from the franchise, with a further 3.75 million excluded by virtue of failing to demonstrate their eligibility for registration. Conversely, some men were allowed to exercise a plural vote, some able to vote as many a ten times in a single election.

The phenomenon of plural voting was often linked to property. Thus the plural voters, some half a million men amounting to 7 per cent of the total, were often to be found in commercial seats, in London, and in county seats close to the parliamentary boroughs. The propertied classes favoured plural voting as signalling the stake that a man might have in society: if a man owned various peices of property in one constituency then he would have only one vote, but six houses in six different constituencies meant that he could vote six times in the same election. At the same time under the old idea that a borough was part of a county it was possible for borough freeholders to vote in a neighbouring county with which they often had no connection.[8]

The British experience had its parallels in Europe and the United States. In America the franchise was linked to property and to white male supremacy – with women, blacks and other ethnic minorities having to struggle over the years for political representation. Thus Amendment 14* (ratified 9 July 1868) to the Constitution of the United States enshrined both racism (untaxed Indians are excluded) and sexism (the Amendment is limited to 'male inhabitants'), and moreover largely failed in its main purpose of pressurising the States to encourage universal white male suffrage. The suffrage provisions of Amendment 14 were intended not to compel but to persuade, by limiting the representation of States that restricted suffrage. Amendment 15 (ratified 3 February 1870) was more direct: 'The right of citizens of the United States to vote shall not be denied or abridged by the United States or by any State on account of race, color, or

---

*Amendment 14(2): 'Representatives shall be apportioned among the several States according to their respective numbers, counting the whole number of persons in each State, excluding Indians not taxed. But when the right to vote at any election . . . is denied to any of the male inhabitants of each State, being twenty-one years of age, and citizens of the United States . . . the basis of representation therein shall be reduced in the proportion which the number of such male citizens shall bear to the whole number of male citizens . . . in such State.'

previous condition of servitude.' Moreover, the Congress 'shall have power to enforce this article by appropriate legislation'. However, it soon became clear that the robust sound of Amendment 15 concealed various persistent problems. For one thing, conservative support for the amendment was purchased only at the cost of dropping the right of nomination to public office, originally designed specifically to aid those persons 'of color, or previous condition of servitude'. Moreover, the wording of the amendment placed no restriction on other impediments – such as literacy and property qualifications – that the individual States might decide to erect. Thus Senator Oliver Morton of Indiana, a supporter of the spirit (if not the letter) of the amendment, commented:

> This amendment leaves the whole power in the States just as it exists now, except that colored men shall not be disfranchised for the three reasons of race, color, or previous condition of slavery. They may be disfranchised for want of education or for want of intelligence . . . They may, perhaps, require property or educational tests, and that would cut off the great majority of colored men from voting in those States, and thus this amendment would be practically defeated in all those States where the great body of the colored people live.

By the early years of the twentieth-century all Morton's doubts had been confirmed. From the time of passing of the Fifteenth Amendment a full century was to pass 'before the federal government took full possession of the field'.[9] And the nineteenth-century debate seldom focused on the question of women's suffrage.

In 1902 the life-long activist Elizabeth Cady Stanton declared her support for general restrictions of the suffrage – for example, that ignorant men and women be not allowed to vote – provided that educated women were granted the franchise. This recommendation, in many ways retrogressive, was similar to ideas that suggested non-racial disqualifications for ignorant or propertyless individuals. Thus Booker T. Washington proposed that both whites and Negroes should be allowed the vote, but that inadequate education or poverty might justify exclusion.

The central point is that the development of political representation has proceeded through various similar phases in different countries. At first the local or national assemblies represent great factional interests or 'estates', often no more than pliant instruments in the hands of hereditary or landed rulers. Then over the course of centuries the focus shifts from élitist factions to individual subjects and citizens. Here the propertied male adult is granted special political privileges, gradually eroded over time in the long drift to the universal franchise. Poor males are granted the franchise before women – who have frequently been grouped with children, criminals and the insane. Ethnic minorities, even in nominal parliamentary democracies, have always been forced to struggle for political representation; and today few would argue that the struggle is over. The problem of representation is that political power is rarely nicely assigned on some consensual principle of human rights, but that it has evolved over centuries in the turbulent reservoir of contending social pressures.

The development of political power in individual countries is analogous to what can be discerned in the evolution of the international community. In particular, for our purposes, it is useful to remember – when we consider the political shape of the United Nations organisation – the priorities and privileges that once obtained in the early parliamentary democracies. There was emphasis on property and influence, as there is in today's United Nations; there were 'rotten boroughs' where seats could be bought (just as post-Soviet Russia was given a permanent seat on the Security Council for reasons that were never democratically explored); propertied individuals could rely on multiple votes (just as Washington has multiple votes, by virtue of its clients and proxies, in the Security Council and the General Assembly); votes could be bought through bribery (just as Washington exploits the IMF and the World Bank to purchase UN support); and any extension of the franchise was calculated in terms of its impact on the ruling party (just as Washington would only consider expanding the Security Council in ways that did not constrain its global hegemony – how about giving Iraq or North Korea a permanent seat on the Security Council?).

The problem of representation in the United Nations is the familiar one of just political representation over the centuries. Great political power – commercial, propagandist, military – can demand political representation, forcing recalcitrant elements (individuals, factions, states) into resentful acquiescence. The problem is how to build political representation on the basis of universal human rights rather than on the weary accommodation to *realpolitik* pressure. Before hinting at an alternative approach to representation in the United Nations it is useful to glance at some crucial UN features and to profile current suggestions for reforming the Security Council.

UN STRUCTURES

At the 1945 San Francisco Conference some four dozen nation states signed the UN Charter. By the mid-1960s there were 120 members; by

1995 no less than 185. No state can become a member without the approval of the United Nations. Article 4(1) states that UN membership is 'open to all peace-loving states which accept the obligations contained in the present Charter', and which 'in the judgment of the Organization, are able and willing to carry out these obligations'. In fact it is the Security Council that decides. Thus Article 4(2) of the Charter states that a state will be admitted 'by a decision of the General Assembly upon the recommendation of the Security Council'. This means that a dominant power in the Council (in reality the United States) can determine whether or not an applicant state is allowed to join the club; and also, according to Article 6, whether it is expelled, for persistent violation of the Charter, 'by the General Assembly upon the recommendation of the Security Council'. Under this arrangement there is no provision for the expulsion of a permanent member of the Security Council since any such member could veto a move to expel it. This is an important matter since some of the worst infractions of the UN Charter have been by permanent members of the Security Council; in particular, by the United States. Thus John Quigley, professor of law at Ohio State University, notes that 'much of the activity' carried out by the United States during the years of the Cold War 'was unlawful under the United Nations Charter'; though of course no mechanism existed to authorise a UN response to such violations.[10] Nor would such a mechanism have been useful: if the United States had been expelled from the United Nations it is likely that the international body would have collapsed, with the *de facto* power centres moving outside its orbit.[11]

There have been a few protracted disputes about membership but no expulsions. For more than two decades the US managed to block the membership of China after the Communists succeeded in expelling the nationalist forces of Chiang Kai-shek from the mainland. This meant that decisions of the Security Council from the late 1940s to the early 1970s were technically invalid since a permanent seat (occupied by a powerless and unrepresentative faction) was illicitly held. One consequence of this clear UN dereliction was the passing of Security Council Resolution 84(1950), authorising the US-orchestrated UN involvement in the Korean War. Other disputes about membership – for example, the recent Greek opposition to the Macedonian application – have had less dramatic consequences. There have been a few brief withdrawals from the United Nations, but, apart from the Soviet absence from the Security Council in 1950, these have had little impact. In 1965 Indonesia withdrew from the General Assembly in protest at the election of Malaysia as a non-permanent member of the Security Council; but resumed its seat a few months later.

The General Assembly – as the only UN body that contains all UN members – is, from a democratic perspective, the most important institution within the United Nations; but it has few powers outside the overarching control by the Security Council. It is essentially a debating chamber: authorised to consider almost anything and to act on almost nothing. Thus Article 10 of the Charter entitles the General Assembly to 'discuss any questions or any matters within the scope of the present Charter or relating to the powers and functions of any organs provided for in the present Charter, and, except as provided in Article 12, may make recommendations . . .'. In a similar vein, Articles 11, 13, 14, 15 and 17 variously entitle the General Assembly 'to consider', to 'initiate studies and make recommendations', to 'recommend measures', to 'receive and consider annual and special reports' (from the Security Council), and to 'consider and approve' the UN budget. However, even these limited powers of discussion, consideration and recommendation are not allowed when the 15-member Security Council is engaged on important matters. Thus Article 12(1) states: 'While the Security Council is exercising in respect of any dispute or situation the functions assigned to it in the present Charter, the General Assembly shall not make any recommendations with regard to that dispute or situation unless the Security Council so requests.'

The Security Council, in contrast to the General Assembly, has considerable powers defined by the Charter, Article 24(1) states that the members of the United Nations 'confer on the Security Council primary responsibility for the maintenance of international peace and security, and agree that in carrying out its duties under this responsibility the Security Council acts on their behalf'. Thus in reality the 180-plus members of the United Nations give the Security Council – carefully manipulated by Washington – a blank cheque to act as it wishes. Article 24(2) notes that the 'specific powers' granted to the Security Council 'are laid down in Chapters VI, VII, VIII and XII' of the Charter; with Article 25 stating that the 'Members of the United Nations agree to accept and carry out the decisions of the Security Council in accordance with the present Charter'. Thus the Security Council – in effect the US-led permanent members – has the power to take binding decisions, not only on UN members but also on 'states which are not Members of the United Nations' (Article 2(6)), with no need to consult the broad membership of the General Assembly. Here we find no balancing of constitutional powers, no 'parliamentary' control over a small and immensely powerful 'executive'.

The voting procedure of the Security Council is defined by Article 27. Here it is stated that each member of the Council 'shall have one vote' (though in reality this means that Washington has as many votes among allies and clients as it can bribe and coerce). Article 27(2) declares that Council decisions on procedural matters 'shall be made by an affirmative vote of nine members'; with (3) decisions on all other matters 'made by an affirmative vote of nine members including the concurring votes of the permanent members'. Thus any permanent member can veto non-procedural questions: so in effect authorising a single powerful UN member to block a resolution that all the rest of the entire UN membership might support.

There is also the question as to whether an abstention on a Security Council vote constitutes a 'concurring' vote. In fact a literal reading of Article 27(3) would require *all* permanent members of the Security Council to vote for a resolution in order for it to be passed: an interpretation that is reinforced by the French draft of the text ('Les décisions du Counseil de Sécurité sur toutes autres questions sont prises par UN vote affirmatif de neuf de ses membres dans lequel sont comprises les voix de tous les membres permanents'). It seems that the original intention behind the drafting of 27(3) has been abandoned, with no attempt to amend the wording. In such a fashion (and other examples could be given), the permanent members of the Security Council assume that they are free to ignore the explicit and unambiguous wording of the Charter, and other members who may disagree with a particular interpretation have no recourse. Thus a few powerful states are in a position to ignore both the spirit and the letter of the UN Charter (see also Chapter 3).[12]

The use of the veto by permanent members in the Security Council has often been criticised for blocking proper UN action, and as representing a serious threat to majority voting power in the Council. In fact the majorities were usually contrived; and without the veto the major powers would not have supported the UN (Washington and Moscow would never have accepted the possibility of being outvoted by the lesser powers on resolutions demanding mandatory compliance). Moreover, the baleful effect of the veto has often been disputed. Thus 'it should be pointed out that the great power veto has not been the constantly growing, indefinitely expansible, cancerous factor in the life of the organization which has sometimes been supposed';[13] and criticism of the exercise of the veto might be lessened by 'examining it in the light of its different dimensions'.[14] In today's post-Cold War world the veto is a changed creature, but it remains important to any consideration of Security Council election procedures.

In the 1950s and 1960s the Soviet Union was the principal user of the veto in the Council (more than 100 Soviet vetoes by the early 1960s), hardly surprising since the Soviet Union was in a permanent minority of one among the five permanent members. However, in later decades, as Washington became increasingly hostile to Third-World blocs keen to criticise Western imperialism, the United States frequently used the veto in the Council (as well as pursuing the time-honoured tactics of vote-buying and intimidation). Today Washington is sufficiently prudent not to bring a resolution to the Security Council unless the vote has already been stitched up in the corridors of the New York headquarters. Other states are unlikely to bring an anti-American resolution to the Council since it is known that the resolution will fall and the state in question will accomplish no more than to incur US wrath in the absence of a Soviet counter-balance. In the rare cases of an anti-American vote in the General Assembly – as with Resolution 47/19 condemning the blockage of Cuba – there is no prospect of mandatory action to force US compliance.

In recent years Washington's use of the veto has signalled more than anything the hostility it has incurred in the Third World (the US predictably blocked resolutions on Namibia, South Africa, Israel, and its own military aggressions against Libya, Grenada and Panama).* Now the United States – in the congenial absence of Soviet opposition – makes some pretence of bringing the United Nations on board before Washington pursues the strategic course that it would follow anyway, so making it impossible for an anti-American resolution to be brought before the Security Council.

The veto itself, nominally a simple device to ensure Great Power membership of the United Nations, has been regarded as having various forms:

The open (or real) veto: any negative vote by a permanent member of the Security Council;

The double veto: one veto preventing a question being considered procedural, another defeating the proposal as a substantive question – used when Council members disagree about whether a proposal is procedural or not (Article 27);

The hidden (or indirect) veto: used when enough Council members are pressured to abstain or vote against a resolution to save a permanent member from the embarrassment of having to record a negative vote;

Artificial and imposed veto: Dag Hammarskjöld stated: 'There is the "artificial" and "imposed veto" problem, that is to say, the attempt by

---

*Since 1970 80 per cent of Security Council vetoes have been by the US and Britain.

this or that Power to make its consent essential for questions which naturally should be solved, let us say, on a majority basis';[15]

Veto by Proxy: used by a permanent member on behalf of a state that does not possess the right of veto.

The various types of vetoes can be used in many different contexts: one authority considers vetoes on membership; on political questions and situations; and on organisational (United Nations) matters and UN operations.[16] The position is plain. Whatever the merits of the veto as a pragmatic device it is obvious that the veto power of the permanent members necessarily protects them (and their allies and clients) from hostile mandatory resolutions.[17]

Hence the problem of representation does not merely focus on the old question of UN membership: today few states are outside the United Nations and yet most members have few powers (most are unable to block mandatory UN decisions that are hostile to their interests). In this context it is hard to avoid the conclusion that the basic constitution of the United Nations is fundamentally flawed; and that, in consequence, radical reform of the UN structure is required. Today there is much talk of proposed changes to the constitution of the Security Council, where due deference is paid to wealth and economic power (the old property qualification). It is also necessary to consider a more fundamental approach to UN reform.

A NEW SECURITY COUNCIL?

One of the most important consequences of the 1990/91 Gulf crisis was to focus attention on the character of the United Nations. With the Soviet Union now moribund and newly pliable (but with China having abstained on the crucial Resolution 678), it was time to re-evaluate the role of the international body. In September 1990 President George Bush had declared that he wanted to see a 'new world order' emerge from the crisis, a development that would demand a revived United Nations with a fresh international authority. Already there was radical speculation about the role and structure of the Security Council. How would it be expected to behave in the new global environment? Would its structure – framed nearly half a century ago in a very different world – be adequate for the new order? In particular, were countries such as Britain and France entitled to permanent seats on the Council when Germany and Japan were excluded? The exclusion of the vanquished nations of the Second World War might have been comprehensible in 1945; by 1990 it was less so.

Sir Anthony Parsons, the British ambassador to the United Nations at the time of the Falklands War (April–June 1982), had urged the development of a new United Nations after the Gulf crisis, one that would be less subject to the whims of powerful states in the Security Council. He failed to explore in detail how the impact of the veto (hidden or otherwise) might be avoided, but such a proposal clearly implied that individual nation states – even if permanent members of the Security Council – should expect to lose some of their sovereignty to the United Nations itself. Any 'new world order' that expected to rely on a traditional Security Council that both allowed a few states immense authority and excluded other powerful nations (and races) from effective influence would be unlikely to win the support of the broad international community. In one view, were the Security Council to be invented from scratch the permanent members 'would probably be the United States, the Soviet Union, Germany, Japan, China and India – the two greatest military powers, the three largest economies and the four most populous nations in the world'[18] – a nice mix of popular democracy and *realpolitik*. But it seemed unlikely that France and Britain, still happy with the 1945 carve-up of world power, would readily sacrifice their permanent seats on the Security Council.

The structure of the Council was thrown into relief by the collapse of the Soviet Union. What was to be done with the permanent Soviet seat? In December 1991, at a time when the Gulf crisis had been partially resolved (at the cost of millions of war-time and post-war Iraqi casualties) and everyone was awaiting the birth of the 'new world order', the Security Council was thrown into temporary confusion. Yuliy Vorontsov was the nominal Soviet ambassador to the United Nations but no-one was now clear who he represented. Was the permanent seat vacant? Would the collapsing Soviet Union be allowed to vote in either the Security Council or the General Assembly? Again there were suggestions that the Soviet demise might lead to a fundamental rethink about the structure of the Council, perhaps with Britain and France losing their permanent seats and with a common European seat (rather than an exclusively German one) being created. It seemed significant that the European Commission had recently been granted permission to act for the twelve EC members in the UN-linked World Food Programme (WFP) in Rome. Perhaps this was the shape of things to come. Britain and France had already subordinated their sovereignty to Europe via the 1958 Treaty of Rome (Britain joined in 1973) and the 1985 Single European Act (the Maastricht Treaty became law in 1993). This course of events encouraged the view that a single permanent European seat might emerge on the Security Council. But in the short term it was necessary first to settle the Soviet question.

Paris and London, fearful of radical changes in the Security Council, expressed a hope that there would be an 'elegant solution' to the problems created by the increasingly defunct Soviet Union. The best solution, from the Western perspective, was for a pliant Russian Federation to take over the permanent Soviet seat (it was judged that Belorussia and the Ukraine, already UN members, would be unlikely to challenge such a move, though Kasakhastan, Tajikistan and the Islamic Soviet regions might present problems). Western UN delegates were keen to warn of an unwieldy Security Council unable to act decisively in the 'new world order'. The simplest ploy would be simply to plant the Russian Federation in the erstwhile Soviet seat; and in the event this is exactly what happened. It is useful in this context to consider what the Charter of the United Nations says about the structure of the Security Council.

The composition of the Council is defined by Article 23(1): 'The Security Council shall consist of fifteen Members of the United Nations. The Republic of China, France, the Union of Soviet Socialist Republics, the United Kindgom of Great Britain and Northern Ireland, and the United States of America shall be permanent members of the Security Council' (with ten non-permanent members to be elected by the General Assembly, to serve for two-year terms, according to 23(2)). It is obvious that the conditions of 23(1) had been overtaken by events. Peking's assumption of Taiwan's permanent seat in 1971, following year-by-year votes in the General Assembly until the necessary majority was secured, followed the stipulations of Article 108, which states that amendments to the Charter can only come into force following a two-thirds vote in the Assembly, 'including all the permanent members of the Security Council'. However, no such procedure was followed in transferring the permanent Soviet seat to the Russian Federation. Boris Yeltsin, president of the Federation, simply sent a letter (24 December 1991) to the UN Secretary-General, informing him that the Federation, with the support of all eleven members of the Commonwealth of Independent States (CIS), would be taking over the Soviet role in the United Nations. This means that *Russia's current occupation of a permanent seat on the Security Council is in violation of Article 108 of the Charter and so is technically invalid*. This detail has relevance to how other changes to the structure of the Security Council might come to be made.

In fact it was the British premier, John Major, who called for an early Security Council meeting to achieve a rapid conversion of the Soviet seat on the Council to a Russian one, so avoiding protracted discussion in the

United Nations that might have called into question the permanent seats of Britain and France. Officials in the US State Department were said to be 'amused but not averse' to this cynical exercise. Britain had a clear interest in discouraging debate. Japan was beginning to agitate for a permanent seat, and Germany was thought to favour a permanent European Community (EC) seat. One British official commented that the speedy move to plant the Russian Federation on the Security Council was neat: 'Since the Germans have been calling more than anyone else for the need to involve Russia on the international stage, they could hardly fail to be satisfied by a proposal to bring Mr Yeltsin to New York and Russian on to the Council as quickly as possible.'[19] This all suggested that future restructuring of the Security Council could be achieved by similar horse-trading among powerful states, even if this entailed a similar violation of the UN Charter.

In January 1992 there were growing signs of dissatisfaction in Germany and Japan about their status in the United Nations. The Japanese prime minister, Kiichi Miyazawa, pointed out that the UN Charter still made reference to the 'enemy'* states of Japan, Germany and Italy of the Second World War. Some argued that Japanese and German claims were hampered by constitutional restrictions (again dating back to World War Two), prohibiting Japanese and German forces being used in an active military role to aid UN peacekeeping operations; but there were few signs of Chinese troops keeping the peace in Cambodia, Bosnia and Angola, and China was seemingly still entitled to its permanent seat on the Security Council. At the same time it was obvious that Japan and Germany were making claims by virtue only of their vast economic strength; poor countries, some observers noted, had as much right to representation in the Council as the rich. A leading article in *The Independent* (London) pointed out the 'great regional powers such as India, Brazil or Nigeria ought to represent their respective continents with a guaranteed place on the Security Council'; and, 'as Germany emerges as economically the strongest country in Europe, there are those who argue that the British and French seats ought to be transferred to the European Community'.[20]

It still seemed unlikely that changes would be made to the structure of the Council. During the negotiations on the Maastricht Treaty's implications for European foreign policy, both Britain and France had rejected proposals that the two permanent Security Council seats be rotated among

---

*See Articles 53, 77 and 107.

the EC members (though the two states were forced to agree to co-ordinate their actions at the UN more closely with the other members of the Community). Again it was clear that neither Britain nor France would readily sacrifice their Security Council privileges. On 15 September 1992 the former West German chancellor, Willy Brandt, made a plea for a stronger United Nations, amid evidence that Bonn was urging reform of the Security Council so that permanent seats could be found for a reunited Germany – and for Japan, Brazil, India, Egypt and Indonesia. Germany was reported to be increasingly dissatisfied with the failure of Britain and France to consult their EC partners on UN matters.[21] Here, as in Japan, there were mounting pressures for change.

In a speech to the UN General Assembly on 21 September 1992 the Japanese foreign minister, Michio Watanabe, again denounced the 'enemy' references in the UN Charter as 'historical relics' from a distant past, and urged their deletion. In response, Secretary-General Boutros-Ghali stated that he hoped that the words would be dropped by 1995, the UN's 50th anniversary. This is a matter of obvious importance. It must be seen as strange that Japan – pressured to offer massive funds for the 1991 Gulf War and today paying one-eight of the UN's expenses – is still branded (along with Germany and Italy) in the Charter of the United Nations as an 'enemy'. The removal of such wording must be seen as an essential first step to any UN reform that gives Japan a more substantial representation. The anguished debate within Japan about reform of the country's 'peace' constitution had already yielded changes that would allow Japanese troops to be sent to Cambodia to support UN peace-keeping, In such circumstances Michio Watanabe felt able to recommend a change to the composition of the UN Security Council.

On 25 January 1993 the US Secretary of State, Warren Christopher, proposed an expansion of the Security Council to include Germany and Japan as permanent members: 'I think it's time for some reorganisation of the UN to bring it into keeping with modern realities. During the [presidential election] campaign President Clinton said that he could envisage the addition of Germany and Japan to the permanent members of the Security Council and I expect we'll see some developments in that direction.' It was significant that there was no reference to the possibility of representation beyond these two wealthy states. And again questions were raised about the likely effects of a German permanent seat on the positions of France and Britain: a Europe with no less than three per-manent seat on the Security Council would seem to be disproportionately represented (Boutros-Ghali had already commented on the organisation's 'Euro-centric' tendencies). France was predictably concerned that changes might dilute its position in the Franco-German partnership, with Britain anxious that its much vaunted (but largely mythical) 'special relationship' with the United States might be eroded. On 26 January, in response to the Christopher proposal, the British Foreign Secretary, Douglas Hurd, commented: 'If it ain't broke, don't fix it.' And in the same speech, to the Royal Institute of International Affairs, he warned that Britain would have to say 'no' more often than 'yes' to UN requests for peacekeeping troops: Britain could not turn its back 'on the wider world' but neither could it become involved in every tragedy. The question of UN reform was a 'huge debate and it will go on for a long time', with any outcome 'very hard and slow to reach and, meanwhile, the Security Council has to get on with its job'.[22]

At the same time Prime Minister John Major was declaring in New Delhi that changes to the composition of the Security Council could be considered; but 'I would not wish to do anything that would make it less effective.' Now the debate was beginning to extend beyond the question of representation to voting procedures. Thus the European commissioner for external affairs, Hans van den Broek, commented to the EC Commission that no single Security Council member should be able on its own to veto a decision ('a veto should at the very least have the support of one other Council member'). It seemed likely that such matters, along with questions of representation, would be unavoidable topics when the European Community expanded in 1994 or 1995 to include such states as Austria, Finland, Norway and Sweden: such a development would necessarily again focus attention on the shared EC foreign, security and defence policy.

On 5 June 1993 Madeleine Albright, the US ambassador to the United Nations, stated that Washington would work actively to bring Germany and Japan onto the Security Council as permanent members, an announcement that produced immediate British alarm (again the cliché, this time from an official: 'The argument remains that if it ain't broke, don't fix it. The Security Council is now working properly for the first time'). Boutros-Ghali, intending to produce a report on the question by 1994, had asked all member states to submit their recommendations. It was made clear that the British Foreign Office, seeing the UN Charter as a 'pretty good read', would be keen to emphasise that the Security Council 'was now working with an unprecedented degree of consensus'; and that a continued permanent British seat, like that of France, might be justified because of their constituents in the former colonies. And there were also signs of an emerging Anglo-French axis to resist the US proposals for the UN reform. France's UN ambassador, Jean-Bernard Mérimée, commented that an increase in the number of Council members would 'diminish its power of decision'; with the British, sympathetic to this view, continuing to insist that states need to have 'global responsibilities to be one of the Permanent Five'. At one level the question was simply a matter of finance: a UN strapped for cash would find it easier to prise funds out of Germany and Japan if it acceded to their demands for more effective representation at the top table, an argument that weighed heavily in a Washington beset by financial deficit problems. Britain continued to urge delay. On 4 July 1993 Douglas Hurd, speaking in Bonn, emphasised that Britain was not fundamentally opposed to every UN reform, 'but we have asked for caution'. However, there were now signs that Britain was bending to the inevitability of change.

On 8 July the British premier, John Major, announced at the Tokyo G7 summit that there was now a policy 'shift of emphasis', not least on the vexed question of an enlargement of the Security Council: 'We recognise that the debate is about widening the Security Council, including the permanent membership . . . There are countries who are, or who are on the way, to being able to carry out their peacekeeping responsibilities' (an obvious reference to the changes in the German and Japanese 'peace' constitutions to allow peacekeeping troops to be sent abroad). But again there was some alarm that poorer countries might seek more effective representation. Said one British official: 'And then we'd have Nigeria knocking at the door. Look at the state they're in.' Significantly enough, Douglas Hurd, after talks with Matthew Mbu, the foreign minister of Nigeria's transitional Council, declared at Tokyo that debate about enlarged membership of the Security Council would not be settled 'simply by adding Germany and Japan to the present list'. The debate was set to continue but no observer thought it likely that the Third World would gain anything from the manoeuvres among the rich states.

In September the Japanese Prime Minister, now Morihiro Hosokawa, continued to press for a permanent Japanese seat on the Security Council, albeit sometimes obliquely, declaring that Japan was now ready to shoulder bigger UN responsibilities. Hosokawa had already issued a general apology for Japanese war-time atrocities (the first from a Japanese leader), and there were repeated claims from Japanese politicians that the country should now be given the status of proper UN representation. But there was no Japanese consensus on the issue. Hosokawa's special advisor, Shusei Tanaka, urged a cautious approach: perhaps other countries could be induced to demand a Security Council seat on Japan's behalf and then Japan would negotiate the terms, And the Leftwing Socialists, predominantly pacifist and worried about the possibility of Japanese military involvement overseas, had the power to disturb Hosokawa's fragile coalition. At times even Hosokawa himself had seemed ambivalent about the prospect of an enlarged military role for Japan, having declared in August that Japan should not aspire to 'mini-superpower status'. However, few could deny the compelling significance of Japan's financial status: with the world's second largest economy it was at the same time the second largest donor to the United Nations (even though its contributions were often delayed); and, already by 1994 the world's largest aid supplier to developing countries, it planned to expand its aid programme to $70 billion over the next five years.

The debate on a possible restructuring of the Security Council continued through 1993 and on into 1994, with no new decisions, despite Secretary-General Boutros-Ghali's acknowledgement that changes were necesssary (and if possible by the time of the UN's 50th birthday). The high-profile consideration given to the claims of Japan and Germany tended to mask the interest of less powerful states in more effective representation on the Council. It was widely recognised that some continents, races and religions were unrepresented at the top table; and that perhaps the matter deserved to be treated in radical terms. What of other countries able to make strong claims (whether based on wealth, geography or religion)? And what of reports (*Reuter*, 23 September 1993) that the 22-member Arab League intended to lobby in New York for a permanent Arab seat on the Security Council? Perhaps, as with the European community, the Arab states in the League could occupy a permanent seat on a rotating basis.

On 12 September 1994 the UN Secretary-General Boutros Boutros-Ghali supported Japan's bid for a permanent seat on the Security Council, delcaring the Japan's war-renouncing constitution was not a barrier. At the same time, during the Tokyo meeting, Japan agreed to pay 15 per cent of the UN budget. On 27 September the Japanese foreign minister, Yohei Kono, addressed the UN General Assembly and there reaffirmed the Japanese position, Japan was prepared, with the endorsement of many countries, to discharge its responsibilities as a permanent member of the Security Council. Now few observers doubted that Japan and Germany would soon be given permanent seats, though attention was also being given to the UN status of such countries as Italy, Nigeria, Egypt, Brazil, Mexico, India and Indonesia. Increasingly it seemed that the fiftieth anniversary of the United Nations would herald important changes to the structure of the Security Council.

The principal criteria for effective representation on the Security Council are today inevitably linked to wealth (the old property qualification), a free-market economic philosophy, and support for (or at least tolerance of) Western strategic and commercial interests. In this context China is the least sympathetic permanent member on the Security Council, and is frequently pressured (for example, by US threats to withdraw 'favoured nation' trading status) to come in line. Washington is unlikely to tolerate new permanent members that might cause fresh difficulties for Western political calculations.

In early 1995 there were growing signs that the Republican control of the US Congress was leading to mounting pressure for a reduction in the US financial contribution to the United Nations. This development – as evidenced, for example, by the House debate (February) on the National Security Revitalisation Act – gave fresh impetus to those reformers wanting to enlarge the Security Council: if US contributions to UN peacekeeping operations were to be reduced perhaps Germany and Japan, as new permanent members, would fill the gap.

The debate has principally focused on enlargement of the Security Council, a likely development that would leave existing power structures largely intact; but there are other voices, seldom heard, that are much more radical. Perhaps the Security Council should be scrapped and new UN organs devised to give the international body a truly democratic character. Perhaps the existing structures, even after substantial reform, would never be well equipped to protect the real interests of 'we the peoples'.

6 The Other United Nations

PREAMBLE

Any attempt to understand the problems faced by the United Nations must take into account the global environment in which it operates. Elements of this environment have already been considered (Chapters 3 and 4), but only as local and discrete problems requiring a peacekeeping or some other initiative. In this context a crisis may focus on particular countries (Somalia, Iraq, Haiti and so on) that need prompt and effective UN intervention. However, there is also a broader question. The UN is interested not only in the tasks of peacekeeping, supplying aid and supervising elections; but in a whole host of other activities. It is the peacekeeping initiatives that receive most of the publicity, with media attention characteristically focusing on military clashes, the level of casualties, what 'our boys' are suffering in the field; but many of the parallel UN activities receive little exposure, and when they are reported in some detail (as with the Uruguay GATT Round) the UN connections and global consequences are seldom made clear. There is in fact another 'United Nations', less transparent than the high-profile peacekeeping UN but equally important for the world community.

The other United Nations is largely represented by the so-called 'specialised agencies' of the UN (Table 6.1). Many of these bodies have

TABLE 6.1   *Specialised agencies of the United Nations*

International Labour Organisation (ILO)
Food and Agriculture Organisation (FAO)
United Nations Educational, Scientific and Cultural Organisation (UNESCO)
International Civil Aviation Organisation (ICAO)
International Bank for Reconstruction and Development (World Bank)
International Monetary Fund (IMF)
Universal Postal Union (UPU)
World Health Organisation (WHO)
United Nations High Commissioner for Refugees (UNHCR)
World Meteorological Organisation (WMO)
Inter-governmental Maritime Consultative Organisation (IMCO)
International Development Association (IDA)
World Intellectual Property Organisation (WIPO)
United Nations Children's Fund (UNICEF)
International Fund for Agricultural Development (IFAD)

been criticised for their management inefficiencies, their staffing policies, their political orientation and so on. They have been depicted as feudal domains, interested more in preserving their own privileges than in fulfilling their charter obligations; criticism has been levelled at the extended rule of particular individuals, such as Edouard Saouma at the Food and Agriculture Organisation and Hiroshi Nakajima at the World Health Organisation; and the radical commitments of such agencies as UNESCO, UNICEF and the ILO have aroused widespread hostility. Inevitably there is frequent talk of corruption, sinecures and the self-serving practices of national governments.[1] Such criticisms are important and deserve attention, but there are other matters – much more significant in their global implications – to be considered. These matters are the province of such UN specialised agencies as the International Monetary Fund (IMF) and the International Bank for Reconstruction and Development (the World Bank); the General Agreement on Tariffs and Trade (GATT) organisation; and the matrix of world capitalist enterprise.

Hence the crucial 'other United Nations' is the global free-market complex defined by the IMF/World Bank/GATT nexus, the transnational corporations (TNCs), and the array of associated pressure groups and governments (powerful states and their clients) working to further the global interests of free-market commerce. The activists and propagandists of the *other United Nations* necessarily portray their endeavours as a benign enterprise, well suited to meeting the needs of the international community. But we need to examine the claim. Today there is mounting evidence that the emerging global free-market system – far from being designed to serve the best interests of 'we the peoples' – is intended mainly to benefit minority commercial groups. At one level this is a quite unremarkable situation: vested interest – commercial, military, ideological – will always tend to protect and enlarge its domain. What is unusual is that world capitalism, despite the malaise of the global economy, now feels equipped to act with unchallenged confidence. The rapid development of the *other United Nations* is one of the most important features of the post-Soviet world.

THE SIGNIFICANCE OF WORLD POVERTY

One of the main purposes of the United Nations is to bring an end to world poverty. Thus in the preamble to the UN Charter there is a declared commitment to the promotion of 'social progress and better standards of life . . .'; 'of the economic and social advancement of all peoples'. In his report to the General Assembly in September 1992 Secretary-General Boutros-Ghali emphasised that the United Nations as an institution 'is uniquely placed to press for global solutions to global problems in the economic field, whether they pertain to aid, trade, technology transfer, commodity prices or debt relief'. In this context the UN 'still has a continuing obligation to put its weight behind those who are most seriously underprivileged and to address the root causes of the economic decline which still characterizes the economic situation of many countries in Africa, Asia and Latin America and is fast reaching crisis proportions in several of them'. Boutros-Ghali declared: '*It is unacceptable that absolute poverty, hunger, disease, illiteracy and hopelessness should be the lot of one fifth of the world's population*' (my italics).[2] It was noted that the situation of Africa was of particular concern, with most Africans poorer than they were when their countries gained independence in the 1950s and 1960s; that, with existing trends, there would be even more Africans living in poverty by the year 2000; and that Africa was the only region of the world whose total debt equals or exceeds its economic output.

A year later, Boutros-Ghali again addressed what he termed the 'humanitarian imperative'. The mass exodus of people from various crisis regions had presented new problems; as had the murder of UN staff members working in humanitarian programmes in Sudan, Afghanistan and elsewhere. There was a growing requirement for emergency humanitarian relief, for increased funding for such UN organisations as the Children's Fund (UNICEF), the World Food Programme (WFP), and the UN High Commissioner for Refugees (UNHCR). Relief operations had continued in such countries as Sudan, Ethiopia and Kenya; and it was noted that in northern Iraq the UN humanitarian efforts had prevented 'another serious refugee crisis'.[3] Boutros-Ghali made no effort to discuss the paradox that many problems in the Third World had been exacerbated by specific UN initiatives, not least the decision to wage war on Iraq in 1991 (and to impose punitive sanctions on that country from August 1990), following its invasion of Kuwait. Thus the UN's response to Saddam's aggression had grave consequences for such countries as Yemen, Bangladesh and Jordan (high-profile losers); and for many other Third World nations. A report prepared for six British aid agencies* revealed that at least 40 Third World countries had suffered the equivalent of a natural disaster as a result of the Gulf War.

---

*Cafod, Christian Aid, the Catholic Institute for International Relations, Oxfam, Save the Children, and the World Development Movement.

The report, prepared by the London-based Overseas Development Institute, called for a new package of support for the worst-affected countries (which together were reckoned to have lost some $12 billion): 'Hundreds of thousands of workers from developing countries have had to flee the Gulf region abandoning their savings, possessions and livelihoods. Millions of people were dependent on receiving financial support from relatives working in the Gulf. Even more have seen their poverty deepened and their opportunities curtailed by the wider effects of the crisis.'[4] More than 40 nations had lost more than 1 per cent of the gross national product (GNP), the UN benchmark for defining a natural disaster, and for some countries (for example, Jordan: GNP loss 25 per cent) the effects had been much worse. Fourteen of the affected countries were sub-Saharan states, already in the grip of poverty but unlikely to derive any benefit from Article 50 of the UN Charter (which states that if any UN enforcement measures cause problems for a state it 'shall have the right to consult the Security Council with regard to a solution of those problems'). Richard Reid, the UNICEF director for North Africa and the Middle East, stated that nearly five million children ('a lost generation') would spend their formative years in deprived circumstances as a result of the Gulf crisis.

Such considerations highlight one of the principal dilemmas facing the United Nations. How is the UN to calculate the true costs of intervention? Should *all* the factors be weighed in the balance? Should a military intervention, even if justified in ethics and law, be undertaken if it is likely to generate massive new aid demands on the international body? And how are such questions to be assessed in the context of the other United Nations, the international matrix concerned above all to protect and develop the practice of global free-market commerce?

The importance of food aid has always been recognised, though continually questioned with regard to politics and effectiveness. Thus the 1980 Brandt Report recognised that food aid 'will continue to be essential', even though in the past it has been criticised 'for its political exploitation' and 'for the disruption of agricultural incentives in the recipient countries'.[5] In 1975 the UN General Assembly recommended that an emergency food reserve be established, but by 1980 no reliable international mechanism had been created to maintain the reserve by annual replenishment; and today (mid-1994) the UN is still forced to address many aid emergencies on an *ad hoc* basis, with too little scope for preventive action and inadequate international support when relief aid is needed on an emergency basis. After commenting that there must be 'an end to mass hunger and malnutrition', the Brandt Report states that the capacity of food-importing developing countries to meet their food needs should be expanded 'and their mounting food import bill reduced' – through their own efforts and through expanded financial flows for agricultural development. Here food aid 'should be increased and linked to employment promotion and agricultural programmes and projects without weakening incentives to food production'; moreover, the liberalisation of trade (hints of GATT) 'in food and other agricultural products within and between North and South would contribute to the stabilization of food supplies'.[6]

So much may seem uncontentious, a description of existing aid philosophy. Even the reference to a 'food financing facility' does not suggest a radical departure from mechanisms already in place. But there were already suggestions that the provision of aid was only rarely a truly ethical venture, a genuine attempt to further the human 'economic and social advancement' urged in the UN Charter preamble. It was already being suggested that aid, as exemplified by the endeavours of such UN-linked bodies as the IMF and the World Bank, was essentially an imperialist initiative intended to secure the continual post-colonial exploitation of the Third World in the interests of small wealthy factions in the developed countries. At times the Western strategy is candidly admitted. Thus in 1961 President John Kennedy was prepared to declare that 'foreign aid is a method by which the United States maintains a position of influence and control around the world . . .'; with a former senior economist of the US Agency for International Development, Professor H. B. Chenery, acknowledging that 'economic assistance is one of the instruments of foreign policy that is used to prevent political and economic conditions from deteriorating in countries where we value the preservation of the present government' (the obvious corollary is that unwelcome governments will not be granted food aid, whatever the emergency needs of their people). In a similar vein – and in language that is today unfashionable (even if accurate) – Teresa Hayter, then of the Overseas Development Institute (ODI) financed by the World Bank, commented: 'In its general role as preserver of the capitalist system, aid can act in more indirect and complex ways than as a mere bribe or concession to sweeten the pill of exploitation.'[7] It can be used to pressure governments into accepting economic reforms that benefit international capitalism; to act against leftist parties that may gain power through the ballot box; to abolish existing workers' rights that 'restrict industrial enterprise'; and to defuse revolutionary situations. In the same vein, Cheryl Payer, political scientist and one-time employee of the Washington-based Agency for International Development (AID), explored how the IMF worked to frustrate the efforts of poor countries to gain some control over their own economies.[8] Writing two decades ago, Payer declared:

The International Monetary Fund is the most powerful supranational government in the world today. The resources it controls and its power to interfere in the internal affairs of borrowing nations give it the authority of which United Nations advocates can only dream . . . The IMF must be seen as the keystone of a total system . . . All the major sources of credit in the developed capitalist world, whether private lenders, government, or multilateral institutions such as the World Bank group, will refuse to lend to a country which persists in defying IMF 'advice' . . . the IMF has been the chosen instrument for imposing imperialist financial discipline upon poor countries under a facade of multilateralism and technical competence.[9]

Today the situation is different, but not in ways that benefit poor countries. The global policies of the IMF/World Bank nexus have remained largely unchanged in principle, though, in the post-Soviet environment, they encounter fewer ideological challenges. The basic aims remain the same; to break down world trade barriers that obstruct the access of international finance capital to sympathetic domestic markets; and to discourage the emergence of political movements that might disturb the developing shape of world trade.[10]

It should not be assumed that it is only the IMF and the World Bank (in concert with GATT pressures for 'free trade' – see below) that are intent on subverting the ethics of aid to serve commercial/political vested interest. To some extent most of the world's official aid institutions and national aid programmes are tainted by the same corrupt culture. Thus Graham Hancock, formerly East Africa correspondent of *The Economist*, argues that 'official development assistance' is not necessary: 'the poor thrive without it in some countries; in others, where it is plentifully available, they suffer the most abject miseries. Such suffering . . . often occurs not *in spite of* aid but *because* of it'. Moreover, the official aid industry is lost to the extremes of corruption, with 'record-breaking standards . . . set in self-serving behaviour, arrogance, paternalism, moral cowardice and mendacity'; the only reasonable option now being for the 'lords of poverty to depart . . . in the best interests both of the taxpayers of the rich countries and the poor of the South'.[11] In this context the official aid agencies are seen as self-serving, massively bureaucratic, and irredeemably corrupted by bribery, easy sinecures and disguised political agendas. It is hardly surprising, if even a significant part of this is true, that the official aid agencies – many of which are linked to the United Nations – are failing adequately to address the global problems of poverty.

In October 1984 publicity was given to an impressive new study produced by the UN Food and Agriculture Organisation (FAO), intended to work out just how many people the land of the Third World should be able to feed.[12] Maps of soils and climates were superimposed to create a detailed mosaic of cells with distinctive combinations of soil, slope, rainfall and so on. Then a computer was employed to check each cell against 15 major food crops to devise a calorie yield for particular terrains. It was found that, political constraints apart, all major regions would be capable of food self-sufficiency in the year 2000 AD. If the Third World countries achieved the farming levels of the West, they would be able to support a massive 33 billion people – more than four times the most likely estimates of the stable populations that such countries might reach around 120 years from now. The basic catch was that all the world's forests would have to be felled to grow vegetables for human consumption (no grain fed to livestock) in egalitarian human societies. The FAO study showed what could be achieved, granted such conditions and the more efficient use of land already overloaded; but with political factors taken into account the study bore little connection with reality.

By 1990 – with the IMF/World Bank/GATT nexus almost half a century old (and with the rich states enjoying a massively developed food production technology) – it was obvious that the plight of the world's poor was not being alleviated. In some areas, the extent of poverty was growing worse by the year: by 1990 some 140 million Africans were hungry, compared with 92 million 20 years earlier and an estimated 200 million that would be hungry by the year 2000. Africa has never had power in the IMF, the World Bank or GATT, and such institutions have never paid attention to the real needs of the African poor. When Robert Macnamara headed the World Bank in the late 1960s there was brief and fruitless talk of eliminating world hunger; but, more significantly, there was commonly an outflow of capital from impoverished Africa to the rich nations of the world. For example, in 1989 the IMF took out of Africa more than $2.5 billion more than it put in, with no attempts to alter the terms of trade or the debt burden in Africa's favour. The former President Nyerere of Tanzania commented that 'our governments have no power over commodity prices, or over the prices of manufactured goods, or over the exchange rate of the dollar'. Through the 1980s the terms of trade for African exports – copper, bauxite, coffee, cotton, sisal, sugar, groundnuts and so on – dropped by 30 per cent, and continued to drop in the 1990s. At the same time the rise of interest rates worldwide at the end of the 1980s meant that the servicing of foreign debts was then amounting to no less than 40 per cent of Africa's foreign exchange earnings: this has meant –

under IMF/World Bank prompting – the slashing of health and education budgets, and a significant drop in calorie intake (by 1990 African children were dying of malnutrition in twice the numbers of a decade earlier). Nyerere declared:

> The worst thing of all in Africa now is that Africa is reeling like an out-weighted boxer after 15 rounds of punishment. There is a feeling of hopelessness, a loss of the will to fight. There is an intolerable feeling of dependence. We can't even scream. We are afraid the aid we now get might stop if we do scream, or if we argue against the powerful in the United Nations or at GATT.[13]

This was (is) the world created by the IMF/World Bank/GATT nexus, with its cynical apologists confident enough to admit the political purposes behind aid. Thus on 6 June 1990 the British Foreign Secretary, Douglas Hurd, defined the political and economic conditions attached to British aid for Africa: 'Countries tending towards pluralism, public accountability, respect for the rule of law, human rights and market principles should be encouraged. Governments who persist with repressive policies, with corrupt management, or with wasteful and discredited economic systems should not expect us to support their folly with scarce aid resources.' Note the reference to 'discredited economic systems' (that is, socialist systems that choose to invest in public services): money should not be wasted on such things but should be devoted to export products of interest to the West, and to the servicing of debt. In response to the Hurd speech, delivered to the Overseas Development Institute, Salim Ahmed Salim, the Secretary-General of the Organisation of African Unity (OAU), commented: 'While Africa must democratise, *our efforts will be hamstrung by the non-democratic international economic system in which we operate and which militates against our development* . . . No matter how many political parties an African state has, that will not alter its economic fortunes. It will not change the price of coffee, cocoa, cotton, sisal or copper' (my italics).[14] Nor was the African crisis helped by the 1990/1991 confrontation in the Gulf: the impact on Third World economies has already been mentioned, but it is important also to remember the impact on aid provision. The African plight was forgotten.[15]

In early 1991 around 27 million Africans were threatened with starvation, with desperate aid agencies struggling to generate interest in donor countries: Oxfam stated that not enough food had been pledged to save millions of African lives, while Save the Children launched an emergency campaign on behalf of 15 million starving African children. In June,

Professor Adebayo Abedeji, the executive secretary of the UN Economic Commission for Africa (ECA), spoke of the 1980s as a 'lost decade', at the same time urging a renewed effort for the new decade. The international community had pledged an extra $9 billion for the UN's emergency economic recovery programme (UN-PAAERD), launched in 1986, but none of the pledged money arrived; and during the same period the IMF took a net $4 billion out of Africa.

In August 1991 the UN Secretary-General, Javier Perez de Cuellar, issued a new report challenging the world to come to the assistance of Africa.[16] The report commented that there had been 'scarcely any change for the better in the structure of the African economies', recognising that conditions had worsened and that even those states that had managed to reverse or halt the decline would not be able to sustain their successes without assistance. However, now it was plain in the post-Gulf War world, in George Bush's 'new world order', that poor countries – African states in particular – could expect little assistance that was not geared to Western strategic interests; now there were those countries 'within the pale and those beyond it'.[17] On 23 April 1992 a report produced by the UN Development Programme (UNDP) proposed a world summit of rich and poor nations to reduce the yawning economic gap by the year 2000. The report stated that in 1960 the wealthiest 1 billion of the world's population of 5 billion were thirty times better off than the poorest 1 billion; whereas in 1992 the richest fifth was just to be around 150 times better off.[18] At the same time, the director of the UN Population Fund, Nafis Sadik, reported that world poverty was rising and that the benefits from economic development should be distributed 'more equitably'.

In June 1992 a report from the Food and Agriculture Organisation (FAO) stated that almost 40 million Africans were threatened with hunger ('The current indications suggest that Africa's minimum needs will not be met'). Somalia, the most seriously affected country, was experiencing 'widespread deaths from starvation', with serious problems also in such countries as Sudan, Kenya, Liberia, Sierra Leone, Togo, Zaire and Rwanda. Andrew Natsios, the assistant administrator for food and humanitarian assistance at the Washington-based Agency for International Development (AID), stated that 110 million Africans lived in areas affected by the current drought, and that 18 million could die without effective UN intervention ('The people most at risk are in Mozambique, Zimbabwe, Zambia, Malawi, Angola and Swaziland'). Jeffrey Clark, a consultant on relief assistance in Africa at the US Committee for Refugees declared: 'Internationally, there is no mobilisation. There is no master plan. There is nobody saying, "Somalia cannot be repeated in

Mozambique or southern Sudan." There is nobody saying, "We have to raise a billion dollars and get food on the boats and get going."'[19]

By 1993 there were indications of progress in the fight against global poverty: a UN sub-committee on nutrition chaired by Secretary-General Boutros-Ghali reported that for the first time the number of hungry people in the world was falling, despite the rapid population increase and the appalling problems in Africa. The study stated that famine had been 'virtually eradicated' outside Africa, suggesting that in 1990 there were about 200 million fewer hungry people than there were in the mid-1970s: a third of people were hungry in developing countries in 1975, around one fifth in 1990. At the same time about one third of all children in developing states were seriously malnourished in 1990 (40 per cent in 1975). John Mason, one of the report's co-authors, commented that we seem 'to have passed the point in history where the earth has the maximum number of underfed people'. An FAO survey of China suggested that it had halved the hunger rate since 1975, with a slow but steady decline (about 0.5 per cent a year) in the number of malnourished children in India.

In sub-Saharan Africa the international trade share had fallen from 14 to 6 per cent in the two decades prior to 1993, a trend that continued to bear heavily on much of Africa. For example, by 1982 Zambia was having to export more than four times as much copper to import the same volume of goods as it had in 1970. Short-term IMF rescue programmes only made matters worse; by 1984 Zambia was paying out an annual $610 million to service its debt – which even then was continuing to rise ($5 billion by May 1987). On 1 May 1987 President Kenneth Kaunda declared that we would be abandoning the failed IMF programme, whereupon the government suspended debt payments to the IMF and the World Bank and launched the interim National Development Plan; but after food riots and growing political disaffection a government climb-down was inevitable. In early 1991 a new programme was agreed with the IMF and the World Bank, a plan that involved the removal of some domestic price controls and the 'reform' of state industries to accord more closely with the demands of a free-market economy.

Elections were called for 31 October 1991, whereupon Kaunda froze the lifting of maize subsidies and relaxed the controls on the money supply. The IMF responded by freezing disbursements in September, bringing fresh tensions to an economy in turmoil. The newly formed Movement for Multi-Party Democracy (MMD) won 125 seats in the 150-seat National Assembly. The new government moved quickly to improve relations with the IMF and the World Bank: the kwacha was devalued (from 85 to the dollar in 1992 to 400 in March 1993); interest rates were pushed up to 75 per cent; and more than 130 state owned or controlled enterprises, including Zambia Consolidated Copper Mines, have been or are being privatised. More than 80 per cent of the population continues to live in poverty. Now, with increased loans from a contented donor community, the Zambian debt has reached almost $8 billion. It is now increasingly recognised that Africa's immense debt burden, linked to harsh IMF/World Bank conditions, represents an enormous obstacle to African development.

In May 1993 the US government suggested a write-off of 50 per cent of the debt of Africa's poorest countries, an important departure from the Reagan/Bush years when Washington routinely blocked similar suggestions from Britain and France. It was thought that the US move might influence the Paris Club, the group of Western nations that schedules the debt repayments from developing countries. However, the conditions for rescheduling were soon made plain: the counties concerned would be required to adopt IMF structural adjustment programmes to bring the domestic economies in line with Western free-market demands. The plight of the poorest sub-Saharan nations would be marginally eased – provided they agree to subordinate their domestic economies still further to the requirements of international capitalism.

The situation was clear. The principal Western donor agencies (in particular, the IMF and the World Bank) would facilitate investment in poor countries – but only if such states agreed to expose their economies to whatever predations might be demanded by financial policy planners in the West. At the same time, through the GATT manoeuvres, further pressure would focus on vulnerable Third World countries to force compliance with the market needs of international capitalism. The Western donors would not be too concerned if the stringent loan conditions meant a collapse of domestic investment in such social services as health and education; or if unemployment and widening circles of destitution were the result. Nor would Western governments worry unduly if itinerant bag men regularly conveyed vast hauls of currency from the world's poorest countries for deposit in Western banks.[20] It is known that banks are discouraged from large-scale cash business such as this by British and European banking regulations, but the 'British authorities have closed their eyes to the bag men, in spite of the risk that this might enable drug money to be laundered – Nigerian drug barons are major distributors of heroin and cocaine – and the damage caused to West African countries by facilitating the illegal flight of capital into European bank accounts'.[21]

The bag men are a nice symbol of the *raison d'être* of modern international finance capital. The central task is to maximise the inflow of funds, the social welfare of 'we the peoples' being of scant concern. It is useful, in this context, to spend a little more time with the IMF and the World Bank, and then with GATT.

THE IMF AND THE WORLD BANK

The Articles of Agreement for the International Monetary Fund (IMF) and the International Bank for Reconstruction and Development (the World Bank) were drawn up at the conference held at Bretton Woods, New Hampshire, 1–22 July 1944. The main purpose of such developments was to enshrine US interests against the rival capitalist countries weakened by the war, laying the basis for a global monetary system to American advantage. In 1944 most Third World peoples lived under colonialism and no effort was made to represent their interests. By the time they gained their independence they had no opportunity to reform the powerful US-dominated financial institutions that determined the conditions of world trade.

The United States worked hard at Bretton Woods to advance its interests against competing schemes recommended by the other industrial nations. Thus the 'Bancor' plan advocated by John Maynard Keynes, head of the British delegation, was rejected in favour of the alternative White plan, named after the US delegation head, which shifted significant burdens onto deficit countries.[22] Such countries would be able to obtain loans, provided that certain conditions were met. Washington had succeeded in creating two immensely powerful financial institutions to impose US interests on a global free-market system: states would only have access to the main sources of world finance if they were prepared to embrace a thorough-going capitalist philosophy, were thereby granted membership of the IMF, and so allowed access to IMF and World Bank funds. The IMF/World Bank axis was created as a strategic force, a circumstance of great political importance through the years of the Cold War and beyond.

The IMF was not set up with the developing countries in mind, since at that time they were not seen as having much economic significance on the global stage. As the colonial peoples gradually gained their independence the IMF evolved to exploit the situation. The original intention was to promote orderly exchange conditions among the developed powers in order to prevent a return to the chaotic circumstances of the 1930s (Figure 6.1). The Fund's resources are provided through the members' subscriptions;

Purposes

The purposes of the International Monetary Fund are:

(i) To promote international monetary cooperation through a permanent institution which provides the machinery for consultation and collaboration on international monetary problems.

(ii) To facilitate the expansion and balanced growth of international trade, and to contribute thereby to the promotion and maintenance of high levels of employment and real income and to the development of the productive resources of all members as primary objectives of economy policy.

(iii) To promote exchange stability, to maintain orderly exchange arrangements among members, and to avoid competitive exchange depreciation.

(iv) To assist in the establishment of a multilateral system of payments in respect of current transactions between members and in the elimination of foreign exchange restrictions which hamper the growth of world trade.

(v) To give confidence to members by making the general resources of the Fund temporarily available to them under adequate safeguards, thus providing them with opportunity to correct maladjustments in their balance of payments without resorting to measures destructive of national or international prosperity.

(vi) In accordance with the above, to shorten the duration and lessen the degree of disequilibrium in the international balances of payments of members.

The Fund shall be guided in all its policies and decisions by the purposes set forth in this Article.

Figure 6.1   Article 1 (Articles of Agreement) of IMF

based on quotas originally negotiated at Bretton Woods. The size of the quotas – which determined the voting rights of the Fund members – were based on financial status and political considerations. Access to funds was made subject to conditions that could be defined on an *ad hoc* basis as political circumstances demanded. Thus Article V, section 5, of the Articles of Agreement states:

Whenever the Fund is of the opinion that any member is using the resources of the Fund in a manner contrary to the purposes of the Fund, it shall present to the member a report setting forth the views of the Fund and prescribing a suitable time for reply. After presenting such a report to a member, the Fund may limit the use of its resources by the member. If no reply to the report is received from the member within

the prescribed time, or if the reply received is unsatisfactory, the Fund
may continue to limit the member's use of the Fund's resources or may,
after giving reasonable notice to the member, declare it ineligible to use
the resources of the Fund.

Put simply, if a Fund member does not abide by the political and
economic philosophy of the IMF then such a member will be prevented
from borrowing from the main sources of international finance. It soon
became clear that Article V and other Fund provisions were designed to
promote the US view of world trade. The Fund – invented and dominated
by the US – claimed discretion to insist on appropriate domestic policies
in its member countries.[23] From the beginning the IMF's interest in the
domestic policies of members gradually increased – to the point that its
extreme rightist posture was transparent and unambiguous: the Fund was,
for example, immensely hostile to large state investments in social
security programmes, and to any efforts to protect fragile domestic
economies from external trade pressures. By the late-1960s there was
mounting criticism of the Fund's impact on poor countries: social programmes for health and education were discouraged, unemployment was
knowingly increased, and economies were destabilised. Some of the early
critics of the Fund were the 'structuralist' economists from the UN
Economic Commission for Latin America (ECLA or CEPAL), prepared to
argue – against the IMF – for egalitarian measures such as a modest
redistribution of income and a more flexible approach to land tenure.

The principal task of the IMF was to safeguard the economic position of
the Western developed countries, particularly the United States. In this
environment, poor countries have always been set at a deliberate disadvantage. Thus Teresa Hayter observes: 'It can . . . be asserted, given the
international purposes of the fund and the biased nature of its government,
that the interests of the developing countries, where they conflict with
those of the developed countries, will regularly be sacrificed.'[24] The Fund
has always been used to promote US objectives, whether the removal of
restrictions on trade, the defining of exchange rates, and policies on
inflation. It is arguable that such measures are advantageous to world
trade, as at one level they are; but this neglects the grossly unequal bargaining positions of the rich and poor countries. In any conflict of interest
the developed states are certain to win.

The World Bank, with headquarters in Washington close to those of the
IMF, has a similar management structure to that of the Fund, and operates
in similar ways. The Bank has the same membership as the IMF: any state
not entitled to become a member of the one would be barred from the

other. Like the Fund, the Bank provides capital for member states, providing that they behave themselves; that is, the Bank interests itself in the domestic policies of member states – sending experts to examine development plans – and puts pressure on governments to ensure compliance with its view of the world.

The IMF/World Bank axis, working primarily to further US economic interests, is supported by other financial/commercial institutions: for example, the International Development Association (IDA), established in 1960 as an affiliate to the World Bank to provide loans to underdeveloped countries; and the International Finance Corporation (IFC), a separate corporate entity that works closely with the Bank. In addition, such bodies collaborate with the General Agreement on Tariffs and Trade (GATT, see below), working to 'liberalise' the conditions of world trade. The central aim of all such bodies is clear: to organise the conditions of world trade to the advantage of the developed countries, in particular the United States. Thus in April 1990, Dr Michael Irwin, a senior British staff member, resigned from the World Bank, accusing it of profiteering at the expense of the world's poor. He declared that the Bank's austerity programmes for poor countries 'result in the poor suffering the most'.[25] Of the GATT negotiations in the Uruguay Round, launched in September 1986, Julius Nyerere commented: '. . . in area after area of the Uruguay Round's detailed negotiations, Economic Colonialism is attacking the independent nations of the Third World and seeking to secure control of strategic points in their economies . . . this attack is being pointed by the Transnational Corporations of the world, in whose interests the Industrialised Countries are acting, while at the very same time their governments protect other domestic industries and economic sectors even contrary to the existing GATT rules which they now wish to extend and twist!'[26]

It is an easy matter to identify the broad economic philosophy that guides the activities of the IMF/World Bank/GATT nexus. It is significant that this philosophy now characterises the attitudes of many of the governments in the developed world. For one thing, the high inflation rates of many poor countries are regarded as caused by excessive demand, a somewhat ironic interpretation in view of the great contrast in the levels of consumption in rich and poor countries. The aim, therefore, of the IMF and its sister bodies is to reduce the excessive demand – which in reality invariably means attacking subsidies for basic goods, investment in social services, state spending on transport, and unproductive state enterprises. The IMF characteristically demands a currency devaluation to make imports more expensive and to boost exports, coincidentally creating favourable conditions for foreign investors, increasing interest rates and restricting the money supply. In this environment the private sector is generally given more scope to raise capital than is the state.

The IMF has no interest in why particular political or social policies have been implemented in this or that poor country. All that concerns the Fund economists is that the domestic 'price distortions' that lead to 'excessive demand' be eliminated in order to restructure the economy in line with international business needs. This means that food prices, no longer state-subsidised, are made to rise; just as unsubsidised petrol will increase the costs of domestic travel. If state enterprises, even those fulfilling important social purposes, do not at least cover their costs they should be closed, an approach that inevitably brings massive unemployment in the public sector. At the same time tax cuts may be demanded to favour foreign investors, while wages are suppressed to maximise the profits flowing to the private sector. Workers are discouraged from organising to increase their wages to offset the rise in food and other prices – a nice IMF departure from the working of the free market. Thus the IMF and the associated UN-linked financial institutions are interested above all in crushing the independence of poor countries in order to expose their domestic economies to foreign capital.

However, it is significant that, even in IMF/World Bank terms, the free-market ideology is failing to deliver the goods. Much of the developed world is facing immense economic problems which existing global finance policies are doing little to solve. Hence the new emphasis on GATT (see below). The traditional IMF/World Bank approach to the Third World gave international capitalism a handle on poor countries, making it relatively easy to expropriate their natural resources and to exploit their labour, but today, with the global business world needing fresh scope for expansion and exploitation, the last vestiges of Third World independence must be abolished (and even the last elements of state subsidy in the developed world must be subordinated to the business needs of international capital). A principal purpose of GATT is to breathe fresh life into the increasingly moribund IMF/World Bank system, to stave off for perhaps another generation the ultimate financial crisis when there are no more markets to tap, no more trade 'restrictions' to abolish, no more protected sources of goods and natural resources to exploit.

The political character of the IMF/World Bank system has long been apparent. There are many historical examples of where radical governments have been offered loans with attached conditions that were incompatible with their survival; while over the same period rightist or even fascist regimes have been offered loans with few conditions. Thus the socialist government of Salvador Allende was given no significant IMF support whereas the successor fascist regime of General Pinochet, having gained power through a bloody revolt against a democratically-elected government, was rapidly offered standby loans. Similarly, while Vietnam, routinely denied any access to international finance for expelling the US invaders, was starved of investment, South Africa, having just crushed the Soweto uprising and still eagerly maintaining the racist policy of apartheid, was given an IMF loan of $464 million in 1976. In November 1982 the UN General Assembly voted by 121 to 3 (with 3 abstentions) for a denial of IMF aid to the apartheid regime, whereupon the IMF granted South Africa a loan of $1.1 billion. In the early 1980s the fascist regime in El Salvador, at that time waging a genocidal war against its own people, was offered several IMF loans, including a standby credit that was remarkable because of its generous terms: the usual IMF conditions on interest rates, subsidies and the price of agricultural goods were waived to favour a military regime of death squads. Brief objections by the Carter administration to IMF loans for the Somoza dictatorship in Nicaragua were abandoned in 1979, and weeks before the collapse of the regime later that year the IMF provided a credit, most of which was used to line the pockets of the fleeing Somoza clan. US pressure resulted in the severe reduction of a promised IMF loan to Grenada, as a prelude to the illegal American invasion in 1983. In a similar vein, during the 1990/91 Gulf crisis Washington used its control of the IMF and the World Bank to buy support for the fragile anti-Iraq coalition.

Since their inception the IMF and the World Bank operated to shape international trade to the advantage of Western capitalism, primarily that of the United States. The initial focus on the North Atlantic states gradually gave way to massive involvement in the Third World, with attempts to suppress leftist-leaning domestic economies, to destabilise radical regimes, and to expose vulnerable states to Western capital penetration.[27] There is now a broad consensus that the Untied States has used its dominant position in the global financial institutions to further its strategic objectives. Thus the economist John Kenneth Galbraith notes: 'The Marshall Plan and the AID [Agency for International Development] programs . . . *the later American influence in the World Bank and the International Monetary Fund*, the compelling need for other countries to gain access to the American market, the perception of the United States as the obvious model of economic success for the world and the extensive resources its private lenders so confidently dispersed with however disastrous consequences *were all central to the success of American foreign policy initiatives*' (my italics).[28] The IMF/World Bank philosophy has been consistently applied over many decades, with results that are manifest and well documented.

In 1984 that stalwart American activist, Henry Kissinger, began to worry that the IMF burden on the Third World might be excessive, not for any reasons of ethics but because the debt crisis might wind up 'spawning radical anti-Western governments', in which case the financial matters might be 'overwhelmed by the political consequences'. Already it seemed apparent that one country after another might become 'completely insolvent'[29] – a situation that would do little to swell the coffers of Western banks. Already it was clear that the GATT negotiations would have to be reactivated to save the IMF/World Bank axis from itself. It was easy to chart the difficulties in the international financial institutions, but far from clear what should be done.[30] The inefficiencies in the IMF and the World Bank – that Michael Irwin had helped to make transparent – were now obvious: in 1991 the Bank had 6000 staff in Washington, 'with annual staff costs of over $900 million, $150,000 a head, bloated by perks such as first-class air travel'. Only one-tenth of the staff worked in poor countries, with around 1000 consultants hired to do the work that Bank staff should have been doing themselves. When 'World Bankers do visit' poor countries, 'unco-ordinated teams fall over each other'.[31] At the same time there seemed little hope of radical reform of the financial institutions. The question of debt cancellation was sometimes discussed but no-one doubted that any changes would be tied to severe conditions. In May 1991 the US Congress announced that it would withhold part of America's 1992 contribution if the World Bank failed to clean up its environmental act, but again the statement was received with scepticism: Congress had no appetite for domestic environmental legislation, so why should it criticise the Bank?

In October 1991 there were signs that the IMF would offer various countries significant relief on their official debts, providing certain conditions were met. Two early candidates for such relief were thought to be the Philippines and Nigeria, with India already having taken steps to qualify for relief. Outflows from the Indian domestic economy were already threatening the stability of the country; and debt relief was one option for assistance. Another, it emerged, was to increase the Indian debt burden. It was announced that about $6.7 billion of support for India had been set aside for the year ending March 1992, of which around $700 million was said to be immediately available. Already, to encourage the IMF economists, India had introduced 'adjustments' to make it easier for foreign investors to acquire stakes in Indian enterprises. It was also announced that the fragile Brazilian economy would earn IMF aid provided that the public sector payroll was slashed.[32]

In August the IMF and the World Bank approved loans of up to $1.6 billion to prop up the tottering Russian economy: the IMF component ($1 billion) was intended for the foreign currency reserves, with the World Bank element to be spent on intended imports. The acting prime minister, Yegor Gaidar, commented that the money 'will make it possible for us to speak more calmly with our creditors'. At that time the Russian foreign debt amounted to around $74 billion, a burden that threatened a collapse in both capital and interest payments. The new loan allocations to Russia clearly signalled a strategic initiative, just as political demands were being intensified on poor countries hoping to attract aid assistance. In 1990 the British Foreign Secretary Douglas Hurd had suggested that aid would not be forthcoming to countries with 'wasteful discredited economic systems'; and it was now obvious that aid (and the withdrawal of aid) would increasingly be used as a means of political leverage.

On 15 December 1992 donor countries around the world agreed to provide $18 billion of concessional foreign loans to the world's poorest countries; though conditions would be attached and it was far from clear that the money would ever materialise. There was now abundant evidence that many earlier IMF and World Bank initiatives, particularly in Africa, had failed to make real progress, with many states showing a fall in industrial output (Figure 6.2). In this context the structural adjustment programmes (SAPs) had been judged to be successful, despite obvious social costs, in such states as Chile and Indonesia, but unsuccessful in much of sub-Saharan Africa. Many observers, 'particularly Africans – blame the harsh cost-cutting of SAPs for cuts in employment, and in health and education budgets, which have put the entire social fabric at risk'.[33] It still remained the case that the World Bank, originally intended as at least in part a development fund, was operating as 'the West's policeman for economic policy in developing countries, particularly Africa'.[34]

Through 1993 the familiar facts were rehearsed to little effect. Africa was seen to be 'facing deeper gloom', profligate World Bank spending on its own Washington headquarters was criticised, and Oxfam urged a fresh approach to aid policies in Africa: 'There cannot be a role for the IMF if it is going to go on sucking Africa dry, as it is at the moment' (Oxfam director, David Bryer, noted that the Fund had drained Africa of more than $3 billion since 1983). There were repeated IMF promises that agreed aid would soon start flowing to Russia, though at the same time it was emphasised that the Yeltsin administration would need to demonstrate 'a commitment to tackling hyper-inflation' and to move towards the establishment of an independent central bank. On 28 April the World Bank president, Lewis Preston, launching a new strategy to reduce global

206

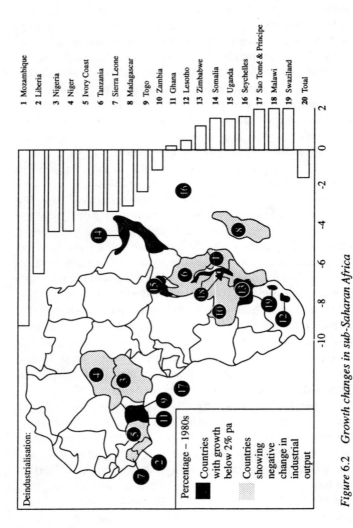

Figure 6.2 Growth changes in sub-Saharan Africa

SOURCE: World Bank Sub Saharan Africa, UNDP.

poverty, admitted that it would be 'a long, long job'. It was acknowledged that in 1990 there were 1.1 billion people living in poverty in developing countries, about 8 per cent more than in 1985.

It was also clear that the IMF, like the World Bank, would remain one of the central institutions of the so-called 'new world order'. In its initiatives on Eastern European and Russian reform the Fund had clearly demonstrated its interest in underwriting Washington's view of the world, despite criticisms that the agency had 'buckled under the load of Russia's problems by failing to facilitate disbursement of the $24bn promised in last year's rescue programme, and by failing to put staff on the ground to provide vital technical assistance'. The Fund's head, Michel Camdessus, has depicted a role for the IMF as the G7's executor on a global stage where *the G7 nations are increasingly taking on the role of the world's steering committee, to resolve global problems ranging from the Gulf War to exchange rate crises.*[35] In this context there would be periodic shifts of policy emphasis on Africa and other problem areas, but the main strategic direction would be maintained. In May 1993 the Russian government and central bank agreed to limit the credits to state enterprises, to remove the remaining barriers to the private ownership of land, and to lift government controls on exports – changes demanded by the Fund as conditions for the release of a $1.5 billion loan from the IMF agreed by the G7 countries. At the same time the International Finance Corporation (IFC), an arm of the World Bank, was threatening a partial pull-out from Ukraine if the country did not quickly pay its membership dues (this followed an earlier similar threat to Russia which resulted in Yeltsin finding the membership fee).

Through 1993, with significant difficulties in the GATT negotiations, there were frequent criticisms of the IMF/World Bank culture. The report from the Bank vice-president, Willi Wapenhans, published in December 1992, had acknowledge many deficiencies in the operation of the institution. There had been a mounting share of projects with 'major problems', a steady deterioration in portfolio performance, and inadequate attention placed on project management. Officials, the report charged, were designing loans to win the approval of management rather than to meet the needs of the borrowers. The Washington-based Environmental Defence Fund (EDF) had called on Congress to lay down stringent conditions for further contributions to the Bank, with emphasis on greater transparency in Bank operations, more public access to project-related documents, and the creation of an independent appeals commission to investigate complaints about Bank behaviour in developing countries. At the same time there were mounting criticisms of the Bank's lavish spending on its own headquarters and officials. The headquarters reconstruction project was already $43 million over budget, and the board had recently backed a $4.7 million proposal to introduce a special air-conditioning system that would enable directors to smoke in their offices once the Bank's general smoke-free policy had been introduced.[36]

By mid-1993 it was clear that the criticisms were having an impact on World Bank attitudes. Lewis Preston, the Bank head, indicated a need for increased transparency in bank operations, with disclosure of information required as a pragmatic development. An internal memorandum, dated 17 May 1993, stated: 'Mr Preston said that this [disclosure of information] was an absolutely vital issue which the bank must handle sensitively. If the bank did not, there was real risk that external pressure would eventually force the bank to make changes which might go well beyond the institution's interest.' This followed a major scare for the Bank when the US House of Representatives voted only 216–210 to approve a payment of $56 million in new funding to the institution. In July there were signs that the Bank, under pressure from the Clinton administration, would be moving to set up an internal watchdog to oversee its environmental policies and to improve the Bank's accountability. However, the in-house Inspection Panel was only intended to make confidential recommendations, so perpetuating the lack of outside accountability. And problems about panel funding, doubts on the part of some borrowers, and opposition from some board members made it highly doubtful that significant reforms would be introduced. While the World Bank ruminated on how it might move to put its own house in order, its annual World Development Report observed that 11 million children were dying needlessly each year in developing countries, all from 'preventable deaths' resulting from such conditions as diarrhoea and respiratory illness exacerbated by malnutrition. Nothing had been done to remove the millstone of external debt: Julius Nyerere's 20-year-old question, 'Must we starve our children to pay our debts?', had been long-since answered by the rich countries with a resounding 'yes'.

In July 1993 the G7 countries pledged a further $3 billion to President Boris Yeltsin to help finance the privatisation of Russian industry. It was now reported that some $43 billion ($28 billion plus $15 billion of relief on Russian debts) had been assembled by G7, the IMF and the World Bank to aid Russia's transition to a free-market economy. While the West was willing to write off $15 billion-worth of Russian debts there was no movement on the plight of Africa. At a time when the international community was spending around $50 a head on Bosnia's 2 million refugees, the 786 million starving people in Africa and Asia were receiving about $2 *a year* in medical aid, with no thought of significant debt cancellation.

It was now clear that the rich countries were moving to reduce their aid disbursements to the developing world. Beset by domestic economic problems, and with an eye on political priorities, increased emphasis was being given to the strategic targeting of available funds. Most of the wealthy countries had manifestly failed to reach the UN targets for official aid (Figure 6.3) and now there were even signs of cut-backs in their modest aid achievements. For example, Britain's aid amounts to 0.31 per cent of GNP and in late-1993 was regarded as frozen at £1.9 billion until 1995, at which time it would represent only 0.26 per cent of GNP (Britain's aid fell in the 1980s, by 1989 worth only 77 per cent of the 1979 figure). To reach the UN-recommended figure Britain's aid would have to more than double, an unlikely prospect. The emphasis was now on the need to secure a GATT agreement, the requirement that aid be politically targeted, and the evident sluggishness of the world economy. In September 1993 the IMF downgraded its forecasts for recovery among the wealthy nations of the world, while the World Bank announced that its loan commitments to Africa, the world's poorest continent, had been reduced by more than $1 billion to $2.82 billion in the year to end-June. The Bank's loan commitments had in fact increased by $3 billion to reach $27 billion for the coming year, but it was obvious that disbursements would be made on political grounds (for example, to Eastern Europe, Russia and the Palestinian territories) rather than according to need. On 23 September 1993 the IMF head, Michel Camdessus, urged the G7 countries to press

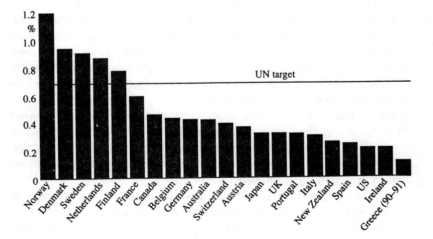

Figure 6.3   Official aid as percentage of GNP

ahead with aid to Russia, even thought it was clear that the economic reforms had stalled. The United States announced it would be accelerating the delivery of its $2.5 billion assistance package to President Yeltsin; while Germany, one of the largest Western donors to Russia, moved to sign a landmark $5 billion debt rescheduling package.

Again it was easy to observe widespread criticism on the IMF/World Bank axis. An Oxfam report, denounced by Camdessus, accused the IMF of 'complacency' and 'undue secrecy' in its approach to the poorest countries of sub-Saharan Africa (Camdessus retorted that he too deplored 'the sinking of a continent'); there were still waves from the hostile Wapenhans report on the quality of World Bank operations; and it remained obvious that the IMF/World Bank bureaucrats' gravy train was necessarily at the expense of the poorest countries of the world (tax-free salaries of $190,000 a year, free travel and pocket-money for employees' families, annual grants for spouses and children, settling-in and resettlement benefits, etc.[37]). At the same time the British Chancellor of the Exchequer, Kenneth Clarke, speaking in Washington after a meeting of the IMF development committee, announced that Britain would be unlikely to make a contribution to the key IMF funding facility used to aid the world's poorest countries.[38]

In March 1994 publicity was given to a secret World Bank report dealing with the controversial subject of 'involuntary resettlement'. Here it was declared that more than 30 million Chinese citizens had been evicted from their homes over the last three decades, forced to resettle as part of road, railway and reservoir projects. The report admitted that a third of the Bank projects underway in China still involve the forced resettlement of people: some 32 projects financed by the Bank will require the removal of 473,000 people from their homes over the coming years. In one case, 150,000 people evicted from their homes 30 years ago were still living in 'temporary shelters'; and one report indicated that of 10 million people moved since 1949 in connection with reservoir projects, over a third were 'living in abject poverty' with another third 'barely getting by'. In April 1994 the World Bank approved funding for the new Xiaolangdi dam on the Yellow River, which would require the forced eviction of 171,000 people; and the project was agreed in the context of workers in the area already denied resettlement benefits.

Fresh interest in the World Bank's resettlement record was sparked by the mounting controversy over India's Sardar Sarovar dam. With this project and others in mind, the Canadian environmental organisation Probe International accused the World Bank of sponsoring the world's 'worst environmental, social and economic disasters . . . in the name of aid to the

Third World'.* It has been emphasised that the Bank often relies on congenial (but dubious) statistics from host countries and that adverse information is often contained in unpublished internal documents.[39] Even the Bank report conceded that 35 per cent more people were being displaced than earlier government estimates had suggested.

It is clear that many World Bank funding decisions have been taken for political reasons rather than to encourage economic development. Thus at a World Bank seminar at the Wye Woods Centre in Queenstown, Maryland, in April 1994 privatisation advocates from Britain, Mexico, Russia and eastern Europe indicated that privatisation was often primarily a political process designed to achieve political ends; industrial and financial benefits may follow but they are secondary. Moreover, such bodies as the International Finance Corporation (IFC), a World Bank offshoot, are only interested in infrastructure improvements if they can be funded from private sector capital: 'the thread which connects many privatisation schemes is political.'[40] In this spirit the World Bank, the IMF and G7 have frequently emphasised that loans to Russia and the Third World are contingent on suitable political reforms – essentially those that signal a more market-friendly posture.[41]

By now there were growing demands for reform of the World Bank and the IMF, both increasingly perceived as ill-suited for operations in the post-Cold War world. It was widely acknowledged that such institutions, now fifty years old, had been created in a quite different political environment. Critics suggested that the World Bank and the IMF ignored local people and their needs, adopted a patronising 'top-down' approach to economic questions, and were indifferent to social and ecological concerns. Some aid agencies even began a campaign '50 years is enough'. Said Justin Forsyth of Oxfam: 'There's a lot of difference between the Bank's rhetoric about alleviating poverty and the reality. In Zambia, Zimbabwe and Uganda they are making economic changes which do nothing to help the poor.'[42] In the same vein Oxfam and Christian Aid together accused the World Bank of impoverishing the Third World by demanding market-oriented policies that involved spending cuts. Of the Bank's Economic Structural Adjustment Programmes (ESAPs) Oxfam noted their imposition of 'unacceptable and unnecessary social costs on the poor'. Christian Aid's Jessica Woodroffe pointed out that an ESAP

Damming the Three Gorges – Probe International's critique of the Canadian Government/World Bank feasibility study in China, published by Earthscan in April 1994, together with *Yangtze, Yangtze*, a collection of essays by Chinese critics of the scheme.

imposed on Bolivia in 1985 had increased unemployment from 16 to 22 per cent; and that a similar programme in Jamaica had reduced health spending from 9 to 5 per cent over a decade. And the Oxfam statement declared: 'Many of the bank's operations . . . result in the (often violent) displacement of communities and gross environmental damage.'[43]

In the post-Soviet world the American role in sustaining the World Bank and the IMF had become increasingly unambiguous. President Clinton, according to Deputy Secretary of State Strobe Talbott, believed that 'international politics and economics are indivisible'. The Bank and the IMF would continue to enjoy US support on the assumption that *they continued to play 'their allotted role in the Clinton administration's global political agenda'* (my italics).[44] There is no acknowledgement in this free-market ideology of what the World Bank and the IMF have come to symbolise throughout much of the world: project failures, expensive foreign experts, increased inequality and hunger, exacerbated ethnic conflicts, political patronage and corruption, brutal evictions, environmental disasters, deforestation, croneyism, increased unemployment, social disruption, food shortages, the crippling of social services, mounting debt and economic decline.[45] In the rationale of global capitalism, such developments are of little concern.

By the mid-1990s the ravages of IMF/World Bank policies were increasingly plain. Despite the occasional nod in the direction of 'green' investment policies, the acknowledgement of past errors, and nominal approval for truly independent policy making in developing countries, the US-dominated global financial institutions continued to steer world investment decisions in the interests of the richest nations on earth. Emphasis continued to be placed on the 'need' for 'structural readjustment' (often leading to massive social dislocation) and to broad global policies designed to underwrite the strategic interests of the G7 countries, particularly the United States. However, there were many signs that the world economic system was failing to meet the needs of international capitalism: free-market economies were sluggish or in crisis, the erosion of social provision was causing domestic tensions in many countries, and it seemed unclear how global GNP could be boosted to remove the problems. In this troubled atmosphere a fresh emphasis was given to the need to secure GATT agreements among the wealthy countries of the world; then the rest, not allowed influence or prior consultation, could be brought on board. Only then, it was argued, could world capitalism be given a shot in the arm and the health of the free-market economies be restored.

GENERAL AGREEMENT ON TARIFFS AND TRADE (GATT)

Features and Progress

The General Agreement on Tariffs and Trade (GATT), with annexes and schedules, is attached to the Final Act of the United Nations Conference on Trade and Development (UNCTAD) that was signed at Geneva on 30 October 1947. GATT came into being in 1948, with 23 countries as signatories, as a temporary arrangement until the planned Havana Charter and the International Trade Organisation (ITO) were created. But in 1950 the US Congress refused to ratify the Charter since this would have meant ceding elements of US trade policy to the ITO. Thus GATT survived as a provisional treaty to encourage sovereign states to negotiate rules on the co-ordination of international trade. The General Agreement was devised by the United States as a means of extending the American free-market model throughout the world. In this aim, the efforts of the GATT negotiators were aided by the parallel endeavours of the IMF and the World Bank.

Between 1948 and 1994 there have been seven rounds of GATT negotiations, the last and most ambitious – the Uruguay Round – ending in December 1993. The earlier talks were relatively modest attempts to encourage trade by reducing tariffs (taxes and duties) and non-tariff restrictions (quotas and licences) on imports. The immensely complicated Uruguay Round went far beyond the earlier negotiations by extending its ambitions into such areas as agriculture, services, foreign investments and intellectual property rights. It became abundantly clear through 1993 that the developing General Agreement would have massive global consequences, not only for the industrialised countries that conducted the negotiations but also for the rest of the planet: the GATT negotiators, drawn almost entirely from the rich countries, had ambitions that embraced the entire world – to the point that there would be 'legal' trade sanctions imposed on any dissident state by the international community. Here was the supreme effort of financial vested interest to impose unified global trading patterns on the entire world. By 1993 there were 108 GATT members, with more joining all the time. By 1994 more than 90 per cent of world trade was governed by the ever expanding GATT rules. Today three enormously powerful financial/commercial bodies – the IMF, the World Bank and GATT – bestride the world: no state is immune from their influence or from the aggressive free-market philosophy that they represent.[46]

The General Agreement was intended from the beginning to benefit the developed rather than the underdeveloped countries. The early negotiations achieved a considerable expansion of world trade, which benefited mostly the industrialised trading regions. Other advantages were brought by IMF/World Bank efforts to ensure free-market trading practices and by such initiatives as the US Marshall Plan, designed as a vehicle for investment and subversion in Europe to defeat popular leftist movements.[47] At the same time the GATT impact on tariff and non-tariff trade restrictions worked to induce the rich countries to remove their mutual trade barriers but not those in respect of Third World exports. In such a fashion the early GATT rounds did little to support the trading efforts of poor countries, but much to secure the dominance by the developed countries (particularly the United States) of the world trade system. There were a number of other GATT features that also worked to place under-developed countries at a serious trading disadvantage.

Whereas Japan, for example, was allowed to join GATT only after securing bilateral restraint on certain exports to the US, efforts by such states as Egypt and Pakistan to export cotton textiles were discouraged by protectionist practices in the developed world. The rich countries would run GATT as they saw fit, allowing various discriminatory and 'managed trade' arrangements in seeming violation of the General Agreement: 'the price paid by the Third World countries for the launch and conclusion of successive GATT' rounds.[48] It is significant that at the outset and for some years afterwards there were few poor countries in GATT. Fewer than half of the 23 original signatories were 'less developed contracting parties', with three of these (Lebanon, Syria and Taiwan) withdrawing by 1951. As the colonised countries gained their independence, most were admitted by the rich states into the United Nations, the IMF and the World Bank, though they were less keen to become GATT members. International trading and loan pressures have forced a growing number of developing countries into GATT, though their interests have rarely been protected by anything more substantial than 'pious exhortations', provisions that 'have not been translated into commitments or obligations like the other parts of the General Agreement'.[49]

The developing countries tried through the 1960s and early 1970s – by dint of what pressure they could exert in the UN General Assembly and in UNCTAD – to bring changes to the rules that governed international trade; but it was impossible to mount a fundamental challenge to the global economic system that had evolved to benefit the industrialised world. The emerging difficulties of the IMF and the World Bank, plus the impact of the Organisation of Petroleum Exporting Countries (OPEC), suggested that the poor countries might at last be able to use their nominal ownership of raw materials to impose changes in the terms of world trade; but again nothing of fundamental importance was achieved. Efforts to organise significant negotiations that might have benefited developing countries were often thwarted by US indifference or hostility. Thus the Non-Aligned Movement (NAM)/G77 initiative for Global Negotiations – placed on the agenda of the 1980 UN General Assembly Special Session on Development – was blocked by US insistence on IMF and GATT jurisdiction. In 1981, following fresh US hostility to negotiations, Julius Nyerere talked of the 'optimism and hope . . . dashed there because Reagan said 'no' and that was it . . . What was very revealing, and very depressing, was that after Reagan said "no", the other leaders from the North said that was the end'.[50] But it was not enough for the West to block Third World efforts to improve the terms of international trade. The financial systems formulated at the 1944 Bretton Woods conference had virtually collapsed in 1973, and the remedy of the floating exchange rate mechanism had created new problems. It was necessary for the industrialised countries to impose a new financial world order; and GATT was chosen as the instrument of the new arrangements. The General Agreement was in place and its underlying philosophy, designed in the US, was highly sympathetic to Western desires to tighten the North's grip on world resources and world trade.

It was recognised that courageous Third World nations might defy the IMF and the World Bank by not asking for financial support, but the need for trade necessarily maintained the vulnerability of poor states. If poor countries could be attacked through their trading practices then the financial hegemony of the rich nations would be assured. This was the main objective of the Uruguay Round: to give the rich nations, led by the United States, a final handle on the resources and commerce of the world. The poor countries, without any co-operative union, remain weak in GATT; by contrast 'the major trading nations, despite their mutual differences and trade quarrels, have always been aware of their general common interest against the South and have been concerting together'. Thus the United States, the European Community, Japan and Canada frequently meet together (at G5, G7, G10 and the OECD) to plan the trade strategies to be adopted in the GATT negotiations and elsewhere.[51] The contest is unequal: a band of collaborating giants against a bunch of disorganised midgets.

The GATT talks of the Uruguay Round ran into 1993 with various tensions and disputes between the negotiators. One contentious issue was the matter of oilseeds. European production had been generously subsidised from Brussels under the terms of the Common Agricultural Policy (CAP), a policy that outraged American oilseed producers as European output increased and prices fell. The US Soya Bean Association, after intensive lobbying against the European subsidies, secured two GATT adjudications against the European Community. Gary Hufbauer, a trade specialist at the Institute for International Economics at Washington, commented: 'We are absolutely right on the legality. We have the highest, strongest ground in terms of free-trade doctrine.' The oilseed dispute was not formally part of the Uruguay Round but no-one doubted that its implications would affect the GATT talks, then (late-1992) stalled on the issue of all farm subsidies.[52] On 16 November 1992 the British premier, John Major, in an address to the Lord Mayor's Banquet at Guildhall in central London, emphasised the need for an early and comprehensive GATT settlement ('We cannot let a handful of oilseeds or a sack of grain stand in the way of the boost such a settlement would give to the world economy'). He declared that Britain's problems with the ratification of the Maastricht Treaty would not be allowed to stand in the way of the vital GATT negotiations ('Nothing would break the clouds of world recession more surely than the boost to confidence of a successful Uruguay round'). The next day the French were defeated in their efforts to toughen the European stance in the trade dispute with the United States, with Jean-Pierre Soisson, the French Agriculture Minister, commenting that 'if there is an agreement it will be bad for the Community and not in conformity with the Common Agricultural Policy'. John Gummer, Britain's Agriculture Minister, suggested that the French did not know their own interests: 'Anybody outside France can see how important it is for France to get a deal. The French economy is as much in need of the kick-start that a GATT deal would bring as any other country in Europe. We need a lot more people to be much more Community minded, much more communautaire . . . and a lot less nationalistic.'[53] Soon there were signs of progress in the GATT talks, though it was clear that the French intended to demand compensation for French farmers if Europe was to agree terms with the United States.

There was still no prospect of an early final agreement. On 25 November 1992 both Belgium and Italy indicated a measure of support for France's opposition to American proposals. Thus Belgium's Economic Minister, Melchior Wathelet, declared that the agreement as it stood was 'unacceptable, both at the economic and social level'; with Italy's Agriculture Minister, Gianni Fontana, 'in the light of new evidence' expressing 'reservations and serious concern over the implications for the [Italian] agricultural sector'. One estimate suggested that some 50,000

French farms would disappear each year during the remainder of the 1990s, a detail that explained French anger and the widespread view in France that Britain was a Trojan Horse for the Americans in a European Community that had simply surrendered to US pressure. Fresh talks in January 1993 to resolve the difficulties were inconclusive, whereupon the US imposed punitive tariffs on $1 billion-worth of EC and other flat-rolled steel exports to America, a significant blow for the European steel industry. In early February seven Latin American presidents met in Ecuador as part of a campaign to reverse EC policy on the banana trade, which they claimed was in violation of GATT rules and which could lead to 'economic ruin' for the region.

On 14 March the European Community hinted at the possibility of reprisals against the United States following the collapse of talks. A week later the US Trade Representative, Mickey Kantor, announced that there was not going to be a trade war and that the US's sole aim was to open up overseas markets for American goods; speaking on CNN, Kantor denied that the United States was acting as a bully and declared that it was simply being 'resolute, practical, pragmatic, engaged and committed'. At the same time the US and the EC continued to accuse each other of rigging their government procurement markets in favour of 'local' suppliers, with one European Community report suggesting that Washington was using Cold War rules to protect its industry by translating 'national security' into 'national economic security': one specific charge was that the US was using 'black' Pentagon funds (that is, funds closed to public scrutiny) to subsidise its aircraft construction industry. It was also emerging that Washington had reservations about many trade issues, going far beyond the high-profile farm dispute. Thus differences with Europe over such matters as foreign shipping in American coastal waters, restrictions on the showing of US films on French television, and US access to the European telecommunications market began to surface. Again there were hints of an impending trade war.

On 13 May 1993 the French premier, Edouard Balladur, called for an armistice between the EC and the US, but still insisted that he was unwilling to sacrifice the interests of French farmers for the sake of a GATT deal. The semi-placatory gesture was welcomed by GATT officials in Geneva while it was made clear that there would be problems if France tried to rewrite the tentative EC–US deals on overall farm subsidies. At this time the oilseed dispute had been resolved in the context of a broader agreement that still had to be ratified by Brussels. Balladur was quoted: 'We intend to put an end to the perception that several hundred French farmers pose an obstacle to the relaunching of world production and activity which would result from a GATT accord . . . All subjects, and not just agriculture, must be really negotiated and all parties, and not just Europeans, must adopt a positive attitude.'[54] On 2 June the European Community agreed to impose tit-for-tat sanctions on some $15 million of US business – a significant departure from conciliation. Six days later – perhaps to mitigate the sanctions on the supply of US telecommunications and construction equipment to Europe – EC foreign ministers meeting at Luxembourg nodded the oilseed agreement through. A final GATT settlement still seemed a long way off.

Pressure for a solution of the outstanding problems remained strong. The Organisation for Economic Co-operation and Development (OECD) had warned in June that the rocketing unemployment in the world's richest countries was jeopardising the social cohesion of the West; and there was broad agreement among the developed nations that a successful conclusion to the Uruguay Round would boost world trade and create many new jobs. At the same time it seemed clear that GATT and accompanying adjustments would be secured at the expense of ordinary people. Thus a confidential G7 report declared that the developed countries should roll back workers' rights, raise retirement ages, and 'rationalise' their health care systems. Here the key to the deeply-rooted problem of unemployment was seen to be lower welfare and unemployment payments to encourage the jobless to search for any kind of work, and new rules to make it easier for employers to hire and fire their workforce: 'Reforms that reduce the structural component of unemployment would enhance the growth potential of the G7 countries and improve the capacity of their economies to adapt to changing economic conditions.' It was clear that such changes would be consistent with an agreed GATT settlement and that most of the industrialised countries hoped to benefit from the final settlement scheduled to emerge not later than 15 December 1993. In July, at the World Economic Summit in Tokyo, the trade ministers of the so-called quadrilateral group (the US, the European Community Commission, Japan and Canada) agreed a framework for agreement for substantial cuts in tariffs on industrial goods. The main elements of the framework 'market access' accord were: to eliminate tariff and non-tariff barriers covering pharmaceuticals, construction equipment, medical equipment and beer (with partial elimination of trade barriers on furniture and farm equipment); the harmonisation of tariffs on chemicals at low levels (with some products zero-rated); the reduction of the highest tariffs of 15 per cent and over (for textiles, clothing, glassware and ceramics) by a maximum 50 per cent; and the reduction of tariffs on all other goods by a third on average (with electronics a key sector in this category). Still it was recognised that the landmark accord – presented to the other 107 GATT members in Geneva on 12 July 1993 – was far from complete. Already the GATT negotiators were agitating for reforms to liberalise services, to define agreements on how trade disputes might be settled, to ban dumping practices, and to create a Multilateral Trade Organisation that would replace GATT and make unilateral trade actions more difficult. It was also being suggested that welfare budgets in almost all the industrialised states would have to be curbed.

There were still many obstacles on the road to a final GATT settlement. European observers were warning that a possible US–Japan 'managed trade' agreement would in principle violate the GATT terms; the French continued to agitate for a degree of protectionism to safeguard French jobs, and for a range of cultural activities to be exempted from the current negotiations;[55] and British premier John Major failed to persuade the Japanese to make adjustments – on taxing Scotch whisky and prohibiting rice imports – to help the GATT negotiations. The mounting dispute in Europe – between Britain and France (with German support) – resulted in 'a draw' on GATT and some related issues, a manifest relief to a Clinton administration increasingly preoccupied with securing the negotiated North Atlantic Free Trade Area (NAFTA) agreement for a free-trade accord between the US, Canada and Mexico.[56] Serious problems remained but there was mounting pressure for a GATT settlement by the deadline date of 15 December 1993. In September, senior officials at the European Commission reckoned that there was a 60 per cent chance of this being accomplished.

On 27 September 1993 the world's three most powerful monetary officials – Michel Camdessus, IMF managing director; Lewis Preston, president of the World Bank; and Peter Sutherland, director-general of GATT – issued a joint statement that failure to conclude the Uruguay Round would fuel a 'rising wave of protectionism', impede economic recovery and lead to social disruption. The statement was immediately endorsed by Britain's Chancellor of the Exchequer, Kenneth Clarke ('I wasn't there to hear any French reply') and his US opposite number, Lloyd Bentsen, in comments to the IMF/World Bank Development Committee. Said the IMF/World Bank/GATT Big Three: if the GATT round were to fail it 'would lead to greater protectionism and loss of confidence, with major economic and social implications for high and low income countries alike. It could also put at risk the new democracies in eastern Europe and the countries of the former Soviet Union . . . With so much at stake, political hesitations and vested interests must be put aside'. In early October the British foreign secretary, Douglas Hurd, sounded a

positive note ('The GATT negotiations are not paralysed, they are pressing ahead'), but at the same time urged the need for an EC summit to clear
the way. Differences between the European Community and the United
States still left the projected global agreement – negotiated for the world
by a handful of states – 'hanging on the edge'. Gunter Rexrodt, Germany's
economics minister, observed that there was no more time for poker if the
15 December deadline was to be met. However, at the end of October the
GATT negotiators in Geneva expressed growing alarm that the talks were
heading for an impasse, with the Czech delegation going so far as to
predict war within ten years if the GATT process broke down. Now the
central problem was the on-going dispute between the EC and the US over
such issues as agricultural subsidies, cultural trade (film and broadcasting)
and barriers to fish imports: such seemingly intractable questions had
stopped the flow of tariff-cut offers on thousands of other products. It also
emerged that Japan was holding up agreement on the question of rice
imports.[57]

Now objections were being raised that the focus of the Clinton administration on the NAFTA deal was endangering the GATT negotiations. A
failure on NAFTA, it was argued, would seriously impede any efforts to
secure a world trade agreement; conversely, a NAFTA success was judged
likely to put new impetus behind the GATT talks. In the event the US
Congress approved NAFTA on 17 November 1993, little more than three
weeks before the GATT deadline. President Clinton, having struck many
expensive deals to buy Congressional votes, had succeeded in establishing
a free-trade bloc to encompass the US, Canada and Mexico. (At the same
time – in gross violation of GATT terms and international law – the
United States maintained its massively punitive trade blockade of Cuba, a
policy that was yet again defeated in the UN General Assembly in
November by 88–4, with 57 abstentions.) But, in terms of progress on
GATT, the NAFTA triumph seemed ambiguous. At one level it represented a blow on behalf of free trade; but at another the price of the
NAFTA victory had disarmed the GATT advocates. In giving a boost to
America's protectionist farmers, Clinton could scarcely object to Japan's
protection of its rice trade or to France's protection of its own farmers.[58]
As the 15 December deadline approached the outcome seemed far from
certain.

The GATT negotiations had mainly focused on differences between the
major trading blocs of the United States, Europe and Japan. This was a
rich man's party, with the beggars outside the gate given scant attention.
For the developed countries the adverse consequences of a GATT settlement might turn out to be minor – though it was known that there would

be a price to pay in social services, environmental protection, employment and other areas; but in the Third World the impact of a GATT deal was a more drastic possibility. It is useful to consider the GATT costs.

The Costs

It was long known that the IMF/World Bank/GATT nexus had evolved to underwrite the interests of the developed countries; in particular, the interests of the large companies, the transnational corporations (TNCs). The Uruguay Round in 1991 inserted proposals for a Multilateral Trade Organisation (MTO) that would have an independent legal personality, allowing the organisation to operate separately from the United Nations and such trade-focused UN bodies as the United Nations Conference on Trade and Development (UNCTAD) and the United Nations Conference on Environment and Development (UNCED). The proposal signals that the MTO would contribute, with the IMF and the World Bank, to a 'greater coherence in global economic policy making'. The MTO would have primary interest in implementing the GATT agreement, but the proposal expresses no concern with controlling restrictive business practices, protecting labour rights, protecting the environment, or improving the terms of trade for the desperately impoverished Third World.[59]

The development non-governmental organisations (NGOs) responded by suggesting that the MTO was essentially an instrument for the rich nations to promote their own interpretation of free trade. The proposal contains no commitment to sustainable economic development and there is little scope for democratic consultation: 'the MTO would be a new world body with extraordinary intervention and regulatory powers over international trade and for arbitrating in trade disputes, which is being introduced by the back door and to by-pass existing bodies . . . many independent observers believe the MTO will do more harm than good.'[60] Some 160 NGOs from 60 countries, now suitably alarmed, protested to their heads of government that their control over their domestic economies was being quietly transferred to an undemocratic global body run by the TNCs and the pliant national representatives. It is significant that discussions about the creation of the MTO have been largely clandestine, in line with the character of most GATT talks: 'while all inter-governmental negotiations are in private, the GATT processes are the least transparent . . . all GATT meetings are behind closed doors, without the obtrusive presence of the media or non-governmental organisations of consumers and other public interest groups.'[61] GATT has no representational system of negotiations, as do most other UN agencies, but only 'green room

consultations' (named after the decor of the GATT director-general's conference room in Geneva). All participation in the consultations follows
invitations issued on a non-transparent basis, with priority being given to
representatives of the rich countries.

In this context it is easy to see why little attention is given to the interests
of poor nations: 'In theory, all contracting parties are equal . . . But in
practice when the small have tried to assert themselves, they have been
ignored or sought to be overawed by arguments that the countries with the
largest share of the world trade have more at stake in the trading system
and its rules, and hence their views should prevail.'[62] It is hardly surprising
to find that the system works to maintain the global disadvantage of poor
countries while the industrialised nations work to sustain the myth that a
GATT settlement would lubricate global trade to the benefit of all.

The opening up of the agricultural sectors of the developing countries
would threaten their food security and make them increasingly dependent
upon the good will of the United States and Europe. The TNCs would be
entitled to export to the unprotected domestic economies; and to have their
mining and manufacturing bases treated on the same basis as locally
owned companies. The new GATT rules on intellectual property rights
would further restrict the access of poor countries to industrial technology
and information; the rules, favouring the TNCs, would force the governments of poor countries to introduce laws to protect TNC patents and
their other intellectual property rights. In such a climate it would be
impossible for poor countries to attempt any measure of independent
industrialisation or development, with the large companies gradually
expanding their grip on the entire world economy. There has been some
opposition to such developments: for example, more than 250 eminent
Indians signed a statement protesting at the GATT threat to the 1970
Indian Patents Act ('Home rule is better than GATT rule'); and there have
been Indian protests about the GATT-led textile agreement and farm deal,
and about the GATT-inspired rise in drug prices.[63] Such GATT consequences – and, for example, the adverse environmental effects of
GATT-induced measures – have been apparent for some years.

The GATT economists make no distinction between, for instance, the
subsidies used in industrialised countries to sustain over-production and
the subsidies used in poor countries to support food self-reliance, rural
employment and ecologically sustainable production. This suggests that
poor countries will be prohibited – on pain of legal sanctions – from
banning cheap imports; which in turn means that small low-technology
producers will be forced to compete with the industrialised food producers
of Europe and the United States. In 1990 the US threatened Nigeria with

sanctions when it tried to restrict US wheat imports in an attempt to develop self-reliant food security. Thus elements of control of poor domestic economies – many of which have been relatively successful in the context of under-development – will be pronounced as illegal, in order to benefit still further the rich corporations in the industrialised world.[64] A principal GATT aim would be to open the markets of the poor countries to the food surpluses of the US and Europe, a move that would provide the rich nations with a total strategic grip on the food prices and supply in all Third World countries.

The likely GATT costs to the poor countries of the world are incalculable. Weak industries, possibly serving some local social purpose, would be exposed to industrial competition; and so would be unlikely to survive. There would be no scope for local independent economic development, the rich countries controlling all access to technology, expertise and information. Workers' rights would be suppressed world-wide, and not just in the Third World, while global environmental standards, the diminished provision for social services, and the levels of employment would all be determined in the boardrooms of the global corporations. The 500 largest TNCs control more than 70 per cent of world trade: and the GATT proposals would work to enlarge this share and to tighten the TNC grip on the resources of the poor countries.[65] There would be fewer controls over the quality of food exports to the Third World, with carcinogens allowed in higher quantities if the GATT terms are fully implemented.[66] Economic enterprises in poor countries would thus be forced to compete in an impossibly unfair trade environment, while at the same time their domestic economies would be totally subject to the strategic and commercial policies of the powerful industrialised nations.[67] The environmental group Friends of the Earth denounced as 'Fools' Gold' a GATT policy that:

- advocates unregulated international trade and puts the interests of trade before those of the environment;

- is dominated by powerful, industrialised nations and is, as a result, unable to cater properly for the needs of poorer countries;

- pays no heed to the Polluter Pays, User Pays or Precautionary Principles;

- threatens to undermine national and international environmental legislation, and

- is negotiated in secret.[68]

The GATT provisions, if fully implemented, would have a 'potentially ruinous effect on food safety and quality by gearing standards to the lowest common denominator', with any country trying to set higher standards branded as acting in a way that is 'GATT-illegal'.[69] It will prove impossible to ban imports for environmental reasons, with the MTO – intended to supervise $6 trillion of world trade – rushing to denounce any protection measures as a barrier to trade. Perhaps even more bizarre – Indian peasants who have traditionally collected oil from neem trees (for use in traditional medicines, pesticides, soap, and so on); farmers who have traditionally harvested and planted particular seeds; peasants in Thailand or Madagascar who have planted in the same way for centuries – all suddenly prohibited from carrying out their traditional practices: because a US or European company has patented the seeds the peasants have relied upon for generations. The US has reckoned that it will earn $61 billion a year from Third World seeds that the industrialised food companies are now beginning to patent.[70] On 1 October 1993 a protest took place outside the London offices of Cargill, a US grain multinational and a strong supporter of GATT's patent plans, that aims to capture 25 per cent of the sunflower seed market in India. At the same time there were mass protests in India against Western moves – encouraged by GATT – to secure legally-enforceable ownership of India's native plants. It was becoming increasingly plain that GATT was emerging as a drastic form of economic imperialism, devoted to the enrichment of the industrialised nations at the expense of the Third World. It now seemed obvious that the GATT plans would lead to the collapse of agrarian communities and peasant traditions, and the consequent disastrous migration of millions of impoverished agricultural workers to swollen Third World cities unable to support even the most basic social provisions: 'The prospect of over a billion ruined peasants being peacefully absorbed into the cities of the Third World will be taken seriously only by those whose support for market institutions is fundamentalist in character'; and even in the developed world, global free trade 'means a massive increase in structural unemployment as workers try vainly to compete with the low-wage economies of the newly industrialised countries. *In both Third and First worlds the GATT proposals are a recipe for social upheaval and political instability on a vast scale*' (my italics).[71] To work for the total abolition of trade barriers, 'as the GATT seeks to do in areas never previously con-sidered, is to further condemn to extinction small farmers, artisans, small shop-keepers and small companies in general throughout the developing world – and also here in the advanced economies.[72] In this context the social costs would be 'enormous'. Even Sir James Goldsmith, the legendary corporate raider, argued in his best-selling book, *Le Piège* (The Trap), that the untrammelled free-trade policies enshrined in GATT would have catastrophic social and economic consequences for both rich and poor countries alike, throwing millions out of work and destabilising whole societies.[73]

The conclusion of the Uruguay GATT round at the end of 1993 was accomplished by means of various backstairs deals, pressures and trade-offs, many conducted in secret and all determined by only a very small minority of the affected factions and states. There was much evident disquiet in developed countries as well as in the Third World. For example, French farmers continued to protest and various dissident voices (mainly Republican) in the United States began complaining that the Clinton administration may not have achieved the best possible result for America. In Europe there were complaints that individual states were allowed no say: the GATT treaty had been negotiated by the European Commission, not by the individual parliaments, and many details of the negotiations remained secret. Third World countries were allowed virtually no influence in the shaping of the final GATT deal agreed clandestinely by the representatives of the United States and the European Union.

On 3 December 1993 more than thirty countries, including India and Malaysia, told GATT Director-General Peter Sutherland that they were being excluded by the US and the EU from a chance to shape the final GATT package, and many of the 80 or so other involved states were showing signs of concern.[74] More than 100 nations were waiting in Geneva to hear the results of the US–EU deliberations, and 'most developing countries remain highly dissatisfied with the lack of progress' in addressing their concerns.[75] Few observers doubted that the new World Trade Organisation (WTO) would serve solely to guard the interests of the multinational corporations; for example, using anti-dumping sanctions to block imports from developing countries.

The impact of the GATT deal was felt around the world. In South Korea, President Kim Young Sam asked for the resignation of premier Hwang In Sung, unhappy at the consequences of GATT for South Korea's rice market, and then sacked the entire cabinet. Just as a French farmer, Thierry Verdier, had articulated the view of thousands when he said 'I never thought I'd see the day the Americans ruled France', so 20,000 South Korean demonstrators protested at the US-imposed threat to their rice market. In Japan the deputy agriculture minister was forced to resign; and in India crowds marched shouting such slogans as: 'This is a sell-out to America!' The Japanese premier Morihiro Hosokawa expressed his 'great remorse' at the fact that he had not been able to 'defend our national interest 100 per cent'. And a report from the Organisation of Economic Co-operation and Development and the World Bank was even prepared to concede that Africa would be further damaged by the patterns of world trade that the GATT deal had been designed to reinforce.[76] Moreover, while massive protests were being staged in Asia, a peasant revolt* erupted in Mexico's poverty-stricken southern state of Chiapas, in large part in protest against the newly-negotiated North American Free Trade Agreement (NAFTA) between Mexico, Canada and the United States, designed – like the GATT deal – to make the rich richer and to marginalise indigenous populations.

On 5 April 1994, as a prelude to the signing of the GATT deal in Marrakesh by the representatives of 125 countries, 100,000 demonstrators protested in Delhi at the effects of the deal on India's agrarian economy. A principal target was the 'intellectual property rights' provision awarded under GATT to the multinational corporations: under this provision Indian farmers would not be allowed to trade with their own seeds – or even to replant them if they had been 'patented' by the multinationals – but would have to buy them from the companies, so inevitably plunging indigenous people into destitution. Moreover, India would no longer be able to subsidise agricultural inputs to protect millions of people on or below the poverty line. At the same time the rich countries were paradoxically proposing that 'social clauses' be inserted into the final agreement, not to protect workers' pay and conditions (no-one would imagine that the British Tory government would be keen to 'burden' industry with extra 'social costs') but to achieve back-door protectionism and to put developing countries at a further disadvantage. Said one Bangladeshi official: 'Yes, we have people earning a dollar a day. But if we are forced by the West to pay five dollars a day, the worker will not only lose his job, he will starve because there is no social safety net.'[77] Again the Western ploy is clear: push Third World industry into terminal collapse and then move in to fill the gap.

The GATT plan – despite the clandestine nature of most of its deliberations – is transparent. In concert with its two ugly sisters, the IMF and the World Bank, it represents a calculated political move to extend the

---

*The uprising led by the Zapatista National Liberation Army (EZLN) – in protest against NAFTA, economic exploitation and abuses of human rights – was followed by a negotiated agreement with the Mexican government, the assassination of presidential candidate Luis Donaldo Collosio, and typically rigged elections (involving a phoney computer breakdown, the 'shaving' of voters' names off the roll, etc.) to consolidate the power of the Institutional Revolutionary Party (PRI). Washington declared itself well pleased with the predictable result.

power and scope of a global capitalist economic system that, even with existing prodigious riches in natural resources and human talent, is quite unable to function in a coherent fashion for the benefit of the peoples of the world.* The GATT *costs*, not only to the poor majority of the global population but also to many of the inhabitants of the rich First World, are equally plain. NAFTA and GATT are designed to thrust rich and poor together in a grotesque economic contest that only the rich can win; the already discredited structural readjustment programmes will be intensified, so bringing widespread social dislocation and impoverishment; the power of multinational corporations over national economies will be massively enlarged; there will be an increased likelihood of food crises in poor countries, ethnic tensions and civil strife. A handful of EU and US negotiators, speaking solely for capitalist wealth and privilege, have demanded through GATT a crippling range of concessions from Third World states who have no power to resist. Under the brutal and peculiar logic of capitalist ambition, there is no alternative. On this stage, the large corporations are principal players.

THE TRANSNATIONAL CORPORATIONS (TNCS)

GATT is essentially a charter for what used to be called the multinational corporations (MNCs) and what are now called the transnational corporations (TNCs): the central underlying thrust of GATT is to assist the efforts of the largest companies in the world to penetrate markets wherever they can be found. There is nothing in this of respect for local conditions, self-reliant peasant communities, or traditional ways of life.†

---

*No one should doubt the power of international capital to act politically to make or break states. For example, Claire Sterling (*Crime without Frontiers*, Little, Brown & Company, 1994) explains how economic means were used to subvert the Soviet Union. She quotes a Western intelligence source: 'I knew there would be a possibility of a Western privately orchestrated Jihad that could help crush the communist ruling powers . . . I decided to play a catalytic role to crash the ruble . . . I was after Ivan's jugular' (p. 165).

†A United Nations Development Programme report (28 October 1994) stated that Third World countries were being deprived of at least $5 billion a year in royalties for plants and local knowledge given to multinational agricultural and drug companies. The situation was worsened by the increasing use of patents giving protection to Western firms for Third-World products: 'Industrialised countries patent material wholly or partially derived from farmers' varieties. As private companies move into the developing countries' seed markets, indigenous farmers are finding themselves paying for the end product of their own genius.'

The aim is to give the powerful TNCs unimpeded access to every country of the world – if there are natural resources to be tapped, cheap labour to exploit, and markets to dominate.

It is important to grasp the scale of the TNC ambitions and the developing role that the TNCs play in the 'other United Nations'. Most of the early multinational companies tended to be primary producers: foreign investment was useful because this safeguarded the supply of the basic products (oil, bananas, meat, coffee, etc.) that such companies needed. In such circumstances there were pressures to co-ordinate the various elements of production, markets and product supply on an international basis. In the twentieth century, as companies have expanded their interests and foreign involvements, their economic activities have become more flexible and more ambitious. Today the TNCs are not limited to any particular product or product family: if the returns from one market look unpromising, resources can be switched elsewhere. Modern transport facilities and communications make particular geographical sites less important unless they offer useful raw materials, suitable cheap labour, or a new untapped market to be exploited. There has long been talk of multinational corporations planning their activities on a global basis, using global management techniques to exploit the global marketplace. As one example, Standard Oil (New Jersey) had built computerised models of their entire worldwide operations by 1970 – to optimise the deployment of their tanker fleets and to analysis particular hypothetical commercial decisions in the context of the company's global trading strategy.

By 1975 there were around 11,000 companies running some 82,000 foreign affiliates, with nearly 400 of these companies active in 20 or more countries. By 1980 more than a quarter of the sales of about a thousand of the world's largest corporations were derived from their foreign affiliates; with some fifty companies deriving more than half of their revenue from foreign sources. At this time the liquid assets of the multinationals were estimated at twice the size of the world's gold and foreign exchange reserves; and through the 1980s – despite recessions, trade disputes and mounting commercial tensions between the major trading regions of the world – the multinational corporations continued to strengthen their position. By 1990 the assets of the multinationals (IBM, ICI, Courtaulds, Exxon, General Motors, Hitachi, ITT, BASF, Nestlé, Bayer, and so on) were estimated at well in excess of $1000 billion. It is important to recognise the vast political and economic power that resides in such a figure: no international organisations not devoted to the accumulation and use of private capital are in a position to deploy resources on such a scale. Today a few thousand global corporations control most of the commercial activity of the planet. Some of the TNCs are more powerful than many of the world's nation states: few countries – perhaps none – are in a position to challenge the owners and planners of the resource system of the world. Today it is largely the multinationals that develop and distribute energy, mine and transport minerals, grow and distribute food, design and manufacture medical products, and supervise the international flow of capital and information. In the early 1960s, George Ball, the chairman of Lehman Brothers International, declared: 'Working through great corporations that straddle the Earth, men are able for the first time to utilise world resources with an efficiency dictated by the objective logic of profit.' This is the sole underlying theme of the evolving commercial system of the world.

It has long been apparent that the global phenomenon of the TNC should be addressed as crucially relevant to the welfare of the human race. Human-rights groups, non-governmental organisations (NGOs), pressure groups of all types have worked to raise the public awareness of the TNC significance. In 1974 the Economic and Social Council of the United Nations adopted Resolution 1913 (LVII), by which it created the Commission on Transnational Corporations (TNCs). One of the main aims was to create a Code of Conduct that might be used to influence the conduct of the multinational corporations around the world. This initiative was largely futile. The Commission created an Intergovernmental Working Group in 1976 to develop a suitable code: after 17 sessions, up to May 1982, the Working Group could offer no more than a partial draft. The draft structure was agreed but there were wide differences on major points of principle. One of the participants, Miguel Rodrigues-Mendoza of Venezuela, said: 'Important differences still remain on fundamental issues that may, in the end, prove to be insurmountable.' It was easy to argue for the need for effective global regulation of TNC activity but hard to imagine that any non-mandatory Code of Conduct – even if agreed by this or that working-party – would have the slightest effect.

The TNCs were increasingly able to operate on an independent basis, oblivious to all concerns but the maximisation of financial profit. The principal objective is to maximise post-tax returns *on a global scale*, with the corollary that there is little commitment to the TNC's home country. In this context there is no guarantee that the outflow profits from a particular region will be counterbalanced by reinvestments in the country of origin. Moreover, the TNC characteristically circumvents exchange-control legislation – where it still exists – by 'transfer pricing'; that is, by deliberately under-invoicing intra-firm imports or exports to evade controls and to guarantee that the highest profits are generated in the countries with the lowest taxes. The TNCs are also in a position to organise oligopolistic pricing and restrictive-practice policies beyond the reach of national governments. Similarly the nation state is often powerless to confront the TNCs over such questions as environmental pollution, workers' protection, and the development of sustainable economic practices for the benefit of local communities.

In this context the United Nations is largely powerless. The putative Code of Conduct seemed doomed: with unresolvable differences over such matters as the 'national treatment' of TNCs (the rights of host governments to discriminate in favour of national companies), the relevance of international law to matters of sovereignty and jurisdiction, and the applicability of international standards on nationalisation and compensation, it seemed unlikely that an agreed code would ever emerge – and if it did, what use would it be? In 1992 the United Nations, seemingly bowing to the inevitable, downgraded its own centre for studying TNCs.[78] The global corporations, long able to confront the nation states of the world, would hardly be likely to tremble at the prospect of being scrutinised by this or that under-funded UN committee.

By the early 1990s more than 35,000 TNCs accounted for some $1.7 trillion in foreign direct investment and global sales totalling $4.4 trillion.[79] They were controlling 70 per cent of world trade, with only 350 TNCs accounting for nearly a half of the world's merchandise trade. Half of the 35,000 TNCs were located in four countries: the US, Japan, Germany and Switzerland; with all the top 500 companies headquartered in the industrialised countries. The total wealth of the top 500 manufacturing and top 500 banking and insurance companies amounted to around $10 trillion, twice the gross domestic product (GDP) of the United States.[80] This represents a vast concentration of commercial and political power: it needs to be addressed in any consideration of how global institutions might be created, developed and regulated in the interests of the peoples of the world.

It is now a straightforward matter to identify the main components of the 'other United Nations'. These comprise the IMF, the World Bank, the GATT, and the TNCs (themselves typically organised into consortia, groups, cartels and so on). To this vast global nexus of commercial/political power – the IMF/World Bank/GATT/TNC alliance – must be added the sympathetic and well-funded army of pundits, politicians, academics and journalists, eager to portray the relentless search for increased private profit as an essentially benevolent enterprise. The various main components of the other United Nations are far from discrete separate entities operating in jealous isolation; instead they mix and mingle, overlap and cross-fertilise – often in seeming contention and dispute, but working to a shared agenda.

The other United Nations operates in parallel with the New York-based UN; but also intermeshes with it at many different levels, always seeking to ensure that the UN does not take initiatives that might seriously conflict with the logic that demands the maximisation of global financial profit. Viewed in idealistic terms, the UN was created in 1945 to benefit 'we the peoples'; not to underwrite the emergence of vast unaccountable institutions with a tightening grip on the economic life of the world and massive covert political power. This prodigious problem facing the UN – that of the other United Nations working to an entirely different agenda – relates closely to all the others. Only the most radical reform of the culture, structure and philosophy of the United Nations will begin to address these problems.

Part III

The Solutions

7 Options for Reform

PREAMBLE

The inevitable imperfection of organisations means that improvement is usually an option: some organisations are basically sound, despite human fallibility, and few reforms are needed; for others there may be no sensible alternative to an early demise. Where on the spectrum does the United Nations lie? Today most observers agree that the United Nations – in its administration, its operations and its structure – is seriously flawed. There are calls on every side for radical reform – unless the very extinction of the UN is the preferred alternative. Thus Richard Gott, writer and Third World specialist, declares: 'I believe now that we should rid ourselves of our residual enthusiasm for the UN; we should regard it with the same kind of suspicion that was once reserved by the Left for the CIA or indeed *any other institution that seeks to protect the privileges of the status quo powers*' (my italics).[1] Here there is no chance of useful reform: the UN 'is an essentially and intrinsically conservative institution, operating almost solely for the benefit of the advanced capitalist world and what used to be thought of as 'the West' . . . no longer capable of reform along lines that would enable it to change in a progressive direction, particularly after the collapse of the Soviet Union and the Third World . . . It is in effect a dangerous and uncontrolled arm of the American government'.[2] However, perhaps the situation is marginally less bleak than this. There *are* circumstances when the Security Council can act as a brake on US caprice, with Washington today committed to preserving the façade of legality. For example, the fresh sanctions imposed on Libya on 1 December 1993, following the passing of Resolution 883 (11 November 1993), were delayed because of Russian doubts, albeit concerning matters of Russian self-interest.

At the other end of the spectrum, the United Nations, admittedly suffering from a deep multi-symptom malaise, requires urgent treatment. Even Secretary-General Boutros Boutros-Ghali, robust pro-UN optimist that he is, is struggling hard to improve the administration of the Secretariat and to lay the basis for a restructured Security Council. Here there is no suggestion of UN demise: 'the world Organization has begun a new chapter . . . the vast potential of the United Nations has been recognized' (Figure 7.1). Instead the UN is perceived as an essential institution that 'everyone should assist . . . at this moment of importance for all

The Solutions

On this United Nations Day 1993 it is clear that the world Organization has begun a new chapter.

In sharp contrast to past decades the vast potential of the United Nations has been recognized.

For international peace and security;
For humanitarian assistance;
For development in all aspects;
For the protection of the planet;
For the promotion of democracy and human rights,
the United nations is indispensable.

In this recognition, Member States have placed more responsibility upon the United Nations than at any time in its history. These new requirements cannot be expected to succeed in the absence of new foundations of support.

This means that Member States must:

- provide adequate levels of resources;
- recognize the changed character of conflict today;
- persevere in seeing missions through to the end;
- realize that the UN can serve, but not substitute for, the concerns of its Members;
- and understand that peace and security must rest upon a foundation of economic and social development.

The successes of the past year outweigh the setbacks.

The year to come will reveal whether the international community is ready for the serious challenges and positive opportunities which now lie before it.

A new chapter in the history of the world has begun. It calls into being a new United Nations. I ask everyone to consider and come forward to assist the United Nations at this moment of importance for all peoples, now and in the decades ahead.

Figure 7.1   Message from Secretary-General Boutros Boutros-Ghali on United Nations Day, 24 October 1993

peoples . . .'. No-one doubts the gravity of the social and political problems facing humankind in the approach to the next millennium; or the countless useful roles that an adequate world body should perform. There is an urgent need to treat the UN, but even with radical attention to its deep-seated and multifaceted malaise the prognosis must remain uncertain.

THE PROBLEM OF POWER

The central problem of power in the United Nations is that, despite Article 2(1) of the Charter, all the member states do not enjoy sovereign equality: some, mainly the Western powers led by the United States, have more sovereign equality than others. Today it is easy to represent the international body as little more than an arm of US government, largely unable to resist American pressures exerted to serve American commercial and strategic interests. So the UN can be activated against Iraq, Libya and Haiti; but not against Israel, Indonesia and Morocco. The UN can be activated to protect the repressed and tortured Kurds, providing they do not live in Turkey. The UN, under broad US tutelage, does not practise double standards; it practises *multiple* standards, with a range of responses to the various behaviours of states, according to how such behaviours impinge on American interests. Thus a country that perpetrates genocide and aggression does not necessarily earn an effective UN response: there may be stern words or no words at all; or there may be sanctions; or military intervention – by a 'UN' coalition of forces – under the terms of Chapter VII of the Charter. Washington orchestrates the response or lack of it, with the criteria for action having little to do with morality and much to do with commercial and military advantage in the world.

There is nothing sacrosanct about the present structure of the United Nations (see 'The Problem of Representation', below), even though it manifestly favours the Big-Power status quo; and even within the present structure there is some scope, albeit limited, for reining in US initiatives that are transparently self-serving, illegal and against the interests of most UN member states. The members should show a greater willingness to offer money and troops to aid UN operations (easy to say: most members are in a dire economic predicament), and thus to dilute the American dominance of the UN peacekeeping operations that bear on US interests. Most Third World states – today crushed by repression, exploitation and impoverishment – aspire to no more than to join the First World (that is, to raise their standards of living); but perhaps their interests would be best served if they combined their efforts, in and outside the UN, to push a common agenda. Support should be given to the development of UN facilities able to transcend the whims of individual states, even if hegemonic powers. It is easy to see that most Third World countries would have an interest in, for example, a standing UN military capability, able to act consistently and quickly to prevent the escalation of civil war or a mounting aggression from an outside state. Such a standing force, widely recommended, would be trained and commanded by UN personnel answerable to no national government. UN military initiatives could be undertaken without the need to begin the *ad hoc* and protracted requisitioning of troops, or to seek the approval of the Pentagon, as often happens today. Boutros-Ghali and many others have urged member states to provide predictable and generous support to the UN, and to agree the concept of a standing UN force.[3] Such developments would gradually erode the American dominance in the Security Council (and for this reason have been opposed by Washington). In short, it may be easier for the vast majority of the member states to assert their own rights under the Charter (for example, under Article 108, giving the General Assembly effective veto powers over any restructuring of the Security Council), than to attack powerful states over non-constitutional matters.

It is important to remember that power – even substantial power – can often be properly restrained by law; and that today much attention is being devoted to how the evolving corpus of international law can be made effective on a global basis. One of the principal charges against the United States is that it is cavalier in its approach to international law, often neglecting its legal obligations in furthering its strategic objectives.[4] But the concept of law still carries weight: we often witness US spokespersons proclaiming American support for the law while Washington violates it. But the international climate remains sympathetic to the idea of a law-abiding community, even when official hypocrisy and frequent violations are transparent.

In this context the increasing resort to the International Court of Justice at The Hague (the World Court) is significant. Thus Secretary-General Boutros-Ghali notes that the World Court has 'in the past few years, experienced a clear increase in contentious cases as opposed to advisory opinions. In 1993, the Court had before it a record number of 12 cases, involving States from nearly every region of the world'.[5] The World Court 'is undergoing a renaissance, as more and more countries enlist its aid'.[6] Marc Weller, a research fellow in international law at Cambridge, England, has observed that it is 'quite remarkable' how the Court has 'increased in popularity within the international community'. The World Court is significant in that it enjoys a degree of independence from the Security Council: the members of the Court are elected by both the Security Council and the General Assembly (Article 4 of the Statute of the International Court of Justice), but there is no equivalent in the Court to the political veto in the Security Council.[7] This means that in reality a conflict may develop between a ruling of the Court and the interest of a member of the Security Council; as happened, for example, when the Court condemned the illegal US support for the Contras in Nicaragua.

Washington rejected this 1986 ruling and when Nicaragua took its complaint to the Security Council Washington vetoed it. It is still possible to envisage how an evolving World Court might be used as an effective tool for the restraining of power.

Reforms to the operation and powers of the Court have already occurred and more are envisaged. Special chambers are now allowed which can enable Third World countries to select judges from lists drawn from outside the powerful Western bloc, so helping to allay suspicions that the Court is pro-US and pro-European. A special chamber is being established to hear environmental disputes, and the possibility of the Court being allowed to hear disputes between states and business organisations is being considered, a radical option in view of the growing impact of the transnational corporations (TNCs) on most of the countries of the world. Another proposal is that the stipulation of Article 34(1) of the Statute be reformed to allow individual citizens, not just states, to bring cases before the Court, as they can to the Court of Justice of the European Community. Some legal experts, even more radically, are suggesting that the powers of the Court be extended *to allow judicial review of UN resolutions*. Such a development would have obvious application to the circumstances in which the US puts pressure on Security Council members to pass US-drafted resolutions: for example the circumstances in which Washington used bribery and intimidation to secure Resolution 678 (on Iraq) and Resolutions 731, 748 and 883 (on Libya).[8] In this connection Marc Weller, noting that the US and the UK 'may well have contributed to, or brought about, an abuse of rights by the Security Council' (in respect of Libya), commented: 'It is now open to question whether the International Court of Justice would have competence to find that such an abuse has taken place.' It has been established that the Court 'can act in parallel with the Security Council . . . and may take action to reinforce a Council resolution'.[9] Whereas upholders of the status quo would want to argue that the Court could not have power that might block the speedy response of the Security Council under Chapter VII of the Charter, it would be possible to argue also that 'the Council is bound to act in accordance with the UN Charter when adopting its decisions, including and especially decisions under Chapter VII'.[10] In fact Article 94(1) of the Charter declares that any UN member party to a dispute is bound by the decision of the Court, a nice stipulation that seemingly admits of no exceptions. However, Article 94(2) gives the Council the right to interpret any claim made to it following a Court ruling. This is what happened with the ruling against the US over Nicaragua (already mentioned); and which effectively placed Washington above the law.

There still remains the possibility that the behaviour of the permanent members of the Security Council might be subject to Court scrutiny. Thus Weller concludes: 'it is perfectly possible to seek judicial review even of decisions of the Security Council without disrupting the functioning of the UN machinery for collective security'; and that 'it may in fact be necessary for the Court to exercise such competence if the constitutional system of the UN Charter is to recover from the blow it has suffered' (over the Lockerbie episode).[11] Here great emphasis is given to the need for proper constraints to be placed by the Court over the 'enormous powers' of the Security Council. There is now a campaign to ensure that all UN members – including the members of the Security Council – recognise the Court's jurisdiction by the year 2000. Malcolm Shaw, a law professor at Leicester University, England, has emphasised the important principle that even a Court decision rejected by a state can help to fashion the climate of opinion: 'Even if a powerful state rejects a ruling, conditions and attitudes are created that ultimately lead to change.'[12]

The point is that UN members keen to redress the power balance in the United Nations should build on the mechanisms that stand a chance of wresting some power away from the Security Council; in particular, away from Washington. In general, this means building up UN resources (funds, troops and so on) to make UN operations less-dependent upon the US Congress and the Pentagon. In particular, it means developing specific UN organs – especially the World Court – which are already well equipped in statute and in ethics to confront the powerful states of the world.

THE PROBLEM OF MANAGEMENT

Many of the management tasks facing the United Nations are relatively mundane, and little need be said here. Already Secretary-General Boutros-Ghali has worked to improve administration at the UN headquarters and elsewhere, but few observers believe that the changes are sufficient. Thus he has appointed an Assistant Secretary-General to oversee the UN's book-keeping, 'but much more needs to be done'.[13] There is much dissatisfaction among UN members about funding arrangements, a circumstance that is not designed to help the management of the organisation. Poor countries, themselves often tardy payers, resent the predictable delays in the payments made by wealthy states; and the wealthy countries are apt to see the assessment arrangements as grossly unfair, a perception that does nothing to aid Boutros-Ghali's management of a 'precarious' financial situation. In his address to the General Assembly on 28 September 1993 President Bill Clinton suggested that the United States was paying too much: 'I am also committed to work with the United Nations to reduce our nation's assessment . . . I believe our rates should be reduced . . .'. Britain, too, often implies that assessments should be frequently reviewed to allow changes in the light of new economic circumstances. What this would mean in practice is that Britain would point to its stumbling economy to justify paying less to the United Nations. Such matters are highly relevant to the question of UN management but they also have deep political implications.

The Department for Development Support and Management Services has been designed to improve the delivery of UN assistance to 'developing countries and countries in transition'. The new department is intended to act as an executing agency for programmes and projects relating to institutional and human resources development in area such as development planning, policies and infrastructure, public administration, private sector development and enterprise management, financial management and accounting, and natural resources and energy planning and management'.[14] Also the Department is seen as a focal point at headquarters for the provision of management services. The development of such roles in 1993 was set against the widespread perception that the United Nations – both at the headquarters and beyond – was a grossly inefficient organisation, paying scant attention to even the most basic management disciplines. It remains to be seen whether the administrative innovations will have much impact.

Suggestions for improvements to UN administration have come from many different sources. A few dissident UN employees have denounced UN inefficiencies (see Chapter 4) but for the most part the criticisms have come from outside observers. The members of the Secretariat, the UN's full-time civil servants, are unlikely to make fundamental criticisms of their employer. Some comments from outside factions have been predictable but useful. For example, the British Liberal Democrats suggested in 1989 that UN machinery should be developed to take rapid action to prevent conflict, that subscriptions arrears should be paid in full, and that Deputy Secretary-General posts should be created to ease the burden on the Secretary-General.[15] Since that time there has been a growing consensus for radical changes to the United Nations, many of the proposals focusing on the need for more effective management. Thus there have been frequent calls for tighter accounting procedures, better staff management policies, improved access to information, a reduction in the prodigious number of UN publications (many of them delayed and repetitive), tighter scrutiny of UN staff perquisitions, and improved management of UN operations in the field. Many of the proposals, nominally within the remit of the Secretary-

General, have a political dimension that cannot be ignored. The management of UN forces in the field is a particularly contentious area, impacting as it does on the rights of the various troop-donating powers.

One suggestion is that the UN might devolve some of its peacekeeping tasks to regional organisations: a burden-sharing ploy for a desperately overcommitted United Nations. This would reduce the controversial involvement of external powers in a local dispute and perhaps reduce the logistical problems of transporting UN troops and equipment around the world (the example of the Economic Community of West African States (ECOWAS), active in Liberia, is sometimes cited as what can be accomplished by regional forces). Here the problem is that such forces, often largely independent of UN control, tend to support local hegemonic interests – which may have been the cause of the problem in the first place. Boutros-Ghali has urged local forces to take on increased responsibilities but any effort to manage UN peacekeeping on such a devolved basis is certain to be fraught with problems. There are enough complications in the UN's organisational structure – which is intended to have a degree of unification – without adding further complex layers.

The proliferation of UN agencies leads to various management difficulties, even though such bodies are intended to function within a defined management structure. For example, the focus of such UN organisations as the United Nations Children's Fund (UNICEF), the World Food Programme (WFP) and the United Nations High Commissioner for Refugees (UNHCR) on similar tasks often leads to problems of co-ordination and optimum use of scarce resources. It has been suggested that the Sudanese government, presented with Operation Lifeline Sudan, has been able to play off one UN agency against another in Khartoum, so weakening the UN's effectiveness. Similarly, in El Salvador the UN Observer Mission (ONUSAL) has experienced problems liaising with the UN Development Programme (UNDP). The creation of the UN Department of Humanitarian Affairs (DHA) in April 1992 has only been partially successful in resolving such difficulties. In the view of Oxfam, one of the principal players, 'the DHA has not been adequately supported by all UN agencies, and its objective has not yet been achieved'.[16] Nor is the situation improved by the fact that UN authority resides almost exclusively in New York and Geneva, making it difficult to co-ordinate the activities of host governments, local civil society, and regional bodies (such as Organisation of African Unity). In such circumstances it is necessary for the UN to delegate decision-making authority to the national level, but without losing overall strategic control. In particular, the DHA 'should generally be responsible for coordinating the humanitarian work of all the UN specialised agencies'.[17]

Management inefficiencies within the UN have often worked to exacerbate social and political problems. For example, the sanctions resolutions on Iraq have nominally permitted the importing of medical supplies but disputes and procrastination in the UN sanctions committee (a pale reflection of the Security Council) and other UN bodies have seriously impeded the availability of such supplies. Is baby formula a food or a medicine? Can surgical scissors be melted down to make bullets? Can some medicines be converted into biological warfare poisons? Such disputes have resulted in the blocking of medical and other aid to Iraq, worsening still further the desperate plight of the civilian population.[18] This is partly a management problem. Are the guidelines clear? Who is responsible for them? Who is responsible for ensuring that urgent questions are speedily resolved? But there is more to the issue than mere management incompetence: some powerful states have an interest in ensuring that some international initiatives go far beyond the terms of the nominal UN authorisation. Thus UN management efforts – in peacekeeping, the delivery of relief aid, the monitoring of peace accords, and so on – are not helped by hidden agendas designed to frustrate them.

The management problem of the United Nations necessarily needs to be addressed on several levels. At the most basic level the standard management disciplines relating to accounting, staff motivation and control, forward planning and so on should be rigorously applied. At many other levels it is necessary to address such questions as the organisational structure, the development of secure funding arrangements, the co-ordination of disparate UN agencies around the world, and the development of adequate management frameworks for operations in the field (peacekeeping, peace monitoring, aid delivery, election supervision, and so on). The problems are compounded by the scale of UN ambitions, the commitment to address all manner of problems wherever they occur around the world – and all in the context of inadequate and uncertain support from member states. And all UN efforts to improve its management structures and practices must consider the interest of powerful factions in working to different agendas, hidden strategic designs that are seen to benefit from UN inefficiencies, confusion and procrastination.

THE PROBLEM OF REPRESENTATION

The problem of political representation at the United Nations is often protrayed in simplistic terms. It seems a straightforward matter: member states, particularly powerful member states, deserve a voice in the most important international forum of the world. But there are important questions to be addressed. Who or what is being represented? Is it only states? Or is it peoples, factions, races, religions and interests? How is a balance to be struck? How are such elements as pragmatism, power and principle to weigh in the balance? Can political structures be created as a matter of conscious design? Or are we bound to accept what we find, entitled to expect no more than gradual and minor evolutionary changes? We might, with John Stuart Mill look upon a political constitution as we might 'a steam plough, or a threshing machine', as an artefact contrived to achieve particular objectives; or we may see that governments 'are not made, but grow'.[19] How are we to interpret such questions in the context of the United Nations?

At the simplest level the question of representation at the UN is addressed by the simple decision to expand the number of permanent members in the Security Council. Here the UN's 'board of directors' must be reformed to include others, 'such as Germany and Japan, whose economic as opposed to military power gives them the right to a permanent seat at the table'.[20] Here the manifest criterion is power and wealth rather than democracy; but any thorough-going adherence to democracy does not weigh long in the scales. The General Assembly, for example, 'is not, and could never be, a democratic organisation' because, if it were, 'the world would be run by the Chinese'.[21] We need to examine why this would be an obvious absurdity. Head counts are always regarded as the principal element of democracy – with franchise restrictions based on education, race, religion, sex and so on seen as historical blots on the political landscape, aberrations from which we have now all escaped. So why should the Chinese, as befits their numbers, not have the dominant voice in the councils of the world; in particular, in the United Nations? It will not do to cite the repression of Tibet or the Tiananmen Square massacre. The United States, Britain, France et al. would not be keen to let even a virtuous China run the show. The politics of the real world is much more about the protection of interest than about the promotion of principle. This singular aspect of reality should be remembered by all those who advocate reforms to the structure and practices of the United Nations.

The straightforward proposal to expand or to otherwise alter the membership of the Security Council is now being widely urged. Few doubt that the arguments for such a change 'are strong'.[22] There may be doubts about whether change should take place in the immediate future since the requirements for peace and security 'make it inadvisable to change a system that can allow decisive action'; but in the longer terms 'it is important that the membership of the Security Council becomes more representative of the global community'.[23] Japan should be admitted, it is argued, simply by virtue of its 12 per cent contribution to the UN budget and its £13 billion contribution to the 1991 Gulf War. In this context it is necessary also to examine the question of the veto. Should a single permanent member be allowed to block a majority decision on the Security Council? Should a permanent member be allowed to vote in a case to which it is a party? And what of 'vetoes by proxy'? If a powerful state were prohibited from voting on a contentious issue in which it had an interest how could it ever be known that a client state was not voting on its behalf? In fact it is obvious that this already happens and that it would continue to happen in a reformed Security Council with a new voting procedure.

On 23 November 1993 the General Assembly began a debate on the question of representation on the Security Council. What would count as equitable representation? And would reform entail an expansion of the total membership? Or just a rejigging of the permanent members? In 1992 the General Assembly asked the Secretary-General to invite member states to submit written comments on reform of the Council: some 75 replies were received. In December 1993 the president of the General Assembly introduced a consensus decision to facilitate the creation of an open-ended working group to examine how the Security Council might be reformed. No-one imagined that anything but piecemeal proposals would be made: perhaps a European seat, perhaps the accession of Japan and Germany, perhaps a nod to the Third World (Brazil? Nigeria?). But is the Security Council capable of reform? It is obvious that any changes that threatened the dominance of Washington would be blocked. In this context would reform achieve any more than merely to extend the grip of the rich nations on the poor majority?

There are more radical options, well outside the remit of the General Assembly working party. Richard Gott has speculated on the total collapse of the United Nations ('We should shed no tears if it were to disappear'). And in the same spirit, Ramsey Clark, former US attorney general, newly sensitised by the US-perpetrated genocide in the Gulf War, demanded an end to the Security Council: '*This institution that people of my generation had placed so much hope in. This institution created as its preamble says 'to end the scourge of war'. We have to go there, as the people of the planet, and demand integrity and demand performance . . . and that means we have to abolish the Security Council.*' It is of course difficult to imagine any powerful states, happy with the UN status quo, agreeing to such a proposal. However, it is equally difficult to see how a Security Council that allows a single state to frustrate the will of the other 180-plus members can long claim legitimacy. Without demanding a totally unrestricted democracy in the United Nations, it is now increasingly unacceptable that the permanent members of the Council should be able to maintain an unhealthy domination of the rest of the world community.

One route to a taming of the Security Council would be to facilitate a progressive transfer of powers from the Council to the General Assembly, a development that would inevitably be opposed by the Council permanent members. Today there are criticisms of the undemocratic representation in the Assembly, a defect that would have to be removed if the Assembly were to have authority as an evolving legislative chamber. Individual countries – irrespective of size, military or economic power, or contributions to the United Nations – are allowed one vote. If the Assembly were to develop the power to pass laws binding on the membership it would have to be seen as a democratic body concerned above all with the general welfare. At the same time it must be stressed that a refined voting system would be far from all that was needed. The gross economic and size differences between the individual members would make it impossible for all members to participate equally in the proceedings of the chamber: a state suffering through famine or other massive social problems would have little motivation to address the broader problems of the world community. Here, as in any legislative body, great disparities of wealth and power would inevitably work against the proper functioning of democracy. Such disparities are likely to be exacerbated by the IMF/World Bank/GATT/TNC nexus (see 'the Other United Nations', below) – a development that is bound to erode democracy still further.

One route to more equitable representation in the General Assembly would be to use 'weighted voting', whereby nations would be assigned different numbers of votes according to various indicators (about which there would certainly be much argument). It is significant that more than two dozen weighted voting formulas have so far been proposed and compared, with nothing like a consensus about their respective merits emerging. Votes may be proportional to population, or to GNP, or to a state's financial contribution to the UN, or – in order to temper simple proportionality – to the square root or the cube root of such indicators; or different indicators might be combined in various ways. In some formulas the number of votes is proportional to 'degree of development' (indicated by, for example, per capita energy consumption), or to expenditure on social services. With votes determined simply by population size, there is an unacceptable disparity between the smallest and the largest nations: four states (the US, Russia, China and India) would always have a majority of votes in the Assembly, though alliances and coalitions might form to produce varying results. Votes based on energy consumption, military power or GNP would necessarily favour the United States – which might serve to convert the General Assembly into a shadow Security Council. Schemes that work against the natural massive disparities of population, wealth or military prowess would seem to have merit, but largely in theoretical terms. The working of a revamped General Assembly with legislative powers could not be known in advance. It is inevitable that there would be imaginative manoeuvring for advantage, so a new Assembly constitution would have to incorporate enough flexibility to block the exposed loopholes.

The extreme differences between voting numbers that the simple proportionality schemes would yield can be mitigated by using square or cube roots of the indicators (already mentioned). Such devices have the effect of flattening out the disparities, decreasing the votes of the larger nations and increasing those of the smaller. Other mathematical devices – for example, logarithms – can be used to reduce the disparities considerably; but here the effects are sometimes excessive, yielding results that are not far removed from the present one-nation/one-vote convention. It should be remembered that none of the proposed schemes can be assessed according to purely objective criteria: every state has interests to protect and this circumstance necessarily influences the choice of critical indicators. We may expect poor countries to favour schemes that give them a 'disproportionate' number of votes in the General Assembly, while the United States is likely to favour schemes that assign votes according to 'degree of development', GNP, or assessed contribution to the UN.

In one evaluation some 25 weighted voting formulas were considered against eight criteria, one of which was the degree of disparity in the number of votes that the scheme produced.[24] Here a principal requirement was that the system should yield approximately equal voting weights between the various political blocs, such as East and West, and North and South. The schemes were applied to earlier voting patterns in the General Assembly to demonstrate what results they would have produced. The scheme that scored highest when judged against the eight criteria was one using population, health expenditure and education expenditure as the indicators. Under this formula – which still could be questioned on various grounds – 'some of the voting weights in a 1000-vote total would be: USA (top) 154, China 126, [erstwhile] USSR 82, India 77, Japan 58, France 38, UK 31, Canada 23, . . . Mexico 10, . . . Philippines 5, . . . Denmark 4, . . . many at the lower end'.[25] This shows, if nothing else, how methodical voting arrangements can be quickly overtaken by political events; and why in consequence any proposed scheme should have scope for on-going reform. In another scheme the world is divided into 100 equal-population districts, a truly 'democratic' approach. Here the erstwhile Soviet Union was granted 60 districts, the US 52 and Canada 7 with two cross-border overlaps; in India and China (alas?) even each province had as many districts as France, with the Pacific Islands region scarcely able to add up to one district.

Under the terms of another system, dubbed the 'Binding Triad' proposal, developed by the Centre for War/Peace Studies, important decisions would still be made with a single vote, but only when three simultaneous majorities were produced.[26] The passing of a resolution – rendered mandatory by changes to the UN constitution – would require: a two-thirds majority of the member states, the support of countries with two-thirds of world's population, and the support of nations making two-thirds of the contributions to the regular UN budget. This means that the reformed General Assembly would be able to pass a mandatory resolution only with strong support 'from most of the countries of the world, most of the population of the world, and most of the political/economic/military strength of the world'.[27]

Any attempt to convert the General Assembly into a legislative body – for example, the 'top level of a global federal system' – must also address the problem of power in the Security Council: it is absurd that a single permanent member (which today means the United States or one of its allies) can block the will of the rest of of world community, and it is equally absurd that a single permanent member of the Security Council, acting under Article 94(2) of the UN Charter, can veto any World Court decision brought to the Council (as happened in the Court ruling against the US over Nicaragua). It is essential in these circumstances that the veto rule (as an obvious 'expression of superior power and privilege'[28]) be modified or abandoned as incompatible with the Article 2(1) stipulation of the 'sovereign equality' of all UN members. There are frequent criticisms of the 'double standards' (I would say multiple standards) employed by the United Nations in confronting the problems of the world), but it is precisely the power and procedures of the Security Council that make such multiple standards inevitable. In fact there has always been widespread dissatisfaction with the veto system and the special interests that it has protected over the years. In the early years of the Security Council an Interim Committee met to propose alternatives to the veto, though the subsequent suggestions were predictably ignored by the Great Powers.

The veto was used to block UN decisions on the Soviet invasions of Czechoslovakia and Afghanistan and on the US invasions of Grenada and Panama. Where, seemingly against the interests of a permanent member, Council resolutions were passed (as with the Israeli occupation of Arab lands), the threat of the veto prevented further resolutions under Chapter VII of the Charter to force compliance. This meant that only states without friends among the permanent members of the Council could be condemned by the UN for aggression, human rights abuses and so on. Today, after the collapse of the Soviet Union, many Third World states are friendless on the Council; and so are totally at the mercy of Washington's strategic policies. Thus Libya, Iraq and Haiti stand condemned; but no UN word is raised against the equally perfidious acts of Indonesia, Burma or Israel. The power of the veto has to be challenged if the UN is to evolve as an ethical organisation rather than one designed to protect the interests of powerful states.[29]

There are also parallel proposals to create a 'Peoples Chamber' (or House or Assembly) that would run in concert with a democratised General Assembly. In particular, the International Network for a UN Second Assembly (INFUSA), sometimes also called 'We the peoples' Assembly (after the Preamble to the UN Charter), has campaigned for democratic UN reforms rather than for a world government or a world federation.[30] It is proposed that a Second Assembly be created under the terms of Article 22 of the UN Charter: 'The General Assembly may establish such subsidiary organs as it deems necessary for the performance of its functions.' There is an obvious advantage in a Charter provision that authorises the General Assembly to take initiatives without having to overcome the problem of the Security Council veto. INFUSA, supported by many international organisations and institutions (Table 7.1) and well over sixty national bodies, has presented its proposals to the UN General Assembly and to the Permanent Missions of all the member states; since 1985 there have been annual appeals to the Assembly for the proposals to be studied by a UN Expert Group or an Independent International Committee. In 1989 a coalition of organisations was formed, under the auspices of the World Citizens Assembly (WCA), to sponsor a series of Conferences on A More Democratic United Nations (CAMDUN).

The basic principle behind the INFUSA proposals is that there should be a UN Second Assembly of non-governmental delegates, representing the global inhabitants as 'world citizens', to complement the current mode of representation by governmental delegates in the General Assembly. Here it is recognised that the world system of national sovereignty is likely to continue into the foreseeable future; but also that a Second Assembly pledged to represent 'we the peoples' as global inhabitants is needed in order to moderate the behavioural power of divisions rooted in political, ethnic, cultural, credal, social and other identities.[31] Such an assembly is seen as having three main advantages: it could be initiated without

TABLE 7.1 *International organisations and institutions participating in the International Network for a UN Second Assembly (INFUSA)*

Action Health 2000 (International Voluntary Health Association)
Anuvrat Global Organization (Anuvibha)
Association for World Education
Campaign for UN Reform
Christians Against Racism and Fascism
Communications Coordination Committee for the United Nations
'Disarmament Campaigns'
Environmental Liaison Centre
European Liaison and Coordination Office of UN University for Peace
Global Education Associates
International Association of University Days for Peace
International Council of Psychologists
International Evangelical Church
International Federation of Social Workers
International Institute of Concern for Public Health
International Peace School on Crete
International Public Policy Institute
Internationale Weltfrieden [World Peace] Partei (IWP)
Pensioners for Peace International
The International People's College
The Networking Institute
The One World Movement of the Ecumenical Community
The Open International University for Complementary Medicines
The Organization Development Institute and The International Registry of
    Organization Development Professionals
Transnational Perspectives
Unitarian Universalist UN Office
United European–African Society
United Nations and Related Agencies Staff Movement for Disarmament and
    Peace (Geneva and New York Branches)
Unity-and-Diversity World Organization
Universala Esperanto-Asocio
Universidad para la Paz (University for Peace)
World Alliance of NGOs for Disarmament, Development and Security
    (VANGUARDS)
World Citizen Diplomats
World Citizens Assembly
'World Democracy News'
World Referendum Association

SOURCE: Barnaby (ed.), *Building a More Democratic United Nations*, 1991.

amendments to the UN Charter; it would not confront the primary significance of governments in the UN system; it would facilitate a dialogue between governmental and non-governmental representatives. Thus a Second Assembly, not seeking to supplant governments in the exercise of tasks under UN auspices, would not disturb existing power relationships within the international organisation. The merits and demerits of such an innovation are obvious: governments might not object to such an assembly since they would not be affected, but an assembly so conceived would be no more than an impotent talking-shop, subsidiary to the General Assembly (under Article 22) and no more able than its parent to do more than consider, discuss, advise and recommend.

It would be necessary also to determine how non-governmental delegates would be elected to the Second Assembly.[32] The aim would be to develop a 'grassroots approach' to a more democratic United Nations, a 'blending harmony between the best features of NGO (non-governmental organisation) efficiency and information-sharing and the creativity of community organizing for open citizen-problem-solving and direct elections'.[33] Above all, the movement of which INFUSA is such a central part demonstrates the widespread perception that the United Nations – in its present structure and operations – is not adequately serving the peoples of the world.

THE OTHER UNITED NATIONS

The efforts of the rich nations – using the mechanisms supplied by the IMF/World Bank/GATT/TNC nexus – to secure a final commanding grip on world trade are transparent in their methods and intent (see Chapter 6). The 'other United Nations', defined by these mechanisms, needs to be addressed in any comprehensive approach to political policies designed to serve the peoples of the world. Some efforts to reduce the growing gap between the world's rich nations and the poor are well-intentioned, even if confused. The UN Development Programme (UNDP) issued a report in April 1992 urging the creation of a 22-member 'Development Security Council' that would work in parallel with the UN Security Council. The new council would comprise the five permanent members of the Security Council (the US, Russia, China, the UK and France), Japan, Germany, Brazil, Egypt, India, Nigeria and eleven rotating members. The UNDP report, criticising the IMF and the World Bank, declared that if these bodies were 'to encourage participatory styles of development, they must also address some fundamental issues about democracy in their own management structures'. To offset some of the effects of IMF/World Bank policies the new council was intended to co-ordinate development policies and humanitarian aid and design global policies to secure food for the hungry, while at the same time protecting the environment, reshaping the current foreign debt system, and developing other complementary policies. The problem remains that such a UNDP-sponsored council would lack clout; its efforts would necessarily be subordinate to the policies of the global financial institutions.

At the same time there are many signs that the traditional financial power centres recognise that changes are necessary if they are to retain and expand their grip on the economics of the global marketplace. Thus the Washington-based think-tank, the Carnegie Endowment (served by, amongst others, former World Bank president Frank Carlucci), has unsurprisingly echoed a number of findings of a Clinton brains trust set up to recommend financial policies. One suggestion is that there should be a new Dumbarton Oaks conference to reconsider the structure of the United Nations, the Security Council, and other UN-linked international organ-isations (suggesting reform of the IMF and the World Bank). Another recommendation is that the G7 group of leading industrialised nations should be reduced to the G3 – the US, Japan and the EC – to achieve 'the reordering of the world economy, possibly at a new version of the Bretton Woods conference . . .'.[34] In this context the US economic advisors, 'like Clinton himself – believe that *the challenges of a global economy require an activist government in Washington to ensure the continuation of US power*' (my italics).[35] In the same spirit the then British Labour Party leader, John Smith, speaking on 4 November 1993 in his Robert Kennedy memorial lecture at Oxford University, urged the G7 industrialised nations to turn themselves into a 'permanent core of an economic equivalent of the Security Council'. The industrialised countries, by one means or another, would work diligently to preserve their control of the world economy. This has always been (and remains) the principal aim of the GATT negotiations.

There is now abundant evidence that IMF/World Bank policies have had a negative impact on many Third World countries. For example, a detailed analysis of structural adjustment policies imposed by the IMF and the World Bank on the Philippines, Ghana and Guyana has reached various important conclusions:[35]

The case studies show that the impact of adjustment on the conservation of tropical forests has been negative;

Forest loss is linked directly and indirectly to economic and export-led policies in the agricultural and timber sectors;

Free-market economic reforms have lacked the regulatory machinery necessary to protect vulnerable groups and the environment;

Whilst structural adjustment has changed relative prices in the economy, the crucial issue of forest pricing has not been addressed;

Structural adjustment has compounded the misery of the poor, damaging tropical forest areas and food self-sufficiency;

Environmental and social problems are exacerbated because of short-sighted policy decisions;

From the 1970s there was a dramatic increase in debt;

Structural adjustment has been responsible for lowering commodity prices in order to protect the existing global order, even where this has led to the collapse of projects (a World Bank Task Force recently confirmed that a third of Bank projects had failed and the number of failures was increasing);

Necessary land redistribution to solve social and environmental problems has been ignored.

In much of this the *political* character of the IMF and the World Bank is clearly exposed. Thus: 'Perhaps the greatest lesson to be learned from the Philippine analysis is that those who produce sterile critiques of the IMF and the World Bank relying solely on economic theory (useful though these may be) miss the critical political dimension of the IMF and the World Bank. Whatever lessons in economics the Bank and IMF may claim to have learned in the past, *they are still political beasts*, a fact which in some cases makes the economics all but irrelevant within the wider discussion' (my italics).[36] This again suggests that the main thrust of so-called development policies espoused by the IMF/World Bank/GATT nexus are principally aimed at securing a world pattern of economic relations that continue to underwrite the commercial hegemony of a few powerful industralised nations.

In this context, in the light of the mounting evidence, it is essential to scrutinise all development projects – however funded but especially where funds derive from institutions that have a global financial presence. Development proposals should be tailored to the specific circumstances of individual countries, with minimal attention paid to broad theoretical arguments about 'free trade', the overarching demand for 'structural readjustment', or the pressing need for growth in the world economy. Development proposals should be judged against a full range of social and environmental indicators, developed and specified with full local and popular participation. And at the same time there should be pressure on the IMF, the World Bank and other related organisations to democratise their internal procedures, to allow broader access to discussions on investment and other policy issues, and to make relevant information more widely accessible – in short to make the activities of the principal financial bodies increasingly transparent.

This means that – against all the thrust of GATT and the linked strategies – *there is a pressing need for economic protectionism in the interests of national populations, traditional practices, sustainable economic patterns, and the environment.* In the words of two significant authors, Tim Lang (Director of Parents for Safe Food) and Colin Hines (co-ordinator of Greenpeace International's Economics Unit), there is a growing need to recognise 'how free trade can discriminate against and hurt the *environment*; how the *economy* of many countries is being damaged by structural unemployment, debt and deregulation; and how *equity* throughout the world – within and between societies – is decreasing' (original italics).[37] There is a pressing requirement to tackle the mounting problems of the three 'E's. And this can best be done within the context of what Lang and Hines dub the 'New Protectionist Agenda' (Figure 7.2), a ten-element scheme designed to serve the interests of 'we the peoples' rather than the commercial factions with global economic power.

It is already abundantly clear that the GATT manoeuvres are essentially designed to strengthen the economic hegemony of the most powerful groups in the industrialised nations. The GATT terms are intended as a

---

1. Economic policy – away from the global towards the regional and local;
2. Building the supporting communities;
3. Aid and trade for self-reliance, fostered by an exchange of appropriate technology and skills;
4. Sharing out the work;
5. Raising environmental and public protection standards;
6. Controlling TNCs;
7. Evening out the money flows;
8. Dismantling or reforming world finance and trade bodies;
9. Curtailing superbloc power to allow local and regional trade;
10. Changing consumption patterns.

Figure 7.2   The New Protectionist Agenda

SOURCE: Lang and Hines, *The New Protectionism* (1993).

complement to the flawed global system currently supported by the IMF, the World Bank, the TNCs, pliant governments and the vast army of sympathetic pundits and propagandists. The system, the 'other United Nations', works in concert with the high-profile international body to protect the prevailing power relationships of the world. It is too rarely noted that the IMF, the World Bank and GATT are UN-linked bodies; and that the TNCs – the great manufacturing, distributing, propaganda and financial institutions – mesh nicely with the UN-linked bodies and with the pliant governments of the industrial nations. This entire global system invites many questions. What is the nature of power? Of democracy? Of political responsibility? What are the resources of the world for? In whose interest are they to be exploited? Sustained? What do the peoples of the world have a right to expect? To demand?

AGENDA FOR REFORM

The following 50-point agenda, given partly as summary, is provided to indicate a possible framework for change. Some of the points are obvious; others less so. Some, based on obvious management disciplines, should attract little criticism; others, deeply political, will necessarily invite opposition from powerful states. Some of the points are general; others particular. It is useful to select out seven general points to serve as a preamble:

1. The authority of the United Nations must be rooted in *ethics*; not in the vested interest of particular factions, groups or states. The UN – by virtue of its Charter, codes, conventions and declarations – is uniquely equipped to serve as the *'conscience of the world'*. This must be borne in mind by all individuals engaged in UN operations and activities.

2. It is essential that the United Nations – as represented by its officials, employees, groups, forces and so on – *observe the law*. In particular, the terms of the UN Charter (when suitably reformed, see below) and the demands of international agreements properly lodged with the UN (under Article 102 of the Charter) must be scrupulously observed.

3. The United Nations must work to enshrine and develop *the democratic principle*. This must be done, not by powerful states as

a pragmatic or cynical ploy, but because the UN exists above all to serve 'we the peoples'. Whatever the hidden agendas of some of its founders and some powerful individuals, groups and states today, the United Nations must be concerned primarily with human welfare, not with the self-serving agitations of powerful vested interests.

4. The United Nations must strive to act with *consistency* in the development of its agendas and the application of its authority. Illegal acts should invite the same odium and UN response whoever perpetrates them, even if the guilty states have powerful friends in the UN. There should be no double standards, no multiple standards.

5. It is essential that the United Nations act with *transparency of purpose*. Its deliberations and decisions must be open to maximum public scrutiny. In any multifaceted organisation there will always be 'corridor deals', private understandings and the rest. Mechanisms should be empowered to discourage clandestine and secret arrangements.

6. The United Nations should always place a premium on *sound judgement*. Its staffing policies should bear this in mind, as should its development of information, archive and other facilities (see below).

7. It is essential that the United Nations develop the concept of *proportionality of response*. This idea, closely linked to the issue of sound judgement, demands that the UN exercise its authority with care and circumspection. The United Nations is authorised to use comprehensive sanctions, massive force and other measures against derelict states. The UN must at all times guard against the abuse of power.

---

8. The resources of the UN (funds, staff and facilities) should be progressively enlarged as a deliberate strategy to reduce the sway of particular powerful member states. This logistical development must be intended to consolidate and enlarge the UN's supranational identity.

9. The method of assessing members' contributions to the general budget and the peacekeeping budget should be revised to achieve

tighter linkage with GNP and other agreed economic indicators. Contributions *in toto* should be increased within the frame of a fair assessment formula.

10. Members should be invited to make commitments to authorise prompt payments. Sanctions, not necessarily financial, on tardy payers, should be introduced (that is, Article 19 should be strengthened).

11. Prompt and robust action must be taken to root out sinecures, 'double dipping' and other inefficient and corrupt practices in the UN organisation that inevitably damage morale in many workers, waste resources and seriously erode UN authority.

12. It is essential to rationalise the UN structure at the macro level to achieve better co-ordination of different agencies nominally addressing the same problems. Resources must be deployed to optimum effect.

13. Staffing policies in the Secretariat must be improved to allow effective career development, to facilitate prompt disciplinary action, to reward effort, to encourage 'the highest standards of efficiency, competence and integrity' (Article 101(3)).

14. A standing military force with adequate logistical support and under clear UN command should be established.

15. The Military Staff Committee, stipulated in Articles 45–47 (with suitable reforms) should be established as a permanent UN body.

16. Increased emphasis should be given to the peaceful settlement of disputes, as stipulated in Article 2(3) and (4). This means that even in the circumstances of an acknowledged crisis, every effort should be made to resolve the situation without resort to force.

17. Peacekeeping operations authorised by the United Nations should be under UN command.

18. The United Nations should develop its own intelligence capability. It is essential that preventive diplomacy and unavoidable enforcement measures be undertaken only on the basis of comprehensive and up-to-date information. The UN should not have to rely on filtered information supplied by member states.

19. The United Nations should build up a general archive, centres of research excellence and so on in all relevant disciplines – so that

UN officials, staff and others are less dependent on 'expertise' supplied by member states.

20. The United Nations should allocate resources to public awareness campaigns on a global basis to enlist popular support for the UN as a supranational body interested in human welfare. National populations should be encouraged to pressure their governments to honour national obligations under UN membership.

21. It is essential that the United Nations monitor the impact of its various initiatives to prevent counter-productive effects. It is short-sighted for the Security Council to authorise sanctions if other UN bodies have then to cope with the aid consequences.

22. The United Nations should develop transparent procurement policies for peacekeeping and other operations. Efforts should be made to ensure that no contractors – in host countries or elsewhere – stand to benefit from inefficient or corrupt UN practices.

23. It is essential to expand the sovereignty clause (Article 2(1) in the Charter and to clarify the associated 'domestic jurisdiction' clause (Article 2(7)). The member states do not today enjoy 'sovereign equality'; and intervention in the domestic affairs of some states is more likely than in the domestic affairs of others. The clauses should be strengthened to protect the equality of members.

24. With most states now members of the United Nations, Article 2(6) should be deleted. Or it should be expanded for clarification. It cannot be assumed that a state is subject to rules imposed by a body of which it is not a member.

25. The Security Council, if it is to survive in a reconstituted United Nations, should be reformed. It is simplistic merely to advocate the granting of permanent seats to one or two extra states on the basis of the old property qualification. The question of representation should be considered in more imaginative and more progressive terms.

26. The working of the Security Council veto should be examined. It is absurd that a single permanent member should be legally entitled to block the combined will of the rest of the UN membership. Consideration should be given also to the significance of hidden vetoes, double vetoes and so on.

27. The powers of the 15-member Security Council should be progressively reduced. In reality it is the five permanent members that

exercise full authority over the United Nations, with a single power typically dominating the five. This travesty of the democratic spirit must end.

28. Where a state is a party to a dispute, such a state should have limited voting powers. It is absurd that a permanent member of the Security Council can veto UN initiatives designed to counter that member's illegal activities. This means that Article 27(3) should be reformed.

29. The election of the Secretary-General should be conducted on a more transparent and democratic basis. There should be less scope for 'corridor deals' struck between powerful states, and the General Assembly should be allowed increased practical involvement in the procedures. No single powerful state should be able to block the appointment of a candidate favoured by the rest of the UN membership.

30. Changes to the composition of the Security Council, to the method of electing the Secretary-General, or to any other procedures and conventions that might demand reform of the Charter should only take place with the approval of the General Assembly. This is already stipulated in Article 108, a provision currently ignored by powerful states in the Security Council.

31. The voting arrangements in the General Assembly should be reformed to facilitate a more reasonable pattern of representation. Any scheme based on simple proportionality (to any parameter) should be rejected as likely to enshrine permanent majorities against the spirit of the Charter. Any adopted scheme should protect the position of the poor.

32. The broad UN membership, not just the powerful states in the Security Council, should be authorised to scrutinise development plans designed and/or operated by UN agencies or UN-linked financial bodies such as the IMF and the World Bank. The broad membership should be authorised, probably through the mechanism of the General Assembly, to influence the shape of UN development initiatives.

33. The aid agencies should have a degree of autonomy at regional and local levels – within the broad scheme of UN co-ordination – to react promptly to sudden crises.

34. Facilities should be created, via the UN archive and other inform-ation-based initiatives, to allow public access to aid and other

deliberations by UN agencies and UN-linked bodies. Emphasis must be given to the UN's democratic ethic and justification.

35. The General Assembly should take initiatives under Article 22 to create bodies that would enhance the weight and effectiveness of the Assembly, at the same time serving as a counter-balance to the Security Council. A Second Assembly (a 'we the peoples' assembly) would be one option if its efforts could be focused and if it did not simply duplicate the 'talking shop' features of the existing General Assembly.

36. It is necessary at every stage to redraft the Charter to reflect the on-going range of reforms. The Charter must be regarded as the reference, albeit supplemented by complementary rulings and codes, for UN operations in the world.

37. Steps should be taken to clarify and expand Article 51, the 'self-defence' provision. It is too easy for powerful states to cite this Article in specious justification of military initiatives that have nothing to do with self-defence. For example, it cannot be reasonable for a state to be able to cite Article 51 to justify a military attack on a country if nationals of that country were involved in an unproven assassination attempt on one of the state's citizens six months before.

38. UN initiatives under Chapter VII of the Charter must be more rigorously controlled. It cannot be right for states to obtain UN authorisation for comprehensive sanctions or military action, and then to act unilaterally in an escalating crisis without further reference to the United Nations.

39. There should be greater transparency in IMF and World Bank deliberations.

40. There should be increased democratic participation in IMF and World Bank decision making and project management.

41. There should be increased UN scrutiny of TNC deliberations and actions throughout the world, following the spirit of Resolution 1913(LVII) from the Economic and Social Council. Work to develop a TNC Code of Conduct should be intensified: new terms of reference should be drawn up and a deadline for a finalised draft specified.

42. Attention should be given to the provision of mandatory powers in the General Assembly to allow its evolution as a truly legislative

body. Such powers would touch every area of UN activity: peace-keeping, fund raising, aid disbursement, TNC monitoring, global health activities, education and training, human rights monitoring and implementation, and so on.

43. The powers of the World Court should be enhanced, with such powers consolidated by the development of the UN's supranational identity.

44. UN members must expect to be bound by World Court decisions. The obligation specified in Article 94(1) should be widened to include states that are not necessarily party to a dispute. The possibility of sanctions to encourage observance of Court decisions should be explored.

45. Individual citizens should be allowed to take cases to an expanded World Court.

46. The World Court should be given unambiguous and wide-ranging powers to scrutinise the passing and implementation of Security Council resolutions. No powerful state should be able to secure Council votes through bribery and threat. No state should be above the law. This means that Article 94(2) should be reformed to abolish the primacy of the Security Council in deciding how to give effect to Court judgements.

47. States should be able to take cases to the World Court in protest against the policies of UN-linked bodies (such as the IMF and the World Court) where adverse effects can be demonstrated.

48. States should be able to take cases to the World Court in protest against the adverse effects of TNC policies (in such areas as pollution and violation of workers' rights).

49. The United Nations should – against the drift of current economic orthodoxy (which in any case is not disinterested) – give strong support to the 'new protectionism', as set out, for example, in the Lang/Hines New Protectionist Agenda (see Figure 7.2). Such an initiative is vital if the United Nations is to demonstrate its commitment to the peoples of the world rather than to powerful economic vested interests.

50. A framework should be created to facilitate an on-going assessment of the reformed Charter. At one level, the simple anachronistic anomalies (for example, the references in Articles 53, 77 and 107 to the 'enemy states' of World War Two) have to be removed. More

fundamentally, there will have to be redrafts of the Charter to allow for the progressive changes to the UN structure, to the rights and duties of the Security Council and the General Assembly, to modes of election, to the creation of new bodies, and so on. The reform process is continuous: there should always be scope for redrafting the UN Charter.

The UN Secretary-General Boutros Boutros-Ghali has repeatedly emphasised that the United Nations is 'indispensable', the 'only global forum'. He is right to urge not only international support for the UN but also the pressing need for the United Nations to adapt in a rapidly changing world; one in which there are massive social dislocation, appallingly destructive military conflicts, and horrendous levels of human suffering. The United Nations – not necessarily for what it is but for what it might become – deserves our commitment and support. It also deserves to be reformed.

Appendix 1
The Charter of the
United Nations

NOTE: The Charter of the United Nations was signed on 26 June 1945, in San Francisco, at the conclusion of the United Nations Conference on International Organization, and came into force on 24 October 1945. The Statute of the International Court of Justice is an integral part of the Charter.

Amendments to Articles 23, 27 and 61 of the Charter were adopted by the General Assembly on 17 December 1963 and came into force on 31 August 1965. A further amendment to Article 61 was adopted by the General Assembly on 20 December 1971, and came into force on 24 September 1973. An amendment to Article 109, adopted by the General Assembly on 20 December 1965, came into force on 12 June 1968.

The amendment to Article 23 enlarges the membership of the Security Council from 11 to 15. The amended Article 27 provides that decisions of the Security Council on procedural matters shall be made by an affirmative vote of nine members (formerly seven) and on all other matters by an affirmative vote of nine members (formerly seven), including the concurring votes of the five permanent members of the Security Council.

The amendment to Article 61, which entered into force on 31 August 1965, enlarged the membership of the Economic and Social Council from 18 to 27. The subsequent amendment to that Article, which entered into force on 24 September 1973, further increased the membership of the Council from 27 to 54.

The amendment to Article 109, which relates to the first paragraph of that Article, provides that a General Conference of Member States for the purpose of reviewing the Charter may be held at a date and place to be fixed by a two-thirds vote of the members of the General Assembly and by a vote of any nine members (formerly seven) of the Security Council. Paragraph 3 of Article 109, which deals with the consideration of a possible review conference during the tenth regular session of the General Assembly, has been retained in its original form in its reference to a 'vote of any seven members of the Security Council', the paragraph having been acted upon in 1955 by the General Assembly, at its tenth regular session, and by the Security Council.

WE THE PEOPLES
OF THE UNITED NATIONS
DETERMINED
to save succeeding generations from the scourge of war, which twice in our lifetime has brought untold sorrow to mankind and
to reaffirm faith in fundamental human rights, in the dignity and worth of the human person, in the equal rights of men and women and of nations large and small, and

to establish conditions under which justice and respect for the obligations arising from treaties and other sources of international law can be maintained, and
to promote social progress and better standards of life in larger freedom,

AND FOR THESE ENDS
to practice tolerance and live together in peace with one another as good neighbours, and
to unite our strength to maintain international peace and security, and to ensure, by the acceptance of principles and the institution of methods, that armed force shall not be used, save in the common interest, and
to employ international machinery for the promotion of the economic and social advancement of all peoples,

HAVE RESOLVED TO
COMBINE OUR EFFORTS TO
ACCOMPLISH THESE AIMS
Accordingly, our respective Governments, through representatives assembled in the city of San Francisco, who have exhibited their full powers found to be in good and due form, have agreed to the present Charter of the United Nations and do hereby establish an international organization to be known as the United Nations.

Chapter I
PURPOSES AND PRINCIPLES

Article 1

The Purposes of the United Nations are:

1. To maintain international peace and security, and to that end: to take effective collective measures for the prevention and removal of threats to the peace, and for the suppression of acts of aggression or other breaches of the peace, and to bring about by peaceful means, and in conformity with the principles of justice and international law, adjustment or settlement of international disputes or situations which might lead to a breach of the peace;

2. To develop friendly relations among nations based on respect for the principle of equal rights and self-determination of peoples, and to take other appropriate measures to strengthen universal peace;

3. To achieve international co-operation in solving international problems of an economic, social, cultural, or humanitarian character, and in promoting and encouraging respect for human rights and for fundamental freedoms for all without distinction as to race, sex, language, or religion; and

4. To be a centre for harmonizing the actions of nations in the attainment of these common ends.

Article 2

The Organization and its Members, in pursuit of the Purposes stated in Article 1, shall act in accordance with the following Principles.

1.   The Organization is based on the principle of the sovereign equality of all its Members.

2.   All Members, in order to ensure to all of them the rights and benefits resulting from membership, shall fulfil in good faith the obligations assumed by them in accordance with the present Charter.

3.   All Members shall settle their international disputes by peaceful means in such a manner that international peace and security, and justice, are not endangered.

4.   All Members shall refrain in their international relations from the threat or use of force against the territorial integrity or political independence of any state, or in any other manner inconsistent with the Purposes of the United Nations.

5.   All Members shall give the United Nations every assistance in any action it takes in accordance with the present Charter, and shall refrain from giving assistance to any state against which the United Nations is taking preventive or enforcement action.

6.   The Organization shall ensure that states which are not Members of the United Nations act in accordance with these Principles so far as may be necessary for the maintenance of international peace and security.

7.   Nothing contained in the present Charter shall authorize the United Nations to intervene in matters which are essentially within the domestic jurisdiction of any state or shall require the Members to submit such matters to settlement under the present Charter; but this principle shall not prejudice the application of enforcement measures under Chapter VII.

Chapter II
MEMBERSHIP

Article 3

The original Members of the United Nations shall be the states which, having participated in the United Nations Conference on International Organization at San Francisco, or having previously signed the Declaration by United Nations of 1 January 1942, sign the present Charter and ratify it in accordance with Article 110.

Article 4

1.   Membership in the United Nations is open to all other peace-loving states which accept the obligations contained in the present Charter and, in the judgment of the Organization, are able and willing to carry out these obligations.

2.   The admission of any such state to membership in the United Nations will be effected by a decision of the General Assembly upon the recommendation of the Security Council.

Article 5

A Member of the United Nations against which preventive or enforcement action has been taken by the Security Council may be suspended from the exercise of the rights and privileges of membership by the General Assembly upon the recommendation of the Security Council. The exercise of these rights and privileges may be restored by the Security Council.

Article 6

A Member of the United Nations which has persistently violated the Principles contained in the present Charter may be expelled from the Organization by the General Assembly upon the recommendation of the Security Council.

Chapter III
ORGANS

Article 7

1. There are established as the principal organs of the United Nations: a General Assembly, a Security Council, an Economic and Social Council, a Trusteeship Council, an International Court of Justice, and a Secretariat.
2. Such subsidiary organs as may be found necessary may be established in accordance with the present Charter.

Article 8

The United Nations shall place no restrictions on the eligibility of men and women to participate in any capacity and under conditions of equality in its principal and subsidiary organs.

Chapter IV
THE GENERAL ASSEMBLY

Composition

Article 9

1. The General Assembly shall consist of all the Members of the United Nations.
2. Each Member shall have not more than five representatives in the General Assembly.

Functions and powers

Article 10

The General Assembly may discuss any questions or any matters within the scope of the present Charter or relating to the powers and functions of any organs provided for in the present Charter and, except as provided in Article 12, may make recommendations to the Members of the United Nations or to the Security Council or to both on any such questions or matters.

Article 11

1.   The General Assembly may consider the general principles of co-operation in the maintenance of international peace and security, including the principles governing disarmament and the regulation of armaments, and may make recommendations with regard to such principles to the Members or to the Security Council or to both.

2.   The General Assembly may discuss any questions relating to the maintenance of international peace and security brought before it by any Member of the United Nations, or by the Security Council, or by a state which is not a Member of the United Nations in accordance with Article 35, paragraph 2, and, except as provided in Article 12, may make recommendations with regard to any such questions to the state or states concerned or to the Security Council or to both. Any such question to which action is necessary shall be referred to the Security Council by the General Assembly either before or after discussion.

3.   The General Assembly may call the attention of the Security Council to situations which are likely to endanger international peace and security.

4.   The powers of the General Assembly set forth in this Article shall not limit the general scope of Article 10.

Article 12

1.   While the Security Council is exercising in respect of any dispute or situation the functions assigned to it in the present Charter, the General Assembly shall not make any recommendation with regard to that dispute or situation unless the Security Council so requests.

2.   The Secretary-General, with the consent of the Security Council, shall notify the General Assembly at each session of any matters relative to the maintenance of international peace and security which are being dealt with by the Security Council and shall similarly notify the General Assembly, or the Members of the United Nations if the General Assembly is not in session, immediately the Security Council ceases to deal with such matters.

Article 13

1.   The General Assembly shall initiate studies and make recommendations for the purpose of:

(a) promoting international co-operation in the political field and encouraging the progressive development of international law and its
codification;

(b) promoting international co-operation in the economic, social, cultural,
educational, and health fields, and assisting in the realization of human
rights and fundamental freedoms for all without distinction as to race,
sex, language, or religion.

2. The further responsibilities, functions and powers of the General Assembly
with respect to matters mentioned in paragraph 1(b) above are set forth in Chapters
IX and X.

Article 14

Subject to the provisions of Article 12, the General Assembly may recommend
measures for the peaceful adjustment of any situation, regardless of origin,
which it deems likely to impair the general welfare or friendly relations
among nations, including situations resulting from a violation of the provisions
of the present Charter setting forth the Purposes and Principles of the United
Nations.

Article 15

1. The General Assembly shall receive and consider annual and special reports
from the Security Council; these reports shall include an account of the measures
that the Security Council has decided upon or taken to maintain international peace
and security.

2. The General Assembly shall receive and consider reports from the other
organs of the United Nations.

Article 16

The General Assembly shall perform such functions with respect to the international trusteeship system as are assigned to it under Chapters XII and XIII,
including the approval of the trusteeship agreements for areas not designated as
strategic.

Article 17

1. The General Assembly shall consider and approve the budget of the
Organization.

2. The expenses of the Organization shall be borne by the Members as
apportioned by the General Assembly.

3. The General Assembly shall consider and approve any financial and
budgetary arrangements with specialized agencies referred to in Article 57 and
shall examine the administrative budgets of such specialized agencies with a view
to making recommendations to the agencies concerned.

Voting

Article 18

1. Each member of the General Assembly shall have one vote.
2. Decisions of the General Assembly on important questions shall be made by a two-thirds majority of the members present and voting. These questions shall include: recommendations with respect to the maintenance of international peace and security, the election of the non-permanent members of the Security Council, the election of the members of the Economic and Social Council, the election of members of the Trusteeship Council in accordance with paragraph 1(c) of Article 86, the admission of new Members to the United Nations, the suspension of the rights and privileges of membership, the expulsion of Members, questions relating to the operation of the trusteeship system, and budgetary questions.
3. Decisions on other questions, including the determination of additional categories of questions to be decided by a two-thirds majority, shall be made by a majority of the members present and voting.

Article 19

A Member of the United Nations which is in arrears in the payment of its financial contributions to the Organization shall have no vote in the General Assembly if the amount of its arrears equals or exceeds the amount of the contributions due from it for the preceding two full years. The General Assembly may, nevertheless, permit such a Member to vote if it is satisfied that the failure to pay is due to conditions beyond the control of the Member.

Procedure

Article 20

The General Assembly shall meet in regular annual sessions and in such special sessions as occasion may require. Special sessions shall be convoked by the Secretary-General at the request of the Security Council or of a majority of the Members of the United Nations.

Article 21

The General Assembly shall adopt its own rules of procedure. It shall elect its President for each session.

Article 22

The General Assembly may establish such subsidiary organs as it deems necessary for the performance of its functions.

Chapter V
THE SECURITY COUNCIL

Composition

Article 23[1]

1.   The Security Council shall consist of fifteen Members of the United Nations. The Republic of China, France, the Union of Soviet Socialist Republics, the United Kingdom of Great Britain and Northern Ireland, and the United States of America shall be permanent members of the Security Council. The General Assembly shall elect ten other Members of the United Nations to be non-permanent members of the Security Council, due regard being specially paid, in the first instance to the contribution of Members of the United Nations to the maintenance of international peace and security and to the other purposes of the Organization, and also to equitable geographical distribution.

2.   The non-permanent members of the Security Council shall be elected for a term of two years. In the first election of the non-permanent members after the increase of the membership of the Security Council from eleven to fifteen, two of the four additional members shall be chosen for a term of one year. A retiring member shall not be eligible for immediate re-election.

3.   Each member of the Security Council shall have one representative.

Functions and powers

Article 24

1.   In order to ensure prompt and effective action by the United Nations, its Members confer on the Security Council primary responsibility for the maintenance of international peace and security, and agree that in carrying out its duties under this responsibility the Security Council acts on their behalf.

2.   In discharging these duties the Security Council shall act in accordance with the Purposes and Principles of the United Nations. The specific powers granted to the Security Council for the discharge of these duties are laid down in Chapters VI, VII, VIII, and XII.

3.   The Security Council shall submit annual and, when necessary, special reports to the General Assembly for its consideration.

Article 25

The Members of the United Nations agree to accept and carry out the decisions of the Security Council in accordance with the present Charter.

Article 26

In order to promote the establishment and maintenance of international peace and security with the least diversion for armaments of the world's human and economic resources, the Security Council shall be responsible for formulating, with the assistance of the Military Staff Committee referred to in Article 47, plans to be submitted to the Members of the United Nations for the establishment of a system for the regulation of armaments.

Voting

Article 27[2]

1. Each member of the Security Council shall have one vote.
2. Decisions of the Security Council on procedural matters shall be made by an affirmative vote of nine members.
3. Decisions of the Security Council on all other matters shall be made by an affirmative vote of nine members including the concurring votes of the permanent members; provided that, in decisions under Chapter VI, and under paragraph 3 of Article 52, a party to a dispute shall abstain from voting.

Procedure

Article 28

1. The Security Council shall be so organized as to be able to function continuously. Each member of the Security Council shall for this purpose be represented at all times at the seat of the Organization.
2. The Security Council shall hold periodic meetings at which each of its members may, if it so desires, be represented by a member of the government or by some other specially designated representative.
3. The Security Council may hold meetings at such places other than the seat of the Organization as in its judgment will best facilitate its work.

Article 29

The Security Council may establish such subsidiary organs as it deems necessary of the performance of its functions.

Article 30

The Security Council shall adopt its own rules of procedure, including the method of selecting its President.

Article 31

Any Member of the United Nations which is not a member of the Security Council may participate, without vote, in the discussion of any question brought before the Security Council whenever the latter considers that the interests of that Member are specially affected.

Article 32

Any Member of the United Nations which is not a member of the Security Council or any state which is not a Member of the United Nations, if it is a party to a dispute under consideration by the Security Council, shall be invited to participate, without vote, in the discussion relating to the dispute. The Security Council shall lay down such conditions as it deems just for the participation of a state which is not a Member of the United Nations.

Chapter VI
PACIFIC SETTLEMENT OF DISPUTES

Article 33

1. The parties to any dispute, the continuance of which is likely to endanger the maintenance of international peace and security, shall, first of all, seek a solution by negotiation, enquiry, mediation, conciliation, arbitration, judicial settlement, resort to regional agencies or arrangements, or other peaceful means of their own choice.
2. The Security Council shall, when it deems necessary, call upon the parties to settle their dispute by such means.

Article 34

The Security Council may investigate any dispute or any situation which might lead to international friction or give rise to a dispute, in order to determine whether the continuance of the dispute or situation is likely to endanger the maintenance of international peace and security.

Article 35

1. Any Member of the United Nations may bring any dispute, or any situation of the nature referred to in Article 34, to the attention of the Security Council or of the General Assembly.
2. A state which is not a Member of the United Nations may bring to the attention of the Security Council or of the General Assembly any dispute to which it is a party if it accepts in advance, for the purposes of the dispute, the obligations of pacific settlement provided in the present Charter.
3. The proceedings of the General Assembly in respect of matters brought to its attention under this Article will be subject to the provisions of Article 11 and 12.

Article 36

1. The Security Council may, at any stage of a dispute of the nature referred to in Article 33 or of a situation of like nature, recommend appropriate procedures or methods of adjustment.

2. The Security Council should take into consideration any procedures for the settlement of the dispute which have already been adopted by the parties.

3. In making recommendations under this Article the Security Council should also take into consideration that legal disputes should as a general rule be referred by the parties to the International Court of Justice in accordance with the provisions of the Statute of the Court.

Article 37

1. Should the parties to a dispute of the nature referred to in Article 33 fail to settle it by the means indicated in that Article, they shall refer it to the Security Council.

2. If the Security Council deems that the continuance of the dispute is in fact likely to endanger the maintenance of international peace and security, it shall decide whether to take action under Article 36 or to recommend such terms of settlement as it may consider appropriate.

Article 38

Without prejudice to the provisions of Articles 33 to 37, the Security Council may, if all the parties to any dispute so request, make recommendations to the parties with a view to a pacific settlement of the dispute.

Chapter VII
ACTION WITH RESPECT TO THREATS TO THE PEACE, BREACHES OF THE PEACE, AND ACTS OF AGGRESSION

Article 39

The Security Council shall determine the existence of any threat to the peace, breach of the peace, or act of aggression and shall make recommendations, or decide what measures shall be taken in accordance with Articles 41 and 42, to maintain or restore international peace and security.

Article 40

In order to prevent an aggravation of the situation, the Security Council may, before making the recommendations or deciding upon the measures provided for in Article 39, call upon the parties concerned to comply with such provisional measures as it deems necessary or desirable. Such provisional measures shall be without prejudice to the rights, claims, or position of the parties concerned. The Security Council shall duly take account of failure to comply with such provisional measures.

Article 41

The Security Council may decide what measures not involving the use of armed force are to be employed to give effect to its decisions, and it may call upon the

Members of the United Nations to apply such measures. These may include complete or partial interruption of economic relations and of rail, sea, air, postal, telegraphic, radio, and other means of communication, and the severance of diplomatic relations.

Article 42

Should the Security Council consider that measures provided for in Article 41 would be inadequate or have proved to be inadequate, it may take such action by air, sea, or land forces as may be necessary to maintain or restore international peace and security. Such action may include demonstrations, blockade, and other operations by air, sea, or land forces of Members of the United Nations.

Article 43

1. All Members of the United Nations, in order to contribute to the maintenance of international peace and security, undertake to make available to the Security Council, on its call and in accordance with a special agreement or agreements, armed forces, assistance, and facilities, including rights of passage, necessary for the purpose of maintaining international peace and security.

2. Such agreement or agreements shall govern the numbers and types of forces, their degree of readiness and general location, and the nature of the facilities and assistance to be provided.

3. The agreement or agreements shall be negotiated as soon as possible on the initiative of the Security Council. They shall be concluded between the Security Council and Members or between the Security Council and groups of Members and shall be subject to ratification by the signatory states in accordance with their respective constitutional processes.

Article 44

When the Security Council has decided to use force it shall, before calling upon a Member not represented on it to provide armed forces in fulfilment of the obligations assumed under Article 43, invite that Member if the Member so desires, to participate in the decisions of the Security Council concerning the employment of contingents of that Member's armed forces.

Article 45

In order to enable the United Nations to take urgent military measures, Members shall hold immediately available national air-force contingents for combined international enforcement action. The strength and degree of readiness of these contingents and plans for their combined action shall be determined, within the limits laid down in the special agreement or agreements referred to in Article 43, by the Security Council with the assistance of the Military Staff Committee.

Article 46

Plans for the application of armed forces shall be made by the Security Council with the assistance of the Military Staff Committee.

Article 47

1.   There shall be established a Military Staff Committee to advise and assist the Security Council on all questions relating to the Security Council's military requirements for the maintenance of international peace and security, the employment and command of forces placed at its disposal, the regulation of armaments, and possible disarmament.

2.   The Military Staff Committee shall consist of the Chiefs of Staff of the permanent members of the Security Council or their representatives. Any Member of the United Nations not permanently represented on the Committee shall be invited by the Committee to be associated with it when the efficient discharge of the Committee's responsibilities requires the participation of that Member in its work.

3.   The Military Staff Committee shall be responsible under the Security Council for the strategic direction of any armed forces placed at the disposal of the Security Council. Questions relating to the command of such forces shall be worked out subsequently.

4.   The Military Staff committee, with the authorization of the Security Council and after consultation with appropriate regional agencies, may establish regional subcommittees.

Article 48

1.   The action required to carry out the decisions of the Security Council for the maintenance of international peace and security shall be taken by all the Members of the United Nations or by some of them, as the Security Council may determine.

2.   Such decisions shall be carried out by the Members of the United Nations directly and through their action in the appropriate international agencies of which they are members.

Article 49

The Members of the United Nations shall join in affording mutual assistance in carrying out the measures decided upon by the Security Council.

Article 50

If preventive or enforcement measures against any state are taken by the Security Council, any other state, whether a Member of the United Nations or not, which finds itself confronted with special economic problems arising from the carrying out of those measures shall have the right to consult the Security Council with regard to a solution of those problems.

Article 51

Nothing in the present Charter shall impair the inherent right of individual or collective self-defence if an armed attack occurs against a Member of the United Nations, until the Security Council has taken measures necessary to maintain international peace and security. Measures taken by Members in the exercise of this right of self-defence shall be immediately reported to the Security Council and shall not in any way affect the authority and responsibility of the Security Council under the present Charter to take at any time such action as it deems necessary in order to maintain or restore international peace and security.

Chapter VIII
REGIONAL ARRANGEMENTS

Article 52

1.   Nothing in the present Charter precludes the existence of regional arrangements or agencies for dealing with such matters relating to the maintenance of international peace and security as are appropriate for regional action, provided that such arrangements or agencies and their activities are consistent with the Purposes and Principles of the United Nations.

2.   The Members of the United Nations entering into such arrangements or constituting such agencies shall make every effort to achieve pacific settlement of local disputes through such regional arrangements or by such regional agencies before referring them to the Security Council.

3.   The Security Council shall encourage the development of pacific settlement of local disputes through such regional arrangements or by such regional agencies either on the initiative of the states concerned or by reference from the Security Council.

4.   This Article in no way impairs the application of Articles 34 and 35.

Article 53

1.   The Security Council shall, where appropriate, utilize such regional arrangements or agencies for enforcement action under its authority. But no enforcement action shall be taken under regional arrangements or by regional agencies without the authorization of the Security Council, with the exception of measures against any enemy state, as defined in paragraph 2 of this Article, provided for pursuant to Article 107 or in regional arrangements directed against renewal of aggressive policy on the part of any such state, until such time as the Organization may, on request of the Governments concerned, be charged with responsibility for preventing further aggression by such a state.

2.   The term enemy state as used in paragraph 1 of this Article applies to any state which during the Second World War has been an enemy of any signatory of the present Charter.

Article 54

The Security Council shall at all times be kept fully informed of activities undertaken or in contemplation under regional arrangements or by regional agencies for the maintenance of international peace and security.

Chapter IX
INTERNATIONAL ECONOMIC
AND SOCIAL CO-OPERATION

Article 55

With a view to the creation of conditions of stability and well-being which are necessary for peaceful and friendly relations among nations based on respect for the principle of equal rights and self-determination of peoples, the United Nations shall promote:

    (a) higher standards of living, full employment, and conditions of economic and social progress and development;

    (b) solutions of international economic, social, health, and related problems; and international cultural and educational co-operation; and

    (c) universal respect for, and observance of, human rights and fundamental freedoms for all without distinction as to race, sex, language, or religion.

Article 56

All Members pledge themselves to take joint and separate action in co-operation with the Organization for the achievement of the purposes set forth in Article 55.

Article 57

1.   The various specialized agencies, established by intergovernmental agreement and having wide international responsibilities, as defined in their basic instruments, in economic, social, cultural, educational, health, and related fields, shall be brought into relationship with the United Nations in accordance with the provisions of Article 63.

2.   Such agencies thus brought into relationship with the United Nations are hereinafter referred to as specialized agencies.

Article 58

The Organization shall make recommendations for the co-ordination of the policies and activities of the specialized agencies.

Article 59

The Organization shall, where appropriate, initiate negotiations among the states concerned for the creation of any new specialized agencies required for the accomplishment of the purposes set forth in Article 55.

Article 60

Responsibility for the discharge of the functions of the Organization set forth in this Chapter shall be vested in the General Assembly and, under the authority of the General Assembly, in the Economic and Social Council, which shall have for this purpose the powers set forth in Chapter X.

Chapter X
THE ECONOMIC AND SOCIAL COUNCIL

Composition

Article 61[3]

1. The Economic and Social Council shall consist of fifty-four Members of the United Nations elected by the General Assembly.
2. Subject to the provisions of paragraph 3, eighteen members of the Economic and Social Council shall be elected each year for a term of three years. A retiring member shall be eligible for immediate re-election.
3. At the first election after the increase in the membership of the Economic and Social Council from twenty-seven to fifty-four members, in addition to the members elected in place of the nine members whose term of office expires at the end of that year, twenty-seven additional members shall be elected. Of these twenty-seven additional members, the term of office of nine members so elected shall expire at the end of one year; and of nine other members at the end of two years, in accordance with arrangements made by the General Assembly.
4. Each member of the Economic and Social Council shall have one representative.

Functions and powers

Article 62

1. The Economic and Social Council may make or initiate studies and reports with respect to international economic, social, cultural, educational, health, and related matters and may make recommendations with respect to any such matters to the General Assembly, to the Members of the United Nations, and to the specialized agencies concerned.
2. It may make recommendations for the purpose of promoting respect for, and observance of, human rights and fundamental freedoms for all.
3. It may prepare draft conventions for submission to the General Assembly, with respect to matters falling within its competence.
4. It may call, in accordance with the rules prescribed by the United Nations, international conferences on matters falling within its competence.

Article 63

1. The Economic and Social Council may enter into agreements with any of the agencies referred to in Article 57, defining the terms on which the agency con-

cerned shall be brought into relationship with the United Nations. Such agreements shall be subject to approval by the General Assembly.

2. It may co-ordinate the activities of the specialized agencies through consultation with and recommendations to such agencies and through recommendations to the General Assembly and to the Members of the United Nations.

Article 64

1. The Economic and Social Council may take appropriate steps to obtain regular reports from the specialized agencies. It may make arrangements with the Members of the United Nations and with the specialized agencies to obtain reports on the steps taken to give effect to its own recommendations and to recommendations on matters falling within its competence made by the General Assembly.

2. It may communicate its observations on these reports to the General Assembly.

Article 65

The Economic and Social Council may furnish information to the Security Council and shall assist the Security Council upon its request.

Article 66

1. The Economic and Social Council shall perform such functions as fall within its competence in connection with the carrying out of the recommendations of the General Assembly.

2. It may, with the approval of the General Assembly, perform services at the request of Members of the United Nations and at the request of specialized agencies.

3. It shall perform such other functions as are specified elsewhere in the present Charter or as may be assigned to it by the General Assembly.

Voting

Article 67

1. Each member of the Economic and Social Council shall have one vote.

2. Decisions of the Economic and Social Council shall be made by a majority of the members present and voting.

Procedure

Article 68

The Economic and Social Council shall set up commissions in economic and social fields and for the promotion of human rights, and such other commissions as may be required for the performance of its functions.

Article 69

The Economic and Social Council shall invite any Member of the United Nations to participate, without vote, in its deliberations on any matter of particular concern to that Member.

Article 70

The Economic and Social Council may make arrangements for representatives of the specialized agencies to participate, without vote, in its deliberations and in those of the commissions established by it, and for its representatives to participate in the deliberations of the specialized agencies.

Article 71

The Economic and Social Council may make suitable arrangements for consultation with non-governmental organizations which are concerned with matters within its competence. Such arrangements may be made with international organizations and, where appropriate, with national organizations after consultation with the Member of the United Nations concerned.

Article 72

1. The Economic and Social Council shall adopt its own rules of procedure, including the method of selecting its President.

2. The Economic and Social Council shall meet as required in accordance with its rules, which shall include provision for the convening of meetings on the request of a majority of its members.

Chapter XI
DECLARATION REGARDING
NON-SELF-GOVERNING TERRITORIES

Article 73

Members of the United Nations which have or assume responsibilities for the administration of territories whose people have not yet attained a full measure of self-government recognize the principle that the interests of the inhabitants of these territories are paramount, and accept as a sacred trust the obligation to promote to the utmost, within the system of international peace and security established by the present Charter, the well-being of the inhabitants of these territories, and, to this end:

(a) to ensure, with due respect for the culture of the peoples concerned, their political, economic, social, and educational advancement, their just treatment, and their protection against abuses;

(b) to develop self-government, to take due account of the political aspirations of the peoples, and to assist them in the progressive development of their free political institutions according to the particular circumstances of each territory and its peoples and their varying stages of advancement;

(c) to further international peace and security;

(d) to promote constructive measures of development, to encourage research, and to co-operate with one another and, when and where appropriate, with specialized international bodies with a view to the practical achievement of the social, economic, and scientific purposes set forth in this Article; and

(e) to transmit regularly to the Secretary-General for information purposes, subject to such limitation as security and constitutional considerations may require, statistical and other information of a technical nature relating to economic, social, and educational conditions in the territories for which they are respectively responsible other than those territories to which Chapters XII and XIII apply.

Article 74

Members of the United Nations also agree that their policy in respect of the territories to which this Chapter applies, no less than in respect of their metropolitan areas, must be based on the general principle of good neighborliness, due account being taken of the interests and well-being of the rest of the world, in social, economic, and commercial matters.

Chapter XII
INTERNATIONAL TRUSTEESHIP SYSTEM

Article 75

The United Nations shall establish under its authority an international trusteeship system for the administration and supervision of such territories as may be placed thereunder by subsequent individual agreements. These territories are hereinafter referred to as trust territories.

Article 76

The basic objectives of the trusteeship system, in accordance with the Purposes of the United Nations laid down in Article 1 of the present Charter, shall be:

(a) to further international peace and security;

(b) to promote the political, economic, social, and educational advancement of the inhabitants of the trust territories, and their progressive development towards self-government or independence as may be appropriate to the particular circumstances of each territory and its people and the freely expressed wishes of the peoples concerned, and as may be provided by the terms of each trusteeship agreement;

(c) to encourage respect for human rights and for fundamental freedoms for all without distinction as to race, sex, language, or religion, and to encourage recognition of the interdependence of the peoples of the world; and

(d) to ensure equal treatment in social, economic, and commercial matters for all Members of the United Nations and their nationals, and also equal treatment for the latter in the administration of justice, without prejudice to the attainment of the foregoing objectives and subject to the provisions of Article 80.

Article 77

1. The trusteeship system shall apply to such territories in the following categories as may be placed thereunder by means of trusteeship agreements:

(a) territories now held under mandate;

(b) territories which may be detached from enemy states as a result of the Second World War; and

(c) territories voluntarily placed under the system by states responsible for their administration.

2. It will be a matter for subsequent agreement as to which territories in the foregoing categories will be brought under the trusteeship system and upon what terms.

Article 78

The trusteeship system shall not apply to territories which have become Members of the United Nations, relationship among which shall be based on respect for the principle of sovereign equality.

Article 79

The terms of trusteeship for each territory to be placed under the trusteeship system, including any alteration or amendment, shall be agreed upon by the states directly concerned, including the mandatory power in the case of territories held under mandate by a Member of the United Nations, and shall be approved as provided for in Article 83 and 85.

Article 80

1. Except as may be agreed upon in individual trusteeship agreements, made under Articles 77, 79, and 81, placing each territory under the trusteeship system, and until such agreements have been concluded, nothing in this Chapter shall be construed in or of itself to alter in any manner the rights whatsoever of any states or any peoples or the terms of existing international instruments to which Members of the United Nations may respectively be parties.

2. Paragraph 1 of this Article shall not be interpreted as giving grounds for delay or postponement of the negotiations and conclusion of agreements for

placing mandated and other territories under the trusteeship system as provided for in Article 77.

Article 81

The trusteeship agreement shall in each case include the terms under which the trust territory will be administered and designate the authority which will exercise the administration of the trust territory. Such authority, hereinafter called the administering authority, may be one or more states or the Organization itself.

Article 82

There may be designated, in any trusteeship agreement, a strategic area or areas which may include part or all of the trust territory to which the agreement applies, without prejudice to any special agreement or agreements made under Article 43.

Article 83

1.   All functions of the United Nations relating to strategic areas, including the approval of the terms of the trusteeship agreements and of their alteration or amendments, shall be exercised by the Security Council.

2.   The basic objectives set forth in Article 76 shall be applicable to the people of each strategic area.

3.   The Security Council shall, subject to the provisions of the trusteeship agreements and without prejudice to security considerations, avail itself of the assistance of the Trusteeship Council to perform those functions of the United Nations under the trusteeship system relating to political, economic, social, and educational matters in the strategic areas.

Article 84

It shall be the duty of the administering authority to ensure that the trust territory shall play its part in the maintenance of international peace and security. To this end the administering authority may make use of volunteer forces, facilities, and assistance from the trust territory in carrying out the obligations towards the Security Council undertaken in this regard by the administering authority, as well as for local defence and the maintenance of law and order within the trust territory.

Article 85

1.   The functions of the United Nations with regard to trusteeship agreements for all areas not designated as strategic, including the approval of the terms of the trusteeship agreements and of their alteration or amendment, shall be exercised by the General Assembly.

2.   The Trusteeship Council, operating under the authority of the General Assembly, shall assist the General Assembly in carrying out these functions.

Chapter XIII
THE TRUSTEESHIP COUNCIL

Composition

Article 86

1. The Trusteeship Council shall consist of the following Members of the United Nations:

  (a) those Members administering trust territories;
  (b) such of those Members mentioned by name in Article 23 as are not administering trust territories; and
  (c) as many other Members elected for three-year terms by the General Assembly as may be necessary to ensure that the total number of members of the Trusteeship Council is equally divided between those Members of the United Nations which administer trust territories and those which do not.

2. Each member of the Trusteeship Council shall designate one specially qualified person to represent it therein.

Functions and powers

Article 87

The General Assembly and, under its authority, the Trusteeship Council, in carrying out their functions, may:

  (a) consider reports submitted by the administering authority;
  (b) accept petitions and examine them in consultation with the administering authority;
  (c) provide for periodic visits to the respective trust territories at times agreed upon with the administering authority; and
  (d) take these and other actions in conformity with the terms of the trusteeship agreements.

Article 88

The Trusteeship Council shall formulate a questionnaire on the political, economic, social, and educational advancement of the inhabitants of each trust territory, and the administering authority for each trust territory within the competence of the General Assembly shall make an annual report to the General Assembly upon the basis of such questionnaire.

Voting

Article 89

1. Each member of the Trusteeship Council shall have one vote.
2. Decisions of the Trusteeship Council shall be made by a majority of the members present and voting.

Procedure

Article 90

1. The Trusteeship Council shall adopt its own rules of procedure, including the method of selecting its President.
2. The Trusteeship Council shall meet as required in accordance with its rules, which shall include provision for the convening of meetings on the request of a majority of its members.

Article 91

The Trusteeship Council shall, when appropriate, avail itself of the assistance of the Economic and Social Council and of the specialized agencies in regard to matters with which they are respectively concerned.

Chapter XIV
THE INTERNATIONAL COURT OF JUSTICE

Article 92

The International Court of Justice shall be the principal judicial organ of the United Nations. It shall function in accordance with the annexed Statute, which is based upon the Statute of the Permanent Court of International Justice and forms an integral part of the present Charter.

Article 93

1. All Members of the United Nations are ipso facto parties to the Statute of the International Court of Justice.
2. A state which is not a Member of the United Nations may become a party to the Statute of the International Court of Justice on conditions to be determined in each case by the General Assembly upon the recommendation of the Security Council.

Article 94

1.   Each Member of the United Nations undertakes to comply with the decision of the International Court of Justice in any case to which it is a party.

2.   If any party to a case fails to perform the obligations incumbent upon it under a judgment rendered by the Court, the other party may have recourse to the Security Council, which may, if it deems necessary, make recommendations or decide upon measures to be taken to give effect to the judgment.

Article 95

Nothing in the present Charter shall prevent Members of the United Nations from entrusting the solution of their differences to other tribunals by virtue of agreements already in existence or which may be concluded in the future.

Article 96

1.   The General Assembly or the Security Council may request the International Court of Justice to give an advisory opinion on any legal question.

2.   Other organs of the United Nations and specialized agencies, which may at any time be so authorized by the General Assembly, may also request advisory opinions of the Court on legal questions arising within the scope of their activities.

Chapter XV
THE SECRETARIAT

Article 97

The Secretariat shall comprise a Secretary-General and such staff as the Organization may require. The Secretary-General shall be appointed by the General Assembly upon the recommendation of the Security Council. He shall be the chief administrative officer of the Organization.

Article 98

The Secretary-General shall act in that capacity in all meetings of the General Assembly, of the Security Council, of the Economic and Social Council, and of the Trusteeship Council, and shall perform such other functions as are entrusted to him by these organs. The Secretary-General shall make an annual report to the General Assembly on the work of the Organization.

Article 99

The Secretary-General may bring to the attention of the Security Council any matter which in his opinion may threaten the maintenance of international peace and security.

Article 100

1.   In the performance of their duties the Secretary-General and the staff shall not seek or receive instructions from any government or from any other authority external to the Organization. They shall refrain from any action which might reflect on their position as international officials responsible only to the Organization.

2.   Each Member of the United Nations undertakes to respect the exclusively international character of the responsibilities of the Secretary-General and the staff and not to seek to influence them in the discharge of their responsibilities.

Article 101

1.   The staff shall be appointed by the Secretary-General under regulations established by the General Assembly.

2.   Appropriate staffs shall be permanently assigned to the Economic and Social Council, the Trusteeship Council, and, as required, to other organs of the United Nations. These staffs shall form a part of the Secretariat.

3.   The paramount consideration in the employment of the staff and in the determination of the conditions of service shall be the necessity of securing the highest standards of efficiency, competence, and integrity. Due regard shall be paid to the importance of recruiting the staff on as wide a geographical basis as possible.

Chapter XVI
MISCELLANEOUS PROVISIONS

Article 102

1.   Every treaty and every international agreement entered into by any Member of the United Nations after the present Charter comes into force shall as soon as possible be registered with the Secretariat and published by it.

2.   No party to any such treaty or international agreement which has not been registered in accordance with the provisions of paragraph 1 of this Article may invoke that treaty or agreement before any organ of the United Nations.

Article 103

In the event of a conflict between the obligations of the Members of the United Nations under the present Charter and their obligations under any other international agreement, their obligations under the present Charter shall prevail.

Article 104

The Organization shall enjoy in the territory of each of its Members such legal capacity as may be necessary for the exercise of its functions and the fulfilment of its purposes.

Article 105

1.   The Organization shall enjoy in the territory of each of its Members such privileges and immunities as are necessary for the fulfilment of its purposes.

2.   Representatives of the Members of the United Nations and officials of the Organization shall similarly enjoy such privileges and immunities as are necessary for the independent exercise of their functions in connection with the Organization.

3.   The General Assembly may make recommendations with a view to determining the details of the application of paragraphs 1 and 2 of this Article or may propose conventions to the Members of the United Nations for this purpose.

Chapter XVII
TRANSITIONAL SECURITY ARRANGEMENTS

Article 106

Pending the coming into force of such special agreements referred to in Article 43 as in the opinion of the Security Council enable it to begin the exercise of its responsibilities under Article 42, the parties to the Four-Nation Declaration, signed at Moscow, 30 October 1943, and France, shall, in accordance with the provisions of paragraph 5 of that Declaration, consult with one another and as occasion requires with other Members of the United Nations with a view to such joint action on behalf of the Organization as may be necessary for the purpose of maintaining international peace and security.

Article 107

Nothing in the present Charter shall invalidate or preclude action, in relation to any state which during the Second World War has been an enemy of any signatory to the present Charter, taken or authorized as a result of that war by the Governments having responsibility for such action.

Chapter XVIII
AMENDMENTS

Article 108

Amendments to the present Charter shall come into force for all members of the United Nations when they have been adopted by a vote of two-thirds of the members of the General Assembly and ratified in accordance with their respective constitutional processes by two-thirds of the Members of the United Nations, including all the permanent members of the Security Council.

Article 109[4]

1.   A General Conference of the Members of the United Nations for the purpose of reviewing the present Charter may be held at a date and place to be fixed by a two-thirds vote of the members of the General Assembly and by a vote of any nine members of the Security Council. Each Member of the United Nations shall have one vote in the conference.

2.   Any alteration of the present Charter recommended by a two-thirds vote of the conference shall take effect when ratified in accordance with their respective constitutional processes by two-thirds of the Members of the United Nations including all the permanent members of the Security Council.

3.   If such a conference has not been held before the tenth annual session of the General Assembly following the coming into force of the present Charter, the proposal to call such a conference shall be placed on the agenda of that session of the General Assembly, and the conference shall be held if so decided by a majority vote of the members of the General Assembly and by a vote of any seven members of the Security Council.

Chapter XIX
RATIFICATION AND SIGNATURE

Article 110

1.   The present Charter shall be ratified by the signatory states in accordance with their respective constitutional processes.

2.   The ratifications shall be deposited with the Government of the United States of America, which shall notify all the signatory states of each deposit as well as the Secretary-General of the Organization when he has been appointed.

3.   The present Charter shall come into force upon the deposit of ratifications by the Republic of China, France, the Union of Soviet Socialist Republics, the United Kingdom of Great Britain and Northern Ireland, and the United States of America, and by a majority of the other signatory states. A protocol of the ratifications deposited shall thereupon be drawn up by the Government of the United States of America which shall communicate copies thereof to all the signatory states.

4.   The states signatory to the present Charter which ratify it after it has come into force will become original Members of the United Nations on the date of the deposit of their respective ratifications.

Article 111

The present Charter, of which the Chinese, French, Russian, English, and Spanish texts are equally authentic, shall remain deposited in the archives of the Government of the United States of America. Duly certified copies thereof shall be transmitted by that Government to the Governments of the other signatory states.

IN FAITH WHEREOF the representative of the Governments of the United Nations have signed the present Charter.

DONE at the city of San Francisco the twenty-sixty day of June, one thousand nine hundred and forty-five.

NOTES

1. Amended text of Article 23 which came into force on 31 August 1965. The text of Article 23 before it was amended read as follows:

    1. The Security Council shall consist of eleven Members of the United Nations. The Republic of China, France, the Union of Soviet Socialist Republics, the United Kingdom of Great Britain and Northern Ireland, and the United States of America shall be permanent members of the Security Council. The General Assembly shall elect six other Members of the United Nations to be non-permanent members of the Security Council, due regard being specially paid, in the first instance to the contribution of Members of the United Nations to the maintenance of international peace and security and to the other purposes of the Organization, and also to equitable geographical distribution.
    2. The non-permanent members of the Security Council shall be elected for a term of two years. In the first election of non-permanent members, however, three shall be chosen for a term of one year. A retiring member shall not be eligible for immediate re-election.
    3. Each member of the Security Council shall have one representative.

2. Amended text of Article 27 which came into force on 31 August 1965. The text of Article 27 before it was amended read as follows:

    1. Each member of the Security Council shall have one vote.
    2. Decisions of the Security Council on procedural matters shall be made by an affirmative vote of seven members.
    3. Decisions of the Security Council on all other matters shall be made by an affirmative vote of seven members including the concurring votes of the permanent members; provided that, in decisions under Chapter VI, and under paragraph 3 of Article 52, a party to a dispute shall abstain from voting.

3. Amended text of Article 61, which came into force on 24 September 1973. The text of Article 61 as previously amended on 31 August 1965 read as follows:

    1. The Economic and Social Council shall consist of twenty-seven Members of the United Nations elected by the General Assembly.
    2. Subject to the provisions of paragraph 3, nine members of the Economic and Social Council shall be elected each year for a term of three years. A retiring member shall be eligible for immediate re-election.

3. At the first election after the increase in the membership of the Economic and Social Council from eighteen to twenty-seven members, in addition to the members elected in place of the six members whose term of office expires at the end of that year, nine additional members shall be elected. Of these nine additional members, the term of office of three members so elected shall expire at the end of one year, and of three other members at the end of two years, in accordance with arrangements made by the General Assembly.

4. Each member of the Economic and Social Council shall have one representative.

4. Amended text of Article 109 which came into force on12 June 1968. The text of Article 109 before it was amended read as follows:

1. A General Conference of the Members of the United Nations for the purpose of reviewing the present Charter may be held at a date and place to be fixed by a two-thirds vote of the members of the General Assembly and by a vote of any seven members of the Security Council. Each Member of the United Nations shall have one vote in the conference.

2. Any alteration of the present Charter recommended by a two-thirds vote of the conference shall take effect when ratified in accordance with their respective constitutional processes by two-thirds of the Members of the United Nations including all the permanent members of the Security Council.

3. If such a conference has not been held before the tenth annual session of the General Assembly following the coming into force of the present Charter, the proposal to call such a conference shall be placed on the agenda of that session of the General Assembly, and the conference shall be held if so decided by a majority vote of the members of the General Assembly and by a vote of any seven members of the Security Council.

Appendix 2
SC Resolution 678
(29 November 1990) on Iraq

The Security Council,

Recalling and reaffirming its resolutions 660 (1990) of 2 August 1990, 661 (1990) of 6 August 1990, 662 (1990) of 9 August 1990, 664 (1990) of 18 August 1990, 665 (1990) of 25 August 1990, 666 (1990) of 13 September 1990, 667 (1990) of 16 September 1990, 669 (1990) of 24 September 1990, 670 (1990) of 25 September 1990, 674 (1990) of 29 October 1990 and 677 (1990) of 28 November 1990,

Noting that, despite all efforts by the United Nations, Iraq refuses to comply with its obligation to implement resolution 660 (1990) and the above-mentioned subsequent resolutions, in flagrant contempt of the Security Council,

Mindful of its duties and responsibilities under the Charter of the United Nations for the maintenance and preservation of international peace and security,

Determined to secure full compliance with its decisions,

Acting under Chapter VII of the Charter,

1. Demands that Iraq comply fully with resolution 660 (1990) and all subsequent relevant resolutions, and decides, while maintaining all its decisions, to allow Iraq one final opportunity, as a pause of goodwill, to do so;

2. Authorizes Member States co-operating with the Government of Kuwait, unless Iraq on or before 15 January 1991 fully implements, as set forth in paragraph 1 above, the foregoing resolutions, to use all necessary means to uphold and implement resolution 660 (1990) and all subsequent relevant resolutions and to restore international peace and security in the area;

3. Requests all States to provide appropriate support for the actions undertaken in pursuance of paragraph 2 of the present resolution;

4. Requests the States concerned to keep the Security Council regularly informed on the progress of actions undertaken pursuant to paragraphs 2 and 3 of the present resolution;

5. Decides to remain seized of the matter.

Adopted by 12 votes to two (Cuba and Yemen), with one abstention (China)

Appendix 3
SC Resolution 748
(31 March 1992) on Libya

The Security Council,

Reaffirming its resolution 731 (1992) of 21 January 1992,

Noting the reports of the Secretary-General,[1][2]

Deeply concerned that the Libyan Government has still not provided a full and effective response to the requests in its resolution 731 (1992) of 21 January 1992,

Convinced that the suppression of acts of international terrorism, including those in which States are directly or indirectly involved, is essential for the maintenance of international peace and security,

Recalling that, in the statement issued on 31 January 1992 on the occasion of the meeting of the Security Council at the level of heads of State and Government,[3] the members of the Council expressed their deep concern over acts of international terrorism, and emphasized the need for the international community to deal effectively with all such acts,

Reaffirming that, in accordance with the principle in Article 2, paragraph 4, of the Charter of the United Nations, every State has the duty to refrain from organizing, instigating, assisting or participating in terrorist acts in another State or acquiescing in organized activities within its territory directed towards the commission of such acts, when such acts involve a threat or use of force,

Determining, in this context, that the failure by the Libyan Government to demonstrate by concrete actions its renunciation of terrorism and in particular its continued failure to respond fully and effectively to the requests in resolution 731 (1992) constitute a threat to international peace and security,

Determined to eliminate international terrorism,

Recalling the right of States, under Article 50 of the Charter, to consult the Security Council where they find themselves confronted with special economic problems arising from the carrying out of preventive or enforcement measures,

Acting under Chapter VII of the Charter,

1.   Decides that the Libyan Government must now comply without any further delay with paragraph 3 of resolution 731 (1992) regarding the requests contained in documents S/23306, S/23308 and S/23309;

---

[1] S/23574.
[2] S/23672.
[3] S/23500.

2.   Decides also that the Libyan Government must commit itself definitively to cease all forms of terrorist action and all assistance to terrorist groups and that it must promptly, by concrete actions, demonstrate its renunciation of terrorism;

3.   Decides that, on 15 April 1992 all States shall adopt the measures set out below, which shall apply until the Security Council decides that the Libyan Government has complied with paragraphs 1 and 2 above;

4.   Decides also that all States shall:

(a)   Deny permission to any aircraft to take off from, land in or overfly their territory if it is destined to land in or has taken off from the territory of Libya, unless the particular flight has been approved on grounds of significant humanitarian need by the Committee established by paragraph 9 below;

(b)   Prohibit, by their nationals or from their territory, the supply of any aircraft or aircraft components to Libya, the provision of engineering and maintenance servicing of Libyan aircraft or aircraft components, the certification of airworthiness for Libyan aircraft, the payment of new claims against existing insurance contracts and the provision of new direct insurance for Libyan aircraft;

5.   Decides further that all States shall:

(a)   Prohibit any provision to Libya by their nationals or from their territory of arms and related material of all types, including the sale or transfer of weapons and ammunition, military vehicles and equipment, paramilitary police equipment and spare parts for the aforementioned, as well as the provision of any types of equipment, supplies and grants of licensing arrangements, for the manufacture or maintenance of the aforementioned;

(b)   Prohibit any provision to Libya by their nationals or from their territory of technical advice, assistance or training related to the provision, manufacture, maintenance, or use of the items in (a) above;

(c)   Withdraw any of their officials or agents present in Libya to advise the Libyan authorities on military matters;

6.   Decides that all States shall:

(a)   Significantly reduce the number and the level of the staff at Libyan diplomatic missions and consular posts and restrict or control the movement within their territory of all such staff who remain; in the case of Libyan missions to international organizations, the host State may, as it deems necessary, consult the organization concerned on the measures required to implement this subparagraph;

(b)   Prevent the operation of all Libyan Arab Airlines offices;

(c)   Take all appropriate steps to deny entry or to expel Libyan nationals who have been denied entry to or expelled from other States because of their involvement in terrorist activities;

7.   Calls upon all States, including States not members of the United Nations, and all International organizations, to act strictly in accordance with the provisions

of the present resolution, notwithstanding the existence of any rights or obligations conferred or imposed by any international agreement or any contract entered into or any licence or permit granted prior to 15 April 1992;

8. Requests all States to report to the Secretary-General by 15 May 1992 on the measures they have instituted for meeting the obligations set out in paragraphs 3 to 7 above;

9. Decides to establish, in accordance with rule 28 of its provisional rules of procedure, a Committee of the Security Council consisting of all the members of the Council, to undertake the following tasks and to report on its work to the Council with its observations and recommendations:

(a) To examine the reports submitted pursuant to paragraph 8 above;
(b) To seek from all States further information regarding the action taken by them concerning the effective implementation of the measures imposed by paragraphs 3 to 7 above;
(c) To consider any information brought to its attention by States concerning violations of the measures imposed by paragraphs 3 to 7 above and, in that context, to make recommendations to the Council on ways to increase their effectiveness;
(d) To recommend appropriate measures in response to violations of the measures imposed by paragraphs 3 to 7 above and provide information on a regular basis to the Secretary-General for general distribution to Member States;
(e) To consider and to decide upon expeditiously any application by States for the approval of flights on grounds of significant humanitarian need in accordance with paragraph 4 above;
(f) To give special attention to any communications in accordance with Article 50 of the Charter from any neighbouring or other State with special economic problems that might arise from the carrying out of the measures imposed by paragraphs 3 to 7 above;

10. Calls upon all States to cooperate fully with the Committee in the fulfilment of its task, including supplying such information as may be sought by the Committee in pursuance of the present resolution;

11. Requests the Secretary-General to provide all necessary assistance to the Committee and to make the necessary arrangements in the Secretariat for this purpose;

12. Invites the Secretary-General to continue his role as set out in paragraph 4 of resolution 731 (1992);

13. Decides that the Security Council shall, every 120 days or sooner should the situation so require, review the measures imposed by paragraphs 3 to 7 above in the light of the compliance by the Libyan Government with paragraphs 1 and 2 above taking into account, as appropriate, any reports provided by the Secretary-General on his role as set out in paragraph 4 of resolution 731 (1992);

14. Decides to remain seized of the matter.

Appendix 4
Convention for the Suppression of Unlawful Acts against the Safety of Civil Aviation (Montreal, 23 September 1971)

The States parties to this Convention

Considering that unlawful acts against the safety of civil aviation jeopardize the safety of persons and property, seriously affect the operation of air services, and undermine the confidence of the peoples of the world in the safety of civil aviation;

Considering that the occurrence of such acts is a matter of grave concern;

Considering that, for the purpose of deterring such acts, there is an urgent need to provide appropriate measures for punishment of offenders;

Have agreed as follows:

Article 1

1. Any person commits an offence if he unlawfully and intentionally;

    (a) performs an act of violence against a person on board an aircraft in flight if that act is likely to endanger the safety of that aircraft; or
    (b) destroys an aircraft in service or causes damage to such an aircraft which renders it incapable of flight or which is likely to endanger its safety in flight; or
    (c) places or causes to be placed on an aircraft in service, by any means whatsoever, a device or substance which is likely to destroy that aircraft, or to cause damage to it which renders it incapable of flight, or to cause damage to it which is likely to endanger its safety in flight; or
    (d) destroys or damages air navigation facilities or interferes with their operation, if any such act is likely to endanger the safety of aircraft in flight; or
    (e) communicates information which he knows to be false, thereby endangering the safety of an aircraft in flight.

2. Any person also commits an offence if he:

(a) attempts to commit any of the offences mentioned in paragraph 1 of this Article; or

(b) is an accomplice of a person who commits or attempts to commit any such offence.

Article 2

For the purposes of this Convention:

(a) an aircraft is considered to be in flight at any time from the moment when all its external doors are closed following embarkation until the moment when any such door is opened for disembarkation; in the case of a forced landing, the flight shall be deemed to continue until the competent authorities take over the responsibility for the aircraft and for persons and property on board;

(b) an aircraft is considered to be in service from the beginning of the preflight preparation of the aircraft by ground personnel or by the crew for a specific flight until twenty-four hours after any landing; the period of service shall, in any event, extend for the entire period during which the aircraft is in flight as defined in paragraph (a) of this Article.

Article 3

Each Contracting State undertakes to make the offences mentioned in Article 1 punishable by severe penalties.

Article 4

1. This Convention shall not apply to aircraft used in military, customs or police services.

2. In the cases contemplated in subparagraphs (a), (b), (c) and (e) of paragraph 1 of Article 1, this Convention shall apply, irrespective of whether the aircraft is engaged in an international or domestic flight, only if:

(a) the place of take-off or landing, actual or intended, of the aircraft is situated outside the territory of the State of registration of that aircraft; or

(b) the offence is committed in the territory of a State other than the State of registration of the aircraft.

3. Notwithstanding paragraph 2 of this Article, in the cases contemplated in subparagraphs (a), (b), (c) and (e) of paragraph 1 of Article 1, this Convention shall also apply if the offender or the alleged offender is found in the territory of a State other than the State of registration of the aircraft.

4. With respect to the States mentioned in Article 9 and in the cases mentioned in subparagraphs (a), (b), (c) and (e) of paragraph 1 of Article 1, this Convention shall not apply if the places referred to in subparagraph (a) of paragraph 2 of this Article are situated within the territory of the same State where

that State is one of those referred to in Article 9, unless the offence is committed or the offender or alleged offender is found in the territory of a State other than that State.

5.   In the cases contemplated in subparagraph (d) of paragraph 1 of Article 1, this Convention shall apply only if the air navigation facilities are used in international air navigation.

6.   The provisions of paragraphs 2, 3, 4 and 5 of this Article shall also apply in the cases contemplated in paragraph 2 of Article 1.

Article 5

1.   Each Contracting State shall take such measures as may be necessary to establish its jurisdiction over the offences in the following cases:

    (a)   when the offence is committed in the territory of that State;

    (b)   when the offence is committed against or on board an aircraft registered in that State;

    (c)   when the aircraft on board which the offence is committed lands in its territory with the alleged offender still on board;

    (d)   when the offence is committed against or on board an aircraft leased without crew to a lessee who has his principal place of business or if the lessee has no such place of business, his permanent residence, in that State.

2.   Each Contracting State shall likewise take such measures as may be necessary to establish its jurisdiction over the offences mentioned in Article 1, paragraph 1 (a), (b) and (c), and in Article 1, paragraph 2, in so far as that paragraph relates to those offences, in the case where the alleged offender is present in its territory and it does not extradite him pursuant to Article 8 to any of the States mentioned in paragraph 1 of this Article.

3.   This Convention does not exclude any criminal jurisdiction exercised in accordance with national law.

Article 6

1.   Upon being satisfied that the circumstances so warrant, any Contracting State in the territory of which the offender or the alleged offender is present, shall take him into custody or take other measures to ensure his presence. The custody and other measures shall be as provided in the law of that State but may only be continued for such time as is necessary to enable any criminal or extradition proceedings to be instituted.

2.   Such State shall immediately make a preliminary enquiry into the facts.

3.   Any person in custody pursuant to paragraph 1 of this Article shall be assisted in communicating immediately with the nearest appropriate representative of the State of which he is a national.

4. When a State, pursuant to this Article, has taken a person into custody, it shall immediately notify the States mentioned in Article 5, paragraph 1, the State of nationality of the detained person and, if it considers it advisable, any other interested States of the fact that such person is in custody and of the circumstances which warrant his detention. The State which makes the preliminary enquiry contemplated in paragraph 2 of this Article shall promptly report its findings to the said States and shall indicate whether it intends to exercise jurisdiction.

Article 7

The Contracting State in the territory of which the alleged offender is found shall, if it does not extradite him, be obliged, without exception whatsoever and whether or not the offence was committed in its territory, to submit the case to its competent authorities for the purpose of prosecution. Those authorities shall take their decision in the same manner as in the case of any ordinary offence of a serious nature under the law of that State.

Article 8

1. The offences shall be deemed to be included as extraditable offences in any extradition treaty existing between Contracting States. Contracting States undertake to include the offences as extraditable offences in every extradition treaty to be concluded between them.

2. If a Contracting State which makes extradition conditional on the existence of a treaty receives a request for extradition from another Contracting State with which it has no extradition treaty, it may at its option consider this Convention as the legal basis for extradition in respect of the offences. Extradition shall be subject to the other conditions provided by the law of the requested State.

3. Contracting States which do not make extradition conditional on the existence of a treaty shall recognize the offences as extraditable offences between themselves subject to the conditions provided by the law of the requested State.

4. Each of the offences shall be treated, for the purpose of extradition between Contracting States, as if it had been committed not only in the place in which it occurred but also in the territories of the States required to establish their jurisdiction in accordance with Article 5, paragraph 1 (b), (c) and (d).

Article 9

The Contracting States which establish joint air transport operating organizations or international operating agencies, which operate aircraft which are subject to joint or international registration shall, by appropriate means, designate for each aircraft the State among them which shall exercise the jurisdiction and have the attributes of the State of registration for the purpose of this Convention and shall give notice thereof to the International Civil Aviation Organization which shall communicate the notice to all State Parties to this Convention.

Article 10

1.   Contracting States shall, in accordance with international and national law, endeavour to take all practicable measures for the purpose of preventing the offences mentioned in Article 1.

2.   When, due to the commission of one of the offences mentioned in Article 1, a flight has been delayed or interrupted, any Contracting State in whose territory the aircraft or passengers or crew are present shall facilitate the continuation of the journey of the passengers and crew as soon as practicable, and shall without delay return the aircraft and its cargo to the persons lawfully entitled to possession.

Article 11

1.   Contracting States shall afford one another the greatest measure of assistance in connection with criminal proceedings brought in respect of the offences. The law of the State requested shall apply in all cases.

2.   The provisions of paragraph 1 of this Article shall not affect obligations under any other treaty, bilateral or multilateral, which govern or will govern, in whole or in part, mutual assistance in criminal matters.

Article 12

Any Contracting State having reason to believe that one of the offences mentioned in Article 1 will be committed shall, in accordance with its national law, furnish any relevant information in its possession to those States which it believes would be the States mentioned in Article 5, paragraph 1.

Article 13

Each Contracting State shall in accordance with its national law report to the Council of the International Civil Aviation Organization as promptly as possible any relevant information in its possession concerning:

(a)   the circumstances of the offence;
(b)   the action taken pursuant to Article 10, paragraph 2;
(c)   the measures taken in relation to the offender or the alleged offender and, in particular, the results of any extradition proceedings or other legal proceedings.

Article 14

1.   Any dispute between two or more Contracting States concerning the interpretation or application of this Convention which cannot be settled through negotiation, shall, at the request of one of them, be submitted to arbitration. If within six months from the date of the request for arbitration the Parties are unable to agree on the organization of the arbitration, any one of those Parties may refer the

dispute to the International Court of Justice by request in conformity with the Statute of the Court.

2.   Each State may at the time of signature or ratification of this Convention or accession thereto, declare that it does not consider itself bound by the preceding paragraph. The other Contracting States shall not be bound by the preceding paragraph with respect to any Contracting State having made such a reservation.

3.   Any Contracting State having made a reservation in accordance with the preceding paragraph may at any time withdraw this reservation by notification to the Depositary Governments.

Article 15

1.   This Convention shall be open for signature at Montreal on 23 September 1971, by States participating in the International Conference on Air Law held at Montreal from 8 to 23 September 1971 (hereinafter referred to as the Montreal Conference). After 10 October 1971, the Convention shall be open to all States for signature in Moscow, London and Washington. Any State which does not sign this Convention before its entry into force in accordance with paragraph 3 of this Article may accede to it at any time.

2.   This Convention shall be subject to ratification by the signatory States. Instruments of ratification and instruments of accession shall be deposited with the Governments of the Union of Soviet Socialist Republics, the United Kingdom of Great Britain and Northern Ireland, and the United States of America, which are hereby designated the Depositary Governments.

3.   This Convention shall enter into force thirty days following the date of the deposit of instruments of ratification by ten States signatory to this Convention which participated in the Montreal Conference.

4.   For other States, this Convention shall enter into force on the date of entry into force of this Convention in accordance with paragraph 3 of this Article, or thirty days following the date of deposit of their instruments of ratification or accession, whichever is later.

5.   The Depositary Governments shall promptly inform all signatory and acceding States of the date of each signature, the date of deposit of each instrument of ratification or accession, the date of entry into force of this Convention, and other notices.

6.   As soon as this Convention comes into force, it shall be registered by the Depositary Governments pursuant to Article 102 of the Charter of the United Nations[1] and pursuant to Article 83 of the Convention on International Civil Aviation (Chicago, 1944).[2]

---

[1] Treaty Series No. 67 (1946), Cmd. 7015.
[2] Treaty Series No. 8 (1953), Cmd. 8742.

Appendices

Article 16

1. Any Contracting State may denounce this Convention by written notification to the Depositary Governments.

2. Denunciation shall take effect six months following the date on which notification is received by the Depositary Governments.

IN WITNESS WHEREOF the undersigned Plenipotentiaries, being duly authorized thereto by their Governments, have signed this Convention.

DONE at Montreal, this twenty-third day of September, one thousand nine hundred and seventy-one, in three originals, each being drawn up in four authentic texts in the English, French, Russian and Spanish languages.

Appendix 5
SC Resolution 883
(11 November 1993) on Libya

The Security Council,

Reaffirming its resolutions 731 (1992) of 21 January 1992 and 748 (1992) of 31 March 1992,

Deeply concerned that after more than twenty months the Libyan Government has not fully complied with these resolutions,

Determined to eliminate international terrorism,

Convinced that those responsible for acts of international terrorism must be brought to justice,

Convinced also that the suppression of acts of international terrorism, including those in which States are directly or indirectly involved, is essential for the maintenance of international peace and security,

Determining, in this context, that the continued failure by the Libyan Government to demonstrate by concrete actions its renunciation of terrorism, and in particular its continued failure to respond fully and effectively to the requests and decisions in resolutions 731 (1992) and 748 (1992), constitute a threat to international peace and security,

Taking note of the letters to the Secretary-General dated 29 September and 1 October 1993 from the Secretary of the General People's Committee for Foreign Liaison and International Cooperation of Libya (S/26523) and his speech in the General Debate at the forty-eighth session of the General Assembly (A/48/PV.20) in which Libya stated its intention to encourage those charged with the bombing of Pan Am 103 to appear for trial in Scotland and its willingness to cooperate with the competent French authorities in the case of the bombing of UTA 772,

Expressing its gratitude to the Secretary-General for the efforts he has made pursuant to paragraph 4 of resolution 731 (1992),

Recalling the right of States, under Article 50 of the Charter, to consult the Security Council where they find themselves confronted with special economic problems arising from the carrying out of preventive or enforcement measures,

Acting under Chapter VII of the Charter,

1.   Demands once again that the Libyan Government comply without any further delay with resolutions 731 (1992) and 748 (1992);

2.   Decides, in order to secure compliance by the Libyan Government with the decisions of the Council, to take the following measures, which shall come into

force at 00.01 EST on 1 December 1993 unless the Secretary-General has reported to the Council in the terms set out in paragraph 16 below;

3.   Decides that all States in which there are funds or other financial resources (including funds derived or generated from property) owned or controlled, directly or indirectly, by:

(a)   the Government or public authorities of Libya, or
(b)   any Libyan undertaking,

shall freeze such funds and financial resources and ensure that neither they nor any other funds and financial resources are made available, by their nationals or by any persons within their territory, directly or indirectly, to or for the benefit of the Government or public authorities of Libya or any Libyan undertaking, which for the purposes of this paragraph, means any commercial, industrial or public utility undertaking which is owned or controlled, directly or indirectly, by

(i)   the Government or public authorities of Libya,
(ii)   any entity, wherever located or organized, owned or controlled by (i), or
(iii) any person identified by States as acting on behalf of (i) or (ii) for the purposes of this resolution;

4.   Further decides that the measures imposed by paragraph 3 above do not apply to funds or other financial resources derived from the sale or supply of any petroleum or petroleum products, including natural gas and natural gas products, or agricultural products or commodities, originating in Libya and exported therefrom after the time specified in paragraph 2 above, provided that any such funds are paid into separate bank accounts exclusively for these funds;

5.   Decides that all States shall prohibit any provision to Libya by their nationals or from their territory of the items listed in the annex to this resolution, as well as the provision of any types of equipment, supplies and grants of licensing arrangements for the manufacture or maintenance of such items;

6.   Further decides that, in order to make fully effective the provisions of resolution 748 (1992), all States shall:

(a)   require the immediate and complete closure of all Libyan Arab Airlines offices within their territories;
(b)   prohibit any commercial transactions with Libyan Arab Airlines by their nationals or from their territory, including the honouring or endorsement of any tickets or other documents issued by that airline;
(c)   prohibit, by their nationals or from their territory, the entering into or renewal of arrangements for:

(i)   the making available, for operation within Libya, of any aircraft or aircraft components, or
(ii)   the provision of engineering or maintenance servicing of any aircraft or aircraft components within Libya;

(d) prohibit, by their nationals or from their territory, the supply of any materials destined for the construction, improvement or maintenance of Libyan civilian or military airfields and associated facilities and equipment, or of any engineering or other services or components destined for the maintenance of any Libyan civil or military airfields or associated facilities and equipment, except emergency equipment and equipment and services directly related to civilian air traffic control;

(e) prohibit, by their nationals or from their territory, any provision of advice, assistance, or training to Libyan pilots, flight engineers, or aircraft and ground maintenance personnel associated with the operation of aircraft and airfields within Libya;

(f) prohibit, by their nationals or from their territory, any renewal of any direct insurance for Libyan aircraft;

7.   Confirms that the decision taken in resolution 748 (1992) that all States shall significantly reduce the level of the staff at Libyan diplomatic missions and consular posts includes all missions and posts established since that decision or after the coming into force of this resolution;

8.   Decides that all States, and the Government of Libya, shall take the necessary measures to ensure that no claim shall lie at the instance of the Government or public authorities of Libya, or of any Libyan national, or of any Libyan undertaking as defined in paragraph 3 of this resolution, or of any person claiming through or for the benefit of any such person or undertaking, in connection with any contract or other transaction or commercial operation where its performance was affected by reason of the measures imposed by or pursuant to this resolution or related resolutions;

9.   Instructs the Committee established by resolution 748 (1992) to draw up expeditiously guidelines for the implementation of paragraphs 3 to 7 of this resolution, and to amend and supplement, as appropriate, the guidelines for the implementation of resolution 748 (1992), especially its paragraph 5 (a);

10. Entrusts the Committee established by resolution 748 (1992) with the task of examining possible requests for assistance under the provisions of Article 50 of the Charter of the United Nations and making recommendations to the President of the Security Council for appropriate action;

11. Affirms that nothing in this resolution affects Libya's duty scrupulously to adhere to all of its obligations concerning servicing and repayment of its foreign debt;

12. Calls upon all States, including States not Members of the United Nations, and all international organizations, to act strictly in accordance with the provisions of the present resolution, notwithstanding the existence of any rights or obligations conferred or imposed by any international agreement or any contract entered into or any licence or permit granted prior to the effective time of this resolution;

13. Requests all States to report to the Secretary-General by 15 January 1994 on the measures they have instituted for meeting the obligations set out in paragraphs 3 to 7 above;

14.   Invites the Secretary-General to continue his role as set out in paragraph 4 of resolution 731 (1992);

15.   Calls again upon all Member States individually and collectively to encourage the Libyan Government to respond fully and effectively to the requests and decisions in resolutions 731 (1992) and 748 (1992);

16.   Expresses its readiness to review the measures set forth above and in resolution 748 (1992) with a view to suspending them immediately if the Secretary-General reports to the Council that the Libyan Government has ensured the appearance of those charged with the bombing of Pan Am 103 for trial before the appropriate United Kingdom or United States court and has satisfied the French judicial authorities with respect to the bombing of UTA 772, and with a view to lifting them immediately when Libya complies fully with the requests and decisions in resolutions 731 (1992) and 748 (1992); and requests the Secretary-General, within 90 days of such suspension, to report to the Council on Libya's compliance with the remaining provisions of its resolutions 731 (1992) and 748 (1992) and, in the case of non-compliance, expresses its resolve to terminate immediately the suspension of these measures;

17.   Decides to remain seized of the matter.

Annex

The following are the items referred to in paragraph 5 of this resolution:

I.   Pumps of medium or large capacity whose capacity is equal to or larger than 350 cubic metres per hour and drivers (gas turbines and electric motors) designed for use in the transportation of crude oil and natural gas

II.   Equipment designed for use in crude oil export terminals:

- Loading buoys or single point moorings (spm)
- Flexible hoses for connection between underwater manifolds (plem) and single point mooring and floating loading hoses of large sizes (from 12" to 16")
- Anchor chains

III.   Equipment not specially designed for use in crude oil export terminals but which because of their large capacity can be used for this purpose:

- Loading pumps of large capacity (4,000 m^3/h) and small head (10 bars)
- Boosting pumps within the same range of flow rates
- Inline pipe line inspection tools and cleaning devices (i.e. pigging tools) (16" and above)
- Metering equipment of large capacity (1,000 m^3/h and above)

IV. Refinery equipment:

- Boilers meeting American Society of Mechanical Engineers 1 standards
- Furnaces meeting American Society of Mechanical Engineers 8 standards
- Fractionation columns meeting American Society of Mechanical Engineers 8 standards
- Pumps meeting American Petroleum Institute 610 standards
- Catalytic reactors meeting American Society of Mechanical Engineers 8 standards
- Prepared catalysts, including the following:

  Catalysts containing platinum
  Catalysts containing molybdenum

V. Spare parts destined for the items in I to IV above.

Appendix 6
SC Resolution 799
(18 December 1992) on Israel

The Security Council,

Recalling the obligations of Member States under the United Nations Charter,

Reaffirming its resolutions 607 (1988), 608 (1988), 636 (1989), 641 (1989), 681 (1990), 694 (1991) and 726 (1992),

Having learned with deep concern that Israel, the occupying Power, in contravention of its obligations under the Fourth Geneva Convention of 1949, deported, on 17 December 1992, hundreds of Palestinian civilians from the territories occupied by Israel since 1967, including Jerusalem,

1.   Strongly condemns the action taken by Israel, the occupying Power, to deport hundreds of Palestinian civilians, and expresses its firm opposition to any such deportation by Israel;

2.   Reaffirms the applicability of the Fourth Geneva Convention of 12 August 1949 to all the Palestinian territories occupied by Israel since 1967, including Jerusalem and affirms that deportation of civilians constitutes a contravention of its obligations under the Convention;

3.   Reaffirms also the independence, sovereignty and territorial integrity of Lebanon;

4.   Demands that Israel, the occupying Power, ensure the safe and immediate return to the occupied territories of all those deported;

5.   Requests the Secretary-General to dispatch a representative to the area to follow up with the Israeli Government with regard to this serious situation and to report to the Security Council;

6.   Decides to keep the matter actively under review.

Appendix 7
GA Resolutions 47/19
(24 November 1992), 48/16
(3 November 1993), and 49/24
(26 October 1994) on Cuba

GA Resolution 47/19

The General Assembly, intent on promoting strict adherence to the principles and aims recognised by the Charter of the United Nations, stressing among other principles, the sovereign equality of nations, non-intervention and non-interference in their internal affairs, the freedom of international trade and navigation, also recognised in other international legal documents;

Concerned for the enforcement and application by member states of laws and regulations whose extraterritoriality affects the sovereignty of other nations and the legitimate interests of entities or persons within their jurisdiction and freedom of trade and navigation;

Having full knowledge of the recent enforcement of similar measures aimed at strengthening and widening the economic, commercial and financial blockade against Cuba;

1. Calls on all member states to abstain from enforcing or applying laws and measures of the kind referred to in the preamble of the current resolution, in compliance with their obligation to adhere to the Charter and international law and the commitments legally entered into by subscribing to international legal procedures which, among others, recognise the freedom of trade and navigation;

2. Urges nations where these kinds of laws or measures exist to fulfil their legal duty by taking whatever measures are necessary to eliminate or annul their effect as quickly as possible;

3. Requests that the Secretary-General draw up a report back on compliance with the current resolution for consideration at the 48th session;

4. Decides to include this issue for discussion on the provisional agenda of its 48th session.

GA Resolution 48/16
Necessity of ending the economic, commercial and financial embargo imposed by the United States of America against Cuba

The General Assembly,

Determined to encourage strict compliance with the purposes and principles enshrined in the Charter of the United Nations,

Reaffirming, among other principles, the sovereign equality of States, non-intervention and non-interference in their internal affairs and freedom of trade and international navigation, which are also enshrined in many international legal instruments,

Taking note of the statement of the heads of State and Government at the third Ibero-American Summit, held at Salvador, Brazil, on 15 and 16 July 1993, concerning the need to eliminate the unilateral application of economic and trade measures by one State against another for political purposes,

Concerned about the continued promulgation and application by Member States of laws and regulations whose extraterritorial effects affect the sovereignty of other States and the legitimate interests of entities or persons under jurisdiction, as well as the freedom of trade and navigation,

Recalling its resolution 47/19 of 24 November 1992,

Having learned that, since the adoption of resolution 47/19, further measures of that nature aimed at strengthening and extending the economic, commercial and financial embargo against Cuba have been promulgated and applied, and concerned about the adverse effects of those measures on the Cuban population,

1. Takes note of the report of the Secretary-General on the implementation of resolution 47/19;

2. Reiterates its call to all States to refrain from promulgating and applying laws and measures of the kind referred to in the preamble to the present resolution in conformity with their obligations under the Charter of the United Nations and international law which, *inter alia*, reaffirm the freedom of trade and navigation;

3. Once again urges States that have and continue to apply such laws and measures to take the necessary steps to repeal or invalidate them as soon as possible in accordance with their legal regime;

4. Requests the Secretary-General, in consultation with the appropriate organs and agencies of the United Nations system, to prepare a report on the implementation of the present resolution in the light of the purposes and principles of the Charter and international law, and to submit it to the General Assembly at its forty-ninth session;

5. Decides to include in the provisional agenda of its forty-ninth session the item entitled 'Necessity of ending the economic, commercial and financial embargo imposed by the United States of America against Cuba'.

GA Resolution 49/24
Necessity of ending the economic, commercial and financial embargo imposed by the United States of America against Cuba

Cuba: draft resolution

The General Assembly,

Determined to encourage strict compliance with the purposes and principles enshrined in the Charter of the United Nations,

Reaffirming, among other principles, the sovereign equality of States, non-intervention and non-interference in their internal affairs and freedom of international trade and navigation, which are also enshrined in many international legal instruments,

Recalling the statements of the heads of State and Government at the third and fourth Ibero-American Summits, held respectively at Salvador, Brazil, in July 1993 and Cartagena, Colombia, in June 1994, concerning the need to eliminate the unilateral application of economic and trade measures by one State against another which affect the free flow of international trade,

Taking note of Decision 356 adopted on 3 June 1994 by the Twentieth Council of the Latin American Economic System, held at the ministerial level at Mexico City, which called for the lifting of the economic, commercial and financial embargo against Cuba,

Concerned about the continued promulgation and application by Member States of laws and regulations whose extraterritorial effects affect the sovereignty of other States and the legitimate interests of entities or persons under their jurisdiction, as well as the freedom of trade and navigation,

Recalling its resolution 47/19 of 24 November 1992 and 48/16 of 3 November 1993,

Concerned that, since the adoption of its resolutions 47/19 and 48/16, further measures of that nature aimed at strengthening and extending the economic, commercial and financial embargo against Cuba continue to be promulgated and applied, and *concerned also* about the adverse effects of such measures on the Cuban people and on Cuban nationals living in other countries,

1.   Takes note of the report of the Secretary-General on the implementation of resolution 48/16;

2.   Reiterates its call to all States to refrain from promulgating and applying laws and measures of the kind referred to in the preamble to the present resolution in conformity with their obligations under the Charter of the United Nations and international law which, *inter alia*, reaffirm the freedom of trade and navigation;

3.   Once again urges States that have and continue to apply such laws and measures to take the necessary steps to repeal or invalidate them as soon as possible in accordance with their legal regime;

4. Requests the Secretary-General, in consultation with the appropriate organs and agencies of the United Nations system, to prepare a report on the implementation of the present resolution in the light of the purposes and principles of the Charter and international law, and to submit it to the General Assembly at its fiftieth session;

5. Decides to include this item in the provisional agenda of its fiftieth session.

Appendix 8
SC Resolution 940
(31 July 1994) on Haiti

Recognizing the 'unique character' of the situation in Haiti, the Security Council this afternoon authorized the formation of a multinational force under unified command and control 'to use all necessary means' to facilitate the departure from Haiti of the military leadership and the prompt return of the legitimately elected President of Haiti, Jean-Bertrand Aristide, as well as the restoration of the legitimate Government authorities, consistent with the Governors Island Agreement.

Acting under Chapter VII of the Charter, the Council adopted, by a vote of 12 in favour to none against, with 2 abstentions (Brazil and China), resolution 940 (1994), which also set out a series of other provisions.

By the resolution's terms, the multinational force will terminate its mission and an expanded, strengthened United Nations Mission in Haiti (UNMIH) will assume the full range of its functions, when a secure and stable environment has been established and UNMIH has the capability and structure to assume those functions. That determination will be made by the Council, taking into consideration recommendations from Member States participating in the multinational force, based on the force commander's assessment, and from the Secretary-General. The cost of implementing the temporary operation of the force will be borne by the participating Member States.

Also by that resolution, the Council approved the establishment of an advance team of UNMIH to determine the appropriate means of coordination with and to monitor the operations of the multinational force. The advance team will also assess requirements and prepare for the deployment of UNMIH when the force's mission is completed.

The Council extended the mandate of UNMIH for a period of six months and increased its troop level to 6,000. It established the objective of completing UNMIH's mission not later than February 1996. Under its revised mandate, UNMIH will assist the democratic government of Haiti in sustaining the secure and stable environment established during the multinational phase and the protection of international personnel and key installations; and the professionalization of the Haitian armed forces and the creation of a separate police force.

Also by the text, the Council requested that UNMIH assist the legitimate constitutional authorities of Haiti in the organization of free and fair legislative elections to be called by the authorities. It further requested the Member States participating in the multinational force, to report to the Council at regular intervals, the first such report to be made within seven days after the deployment of the force. The Secretary-General was asked to report on the activities of the advance teams within 30 days of the deployment of the multinational force, and on the implementation of the resolution at 60-day intervals.

Speaking before the action on the resolution, the representative of China said he would abstain on the vote as he could not agree with the use of military means to solve the problems of Haiti, adding that trying to solve that country's problems by those means did not conform with the Charter. The representative of Brazil said the defence of democracy should always be consistent with principles governing relations between States and did not entail the recourse to force, under the terms contained in the draft. Those terms constituted a worrisome departure from the principles and customary practices adopted by the United Nations as regarded peace keeping, he added.

Speaking after the text's adoption, the representative of the United States said the resolution brought to a climax the Council's effort to restore democracy to the Haitian people, from whom it had been stolen 34 long months ago. The Council's message to the Haitian military was a simple one: 'You too have a choice. You can depart voluntarily and soon, or you can depart involuntarily and soon'.

Addressing the Council under rule 37 of its rules of procedure, the representatives of Mexico, Cuba, Uruguay and Venezuela said the activities proposed in the text were not provided for in the Charter as the crisis in Haiti was not a threat to international peace and security. They expressed their opposition to any military intervention in Haiti, whether multilateral or unilateral, and called for the use of the Charter's provisions on the peaceful settlement of disputes in the Haitian situation.

Also addressing the Council under rule 37, Fritz Longchamp, the Permanent Representative of Haiti to the United Nations, said 'commendable initiatives' had been taken to end the Haitian crisis by diplomatic means, but the military had resisted all appeals to leave power and a climate of terror prevailed in Haiti. Expressing the consent of President Jean-Bertrand Aristide to the draft resolution, he called on the international community to respect Haiti's sovereignty.

Statements were also made by the representatives of Nigeria, France, Argentina, United Kingdom, Spain, New Zealand, Djibouti, Russian Federation, Czech Republic, Oman and Pakistan. The representative of Canada also spoke under rule 37.

END OF SUMMARY

TEXT OF RESOLUTION·

The Security Council,

Reaffirming its resolutions 841 (1993) of 16 Jun 1993, 861 (1993) of 27 August 1993, 862 (1993) of 31 August 1993, 867 (1993) of 23 September 1993, 873 (1993) of 13 October 1993, 875 (1993) of 16 October 1993, 905 (1994) of 23 March 1994, 917 (1994) of 6 May 1994, and 933 (1994) of 30 June 1994,

Recalling the terms of the Governors Island Agreement (S/26063) and the related Pact of New York (S/26297),

Condemning the continuing disregard of those agreements by the illegal de facto regime, and the regime's refusal to cooperate with efforts by the United Nations and the Organization of American States (OAS) to bring about their implementation,

Gravely concerned by the significant further deterioration of the humanitarian situation in Haiti, in particular the continuing escalation by the illegal de facto regime of systematic violations of civil liberties, the desperate plight of Haitian refugees and the recent expulsion of the staff of the International Civilian Mission (MICIVIH), which was condemned in its Presidential statement of 12 July 1994 (S/PRST/1994/32),

Having considered the reports of the Secretary-General of 15 July 1994 (S/1994/828 and Add. 1) and 26 July 1994 (S/1994/871),

Taking note of the letter dated 29 July 1994 from the legitimately elected President of Haiti (S/1994/905, annex) and the letter dated 30 July 1994 from the Permanent Representative of Haiti to the United Nations (S/1994/910),

Reiterating its commitment for the international community to assist and support the economic, social and institutional development of Haiti,

Reaffirming that the goal of the international community remains the restoration of democracy in Haiti and the prompt return of the legitimately elected President, Jean-Bertrand Aristide, within the framework of the Governors Island Agreement,

Recalling that in resolution 873 (1993) the Council confirmed its readiness to consider the imposition of additional measures if the military authorities in Haiti continued to impede the activities of the United Nations Mission in Haiti (UNMIH) or failed to comply in full with its relevant resolutions and the provisions of the Governors Island Agreement,

Determining that the situation in Haiti continues to constitute a threat to peace and security in the region,

1.   Welcomes the report of the Secretary-General (S/1994/828) and takes note of his support for action under Chapter VII of the Charter of the United Nations in order to assist the legitimate Government of Haiti in the maintenance of public order;

2.   Recognizes the unique character of the present situation in Haiti and its deteriorating, complex and extraordinary nature, requiring an exceptional response;

3.   Determines that the illegal de facto regime in Haiti has failed to comply with the Governors Island Agreement and is in breach of its obligations under the relevant resolutions of the Security Council;

4.   Acting under Chapter VII of the United Nations Charter of the United Nations, authorizes Member States to form a multinational force under unified command and control and, in this framework, to use all necessary means to facilitate the departure from Haiti of the military leadership, consistent with the Governors Island Agreement, the prompt return of the legitimately elected President and the restoration of the legitimate authorities of the Government of Haiti, and to establish and maintain a secure and stable environment that will permit implementation of the Governors Island Agreement, on the understanding that the cost of implementing this temporary operation will be borne by the participating Member States;

5.   Approves the establishment, upon the adoption of this resolution, of an advance team of UNMIH of not more than sixty personnel, including a group of observers, to establish the appropriate means of coordination with the multi-national force, to carry out the monitoring of the operations of the multinational force and other functions described in paragraph 23 of the report of the Secretary-General of 15 July 1994 (S/1994/828), and to assess requirements and to prepare for the deployment of UNMIH upon completion of the mission of the multi-national force;

6.   Requests the Secretary-General to report on the activities of the team within thirty days of the date of deployment of the multinational force;

7.   Decides that the tasks of the advance team as defined in paragraph 5 above will expire on the date of termination of the mission of the multinational force;

8.   Decides that the multinational force will terminate its mission and UNMIH will assume the full range of its functions described in paragraph 9 below when a secure and stable environment has been established and UNMIH has adequate force capability and structure to assume the full range of its functions; the deter-mination will be made by the Security Council, taking into account recom-mendations from the Member States of the Multinational Force, which are based on the assessment of the commander of the multinational force, and from the Secretary-General;

9.   Decides to revise and extend the mandate of the United Nations Missions in Haiti (UNMIH) for a period of six months to assist the democratic Government of Haiti in fulfilling its responsibilities in connection with:

   (a)   sustaining the secure and stable environment established during the multinational phase and protecting international personnel and key installations; and
   (b)   the professionalization of the Haitian armed forces and creation of a separate police force;

10.   Requests also that UNMIH assist the legitimate constitutional authorities of Haiti in establishing an environment conducive to the organization of free and fair legislative elections to be called by those authorities and, when requested by them, monitored by the United Nations, in cooperation with the Organization of American States (OAS);

11.   Decides to increase the troop level of UNMIH to 6,000 and establishes the objective to completing UNMIH's mission, in cooperation with the constitutional Government of Haiti, not later than February 1996;

12.   Invites all States, in particular those in the region, to provide appropriate support for the actions undertaken by the United Nations and by Member States pursuant to this and other relevant Security Council resolutions;

13.   Requests the Member States acting in accordance with paragraph 4 above to report to the Council at regular intervals, the first such report to be made not later than seven days following the deployment of the multinational force;

14.   Requests the Secretary-General to report on the implementation of this resolution at sixty-day intervals starting from the date of deployment of the multinational force;

15.   Demands strict respect for the persons and premises of the United Nations, the Organization of American States, other international and humanitarian organizations and diplomatic missions in Haiti, and that no acts of intimidation or violence be directed against personnel engaged in humanitarian or peace-keeping work;

16.   Emphasizes the necessity that, inter alia:

    (a)   All appropriate steps be taken to ensure the security and safety of the operations and personnel engaged in such operations; and

    (b)   the security and safety arrangements undertaken extend to all persons engaged in the operation;

17.   Affirms that the Council will review the measures imposed pursuant to resolutions 841 (1993), 873 (1993) and 917 (1994), with a view to lifting them in their entirety, immediately following the return to Haiti of President Jean-Bertrand Aristide;

18.   Decides to remain actively seized of the matter.

Notes

NOTES TO THE INTRODUCTION

1. *State of the World's Refugees*, United Nations, New York, commissioned by Sadako Ogata, UN High Commissioner for Refugees, published 9 November 1993.

2. Annika Savill, 'Top UN official "to resign" ', *The Independent*, London, 24 November 1993; Hella Pick, 'UN aid chief driven out by "betrayal and inadequate support" ', *The Guardian*, London, 25 November 1993.

3. Two examples will suffice: recent UK law and order measures involving the imprisonment of children breach international law and violate the UN Convention on the Rights of the Child (Alan Travis, 'Child "jails" plan "breaks UN rules" ', *The Guardian*, London, 20 December 1993). Many states are ignoring the conservation treaty signed at the 1992 Rio Earth Summit (Nicolas Schoon, 'Rich nations accused of stifling wild life treaty', *The Independent*, London, 30 December 1993.

4. Barrie Hudson, British IFAD governor, has depicted the agency as 'facing a dark and uncertain future' (James Hansen, 'UN aid agency in shambles', *The Daily Telegraph*, London, 29 January 1994).

5. Conor Cruise O'Brien, 'When cowboy hats replace blue berets', *The Independent*, London, 16 July 1993.

6. *FAO/WFP Crop and Food Supply Assessment Mission to Iraq*, Food and Agriculture Organisation of the United Nations, World Food Programme, No. 237, July 1993.

7. Erlend Clouston, 'Doubt cast on key Lockerbie blast clue', *The Guardian*, London, 5 January 1994.

8. Patrick Cockburn, 'Haitians decide to give war a chance', *The Independent*, London, 16 February 1994; Patrick Cockburn, 'Sanctions drive brings Haiti to the edge of ruin', *The Independent*, London, 18 February 1994.

9. Michael Sheridan, 'Chaotic harmony or just chaos?', *The Independent*, London, 1 November 1993.

10. *Ibid.*

11. Jeffrey Sachs, 'The bank that foreclosed on Russia', *The Independent*, London, 26 January 1994.

12. Ruth Kelly, 'African debt deepening says Bank', *The Guardian*, London, 16 December 1993; Sue Branford, 'Plight of Indians at sharp end of World Bank loan', *The Guardian*, London, 28 September 1993; Paul Brown, 'World Bank projects "evicting millions" ', *The Guardian*, London, 5 November 1993.

13. Mark Tran, 'US slashes Chinese textile quotas as trade row simmers', *The Guardian*, London, 7 January 1994.

14.   David Smith, 'Clinton threatens to force up yen', *The Sunday Times*,
      London, 13 February 1994; Rupert Cornwell and Terry McCarthy, 'US pre-
      pares sanctions against Tokyo', *The Independent*, London, 14 February
      1994; Terry McCarthy, 'Japan buckles under threat of sanctions', *The
      Independent*, London, 16 February 1994.
15.   Kevin Rafferty, ' "Outlaw" US is breaking trade rules, says Japan', *The
      Guardian*, London, 1 June 1994.
16.   Kate Rankine, 'US "ready to use trade laws against Japan" ', *The Daily
      Telegraph*, London, 8 June 1994; Mark Tran, 'US hits Japan with
      sanctions', *The Guardian*, London, 1 August 1994; Kate Rankine, 'Dollar
      falls amid fears of trade war', *The Daily Telegraph*, London, 2 August 1994.
17.   In December 1990, a CIA official declared that the CIA had been 'involved
      in GATT and every trade negotiation. We take tasks from US negotiators to
      find out about the [other countries'] positions. We usually have someone
      who's right there, or within cable reach . . . We tell our negotiators "Here's
      what the other side left out or is holding back" ' (*The Independent*, London,
      14 November 1990; *The Guardian*, London, 29 December 1990; *The Daily
      Telegraph*, London, 24 January 1992).

NOTES TO CHAPTER 1

1.   Peter H. Lindsay and Donald A. Norman, *Human Information Processing*,
      Academic Press, New York, 1977, p. v.
2.   James Grier Miller, *Living Systems*, McGraw-Hill, New York, 1978,
      Chapter 12.
3.   A. Etzioni, *The Active Society*, Free Press, New York, 1968, pp. 564–565.
4.   Miller, *op. cit.*, pp. 907–910.
5.   Rebecca M. M. Wallace, *International Law*, Sweet & Maxwell, London,
      1992, p. 69.
6.   Immanuel Kant, *Perpetual Peace: A Philosophic Essay*, 1795, translated by
      E. Campbell Smith, Garland Library of War and Peace, London, 1972.
7.   M. Gravel, *The California Initiative*, New Forum, Carmel, CA, 1989;
      G. Clark and L. Sohn, *World Peace through World Law*, Harvard University
      Press, Cambridge, MA, 1958; H. Stassen, *Draft Charter for a Better United
      Nations Organisation*, Glenview Foundation, St Paul, MN, 1987; Frank
      Barnaby (ed.), *Building a More Democratic United Nations*, Proceedings
      of the First International Conference On A More Democratic UN
      (CAMDUN-1), Frank Cass, London, 1991.
8.   Leopold Kohr, *The Breakdown of Nations* (1957), E. P. Dutton, New York,
      1978.
9.   E. F. Schumacher, *Small is Beautiful*, Blond & Briggs, London, 1973.
10.   Jeffrey J. Segall, 'The world's power system', in N. Albery and Y. Peeters
      (eds), *How to Save the World: A Guide to the Politics of Scale*, Fourth
      World Educational and Research Association, London, 1982.
11.   Inis L. Claude, *Swords into Plowshares*, first published by Random House,
      New York, 1956; revised third edition, University of London Press, London,
      1964, p. 7.

12. Walter Lippmann, 'International control of atomic energy', in Dexter Masters and Katherine Way (eds), *One World or None*, McGraw-Hill, New York, 1946, p. 74.

13. For a full statement of the UN Universal Declaration of Human Rights see, for example, Ian Brownlie (ed.), *Basic Documents in International Law*, Clarendon Press, Oxford, 1975, Part 6, I.

14. *Ibid.*

15. Boutros Boutros-Ghali, *An Agenda for Peace*, United Nations, New York, 1992, pp. 1–2.

16. Special Alert, '*FAO/WFP Crop and Food Supply Assessment Mission to Iraq*', Food and Agriculture Organisation of the United Nations, World Food Programme, Rome, July 1993.

17. J. L. Brierly, *The Law of Nations*, sixth edition, Clarendon Press, Oxford, 1963, p. 48.

18. It has been argued (e.g. in Bertrand Russell, *Which Way to Peace?*, Michael Joseph, London, 1936, p. 63) that a principal weakness of the League of Nations was that it left state sovereignties intact with no means of compelling respect for the Covenant.

19. J. William Fulbright, *The Arrogance of Power*, Penguin, Harmondsworth, England, 1970, p. 17.

20. Mortimer Lipsky, *The Quest for Peace: The Story of the Nobel Awards*, Yoseloff, London, 1966, pp. 213–214.

21. Boutros-Ghali, *op. cit.*, p. 9.

22. Richard Gott, 'Mr Fixit seeks a new role', *The Guardian*, London, 27 December 1991.

23. *Ibid.*

24. Julie Flint, 'UN crisis over West's "tyranny" ', *The Observer*, London, 2 August 1992.

25. The current involvements were: the UN Truce Supervision Organisation (UNTSO) in Jerusalem; the UN Military Observer Group in India and Pakistan (UNMOGIP); the UN Disengagement Observer Force (UNDOF) on the Syrian Golan Heights; the UN peacekeeping force in Cyprus (UNFI-CYP); the UN Interim Force in Lebanon (UNIFIL); the UN Iraq–Kuwait Observation Mission (UNIKOM); the UN Angola Verification Mission (UNAVEM II); the UN Observer Mission (ONUSAL) in El Salvador; the Western Sahara Referendum Mission (MINURSO); the UN Protection Force (UNPROFOR) in former Yugoslavia; the UN Transitional Authority in Cambodia (UNTAC); and the UN Operation in Somalia (UNOSOM).

26. Richard Dowden, 'Making war to secure peace', *The Independent*, London, 24 November 1992; Adam Roberts, 'All the troubles of the world on its shoulders', *The Independent*, London, 21 December 1992.

27. Hella Pick, 'When relief adds misery', *The Guardian*, London, 15 July 1993.

28. Conor Cruise O'Brien, 'Two UNs at war with each other', *The Independent*, London, 13 August 1993.

29. Boutros Boutros-Ghali, 'UN Multilateralism: a cure for ugly new nationalisms', *International Herald Tribune*, New York, 21–22 August 1993.

30. *Ibid.*

31. Brian Urquhart, 'The United Nations and its discontents', *The New York Review of Books*, 15 March 1990.

32. Boutros-Ghali (1992), *op. cit.*, pp. 7–8.
33. *Ibid.*, pp. 9–10.
34. Boutros Boutros-Ghali, *Report on the Work of the Organization from the Forty-sixth to the Forty-seventh Session of the General Assembly*, United Nations, New York, September 1992.
35. *The Military Balance 1993–1994*, Brassey's (UK), London, published for the International Institute for Strategic Studies (IISS), 1993.

NOTES TO CHAPTER 2

1. James Barros, *Office Without Power, Secretary-General Sir Eric Drummond 1919–1933*, Clarendon Press, Oxford, England, 1979.
2. Churchill to Roosevelt (letter, 'Morning Thoughts, Note on Post-War Security'), Document 210, 2 February 1943; in Francis L. Loewenheim, Harold D. Langley and Manfred Jonas, (eds), *Roosevelt and Churchill, Their Secret Wartime Correspondence*, Barrie and Jenkins, London, 1975, p. 311.
3. Jim Bishop, *FDR's Last Year*, Hart-Davis, MacGibbon, London, 1975, pp. 42–43.
4. *Ibid.*, p. 43.
5. T. R. Fehrenbach, *This Kind of Peace*, Frewin, London, 1967, p. 25.
6. Bishop, *op. cit.*, p. 54.
7. *Postwar Foreign Policy Preparation 1939–1945*, Department of State publication, 3580, Government Printing Office, Washington, 1949.
8. Leonard Mosley, *Dulles*, Hodder and Stoughton, London, 1978, pp. 150–151.
9. Bishop, *op. cit.*, p. 131.
10. Mosley, *op. cit.*, pp. 153–154.
11. Fehrenbach, *op. cit.*, p. 20.
12. *Ibid.*, p. 21.
13. *Ibid.*, p. 68.
14. Ernst B, Hass, *The Web of Interdependence: The United States and International Organisations*, New Jersey, 1970, p. 3.
15. On 13 August 1940 Roosevelt agreed to give the British fifty destroyers in exchange for long-term bases on Newfoundland, Bermuda and five West Indian colonies: 'it was the British who made all the concessions . . . The number of ships they received was half that requested, the number of bases acquired by the US was twice the initial British offer' (Clive Ponting, *1940: Myth and Reality*, Sphere, London, 1990, p. 203).
16. James Reston, *New York Times*, 12 June 1945.
17. Cited by D. F. Fleming, *The Cold War and Its Origins, 1917–1960*, Doubleday, New York, 1961, p. 207.
18. Sallie Pisani, *The CIA and the Marshall Plan*, Edinburgh University Press, Edinburgh, Scotland, 1991.
20. Thomas Bodenheimer and Robert Gould, *Rollback: Right-wing Power in US Foreign Policy*, South-End Press, Boston, Mass., 1989.
20. Fehrenbach, *op. cit.*, p. 139.

21. Michael C. Sandusky, *America's Parallel*, Old Dominion Press, Alexandria, Virginia, 1983, p. 145.

22. E. Grant Meade, *American Military Government in Korea*, Oxford University Press, Oxford, England, 1951, pp. 59–62.

23. George M. McCure, *Korea Today*, Harvard University Press, Harvard, Mass., 1950, pp. 51–52, 201–207.

24. A. Wigfall Green, *Epic of Korea*, Public Affairs Press, Washington, 1950, p. 95.

25. Quoted in William Manchester, *American Caesar, Douglas MacArthur 1880–1964*, Hutchinson, London, 1978, p. 539.

26. John Gunther, *The Riddle of MacArthur: Japan, Korea and the Far East*, New York, 1951, p. 178.

28. Hodge to MacArthur, 24 September 1945, Record Group 9, 'Radiograms, 1945–1951', MacArthur Archives, Norfolk, Virginia.

28. Sandusky, *op. cit.*, pp. 16–17.

30. Owen Lattimore, *The Situation in Asia*, Little, Brown & Company, New York, 1949, p. 97.

31. W. Douglas Reeve, *The Republic of Korea*, Oxford University Press, Oxford, England, 1963, pp. 31–32.

31. See, for example, David Horowitz, *From Yalta to Vietnam, American Foreign Policy in the Cold War*, Penguin, Harmondsworth, England, 1967, pp. 117–123; I. F. Stone, *The Hidden History of the Korean War*, Monthly Review Press, New York, 1952; William Blum, *The CIA: A Forgotten History*, Zed Books, London, 1991; John Quigley, *The Ruses for War, American Interventionism Since World War Two*, Prometheus Books, New York, 1992, Chapters 3–5.

32. Fleming, *op. cit.*, pp. 603–604.

33. Trygve Lie, *In the Cause of Peace*, Macmillan, New York, Chapters 18 and 19.

34. Fleming, *op. cit.*, p. 656.

35. *Ibid.*, p. 654.

36. *US News and World Report*, 7 July 1950, p. 29.

37. Gunther, *op. cit.*, p. 166.

38. Bruce Cumings, *The Roaring of the Cataract, 1945–1950*, Volume 2, *The Origins of the Korean War*, Princeton University Press, Princeton, New Jersey, 1990, pp. 572–573, 578–579.

39. Quigley, *op. cit.*, p. 38.

40. Robert Leckie, *The Korean War*, Putnam, New York, 1962.

41. Fleming, *op. cit.*, p. 656.

42. Manchester, *op. cit.*, p. 610.

43. See Geoff Simons, *The United Nations, A Chronology of Conflict*, Macmillan, Basingstoke, England, 1994.

44. J. William Fulbright, *The Price of Empire*, Fourth Estate, London, 1989, p. 21.

NOTES TO CHAPTER 3

1. Lord John Acton: 'Power tends to corrupt, and absolute power corrupts absolutely' (letter in *Life and Letters of Mandel Creighton*, 1904).

Commentators less frequently quote what follows: 'Great men are also always bad men, even when they exercise influence and not authority'. Compare Anthony Trollope: 'We know that power does corrupt, and that we cannot trust kings to have loving hearts', *Prime Minister IV*, viii, 1876; and William Pitt, Earl of Chatham: 'Unlimited power is apt to corrupt the minds of those who possess it', House of Lords, 9 January 1770.

2. John Bowle, *Politics and Opinion in the Nineteenth Century*, Jonathan Cape, London, 1954, pp. 391–392.

3. Lord John Acton, *The History of Freedom and Other Essays*, London, 1907, p. 299.

4. Boutros Boutros-Ghali, *An Agenda for Peace*, United Nations, New York, 1992.

5. Boutros Boutros-Ghali, 'UN multilateralism: a cure for ugly new nationalisms', *International Herald Tribune*, 21–22 August 1993.

6. Boutros-Ghali (1992), *op. cit.*, p. 46.

7. Margaret Thatcher, *The Downing Street Years*, HarperCollins, London, 1993.

8. James Adams, 'Britain opposes UN ban on land-mines', *The Sunday Times*, London, 17 October 1993.

9. Stephen Bates, 'UN committee calls on Britain to ban racist political groups', *The Guardian*, London, 21 August 1993; Hugh Muir, 'Britain lags in battle to beat racism, says the UN', *The Daily Telegraph*, London, 21 August 1993.

10. Alexis Rowell, 'Shevardnadze asks the world for urgent help', *The Guardian*, London, 10 July 1993.

11. Alexis Rowell, 'Exhausted Georgian refugees flee one war for another', *The Guardian*, London, 7 October 1993.

12. I describe this episode, the history that led up to it and the consequences that followed — in *Iraq: from Sumer to Saddam*, Macmillan, Basingstoke, England, 1993.

13. Boutros Boutros-Ghali, *Report on the Work of the Organization from the Forty-seventh to the Forty-eighth Session of the General Assembly*, United Nations, New York, September 1993, p. 114.

14. Consider: 'If Kuwait grew carrots we wouldn't give a damn', Lawrence Korb (former US Assistant Defence Secretary), 1992; 'I venture to say that if Kuwait produced bananas, instead of oil, we would not have 400,000 American troops there today', Congressman Stokes, Ohio, 12 January 1991.

15. Resolution 660 also called upon Iraq and Kuwait to begin immediate 'intensive negotiations' to resolve their differences. Washington, quite prepared to tolerate Kuwait's refusal to talk to Iraq (despite Kuwait's acceptance of 660), made no effort to ensure compliance with this requirement (660(3)).

16. I owe the details of this account to Bob Woodward, *The Commanders*, Simon and Schuster, London, pp. 333–335.

17. Mohamed Heikal, *Illusions of Triumph*, HarperCollins, London, 1992, p. 215.

18. Robert Fisk, 'US withholds death toll from Red Cross', *The Independent*, London, 5 August 1991; Caroline Moorehead, 'Allies "breached Geneva rules" in Gulf conflict', *The Independent on Sunday*, London, 17 November 1991; Victoria Brittain, 'Allies accused of violating war laws', *The Guardian*, London, 18 November 1991.

19. In a letter made available to me, following communication with a British M.P., a researcher in the International Affairs and Defence Section of the House of Commons Library comments that 'It is certainly true that neither [no fly] zone was directly created by a UN Security Council Resolution . . . It is, therefore, true to say that the Iraqi no-fly zones were created unilaterally by the Gulf war coalition allies . . .'.

20. Special Alert, Number 237, *FAO/WFP Crop and Food Supply Assessment Mission to Iraq*, Food and Agriculture Organisation of the United Nations, World Food Programme, July 1993.

21. 'Iraq faces health crisis', *The Guardian*, London, 13 September 1993.

22. I have described the Libyan case in *Libya: the Struggle for Survival*, Macmillan, Basingstoke, England, 1993.

23. George Wilson, 'Colonel "was the target"', *The Guardian*, London, 19 April 1986.

24. Leonard Doyle, 'Ghali finds merit in Tripoli shift', *The Independent*, London, 5 March 1992.

25. Francis A. Boyle, 'Memorandum of Law on the Dispute between Libya and the United States and the United Kingdom over the Lockerbie bombing allegations', University of Illinois, Urbana-Champaign, 1992; see also Memorandum extract, *Third World Resurgence*, Number 21, p. 28.

26. *Ibid.* See also Marc Weller, 'The Lockerbie Case: a premature end to the "New World Order"?', *African Journal of International and Comparative Law*, Number 4, 1992; Erskine Childers, 'Law of the jungle reigns in the UN', *Third World Resurgence*, Number 21, p. 29. It is important also that international law is part of US law (see discussion in Rebecca M. M. Wallace, *International Law*, Sweet and Maxwell, London, 1992). Thus in violating the Montreal Convention, Washington also violates the US Constitution.

27. Weller, *op. cit.*, p. 14.

28. The Jamahirya News Agency (JANA), an official Libyan organ, reported (*News Bulletin*, 20 October 1993) that China had agreed to run Libya's medicine production factories 'to minimise the effects of harsh sanctions'.

29. Weller, *op. cit.*, p. 14.

30. Anton La Guardia, 'Israel backs down over Palestinians', *The Daily Telegraph*, London, 2 February 1993.

31. I have given a more detailed profile of the Yugoslavian quagmire in *The United Nations: A Chronology of Conflict*, Macmillan, Basingstoke, England, 1994.

32. Mark Tran and David Fairhall, 'US resists call for UN control of troops', *The Guardian*, London, 6 May 1993.

33. Annika Savill, 'US may boycott UN meeting over Bosnia', *The Independent*, London, 18 May 1993.

34. John Palmer, 'US and EC fail to agree on response', *The Guardian*, London, 10 June 1993.

35. Peter Pringle, 'US and UN vie for control of air strikes', *The Independent*, London, 5 August 1993.

36. Edward Cowan, 'Betrayed Bosnians await their fate', *The Sunday Times*, London, 8 August 1993.

37. Maggie O'Kane, 'Giving thanks for little Irma', *The Guardian*, London, 10 August 1993.

38. Stephen Castle, Nick Cohen and Michael Sheridan, 'Children, pity and politics', *The Independent on Sunday*, London, 15 August 1993.

39. John Palmer and Hella Pick, 'US seeks to veto UN command in Bosnia', *The Guardian*, London, 13 September 1993.

40. Ian Traynor, 'Serbs gain victory from international confusion', *The Guardian*, London, 18 April 1994.

41. Simon Tisdall, 'Clinton shies away from ordering punitive action', *The Guardian*, London, 18 April 1994; Patrick Cockburn, 'Clinton supports further NATO air strikes', *The Independent*, London, 20 April 1994.

42. Tim Butcher, 'UN humiliated as Serbs move more tanks', *The Daily Telegraph*, London, 7 May 1994.

43. Patrick Bishop, 'American indifference heightens UN impotence', *The Daily Telegraph*, London, 14 May 1994.

44. David Smith and James Adams, 'Britain prepares to quit after U-turn in Bosnia', *The Sunday Times*, London, 10 July 1994; Ian Traynor, 'UN warns troops will quit Bosnia', *The Guardian*, London, 13 August 1994.

45. James Adams, 'CIA plans to arm Bosnian Muslims', *The Sunday Times*, London, 14 August 1994.

46. Rakiya Omaar and Alex de Waal, 'Uneasy landfall for US Marines', *The Guardian*, London, 5 December 1992.

47. Mark Huband, 'US marines met by television crews', *The Guardian*, London, 9 December 1992; Richard Dowden, 'Ill met by moonlight in Mogadishu', *The Independent*, London, 10 December 1992.

48. Patricia Clough, 'UN dismisses Italian general in Somalia', *The Independent*, London, 15 July 1993; Angus Shaw, 'Italy refuses to withdraw Somalia chief', *The Guardian*, London, 17 July 1993; Peter Pringle, 'Mutiny simmers under the blue helmet', *The Independent*, London, 18 July 1993.

49. Richard Ellis, 'Can "Delta farce" now get it right?', *The Sunday Times*, London, 5 September 1993.

50. Richard Ellis, 'UN paid protection money to warlord', *The Sunday Times*, London, 5 September 1993.

51. David Usborne, 'Somalia cuts Clinton down to size', *The Independent on Sunday*, London, 10 October 1993.

52. Hella Pick, 'Between Clinton's rock and Somali hard place', *The Guardian*, London, 16 October 1993.

53. 'For UN read US' (leading article), *The Guardian*, London, 15 October 1993.

54. Pick (16/10/93), *op. cit.*

55. Mark Huband and Hella Pick, 'United Nations irate at casting as whipping-boy', *The Guardian*, London, 11 October 1993.

56. Rick Atkinson, 'A bitter tale of two estranged worlds in one divided city', *The Guardian*, London, 27 November 1993.

57. Mark Huband, 'Operation Disaster born out of lie', *The Observer*, London, 12 December 1993.

58. Jonathan Clayton, 'US leaves Somalia to its agony', *The Guardian*, London, 26 March 1994.

59. Thomas Lippman, 'UN chief "failed Somalia"', *The Guardian*, London, 30 August 1994.
60. Raymond L. Garthoff, *Reflections on the Cuban Missile Crisis*, Brookings Institution, 1987, p. 17.
61. William Blum, *The CIA: A Forgotten History*, Zed Books, London, 1991, pp. 206–216; Noam Chomsky, 'International terrorism: image and reality', in Alexander George (ed.), *Western State Terrorism*, Polity Press, Cambridge, England, 1991, pp. 22–23; John H. Davis, *The Kennedys, Dynasty and Disaster*, SPI Books, New York, 1992, Chapters 41 and 49; William Colby, *Honourable Men, My Life in the CIA*, Hutchinson, London, 1978, p. 188.
62. Chomsky, *op. cit.*, pp. 210–211.
63. *Ibid.*
64. Lynne Wallis, 'Cuba's hunger feeds an epidemic of pain', *The Observer*, London, 23 May 1993.
65. Edward Luce, 'Swift Cuban action beats eye disease', *The Guardian*, London, 30 September 1993.
66. Phil Gunson, 'Cuba blockade ruled out by US', *The Guardian*, London, 29 August 1994.
67. Ian Aitken, 'Our man in Havana the night the revolution happened', *The Guardian*, London, 29 August 1994.
68. Christine Toomey, 'Boat people prefer death to Castro', *The Sunday Times*, London, 28 August 1994.
69. Lisandro Perez, 'The fault line that runs through Washington', *The Observer*, London, 28 August 1994.
70. Mark Huband, 'UN troops stand by and watch carnage', *The Guardian*, London, 12 April 1994.
71. 'Terrified UN soldiers pull out of Rwanda', *The Independent*, London, 21 April 1994.
72. Mark Huband, 'UN leaves Rwanda in grip of killers', *The Observer*, London, 24 April 1994.
73. Buchiyza Mseteka and Victoria Brittain, 'UN chief calls for force as human tide flees Rwanda', *The Guardian*, London, 30 April 1994; 'Rwanda exodus overwhelms UN', *The Sunday Times*, London, 1 May 1994; Mark Huband, 'Church of stinking slaughter', *The Observer*, London, 1 May 1994.
74. Larry Elliot, 'US and Russia sink plans to send 5500 troops', *The Guardian*, London, 13 May 1994.
75. Peter Pringle, 'America hampers dispatch of UN troops for Rwanda', *The Independent*, London, 18 May 1994; Larry Elliott, 'Fury greets US block on peace force', *The Guardian*, London, 18 May 1994.
76. Mark Huband, 'Rwanda genocide probe chief quits over UN blunders', *The Observer*, London, 11 September 1994.
77. Hugh Shaughnessy, 'How Joseph lost an American dream', *The Observer*, London, 7 March 1993.
78. Patrick Cockburn, 'UN forces clear the way for Aristide comeback', *The Independent*, London, 5 October 1993.
79. Martin Walker, 'US uses Haitian MPs' visit to put pressure on Aristide', *The Guardian*, London, 17 February 1994.
80. Phil Gunson, 'Aristide attacks refugee policy', *The Guardian*, London, 8 April 1994.

81. Ambrose Evans-Pritchard, 'US braced for Haiti invasion', *The Sunday Telegraph*, London, 10 July 1994.
82. Maurice Weaver, 'Perry on standby for Haiti invasion', *The Daily Telegraph*, London, 5 September 1994.
83. Inis L. Claude, *Swords into Plowshares*, University of London Press, London, 1965, p. 246.
84. Boutros-Ghali (September 1993), *op. cit.*
85. John Quigley, *The Ruses for War, American Interventionism since World War II*, Prometheus Books, New York, 1992, p. 291.
86. Wallace, *op. cit*, p. 46.
87. Adam Roberts, 'All the troubles of the world on its shoulders', *The Independent*, London, 21 December 1992.
88. Hella Pick, 'When relief adds misery', *The Guardian*, London, 15 July 1993.
89. Hella Pick, 'Hurd tells UN to limit its goals and cut expenses', *The Guardian*, London, 29 September 1993.
90. Thatcher, *op. cit.*
91. Martin Walker, 'Clinton, the worrier king', *The Guardian*, London, 14 October 1993.
92. Hella Pick, 'Between Clinton's rock and Somali hard place', *The Guardian*, London, 16 October 1993.
93. 'Clinton foreign policy in tatters', *The Sunday Times*, London, 17 October 1993.

NOTES TO CHAPTER 4

1. Mats R. Berdal, *Whither UN Peacekeeping?*, Adelphi Paper 281, International Institute for Strategic Studies, Brassey's (UK), London, 1993, p. 31.
2. Hella Pick, 'Between Clinton's rock and Somali hard place', *The Guardian*, London, 16 October 1993.
3. Michael Sheridan, 'The high cost of peace-keeping', *The Independent*, London, 1 November 1993.
4. Boutros Boutros-Ghali, *Report on the Work of the Organization from the Forty-seventh to the Forty-eighth Session of the General Assembly*, United Nations, New York, September 1993.
5. David Bryer (letter), *The Sunday Times*, London, 12 September 1993.
6. Conor Cruise O'Brien, 'Disorder between war and peace', *The Independent*, London, 18 June 1993.
7. Pick, *op. cit.*
8. Boutros Boutros-Ghali, 'UN multilateralism: a cure for ugly new nationalisms', *International Herald Tribune*, 21–22 August 1993.
9. Conor Cruise O'Brien, 'Two UNs at war with each other', *The Independent*, London 13 August 1993.
10. Mark Huband, Simon Tisdall and Hella Pick, 'Clinton builds up to withdrawal from Somalia', *The Guardian*, London, 7 October 1993.
11. Hugh O'Shaughnessy, 'Jakarta's spider web of oppression', *The Observer*, London, 30 May 1993.

12. John Gittings, 'East Timorese accuse Britain of blocking action on Indonesia', *The Guardian*, London, 17 June 1992.
13. A copy of the full text is given in *The Guardian*, London, 5 August 1993.
14. Hella Pick, 'Hurd tells UN to limit its goals and cut expenses', *The Guardian*, London, 29 September 1993.
15. Raymond Whitaker, 'Cambodians fall out with the UN peace-keepers', *The Independent*, London, 26 January 1993.
16. Boutros Boutros-Ghali, *An Agenda for Peace*, United Nations, New York, 1992, p. 2.
17. Crispin Tickell, 'Why it would be folly to tear up the Charter', *The Observer*, London, 18 July 1993.
18. 'Draft Statement by the President of the Security Council on the Report *An Agenda for Peace*', United Nations, New York, 28 October 1992; in June 1959 Secretary-General Dag Hammarskjöld proposed the earmarking of troops for UN tasks.
19. Madeleine Bunting, 'British brass cool to UN standing army', *The Guardian*, London, 24 September 1993.
20. 'Trouble spots within the UN' (editorial), *The Independent*, London, 28 August 1993.
21. Boutros Boutros-Ghali, *Report on the Work of the Organization from the Forty-sixth to the Forty-seventh Session of the General Assembly*, United Nations, New York, September 1992, pp. 8–9.
22. *Ibid.*, p. 9.
23. *Ibid.*, pp. 10, 11, 15.
24. Boutros-Ghali (September 1993), *op. cit.*, p. 20.
25. *Ibid.*, pp. 26–27.
26. Berdal, *op. cit.*, p. 51.
27. *Ibid.*, pp. 52–59.
28. See, for example, William J. Durch, 'Building on sand; UN peacekeeping in the Western Sahara', *International Security*, Volume 17, Number 4, Spring 1993, pp. 158–160.
29. Boutros-Ghali (September 1992), *op. cit.*; (September 1993), *op. cit.*
30. Berdal, *op. cit.*, p. 59.
31. Boutros-Ghali (September 1992), *op. cit.*, pp. 42–43.
32. *Ibid.*, p. 43.
33. *Ibid.*, p. 44.
34. Boutros-Ghali (September 1992), *op. cit.*, p. 17.
35. Boutros-Ghali (September 1993), *op. cit.*, p. 34.
36. *Ibid.*, p. 35.
37. Berdal, *op. cit.*, p. 11.
38. Karl Maier, ' "Raw deal" for UN in Angola', *The Independent on Sunday*, London, 18 October 1992; Karl Maier, 'UN despairs of Angola's see-saw war', *The Independent*, London, 31 January 1993; Mark Huband, 'Solace for Angola's tears in the bar americano', *The Observer*, London, 29 August 1993.
39. David Orr, 'The town where most children are corpses', *The Observer*, London, 31 October 1993.
40. Vanessa Redgrave (letter), 'UN urged to save the day for Georgia', *The Guardian*, London, 29 September 1993; Alex Rowell, 'Exhausted Georgian refugees flee one war for another', *The Guardian*, London, 7 October 1993.

41. Richard Dowden, 'War strips southern Sudan bare', *The Independent*, London, 4 May 1993; Richard Dowden, 'Why the food just stopped', *The Independent on Sunday*, London, 6 June 1993.
42. Richard Dowden, 'Boutros-Ghali keeps Liberia off UN agenda', *The Independent*, London, 26 March 1993.
43. Richard Dowden, 'Liberia lives at risk as UN blocks food aid', *The Independent*, London, 2 September 1993.
44. Patrick Cockburn, 'Clinton purges foreign advisors', *The Independent*, London, 10 November 1993.
45. Phil Davison, 'Death squads in El Salvador on prowl again', *The Independent*, London, 11 November 1993; *Report of the Commission on the Truth for El Salvador* S/25500, 1 April 1993.
46. *Ibid.* Information in more than 12,000 documents released in November 1993 by the CIA, the Pentagon and the State Department provide 'powerful evidence' (*The New York Times*) that both the Reagan and Bush administrations were prepared to work with known death-squad leaders during the 1980s.
47. Berdal, *op. cit.*, p. 45.
48. Tim Weiner, 'Haiti military "worked as CIA agents" ', *The Guardian*, London, 2 November 1993.
49. Conor Cruise O'Brien, 'Forces for the good, and bad', *The Independent*, London, 27 August 1993.
50. *Ibid.*
51. Leonard Doyle, 'UN officials "worked against Polisario" ', *The Independent*, London, 15 November 1991.
52. Louise Branson, 'Fury over UN's Russian troops', *The Sunday Times*, London, 21 February 1993.
53. Nick Rufford, Ian Burrell and David Leppard, 'Talk poor by day; live rich by night: The corrupt heart of the UN bureaucracy', *The Sunday Times*, London, 15 August 1993.
54. 'The UN and The Sunday Times', Information Centre, United Nations, 20 Buckingham Gate, London SW1E 6LB, 9 September 1993.
55. 'UN acts on report of waste and fraud', *The Sunday Times*, London, 29 August 1993.
56. Peter Hillmore, 'British officer blows whistle on UN corruption', *The Observer*, London, 29 August 1993.
57. *Ibid.*
58. Nick Cumming-Bruce, 'Cambodian thieves drive UN to despair', *The Guardian*, London, 16 July 1993.
59. 'French general criticises peace-keeping troops' conduct', *The Guardian*, London, 16 July 1993.
60. Maggie O'Kane, 'The soldiers are out of control – feasting on a dying city', *The Independent*, London, 26 August 1993.
61. *Ibid.*
62. Maggie O'Kane, 'UN troops in corruption enquiry', *The Independent*, London, 26 August 1993.
63. Terry McCarthy, 'Hot tempers rise on the seamier side', *The Independent*, London, 19 October 1992.
64. *Ibid.*
65. Jon Swain, 'UN losing battle for Cambodia in the brothels of Phnom Penh', *The Sunday Times*, London, 27 December 1992.

66. Edward Luce, 'Child sex boom blamed on UN', *The Independent*, London, 4 November 1993.
67. *Ibid.*
68. 'Today', BBC Radio, 2 November 1993; quoting *Newsday* publication, New York.
69. *Somalia: Human Rights Abuses by the United Nations Forces*, African Rights, 11 Marshalsea Road, London SE1 1EP, July 1993.
70. *Ibid.*
71. Peter Hillmore, 'Where peace dawns only the grave-diggers aren't smiling', *The Observer*, London, 25 July 1993.
72. Richard Dowden, 'UN detainees "denied rights" ', *The Independent*, London, 18 October 1993; Mark Huband, 'UN forces deny Somali detainees legal rights', *The Guardian*, London, 25 September 1993.
73. 'Canada sent racist troops to Somalia', *The Guardian*, London, 1 September 1993.
74. *Getting Away with Murder: Political killings and 'disappearances' in the 1990s*, 1 Easton Street, London WC1X 8DT, October 1993, p. 106.
75. *Ibid.*, pp. 106–107.

NOTES TO CHAPTER 5

1. See, for example, Gustavus Myers, *History of the Great American Fortunes*, Random House, New York, 1936.
2. R. Hoftstadter, *The American Political Tradition*, London, 1962, pp. 26–32.
3. Quoted in R. A. Dahl, *Democracy in the United States*, Chicago, 1976, p. 73.
4. John Stuart Mill, *Representative Government*, Everyman's Library, London, 1960, Chapter VIII, pp. 280–281.
5. *Ibid.*, p. 281.
6. Roger Fulford, *Votes for Women, the story of a struggle*, Faber & Faber, London, 1958, p. 32.
7. Martin Pugh, *The Making of Modern British Politics 1867–1939*, Basil Blackwell, Oxford, England, 1982, p. 3.
8. *Ibid.*, p. 8.
9. J. R. Pole, *The Pursuit of Equality in American History*, Jefferson Memorial Lectures, University of California Press, Berkeley and Los Angeles, 1978, p. 173.
10. John Quigley, *The Ruses for War. American Interventionism since World War II*, Prometheus Books, New York, 1992, p. 291.
11. Since US membership of the United Nations makes its legal obligations under the Charter an effective part of US law (according to provisions in the Constitution), US violations of the Charter have rendered successive American presidents liable to impeachment by Congress. Such a course, though technically sound, was never a likely option.
12. A useful description of the practical working of the Security Council is given in Evan Luard, *The United Nations, How it works and what it does*, Macmillan, London, 1979, pp. 9–31.

13. Inis L. Claude, *Swords into Plowshares*, University of London Press, London, 1965, p. 140.
14. Anjali V. Patil, *The UN Vote in World Affairs, A Complete Record and Case Histories of the Security Council's Veto*, UNIFO Publishers, Sarasota, Florida, 1992, p. 16.
15. Dag Hammarskjöld, *The Servant of Peace*, Bodley Head, London, 1962, p. 350.
16. Patil, *op. cit.*, Chapters III to V.
17. It may be thought that a permanent member should not be allowed to use the veto if that state is a party to the dispute and has a vested interest in the outcome. In fact Article 27(3) states that 'a party to a dispute shall abstain from voting'. No state takes any notice of this unambiguous Charter provision.
18. Peter Kellner, 'Britain's UN sacrifice for a "new world order" ', *The Independent*, London, 25 January 1991.
19. Annika Savill, 'UK finds a way to hold on to the mother of all seats', *The Independent*, London, 7 January 1992.
20. 'An international interest' (leading article), *The Independent*, London, 31 January 1992.
21. David Gow, 'Brandt urges stronger UN to guarantee world peace', *The Guardian*, London, 16 September 1992.
22. Leonard Doyle, 'Hurd warning over "slide into disorder" ', *The Independent*, London, 28 January 1993.

NOTES TO CHAPTER 6

1. See, for example, the protracted dispute over the role of the WHO head, Hiroshi Nakajima: Leonard Doyle, 'Sick tactics in battle for health chief's job', *The Independent on Sunday*, London, 10 January 1993; Michael Sheridan, 'World health chief faces fraud enquiry', *The Independent on Sunday*, London, 28 February 1993; James Adams, 'Critics battle to oust "disastrous" WHO chief', *The Sunday Times*, London, 18 April 1993; Ian Black, 'West fails to block Japanese chief of world health body', *The Guardian*, London, 6 May 1993.
2. Boutros Boutros-Ghali, *Report on the Work of the Organization from the Forty-sixth to the Forty-seventh Session of the General Assembly*, United Nations, New York, September 1992, pp. 24–25.
3. Boutros Boutros-Ghali, *Report on the Work of the Organization from the Forty-seventh to the Forty-eighth Session of the General Assembly*, United Nations, New York, September 1993, p. 167.
4. Michael Simmons, ' "Disaster" for Third World economies', *The Guardian*, London, 4 March 1991.
5. *North – South: A Programme for Survival*, The Report of the International Commission on International Development Issues, Chairman: Willy Brandt, Pan Books, London, 1980, p. 101.
6. *Ibid.*, pp. 103–104.
7. Teresa Hayter, *Aid as Imperialism*, Penguin Books, Harmondsworth, England, 1971, p. 10. The ODI refused to publish this report (Hayter: 'The study was written with care and caution and a certain amount of evasion,

since it had at least to give an appearance of being publishable by the ODI. It was also rewritten, at the behest of ODI, back to front, "so as to present the agencies' case more fairly" . . . The ODI was, nevertheless, unable to publish it').

8. Cheryl Payer, *The Debt Trap, The IMF and the Third World*, Penguin Books, Harmondsworth, England, 1974.

9. *Ibid.*, pp. ix–x.

10. See, for example, Susan George, *How the Other Half Dies*, Penguin Books, Harmondsworth, England, 1991; Peter Körner, Gero Maass, Thomas Siebold and Ranier Tetzlaff, *The IMF and the Debt Crisis*, Zed Books, London, 1992; Graham Hancock, *Lords of Poverty*, Macmillan, London, 1989.

11. *Ibid.*, pp. 192–193.

12. Paul Harrison, 'Trapped in the food maze', *The Guardian*, London, 11 October 1984.

13. Quoted by Victoria Brittain, 'Why is Africa hungry', *The Guardian*, London, 21–22 October 1989.

14. Richard Dowden, 'Hurd sets out rules for aid to Africa', *The Independent*, London, 7 June 1990; writing in *Crossbow*, the quarterly journal of the Conservative Bow Group, a few months later, Hurd again emphasised how aid could be used as a political lever (*The Independent*, London, 1 October 1990).

15. John Vidal, 'Long shadows over the parched land', *The Guardian*, London, 18 January 1991; Judy Jones, 'African famine is "a forgotten crisis" ', *The Independent*, London, 31 January 1991.

16. Javier Perez de Cuellar, *New Compact for Co-operation: Report and Recommendations of the Secretary-General on the Final Review of the UN Recovery Programme*, United Nations, New York, August 1991.

17. Richard Dowden, 'Building a wall around the West', *The Independent*, London, 13 March 1992.

18. *Human Development Report 1992*, UN Development Programme (UNDP), United Nations, New York, 1992.

19. Barbara Crosette, 'Relief groups see disaster across southern Africa', *International Herald Tribune*, 18 September 1992.

20. Michael Gillard, 'Bag men bleeding Africa', *The Observer*, London, 26 September 1993.

21. *Ibid.*

22. J. K. Horsefield et al., *The International Monetary Fund, 1945–1965: Twenty Years of International Monetary Co-operation*, Washington, D.C., 1965, Volume III.

23. R. F. Harrod, *The Life of John Maynard Keynes*, Macmillan, London, 1951; W. M. Scammel, *International Monetary Policy*, Macmillan, London, 1961.

24. Hayter, *op. cit.*, p. 45.

25. Hugh O'Shaughnessy, 'UN's World Bank condemned for 'immoral' profits', *The Observer*, London, 22 April 1990; Michael Irwin joined the World Bank as director of the health services department after a distinguised 32-year career with the UN Development Programme (UNDP) and the UN Children's Fund (UNICEF). See also Ken Ringle, 'The man who broke open the World Bank', *The Sunday Times*, London, 30 September 1990.

26. Julius Nyerere, Foreword to Chakravarthi Raghavan, *Recolonization: GATT, the Uruguay Round and the Third World*, Zed Books, London, 1990.

27. There is abundant literature on the impact of the IMF and the World Bank. See, for example, Hayter, *op. cit.*, for a description of early Fund involvements in Brazil and Peru; Payer, *op. cit.*, for a description of Fund involvements in Indonesia, Indochina, Yugoslavia, Brazil and India, and of the 'breakaways' (Chile, Ghana and North Korea); Körner *et al.* for an account of Fund involvements in Brazil, Portugal, Sudan, Zaire, Jamaica and Ghana; Sue Branford and Bernardo Kucinski, *The Debt Squads; The US, the banks and Latin America*, Zed Books, London, 1990, for an account of the 'bleeding of Latin America', the 'human cost of the debt crisis', and so on; *The SAP in the Forest, The Environmental and Social Impacts of Structural Adjustment Programmes in the Philippines, Ghana and Guyana*, Friends of the Earth, London, 1993.

28. John Kenneth Galbraith, *The Culture of Contentment*, Sinclair-Stevenson, London, 1992, p. 117.

29. Andre Gunder Frank, 'A debt bomb primed for the next recession', *The Guardian*, London, 12 October 1984.

30. William Keegan, 'The IMF: A consensus not to agree', *The Observer*, London, 5 October 1986.

31. 'A job for Atlas and Hercules combined', *The Economist*, London, 30 March 1991.

32. Alex Brummer, 'IMF to ease burden on troubled nations', *The Guardian*, London, 11 October 1991.

33. Victoria Brittain, 'Donors fail dark continent in decline', *The Guardian*, London, 13 February 1993 (review article: Frances Stewart, Sanjaya Lall and Samuel Wangwe (eds), *Alternative Development Strategies in SubSaharan Africa*, Macmillan, London, 1993; Giovanni Andrea Cornia, Rolf van der Hoeven and Thandika Mkandawire (eds), *Africa's Recovery in the 1990s*, Macmillan, London, 1993).

34. Richard Dowden, 'Inside the building the officials are deciding what's best for Africa', *The Independent*, London, 28 March 1993.

35. Bailey Morris, 'World shaker emerges at IMF', *The Independent on Sunday*, London, 2 May 1993.

36. 'World Bank board demands first class', *The Financial Times*, London, 8 June 1993.

37. Greg Hadfield, 'Poor countries pay dearly for bankers' global gravy train', *The Sunday Times*, London, 26 September 1993.

38. Janet Bush, 'Clarke says UK has no cash for IMF poverty fund', *The Times*, London, 28 September 1993; Alex Brummer, 'Comfortable Clarke defies convention', *The Guardian*, London, 29 September 1993.

39. John Gittings, 'Bank aids people its work uproots', *The Guardian*, London, 11 April 1994.

40. Alex Brummer, 'Policymakers ponder privatisation pitfalls', *The Guardian*, London, 20 April 1994.

41. Peter Torday, 'World Bank under pressure to reform', *The Independent*, London, 27 April 1994; Peter Torday, 'Loans go hand in hand with reform, G7 tells Moscow', *The Independent*, London, 25 April 1994.

42. Peter Torday, 'What role for the over-fifties?', *The Independent*, London, 3 June 1994.

43. Walter Schwarz, 'World Bank makes poor poorer, say aid charities', *The Guardian*, London, 20 July 1994.

44. Christopher Johnson, 'Strings on US aid package', *The Observer*, London, 24 July 1994.

45. Victoria Brittain and Kevin Watkins. 'A continent driven to economic suicide', *The Guardian*, London, 20 July 1994.

46. Detailed descriptions and anaylses of GATT are given in Raghavan, *op. cit.*, and in Tim Lang and Colin Hines, *The New Protectionism, Protecting the future against free trade*, Earthscan, London, 1993, pp. 46–57.

47. Sallie Pisani, *The CIA and the Marshall Plan*, Edinburgh University Press, Edinburgh, Scotland, 1991.

48. Raghavan, *op. cit.*, p. 51.

49. *Ibid.*, p. 52.

50. *Ibid.*, p. 55; quoted Raghavan interview with Julius Nyerere.

51. *Ibid.*, p. 61.

52. Andrew Marshall, Sarah Lambert and Peter Torday, 'The war of the seeds', *The Independent on Sunday*, London, 8 November 1992.

53. Tim Jackson, ' "Non" to a GATT compromise', *The Independent*, London, 18 November 1992.

54. Larry Elliott and Jonathan Fenby, 'France urges global deal to end trade row', *The Guardian*, London, 14 May 1993.

55. David Smith, 'Defiant France set to scupper vital trade deal', *The Sunday Times*, London, 19 September 1993; James Nicholson, 'French brinkmanship threat to Gatt', *The Guardian*, London, 20 September 1993.

56. George Brock, 'Hurd bolsters threat of EC sabotage over GATT', *The Times*, London, 21 September 1993; Sarah Lambert, 'France allies with Germany on Gatt', *The Independent*, London, 21 September 1993; Sarah Lambert, 'EC battle over Gatt ends in a draw', *The Independent*, London, 22 September 1993.

57. Kevin Rafferty, 'Japan in paddy over rice', *The Observer*, London, 7 November 1993.

58. Irwin Stelzer, 'Nafta victory swells protectionist army', *The Sunday Times*, London, 21 November 1993.

59. Lang and Hines, *op. cit.*, p. 48.

60. *Ibid.*, p. 49.

61. Raghavan, *op. cit.*, pp. 62–63.

62. *Ibid.*, p. 64.

63. Lang and Hines, *op. cit.*, pp. 50–51.

64. Kevin Watkins, Stephanie d'Orey and Dieneke Ferguson, 'Profit without honour in other lands', *The Guardian*, London, 11 January 1991.

65. John Vidal, 'Can the world afford free trade?', *The Guardian*, London, 13 November 1992.

66. Oliver Gillie, 'Trade agreement raises fear over food safety', *The Independent*, London, 19 April 1993.

67. Rachel Watson, 'The GATT negotiations on agriculture: What are the implications for developing countries?', *CAP Tales*, September 1993.

68. *Fool's Gold, The General Agreement on Tariffs and Trade and the threat of unsustainable development*, Friends of the Earth, London, May 1992.

69. Joanna Blythman, 'The GATT deal is a recipe for disaster', *The Independent*, London, 25 September 1993.
70. John Vidal, 'Seeds of discontent', *The Guardian*, London, 1 October 1992.
71. John Gray, 'When no deal is a good deal', *The Guardian*, London, 9 November 1993.
72. Teddy Goldsmith, 'Trading places', *The Guardian*, London, 12 November 1993.
73. Simon Caulkin, 'Europe's St George in a war on free trade', *The Observer*, London, 21 November 1993.
74. Edward Luce, Julie Wolf and Larry Elliott, 'Gatt bargaining encounters new hitch', *The Guardian*, London, 4 December 1993.
75. Larry Elliot and Edward Luce, 'Gatt envoys fear pitfalls in path', *The Guardian*, 7 December 1993.
76. Richard Dowden, 'Seeds sown for clashes with the Third World', *The Independent*, London, 15 December 1994.
77. Larry Elliott, 'Finishing tape in sight for the marathon Gatt talks', *The Guardian*, London, 14 April 1994.
78. K. Watkins, 'The foxes take over the hen house', *The Guardian*, London, 17 July 1992.
79. *UN World Investment Report*, New York, 1992.
80. F. Clairmonte, 'The debacle of the Uruguay Round – an autopsy', *Third World Economics*, 16–31 January 1991, p. 11.

NOTES TO CHAPTER 7

1. Richard Gott, 'Nations divided by a lost vision', *The Guardian*, London, 28 August 1993.
2. *Ibid.*
3. Boutros Boutros-Ghali has supported the idea of a standing UN force (in *Agenda for Peace*, 1992, and elsewhere); as have, for example, Sir Brian Urquhart (in the *New York Review of Books*), the British Labour Party, and the British Liberal Democrat Party (in *Beyond the Nation State*, Federal Green Paper, Number 25, July 1992).
4. Thus Washington has denounced the World Court (when there was an adjudication against the US over Nicaragua), ignored General Assembly Resolution 47/19 condemning the illegal 35-year-long trade blockade of Cuba, and violated the UN Charter by invading Grenada and Panama, bombing Libya and more recently (October 1993) launching cruise missiles at Baghdad.
5. Boutros Boutros-Ghali, *Report on the Work of the Organization from the Forty-seventh to the Forty-eighth session of the General Assembly*, United Nations, New York, September 1993, p. 17.
6. Vivek Chaudhary, 'Justice sans frontières', *The Guardian*, London, 5 October 1993.
7. Article 55(1) of the Statute states: 'All questions shall be decided by a majority of the judges present.'

8. See 'Manipulating the UN: over Iraq' and 'Manipulating the UN: over Libya' in Chapter 3.
9. Marc Weller, 'The Lockerbie Case: A premature end to the "New World Order"?', *African Journal of International and Comparative Law*, Number 4, 1992, p. 14.
10. *Ibid.*, p. 15.
11. *Ibid.*
12. Quoted by Chaudhary, *op. cit.*
13. Peter Pringle, 'UN searches for a brave new world', *The Independent*, London, 21 September 1993.
14. Boutros-Ghali (September 1993), *op. cit.* p. 49.
15. *After the Cold War*, Federal Green Paper, Number 9, Liberal Democrats, London, 1989.
16. 'Improving the UN's response to conflict-related emergencies', *Oxfam briefing*, Oxfam, London, Number 6, November 1993, p. 5. Boutros-Ghali has said little about the DHA: 'An inter-agency early warning mechanism for examining possible situations of mass population displacement is being managed by the Department of Humanitarian Affairs. One of its purposes is to assist in determining when preventive humanitarian action may be appropriate' (Boutros-Ghali, September 1993, *op. cit.*, p. 101).
17. *Oxfam briefing, op. cit.*, p. 5.
18. I give a brief description of the post-Gulf War plight of the Iraqi people in *Iraq: from Sumer to Saddam*, Macmillan, London, 1994, pp. 9–15.
19. John Stuart Mill, *Representative Government*, Dent, London, 1960, pp. 175–176.
20. Pringle, *op. cit.*
21. Gott, *op. cit.*
22. *Beyond the Nation State*, Federal Green Paper, Number 25, Liberal Democrats, London, July 1992, p. 12.
23. *Ibid.*
24. Hanna Newcombe, 'Democratic representation in the UN General Assembly', in Frank Barnaby (ed.), *Building a More Democratic United Nations*, Proceedings of the First International Conference On a More Democratic UN, Frank Cass, London, 1991, pp. 226–228.
25. *Ibid.*, p. 228.
26. Richard Hudson, 'The Binding Triad', in Barnaby (ed.), *op. cit.*, pp. 232–237.
27. *Ibid.*, p. 233.
28. Sidney Bailey, *Veto in the Security Council*, New York, 1968, pp. 66.
29. See, for example, the useful discussion in Hans Koechler, 'The United Nations Security Council and the New World Order', in Barnaby (ed.), *op. cit.*, pp. 238–245.
30. See Barnaby (ed.), *op. cit.*
31. Jeffrey J. Segall, 'Building world democracy through the UN', *Medicine and War*, Volume 6, Number 4, 1990, pp. 275–285.
32. Specific proposals are detailed in Jeffrey J. Segall, 'A UN Second Assembly', in Barnaby (ed.), *op. cit.*, pp. 107–109; see also David Chapman, 'A method for the direct election of a popular second assembly of the UN', in Barnaby (ed.), *op. cit.*, pp. 128–136.

33. Harry H. Lerner, 'INFUSA and the dynamics of democracy', in Barnaby (ed.), *op. cit.*, p. 115.
34. Mark Tran, 'New world order could replace tanks with banks', *The Guardian*, London, 9 November 1992.
35. Dominic Hogg, *The SAP in the Forest*, Friends of the Earth, London, September 1993, p. 156.
36. *Ibid.*, p. 97.
37. Tim Lang and Colin Hines, *The New Protectionism*, Earthscan, London, 1993, p. 125.

Select Bibliography

Akehurst, Michael, *A Modern Introduction to International Law* (London: HarperCollin Academic, 1991).

Ambrose, Stephen E., *Rise to Globalism: American Foreign Policy since 1938*, 5th edition (Harmondsworth, England: Penguin, 1988).

Baehr, P. R. and Gordenker, L., *The United Nations: Reality and Ideal* (London: 1984).

Bailey, Sydney D., *The Procedure of the UN Security Council* (Oxford: Clarendon Press, 1988).

Barnaby, Frank (ed.), *Building a More Democratic United Nations: Proceedings of the First International Conference on A More Democratic UN* (London: Frank Cass, 1991).

Barros, James, *Office Without Power: Secretary-General Sir Eric Drummond, 1919–1933* (Oxford: Oxford University Press, 1979).

Bennis, Phyllis and Moushabeck, Michel, *Beyond the Storm: A Gulf Crisis Reader* (Edinburgh: Cannongate Press, 1992).

Boyd, Andrew, *Fifteen Men on a Powder Keg: A History of the UN Security Council* (London: Methuen and Co., 1971).

Branford, Sue and Kucinski, Bernardo, *The US, the Banks and Latin America* (London: Zed Books, 1990).

Brierly, J. L., *The Law of Nations, An Introduction to the International Law of Peace* (London: Oxford University Press, 1963).

Castberg, Frede, *The Voting Procedure in the League of Nations and the United Nations* (Oslo: F. Castberg and E. Dons, 1949).

Cecil, Lord Robert, *A Great Experiment* (Oxford: Oxford University Press, 1941).

Choate, J. H., *The Two Hague Conferences* (Princeton and London, 1913).

Chomsky, Noam, *Deterring Democracy* (London and New York: Verso, 1991).

Claude, Inis L., *Swords into Plowshares: The Problems and Progress of International Organization* (New York: Random House, 1967).

——, *The Changing United Nations* (New York: Random House, 1967).

Eagleton, Clyde, *United Nations and United States* (Dallas: Southern Methodist University Press, 1951).

Echelberger, Clark, M., *United Nations – The First Ten Years* (New York: Harper and Brothers, 1955).

Evatt, Herbert Vere, *The United Nations* (Massachusetts: Harvard University Press, 1948).

Falk, Richard A. (ed.), *The Vietnam War and International Law* (Princeton, New Jersey: Princeton University Press, 1968).

Fehrenbach, T. R., *This Kind of Peace* (London: Frewin, 1967).

Fleming, D. F., *The Cold War and its Origins, 1917–1960* (New York: Doubleday, 1961).

Foley, Hamilton, *Woodrow Wilson's Case for the League of Nations* (Princeton, New Jersey: Princeton University Press, 1923).

Frankel, Joseph, *International Relations in a Changing World* (Oxford: Oxford University Press, 1964).

Fromkin, David, *A Peace to End All Peace* (London: Deutsch, 1989).

Fulbright, J. William, *The Price of Empire* (London: Fourth Estate, 1989).

George, Susan, *How the Other Half Dies: The Real Reasons for World Hunger* (Harmondsworth, England: Penguin, 1991).

——, *The Debt Boomerang: How Third World Debt Harms Us All* (London: Pluto Press, 1992).

Gildersleeve, Virginia, C., *The Making of the United Nations Charter* (New York: Macmillan, 1954).

Goodrich, Leyland and Simmons, Anne P., *United Nations and Maintenance of International Peace and Security* (Washington, DC: The Brookings Institution, 1955).

Griffin, G. Edward, *The Fearful Master: A Second Look at the United Nations* (Belmont, Massachusetts: Westward Islands, 1964).

Hancock, Graham, *Lords of Poverty* (London: Macmillan, 1992).

Hayter, Teresa, *Aid as Imperialism* (Harmondsworth, England: Penguin, 1971).

Hiro, Dilip, *The Longest War: The Iran–Iraq Military Conflict* (London: Paladin, 1990).

——, *Desert Shield to Desert Storm: The Second Gulf War* (London: Paladin, 1992).

Hiscocks, Richard, *The Security Council* (London: Longman, 1973).

Holcombe, Arthur N., *The United Nations and American Foreign Policy* (Urbana: University of Illinois Press, 1957).

Körner, Peter; Maass, Gero; Siebold, Thomas; and Tetzlaff, Rainer, *The IMF and the Debt Crisis* (London: Zed Books, 1992).

Lang, Tim and Hines, Colin, *The New Protectionism* (London: Earthscan, 1993).

Lie, Trygve, *In the Cause of Peace* (New York: Macmillan, 1954).

Luard, Evan *The United Nations: How it Works and What it Does* (London: Macmillan, 1979).

Nicholas, H. G., *The United Nations as a Political Institution* (London: Oxford University Press, 1959).

Northedge, F. S., *The League of Nations: Its Life and Times 1920–1946* (Leicester, England: Leicester University Press, 1986).

O'Brien, Conor Cruise and Topolski, Felix, *The United Nations: Sacred Drama* (London, 1968).

Osmanczyk, Edmund Jan, *Encyclopedia of the United Nations and International Agreements* (New York: Taylor and Francis, 1990).

Padelford, Norman J. and Goodrich, Leyland N., *United Nations in the Balance* (New York: Frederick Praeger, 1965).

Patil, Anjali V., *The UN Veto in World Affairs 1946–1990, A Complete Record and Case Histories of the Security Council's Veto* (Sarasota, Florida: UNIFO/Mansell, 1992).

Payer, Cheryl, *The Debt Trap: The IMF and the Third World* (Harmondsworth, England: Penguin, 1974).

Pisani, Sallie, *The CIA and the Marshall Plan* (Edinburgh: Edinburgh University Press, 1991).

Raghavan, Chakravarthi, *Recolonization: GATT, the Uruguay Round and the Third World* (London: Zed Books, 1990).

Reynolds, E. E., *The League Experiment* (London: Nelson, 1940).

Rikhye, Indar Jit and Skjelsbaek, K., *The United Nations and Peacekeeping* (London: Macmillan, 1990).

Sandusky, Michael C., *America's Parallel* (Alexandria, Virginia: Old Dominion Press, 1983).

Schiavone, Giuseppe, *International Organizations: A Dictionary and Directory* (London: Macmillan Reference Books, 1986).

Scott, George, *The Rise and Fall of the League of Nations* (London: Hutchinson, 1973).

Simons, Geoff, *Libya: The Struggle for Survival* (London: Macmillan, 1993).

——, *Iraq: From Sumer to Saddam* (London: Macmillan, 1994).

——, *The United Nations: A Chronology of Conflict* (London: Macmillan, 1994).

Stettinius, Edward R., *Roosevelt and the Russians: The Yalta Conference* (New York: Doubleday, 1949).

Twitchett, Kenneth J., *The Evolving United Nations: A Prospect for Peace?* (London: Europa Publications, 1971).

The United Nations Conference on International Organization; San Francisco, California, April 25 to June 26, 1945; Selected Documents (Washington, DC: U.S. Government Printing Office, 1946).

Walters, F. P., *A History of the United Nations* (Oxford: Oxford University Press, 1960).

Wilcox, Francis O. and Marcy, Carl M., *Proposals for Changes in the United Nations* (Washington, DC: The Brookings Institution, 1955).

Index

Index